MW01008709

Mavericks of War

The Unconventional, Unorthodox Innovators and Thinkers, Scholars, and Outsiders Who Mastered the Art of War

Jason S. Ridler

STACKPOLE BOOKS
Guilford, Connecticut

Published by Stackpole Books
An imprint of The Rowman & Littlefield Publishing Group, Inc.
4501 Forbes Blvd., Ste. 200
Lanham, MD 20706
www.rowman.com

Distributed by NATIONAL BOOK NETWORK
800-462-6420

British Library Cataloguing in Publication Information available

Library of Congress Cataloging-in-Publication Data available

ISBN 978-0-8117-1986-5 (hardback)
ISBN 978-0-8117-6776-7 (e-book)

∞™ The paper used in this publication meets the minimum requirements of American National Standard for Information Sciences—Permanence of Paper for Printed Library Materials, ANSI/NISO Z39.48-1992.

Printed in the United States of America

To Little-Bit. I remain in your debt.

Contents

Acknowledgments

In 2014 I won the Smith Richardson Foundation Fellowship for Foreign Policy and National Security. The research for that project has been modified into *Mavericks of War*, and thus this monograph could not have been produced without the support of the Smith Richardson Foundation. I'd also like to thank some of the many people who directly or indirectly helped or inspired this work to come to fruition: Priya Satia, Edward Said, Kalev Sepp, Thomas Ricks, Rufus Philips, Sean Maloney, Thomas Vincent, Mike Hennessy, David Last, Brian McKercher, Modris Eksteins, Jonathan Vance, Michael Reynolds, Dorothy Fall, Sarah Chayes, Carter Malkasian, and Emma Sky. I'd also like to thank the following institutions for their support: Norwich University, who backed my fellowship proposal, Johns Hopkins University, and the Bayview Branch of the Richmond, California, Public Library System, including the invaluable Link+ system in California and Nevada. Thanks to Dave Reisch at Stackpole, my agent Peter Rubie at Fine Print Literary Management for his expert guidance, Janet Reid for her early efforts on the project, and to the gang at The Ark who watched as this book emerged from the "Lair." Finally, thanks to Sunny for her love and support.

Note

Small parts of this work originally appeared as part of articles for *War on the Rocks* and *Small Wars and Insurgencies*.

Introduction

Leachman's Ghost

The Triumph Leader Museum in central Baghdad was a bizarre and gilded shrine to the avarice, brutality, and ego of President Saddam Hussein. It was filled with whips, Kalashnikovs, and pictures of famous statesmen and women greeting the dictator, from Indira Gandhi to Fidel Castro.[1] It also held a prized possession of the Iraqi dictator, a Brno rifle, almost a century old.

As the United States prepared for the invasion of Iraq in 2003, the rifle was hidden.

"Any Decent Servant Would Have Shot Him"

—August 12, 1920, just outside Fallujah, Mesopotamia.

British colonel Gerard Evelyn Leachman, political officer of the British Mandate in Mesopotamia, met with Sheik Dhari al Mahmud of the Zorba tribe, his sons Khamis and Sulaiman, a retainer, and one of his slaves. It was a period of violent and relentless uncertainty as Western nations decided the fate of peoples who had suffered under the thrall of the Ottoman Empire. Independence and freedom were craved, but the Arabs, Christians, Kurds, Turkmen, and other peoples of Mesopotamia would now be subjects of a British mandate instead of the Sultan. Arabia would be independent and Syria a French imperial holding. Demonstrations and violence followed this declaration of April 20. British air power as much as diplomacy quelled dissent.[2]

Dhari was no fan of the British, but his people were not part of the growing rebellions against their new imperial master. While some mystery remains on the origins of the visit, Leachman took the initiative to help waive loans paid to Dhari for agricultural support. The goal was to reduce tensions between the leadership of Baghdad and Fallujah, and strengthen

Dhari's support for the British. Local issues were also discussed, including rivals and crime, and according to some sources the dialog became heated. Leachman's style of diplomacy was frank and sharp, every ounce a British officer talking to an colonial underling. Such attributes made him a hero to some.

Leachman was a career imperial soldier. A veteran of South Africa and decorated explorer of Arabia (1909–1912), he had distinguished himself escaping the siege of Kut before working with the Arabs of Mesopotamia to hold ground against a violent but disintegrating arena of the Ottoman Empire. The "Officer Commanding: Desert" was a man of action and in perpetual motion. He worked among the tribes and people he had studied before the war, dressed in Arab fashion, and excelled in intelligence gathering and commanding his men with a fierce temper. Tough, resilient, and cunning, *Lijman*, as the Bedouin called him, was seen as one of the foremost soldiers of the Middle East theater.[3]

Outside of Fallujah, Leachman turned and left Dhari's building.

A Brno rifle fired.

Leachman was shot in the back and killed by one of the sheik's sons. Outrage against the mandate and the fury at Leachman's murder unleashed another revolt, this time Arab against the British. Brutal repressions and diplomatic machinations led to the establishment of Prince Feisal, son of the Sharif of Mecca and leader of the first Arab Revolt as the king of the newly created Kingdom of Iraq (see chapter 7).[4]

In death, Leachman was championed by many imperialists as a soldier whose knowledge and appreciation of the Arabs was instrumental in the protection of British interest during and after the war. He was praised for his ability to live among the Bedouins in their garb and among their traditions as a means to gather information, and for his ability to command and lead foreign soldiers.[5] Indeed, he appeared to be a kindred spirit to the more celebrated T. E. Lawrence "of Arabia" or Gertrude Bell, "mother" of modern Iraq. But there was also critique. St. John Philby, himself a heralded British agent in Arabia, was tasked by Leachman's kin to write his biography. The results were unacceptable to family and publisher and it was never published.[6] One reason may be that Leachman was far less worthy of praise than at first blush.

"Leachman wasn't quite what you call a decent fellow," noted T. E. Lawrence to a friend after Leachman's death. "Don't make him a hero in your book. He was too shrill, too hot-tempered, too little generous."[7] In 1925, Lawrence elaborated, "He was full of courage, and as hard as nails. He had an abiding contempt for everything native (an attitude he picked up in India). Now this contempt may be a conviction, an opinion, a point of view. It is inevitable perhaps, and therefore neither to be praised of blamed. Leachman allowed it to be a rule of conduct. This made him considerate, harsh, overbearing toward his servants and subjects: and there was, I stake my oath, *no justification for the airs he took.*" Leachman was of ordinary intellect, but extraordinary toughness, but lacking too much to do great works among the Arabs, "a man *too little sensitive to be aware of other points of view than his own*: too little fine to see degrees of greatness, degrees of rightness in others. He was blunt and outspoken to a degree. Such is a good point in a preacher, a bad point in a diplomat." He may have been a big deal in Mesopotamia, "a land of forth-raters," but after a week with Lawrence in Arabia "we had to return him on board ship, not for anything he said, though he spoke sourly always, but because he used to chase his servant so unmercifully that our camp took scandal at it. The servant was a worm, a long worm, who never turned or shows a spark or spirit. Any decent servant would have shot him."[8]

Eventually, one did.

The Brno rifle that killed Leachman had been given to Hussein by a descendent of Dhari shortly before the U.S. invasion of 2003.[9] It was hidden in the prelude to the "shock and awe" campaign, and has yet to be recovered. But the air campaign that crippled a regime, the brutality of Abu Ghraib, the bullying nature and reliance on power instead of diplomacy that characterized the U.S. invasion of Iraq would have made the ghost of Leachman proud.

Leachman's example, however, is a strange paradox compared to his contemporary. Lawrence is the more famous and celebrated (for good and ill, as we shall see). Leachman is almost forgotten. Yet Leachman's attitudes, methods, and conduct as an imperial soldier fighting in foreign wars have been more common than not as Western nations find themselves in wars across the globe. Leachman's lack of empathy was matched by cultural knowledge that had little respect for the Arabs whom he worked with. The same could not be said of Lawrence, who earned respect and admiration for his conduct, but also his appreciation of a complex people's culture, religion, traditions, and practices. It would seem that for every dozens of Leachmans, there are very few Lawrences. So, after a fashion, Leachman's most celebratory biographer was right. "To this day many think that he still lives."[10] Alongside the ghost of Leachman, however, is an invisible path that ran counter to his legacy of brutality and ignorance in foreign lands. These footsteps begin with Lawrence.

For fifteen years I have studied the role of "outsiders" in warfare and found the footsteps of many of Lawrence's brethren. Initially I had studied scientists involved in military affairs. Industrial warfare in the modern era created an increasing demand for scientific and technical prowess. It brought scientists of all stripes into increasing contact with soldiers. This necessity was fraught with frictions due to competing cultures, professional goals, and ethos of each profession, yet, the value of science to warfare could be demonstrated with measurable results from efficiency in training regimes, optimizing of weapons systems, and the creation of new weapons, most notably the atomic bomb. Among the most compelling aspects of this clash of cultures was the development of operational research in Britain and operations research (OR) in the United States. Scientists of various stripes were employed within military structures and even close to battle to solve problems ranging from air defense against the Luftwaffe, naval strategy to do with armadas during the Battle of the Atlantic, to battle analysis during the Normandy campaign. With rare exceptions, soldiers bristled at the need of outside experts entering their realm of professional expertise and telling them their business. Worse, the OR scientists had to tell them why they were doing it poorly and how to do it better, all without having to have come up through the ranks. The best OR scientists found common cause with their military peers and started from a place of respect for current knowledge, avoiding judgment on culture, and studying how and why things were in reality before considering how best to make things better in the future. Shared experiences built trust between the "eggheads" and "martinets." Soon the value of OR was noted in better training regimes, weapons, and doctrine. OR championed the use of battle data and even sent OR teams into the field to collect it fresh from the battlefield. By the end of the Second World War, one of the defining characteristics of Western victory against the Axis was the application of science and technology, including the creation of OR.[11]

In other words, outsiders who have a distinct skill set or expertise that is required by the military can have a profound impact on warfare. I'd seen this demonstrated conclusively within the realm of scientists and applied technical trades. Yet, I began to wonder about other fields, ones less empirical but no less valid or valuable. Could other kinds of experts, ones facing similar frictions with the armed services, have similar impacts on military affairs?

My answer is *Mavericks of War*.

Since the Great War, Western nations having increasingly found themselves waring outside the confines of conventional battle in Europe and North America. As imperial wars birthed global conflicts, many nations have required unique or unconventional experts with skills, knowledge, and abilities the military needs but does not want to learn and may even disdain. Scientific expertise dominated much of the West's wars against each other, but in foreign lands the great lack was in the arena of cultural knowledge. Concurrently, operating in foreign lands demanded a different skill set and acumen than the great maw of conventional warfare and industrial violence on the Western Front. The traditions of "small wars" and "savage wars of peace" were stained with racism and brutality, too, but also seeds of empathy and, at the very least, the practical necessity of knowing about foreign cultures in order to survive, let alone maximize intelligence against one's adversary. Thus, unlike conventional warfare, unconventional warfare required cultural acumen in some measure. There was a "knowledge gap" about people, religion, social organization, and more whose value ranged from the tactical to the strategic.[12]

The paragon of this tradition was T. E. Lawrence, subject of chapter 1, for he set a standard that has yet to be eclipsed: a Western archeologist brings his knowledge of distinctly non-Western regions and peoples to help an indigenous revolt defeat of an imperial overlord. He was the paragon maverick of war: disliked by conventional soldiers, confident in his abilities, interested and empathetic to foreign cultures, and disdained the straight jacket of conventional warfare. It led him to become an innovative theorist and practitioner of guerrilla warfare, despite never having set foot in Royal Military Academy, Sandhurst, or anything but minor military service before 1914 (much of which he disliked). When the war began, he was truly a "maverick" who bucked the system, succeeded against the odds, and made a demonstrable contribution to the British and Arab forces fighting against the Turks. But similar mavericks have appeared throughout the twentieth and into the twenty-first century, men and women of exceptional skills and insights who found themselves needed within the ranks of professional armed services.

Wilhelm Wassmuss, scholar and diplomat of Persia, was sent on the most audacious German mission of the Great War, to spark an Islamic rebellion against Britain and France that would spread from Persia to Afghanistan and India. The bold nature of the plan matched his personality, but the mission collapsed due to a range of factors for this "German Lawrence." Most tellingly, Imperial Germany had no grand tradition of working among foreign nations outside of Africa, where their interest in conventional warfare had turned their wars against West Africans into brutal prelude to the Eastern and Western Front.[13] Wassmuss tried, with almost no support, to carry off a grand scheme while other members of his team abandoned their mission. His failure was as instructive as Lawrence's victories, and how much havoc one man can cause in an insurgency.

During the Second World War, the conflict's global dimensions created demands for knowledge and expertise that even dwarfed the efforts of the Great War. Britain and the United States created two organizations to help fill the knowledge gap to pursue their efforts against the Axis, the Special Operations Executive (SOE), and the Office of Strategic Services (OSS). Despite being embryonic, the SOE and OSS developed into controversial but innovative assets and predecessor organizations for modern Special Forces and intelligence services. C. M. Woodhouse was a classicist and archeologist whose command of Greek found him involved in the SOE-organized guerrilla war of occupied Greece. Cora Du Bois was a rising star in anthropology and then the OSS, where her command of the Research and Analysis Branch in Kandy (Sri Lanka) became a vital intelligence hub for both South East Asia Command (SEAC) and OSS operations throughout the region. She became the only woman to lead an R&A unit outside of the United States. Both Woodhouse and Du Bois were mavericks against the enemy and their own government's mixed view of their efforts. Woodhouse contended with the complexity of a war of liberation, a civil war, and the coming of the Cold War, batting heads with communist guerrillas and Winston Churchill to keep the fight focused on the Germans instead of everyone else. Du Bois, as a woman and closeted lesbian, contended with both the sexism of the limited appreciation for Southeast Asia to the OSS, only to have her career snuffed out due to the paranoia of the Cold War.

Indeed, the Cold War and anti-imperial wars in Southeast Asia saw the rise and resistance of three mavericks. Advertising executive Edward Lansdale and archeologist Charles Bohannan formed a partnership in the Philippines that produced America's first postwar counterinsurgency success. Yet their novel ideas and strategies, which emphasized political, psychological, and legal elements along with military reform, made them mavericks within their services. Enemies grew with their successes. Despite critical roles in South Vietnam in the 1950s, their influence dwindled as the war became dominated by conventional leaders, doctrines, and reliance on firepower. Yet they achieved far more decisive results than Dr. Bernard Fall, perhaps the greatest expert on war in Indochina of the era. A child soldier in occupied France, Fall learned to speak truth to power as a researcher for the Americans during the Nuremberg War Crimes trials. When he applied this conviction to the French failure in Indochina, he was praised in America for his penetrating intellect and boots-on-the ground research. When he fixed his gaze on the growing United States presence in Vietnam, he became blacklisted and investigated as a possible foreign spy or communist provocateur. He did his best to influence the war through words and analysis outside the corridors of power before his research in Vietnam got him killed.

Over twenty years from the failure of Vietnam, the United States created the most technically lethal and sophisticated armed forces on earth. Yet, after the attacks of 9/11, it again found itself suffering a knowledge gap so big and serious that it needed to be filled before "victories" in

Afghanistan and Iraq became civil wars or regional conflicts. Former Peace Corps member and NPR journalist Sarah Chayes found meaning in rebuilding Kandahar among the rubble of U.S. victory. As a civic rights and business leader Chayes fought corrupt warlords who replaced the Taliban while U.S. interest in Afghanistan bled into the sinkhole of Iraq. Her understanding of the people, the systems of corruption, and more led her to become advisor to three International Security Force (ISAF) commanders and special advisor to the Chairman of the Joint Chiefs of Staff. But when the underlying corruption of the political elite was uncovered as the chief enemy of stability in the country, Chayes found herself a maverick against the interests of the Central Intelligence Agency (CIA) and others who preferred strongmen to functional government. Emma Sky was an anti-war protestor who had cut her teeth in development, diplomacy, and conflict management in Palestine when she took a job to work with the Coalition Provisional Authority in Iraq. Her refusal to worship military conformity and respect for the Iraqi people earned her the respect of senior commanders as the "victory" of 2003 slid into the mire of violence. Sky would become political advisor to both Lt. Gen. Raymond T. Odierno and Gen. David Petraeus during the "surge" in Iraq, and was a driving force of reconciliation within the warring parties of Iraq until 2010. Like Chayes, she left for academia, only to watch the successes bought by her efforts begin to unravel.

This is the story of how mavericks of war have succeeded, failed, recovered, died, and what their efforts have meant in their time and, perhaps, for the future. A general assertion based on this research is simply this: the increasingly unconventional and global conflicts mean we need more Lawrences and Skys, and far less Leachmans.

Limitations

Mavericks of War cannot cover every "subject matter expert" involved in foreign wars. Many have not left detailed records and, in the case of the Research and Analysis Branch of the OSS, the vast amount of work done by this organization has paled in comparison to the more "exciting" world of the Jedburghs and other combat-oriented missions.[14] Thus I had to be deliberate instead of comprehensive in my choices.

The selections here held because they all demonstrated the value (good and bad) of using unconventional experts in war. All had demonstrable skills in nonmilitary arts before becoming invested in military affairs. They represented a spectrum of skills, genders, attitudes, and relative rates of success to make comparisons. Breadth was as important as depth. They are the result of research across the United States, the United Kingdom, and the Philippines, as well as years of reflection on the role of outsiders in military affairs.

Mavericks of War also has limits of compression. Each subject is worthy of a detailed biography, and many have been treated to more than one. Each chapter could be a biography, even though no maverick was ever in theater for the same amount of time. Lawrence's three years in the Arab Revolt fill volumes of texts and require intense scrutiny. Yet, Edward Lansdale and Charles Bohannan served in three major conflicts (the Second World War and COIN operations in the Philippines and Vietnam), not including smaller advisory and planning missions (Cuba and Colombia), over a span of twenty-five years. Only one biography of Lansdale has been written (though a second is on the way) and no biography of Bohannan has been completed (though I am working on it). Due to the realities of compression, omissions were regrettable but necessary. Further study can be taken from the bibliography.

Here the goal is to establish the narrative of how and why mavericks emerged from their unmilitary lives into ones of import. I highlight the common threads and unique circumstances of each and offer insights on how and why they occurred. To keep the narrative flowing, the conclusion includes a detailed comparative analysis on the major themes that established the successes and failures of mavericks of war over the past one hundred years.

Other limitations were on scope of related subjects. I have excluded professional soldiers who became experts in other fields or held senior degrees outside of professional military education institutes (though work on the influence and role of PMEs on the knowledge gap of modern war is worthy of intensive scrutiny and study). I consider "Soldier-Scholars" to be a kindred spirit to *Mavericks of War*, and worthy a separate monograph. But products of the military profession who obtain senior degrees or certification are a very different animal than mavericks of war. Gen. David Petraeus may be able to quote *Seven Pillars of Wisdom* verbatim, but he would have never lived in poverty among the Arabs of Lebanon. As you will see, that distinction has a value.

Space and time restrictions also meant limited time spent on the relationship of mavericks and formal and wartime organizations or institutions. Each war produced innovative groups and organizations, including the Arab Bureau, the *Nachrictenstelle für den Orient*, the SOE and OSS, the Michigan State University Advisory Program, and, in the last two modern wars, the Human Terrain System. All of these organizations brought together academics and experts from around the world to serve in various capacities. Much work has been written on all of them, though detailed comparative work remains to be done. The Arab Bureau, SOE, and OSS are included as part of this discussion, but are not the focus.[15]

The greatest limitation here is lingual. My focus on English-only text has denied me panoply of material in German, French, Arabic, Farsi, Pashto, Vietnamese, Japanese, and Tagalog. Indeed, the greater story of these peoples dealing with British, German, and American imperialism, while not absent, is generalized due to the discrete limitations of this author. A much more impressive study would have included a detailed analysis of the actual peoples forced to deal with the imperial agents of the United States, Britain, and Germany. One presumes that such a study would see very little good in these mavericks and for some my linguistic limitations would be enough to invalidate my efforts, and not without cause, but I will let the merits of the work stand on their own. It is hoped others with greater gifts will challenge and build upon what I've researched and argued, be they from those oppressed by imperialism or those who love it. I sincerely look forward to reading such a work.

Here, we look at the outsiders and outcasts, strangers in uniform, the pacifists and combat veterans who found themselves shaping wars in foreign lands for good or ill, and causing friction and sometimes havoc with the conventional thinkers, soldiers, and statesmen.

Our first set the standard. His approach, influence, and reputation echoes across the century. He remains the paragon of eccentric scholars who go to war.

Part I

Mavericks of the Great War

The First World War offers few traditions anyone should champion today. Nations harnessed the power of the industrial revolution, applied it to nationalistic wars of empire, and turned Europe into a hungry graveyard. Million-man armies churned behind walls of screaming shells and tried to break each other's defenses by storming through the fetid waste of barbed wire and corpses known as no-man's-land, a lunar landscape where poison gas and bloated rats stalked the trenches for ever more victims. Despite the greatest military minds of the Edwardian period believing that offensive operations would lead to short, bloody wars, the defensive proved itself more powerful than the cult of the offensive. The result was a generation bled white.[1] When it ended in 1918, ten million were dead, and even more were mangled in mind and body. The war was "a dreadful place, a place of horror and desolation which no imagination could have invented," recalled Siegfried Sassoon, a British officer, decorated combatant, and critic. A place where "a man of strong spirit might know himself utterly powerless against death and destruction, and yet stand up and defy gross darkness and stupefying shell-fire, discovering in himself the invincible resistance of an animal or an insect, and an endurance which he might, in after days, forget or disbelieve."[2] This war of human endurance against industrial wreckage was a nightmare from which many of the "Lost Generation" thought they would never wake.[3]

Despite the orgy of innovation required to solve the "riddle of the trenches," from the creation of tanks to the best use of airpower, the First World War is justly remembered as a military horror show, littered with ideas about using men and machines in modern combat that took years to undo and redress. The symbolic heart remains the infamous Battle of the Somme, with its biblical seven-day rain of a million shells that failed to break German defenses, a battle that cost the British Army 60,000 casualties in a single day and nearly half a million casualties by November. The results were carnage and no tangible measure of success. When the armistice was signed in 1918, the race to learn the lessons of the war began. The catastrophic cost led many to enshrine monuments with much greater meaning than the *realpolitik* that led to the outbreak of violence in 1914.[4] Much ink was spilt from authors and visionaries that the conduct of the Great War should never be repeated. From this disdain emerged modern ideas of mobile tank warfare, strategic bombing, and more. The major tradition, it would seem, would be to avoid fighting as they had in 1914–1918.

And yet, one tradition of fighting emerged that shaped the nature of armed conflict ever since. The Great War's size, scope, and complexity proved, as French Prime Minister George Clemenceau noted, "too serious a business to be left to the generals."[5] Clemenceau was referring to the primacy of politicians in strategy, but a primacy that needed to be reasserted during the Great War; it also spoke to the growing need of outsiders to influence military events. The demands of the Great War were so vast that civilian experts of all shapes and sizes were called upon to become part of the machinery of war like never before. Scientists, economists, railway workers and engineers, doctors, and academics of all stripes found themselves in increasing demand to solve problems from defending London from air raids from zeppelins to pulling together the shattered psyche of soldiers suffering from shellshock, and more. And not just in Europe. The Great War was the first truly global conflict, involving Eurasia, Africa, Asia, and North America, as well as the supposed "sideshow" of fighting within the Middle East. Compared to the titanic bloodletting in Europe, the Middle Eastern theater was the fringe. Yet it was here that the most brilliant maverick to military affairs established a tradition of warfare that outlived his short life, whose ideas and approach were absorbed into revolutions and counterrevolutions that touch the world today, who defined the value of the military outsider to the world of war.

Chapter 1

"Those Who Dream in Daylight": T. E. Lawrence and the Impact of a Maverick of War

All men dream: but not equally. Those who dream by night in the dusty recesses of their minds wake in the day to find that it was vanity: but the dreamers of the day are dangerous men, for they may act their dreams with open eyes, to make it possible. This I did.[1]

—T. E. LAWRENCE, *Seven Pillars of Wisdom: A Triumph*

"We Were a Rebellion of the Arabs against the Turks"

—Wadi Sirhan, Arabia, June 1917.

"Clayton. I've decided to go off alone to Damascus, hoping to get killed on the way: for all sakes try and clear this show up before it goes any further. We are calling them to fight for us on a lie, and I can't stand it."[2] The message was scribbled into a notebook and left at Wadi Sirhan. Its author, Capt. T. E. Lawrence, was preparing to execute an unsanctioned operation in the north, a quixotic plan that appealed to no one within the British military in the Middle East. If Lawrence died, this note, addressed to his superior Gilbert Clayton, would be the last his name would have been etched on during the Arab Revolt. The British had promised support for an independent Arab State, and the Emir of Mecca sanctioned the revolt under his sons and against the Ottoman Empire. But British diplomats had secretly carved out the Ottoman's territories among itself and wartime ally France. Lawrence believed the Arabs had the right to their own state, but he could not bring himself to reveal the truth. From Wadi Sirhan he would exhaust himself to put them in the strongest position to resist British and French intrigue by war's end, or die trying. What happened next became legend and controversy.

Lawrence began a journey of a thousand miles in the Arabian Desert. He joined Prince Feisal, son of the Emir and leader of the Western revolt, and Auda abu Tayi, battle-hardened leader of the Howeitat tribe, on a reconnaissance behind Turkish lines to Damascus. The Bedouin and Howeitat were joined by other groups as the vanguard moved. They climbed, as Lawrence called it, "the ladder of tribes," with the intent of storming the port fortress of Aqaba. Lawrence knew that Aqaba was built to resist an assault from the Mediterranean. All guns and defensive structures pointed west. If taken from the east, they would have a rich northern port to wage war on the Hejaz railway and keep the Turks imprisoned in Medina with raids. Lawrence had learned of Aqaba's weaknesses before the war. As an archeologist, he had been hired to do amateur espionage against the Ottoman possessions in the Holy Lands for the British government under the cover of writing a work on religious structures in Palestine. He'd also taken the opportunity to snoop around the fortress while seconded to an intelligence mission three years prior. But success for an eastern assault required a journey among the Bedouin against the unrelenting sun and sand of the Arabian Desert. Like Xenophon and the Ten Thousand, lost in Persia after a failed expedition in 401 BC, he was about to have his endurance tested until there could be the cry, "The Sea! The Sea!"[3]

Aqaba sits at the end of a one-hundred-mile link of water and forms the boundary of the Sinai Peninsula; it offered Lawrence and the Arabs a powerful strategic target that could serve as the launching point for raids through Southern Palestine. Just sixty miles east was the Hejaz Railway, the strategic lifeline of 40,000 Turkish soldiers at Medina who had perpetually threatened to march out and crush the revolt's symbolic heart and birthplace in Mecca.[4] Most British officers wanted the Turks crushed at Medina and grew increasingly frustrated with Arabs who could not or would not form into formal and conventional battle lines for a decisive confrontation. Lawrence's own strategy, the one he abandoned the war to prove, rested on a different goal than decisive battle. "We wanted the enemy to stay in Medina," he said with hindsight, using the royal "we," "and in every other harmless place, in the largest numbers. Our ideal was to keep his railway just working, but only just, with the maximum of loss and discomfort to him."[5] Attacking the railway, blowing up bridges and trains, raids that struck hard and fast and vanished before a decisive counterattack could be made, all would secure the Turks as prisoners of Medina and allow the Arab Revolt to head north so that Feisal could be in Damascus before the British or French. Aqaba was the most important rung on the ladder to prove Lawrence's strategy.

Lawrence rode into Syria with Auda and Nasir, Feisal's chief officer, raising Howeitat and other tribesmen for the assault. He met in secret with Arab leaders, warned against independent uprisings, and found more recruits. Eight miles north of Damascus, he dynamited a bridge at Ras Baalbek and met with prominent figures such as the mayor of Damascus, Sheikh Hussein of the Druse, and Nuri Shaalan of the powerful Ruwalla tribe. Nuri, a tough and dangerous leader, unrolled differing scrolls with differing promises to the Arabs and the French. Controversy remains over what Lawrence promised Nuri. He may have "bought" loyalty with a promise to hand himself over for retribution if Britain failed its earlier obligations. On June 18, 1917, at Nebk, north of Aqaba, Lawrence and the Howeitat destroyed stretches of rail to draw the Turks away for five days before launching south on Aqaba. Deception forces were sent to keep the main force's movements unknown, lulling the Turks into thinking their only threat was a few bands of angry tribes. Underestimating the Arabs was one of their chief assets.[6] The assaults were planned in series of steps to maximize surprise on Aqaba. In the days ahead, however, Lawrence learned that the war had momentum beyond his control. Turkish responses to the first assault on Fuweilah was a brutal reprisal on the Dhumaniyeh, slitting fourteen throats, for which the Arab force under Zaal responded in kind with the garrison, leaving no prisoner. Lawrence misjudged by a day how long it would take the Turks to respond. They retook Fuweilah without a single loss. The revolt had just lost the Aba el Lissan pass.

Instead of confrontation, Lawrence, Auda, and Nasir realized that the Turkish position was still defensive and remained under the illusion that there was no significant force to contend with. With surprise on their side and fresh recruits from the Dhumaniyeh onside, they returned to Fuweilah. Snipers filled the air with shots through the day, the sun burning down and making the gunmetal sizzle. The assault required all hands, so water was scarce. Lawrence and Nasir drank from a puddle of mud while Auda chastised them. "All talk and no work?" Growing animosity between them leaked into poor words. "By god, they shoot a lot," Lawrence said of Auda's men, "and hit little." Auda challenged them to follow where the "old man" was heading and then led a flanking maneuver with mounted men into the Turks' exposed rear position. As the Turks headed north, 400 horses and camels charged with Nasir, joining the assault. As the battle hit its crescendo, Lawrence drew his Webley revolver and in his excitement shot his horse.

He landed on the ground, stunned, and then fought to right himself and saw the carnages of corpses from the Turkish battalion. He helped Auda stabilize his senses after the exhaustion of battle, interrogated prisoners, and discovered that Maan, where the battalion had come from, was now weak. Better yet, their secret operation was still dismissed as the vagaries of tribal conflict. As Arabs planned to take the city, Lawrence argued the need to stay on target. Fight on the move, paralyze the Turks with fear and crippled telegraph/rail lines, and avoid holding territory they could not defend. "We have no supporters," he told them, "no regulars, no guns, no base nearer than Wejh, no communications, no money, for our gold is exhausted, and we've had to issue our own scrip, with promises to pay 'when Aqaba is taken,' for daily expenses. Besides, a strategic scheme must not be changed to follow up a tactical success we must push on to the coast, and reopen sea-contact with Suez."[7] Auda pushed them to leave the plundered dead in the moonlight and head as fast as possible for Aqaba. As they approached, they discovered a series of Turkish posts had been abandoned. "Their men had been drawn to Khadra, the entrenched position (at the mouth of Itm), which covered Akaba [*sic*] so well against a landing from the sea. Unfortunately for them the enemy had never imagined attack from the interior, and all of their great works not one trench or post faced inland. Our advance from so new a direction threw them into panic."[8]

A flurry of bullets and surges of men fed a single day of fighting. Lawrence watched as locals joined in the assault against the Turks until

Nasir marched with other leaders, forcing the Arabs to ceasefire. The Turks stopped, too. Aqaba fell to the Arabs, a bloodless victory a year after the horror of the Somme, and Lawrence found a single German working as a well borer. The fellow stranger in a strange land spoke to him in German. "Recent doings had amazed him," Lawrence recalled, "and he begged me to explain what we meant. I said that we were a rebellion of the Arabs against the Turks. This, it took him time to appreciate. He wanted to know who was our leader. I said the Sherif of Mecca."[9]

The city surrendered on July 6, 1917, and Lawrence raced to Cairo to inform British GHQ of what the Arabs had accomplished without their authorization or knowledge. He then requested immediate supplies and support. The commander of British forces, Gen. Edmund Allenby, obliged. Victory at Aqaba sustained the Arab Revolt as a viable tool for the rest of the war. Diplomat and colleague Robert Storrs called Lawrence's "performance" at Aqaba "nothing short of miraculous." Even Clayton, who was highly critical of Lawrence's ideas, said his 300 miles on camelback in thirty days against the brutality of the desert was, in classic British understatement, a "very remarkable performance, calling for a display of courage, resource, and endurance."[10] He was considered for a Victoria Cross and rewarded for his improvised and near-treasonous operation with the rank of major. Of this time in command, Lawrence reflected that as an advisor he had

> *had options and requests, never an order: and I was surfeited, tied to death of free-will. For a year and a half I had been in motion, riding a thousand miles each month upon camels, which added nervous hours in crazy aeroplanes, or rushing across country in powerful cars. In my last five actions I had been hit, and my body so dreaded further pain that now I had to force myself under fire. Generally I had been hungry: and later always cold: and that and the dirt had poisoned my hurts into a festering mass of sores.*[11]

Aqaba also sparked Lawrence's celebrity. Members of Parliament would anxiously read his reports in the *Arab Bulletin*, intelligence briefs that ranged from political and military analysis to his "27 Articles," a primer on Arab culture that Lawrence had created, to help British officers with zero knowledge of Arabs achieve a modicum of success in mitigating their own racial and Western biases in working with the revolt.[12] Aqaba transformed Lawrence into a sought-out advisor, and the Arab Revolt became Allenby's right wing as British and Arab forces headed north to unseat the Turks from Damascus. That adventure would see him captured and abused by the Turks (by luck he escaped); he advised on the revolt and led some conventional battles as well as "shuttle diplomacy" between his front and Allenby's forces. By the time of the Ottoman surrender, Lawrence's preference for the Arabic dress, his eccentric attitude, and his exotic war experience made him among the few celebrities of the horrific war. His ideas on "irregular" and "guerrilla" warfare would soon go viral across the globe, influencing wars in the Middle East, Southeast Asia, Africa, and South America.[13]

This was a phenomenal achievement, made all the more incredible because Lawrence wasn't a professional soldier and, before the war, his major preoccupation was to focus on "Medieval Lead-Glazed Pottery from the Eleven to the Sixteenth Centuries" and perhaps become a travel writer. "He had no habit of unquestioning obedience to help him cope with his predicament," biographer Jeremy Wilson noted, and relied on his own knowledge, skills, and abilities, forged before the Great War. Indeed, it's because he was not a soldier that he was able to view his war with a different frame of reference than his contemporary and professional colleagues. He did not worship the doctrines of the offensive. He had read as much if not more military theory than many of his professional contemporaries, who held "inky fingered" officers who read books with contempt.[14] The war provided him the opportunity to bring a unique personality and skill set to bear on an arena of warfare that most soldiers thought of as a sideshow. For Lawrence, who had lived and worked in the region as an archeologist, it was the main event.

And the inspiration for Aqaba was seeded before the war.

"... A Very Attractive Kind of Native Dignity"

Thomas Edward Lawrence was born on August 16, 1888, the illegitimate son of a Welsh noble and the governess of his wife's children.[15]

A dislike of his mother and general precociousness led him to run away from home when he was seven and enlist in the local garrison, the Royal Garrison Artillery. Military life shocked him with its violence and brutality. Everyone was beaten, and every dispute settled with fists. Black eyes were common on the parade ground. Every "barrack court martial" ended with "mass bullying of anyone unlike the mass," and one weekend the boys "frightened me with their roughness."[16] Eventually, his father secured his release.

Lawrence attended Oxford High School before being admitted to Oxford University in 1907. He was brilliant, individualistic, and driven. He despised team sports that emphasized competition and rules[17] and channeled his energies into studying medieval history and architecture, enjoying the stories of older civilizations.[18] Preparing for a life of adventure, Lawrence made himself as tough as any knight of the age of chivalry, and a crack shot with a pistol.[19] While eccentric, he was no loner but a natural leader among his friends. While in high school he secured a job at the famous Ashmolean Museum and became acquainted with David Hogarth, archeologist and museum curator.[20]

He entered Oxford on October 12, 1907,[21] and was among the intellectual elite of his country. His tutors and administrators had powerful connections in academia and government, which would help his career find opportunities. He continued developing a capacity for hardship, abstaining from meals, never sitting in chairs, and long and tough journeys by bicycle. Mastering his body through willpower was an explicit goal.[22] Lawrence conducted an intensive French cycling tour in the summer of 1908 (2,400 miles). At Oxford, he made military history and strategy his alternative special subjects so that he could continue investigating medieval architecture. He also read voluminous military history beyond his subject matter,[23] served briefly in the new Oxford University's Training Corps, and was an officer in the St. Aldate's Church Lads' Brigade.[24]

Syria, then under the control of the Ottoman Empire, was Lawrence's next stop. Sir John Rhys, principal of Jesus College, arranged through the British government for the Turks to provide an *irades* (letter of safe conduct) for Lawrence's journey.[25] Hogarth failed to deter Lawrence from going to Syria alone. It wasn't "safe or pleasant," and Europeans do not travel alone on foot. "Well," Lawrence said, "I do."[26] Lawrence met acclaimed travel writer Charles Doughty, who suggested he travel with aid, as Lawrence's plan for the work was hazardous. "The distances to be traversed are great," Doughty noted. "You would have nothing to draw upon but the slight margin of strength which you bring with you from Europe. Insufficient food, rest and sleep would soon begin to tell."[27] Doughty connected him with explorer H. Pirie-Gordon, who had toured Syria the previous year, who lent him an annotated map of the region.

Lawrence arrived in Sidon (in modern Lebanon) on July 8 and traveled alone on foot, conducting his thesis research.[28] He compared French designs and structures with those of the Crusader States in Syria and Lebanon. During the trip, he became an expert photographer, cartographer, and sketch artist and worked with clay or stone. Sculptures had become a favorite.[29] Lawrence enjoyed the peoples of Syria and Lebanon and shared their contempt for the Turkish government who mistreated them.[30] The Arabs of Syria were very hospitable. "[T]here are the common people each one ready to receive one for a night," he wrote at the time, "and allow one to share in their meals; and without thought of payment from a traveler on foot. It is so pleasant, for they have a very attractive kind of native dignity."[31] Kindness and hospitality abounded. "Then comes sometimes coffee and aft that a variety of questions, as to whether my tripod is a revolver, and what I am, and where I come from, and where I am going, and why I'm on foot, and am I alone, and every other thing conceivable." It was also a place of crime and corruption, rooted in poverty. "[E]veryone is dreadfully afraid of thieves: they travel very little."[32] Lawrence carried a Mauser for protection but was both robbed and beaten during the trip.[33] Still, he pressed on. Unlike most Westerners, Lawrence preferred to travel poor, with a threadbare existence, and did so in "my beggar-fashion" to stay light and a less tempting target.[34]

During the winter of 1909–1910 Lawrence finished his thesis "The Influence of the Crusades on European Architecture to the End of the XIIth Century."[35] He took "first class"[36] and impressed Hogarth,[37] then invested in the archeological digging of Hittite mounds in Carchemish, a capital and famous battleground of the ancient world. Lawrence was now studying for a bachelor of arts in literature, with the focus on "Medieval

Lead-Glazed Pottery from the Eleven to the Sixteenth Centuries," but when Hogarth offered him a chance to return, he took it and a junior research fellowship. From December 14, 1910, to the summer of 1914, Lawrence would become a junior archeologist under Hogarth.[38]

Archeology at Carchemish required a variety of skills. Over a thousand fragments of carved and incised basalt had been recovered, and fitting them together was painstaking.[39] By 1913, he'd become proficient in using dynamite to blast Roman concrete. He relied on visual memory for inscription work and studied both ancient and modern cultures with an intense eye. Ancient Assyrian pottery, weapons, and structures, as well as the challenge of language and deciphering text, were his spoils. He was invested in understanding those that were foreign to his own culture. While Lawrence suffered from the European biases and exceptionalism of his era, including anti-Semitism, he was not enamored with the idea of progressive civilizations and held in high regard those that, to others, would be deemed primitive or even savage, in the language of the era.[40]

"In Military Theory I Was Tolerably Read . . ."

Lawrence led gangs of labor for excavation. His "street Arabic" was stronger than his formal language skills, and he got on well with the variety of peoples of the region. He also had a fascination with the nomadic Soleyb, whom he wished to travel with and study. "But I have no intention of making a book of it," he wrote at the time. "I would not even go down in Arabia proper. I do not like the modern habit of wrenching all legend into the purpose of anthropology."[41] In all his writing and review he'd carry a more romantic notion of foreign peoples and cultures. He befriended a young Syrian named Dahoum. While Lawrence mentored him in photography and turned him into an executive officer, Dahoum helped Lawrence with improving his Arabic.[42] His visits to Egypt provided stark contrasts. He was not impressed with the digging there, which was akin to body snatching. He watched a graveyard excavation where the heads were ripped off the dead. He worked for a time under Sir William Mathews Flinders Petrie, painstaking groundbreaker of Egyptology research and methodologies.[43] Compared with the Syrians,

Lawrence found the Egyptians “frenetic, and querulous, foulmouthed, and fawning.”[44]

Local and international politics permeated Carchemish. The Berlin-Baghdad Railway remained under construction and ran through the region. The railway was part of Kaiser Wilhelm II’s eastern strategy to use alliances with the Ottoman Empire to project power that could directly threaten British interest in Persia and India. In 1912, German workers took Carchemish city walls for their embankment while Lawrence was absent. So he ran back, got Turkish order to stop the Germans and the minister of public instruction who came there. The Balkan War of 1912 depleted the camp’s labor pool as men were conscripted to serve in the Turkish Army. Still considering a career as a travel writer, Lawrence thought the plight of the Arabs and others would give “vividness to what I write.”[45] Rumors rose of Kurds going to sack Aleppo and murder Germans in the Baghdad railway. Many Kurds worked on their digs. Lawrence cultivated their friendship and understood their grievances.[46] Armenian revolutionaries had also talked with Lawrence, and Kurds tried to enlist his aid. Lawrence’s chief biographer dismisses these activities as intelligence gathering and more to do with survival in a turbulent region and time. Lawrence also spent time improving his aim with pistol and rifle in 1913.[47]

By the fourth season at Carchemish in March he led groups of seventy men in excavation, and the site grew to over 200 members. It needed more than Lawrence and his senior partner Leonard Woolley to run it.[48] The site’s efforts were funded in part by the Palestinian Exploration Fund (PEF), and one of their chief members, Walter Morrison, had also independently financed £5,000 for the work at Carchemish after hearing Hogarth’s lecture.[49] The PEF was also a cover used by the British government to obtain geographical and other intelligence in this region of the Ottoman Empire. Soon, Lawrence would begin his foray to government-led espionage. According to the proposal, “[t]he eastern limit of the new survey will be a line running north through the Akabah, from the Gulf of Akabah to the southern end of the Dead Sea.”[50] Lawrence worked directly under Capt. Stewart Francis Newcomb of the Royal Engineers, a future wartime ally. The value of biblical archeology was sheen for intensive focus on Turkey; the Balkan Wars had raised concern about Ottoman goals, strength, and more.[51] The PEF mission and Newcomb taught Lawrence new skills in surveying, map making, and studying land formations of different geography. This included Aqaba, where Lawrence was denied access to see some ruins off shore. He went anyway in a makeshift raft.[52] Lawrence would later finish the report *The Wilderness of Zin* while in England. Newcombe also asked Lawrence and Woolley to conduct intelligence on the railway through the Taurus Mountains, which they did, and Woolley's interview with a fired Italian from the site helped them write a report.[53]

Before returning to England to work on *The Wilderness of Zin*, Lawrence and Woolley were waiting at Jerablus for a digging permit and witnessed the growing tension in the region break out into violence. In a dispute over work, Kurdish workers on the railway attacked a German rail establishment. It escalated into a firefight with 250 Kurds. Both Lawrence and Woolley intervened to help diffuse the violence and save their own hides. The Germans were grateful for their effort and agreed to loan them wagons for Carchemish.[54] Lawrence worked to complete *The Wilderness of Zin* as the diplomatic intrigues of the summer gave way to violence and the outbreak of the Great War.

By this time, Lawrence was a young professional with distinct expertise. He had a bastion of knowledge of Turkish lands and their oppressed people and could live as they lived without the requirements or comforts of most Westerners. He'd led teams of local men in excavation and recovery, demolition, and meticulous documentation. He contended with harsh Turkish authorities and skirmishes between Arab workers and the German railway men. He dressed in Arabic fashion and took their habits, including reading the *Koran*. He and coworker Leonard Woolley inspired a visitor with their "remarkable knowledge of men: they know more about handling Orientals than any man I have ever met during my two years in Syria."[55] He was responsible for "recording and photographing finds, gluing fragments together, keeping accounts, bargaining for goods, serving as Arabic-English interpreter, helping Gregorios Antoniou, the experienced Cypriot foreman who had worked for Hogarth on other digs, to manage the work crew."[56]

He'd never contemplated a life in military affairs, nor was he schooled at the Royal Military Academy at Sandhurst. And yet, because his mind and schooling had martial ethos, Lawrence was exceptionally well read in military affairs. "In military theory I was tolerably read," he noted later, "my Oxford curiosity having taken me past Napoleon to Clausewitz and his school to Caemmerer and Moltke, and the recent Frenchmen." He found Carl von Clausewitz "intellectually so much the master of them."[57] Clausewitz was the great interpreter of Napoleon, who reshaped Europe by harnessing the revolutionary potential of nationalism. As Clausewitz and others sought to unlock Napoleon's genius, the industrial revolution gave modern nation-states even more powerful and technical means to wage war in greater lethality and numbers. Battles grew. Wars consumed greater resources as nations and empires became industrialized and able to project and withstand mass-produced warfare. By 1914, the doctrine of the offensive had taken hold of most senior officers and strategists. Emphasis lay on the willingness to use maximum amounts of industrial means and men in direct battle. Helmut von Moltke, a brilliant mind and student of Clausewitz, had orchestrated for Prussia and German city states three rapid wars, utilizing advanced industrial organization and deployment of million-man armies forged together with nationalist zeal. Three quick victories emerged against the Danes, the Austrians, and, most humiliatingly, the French. As nations tried to imitate Moltke's mass use of force and industrial support, the Great War started with Lawrence an outsider already by inclination, but now also by military thinking. He would later be appalled by the war of the Western Front, one that consumed two of his three brothers, along with millions of others.[58] Lawrence was no soldier when he answered the call. But his deep reading of warfare would provide him alternative intellectual models to use in a theater that looked nothing like the horrific carnage of No-Man's-Lands.

"Is This Man a God, To Know Everything?"

With *The Wilderness of Zin* and *Military Report on the Sinai Peninsula* completed, Lieutenant Lawrence largely worked with the Intelligence Department of Cairo GHQ as liaison between military intelligence and the civilian Survey of Egypt. He entered dialogues on tactics and strategy as he saw it with colleagues, including Maj. Gen. John Maxwell and High Commissioner Sir Henry McMahon, Sir Gilbert Clayton (representative of Sir Reginald Wingate, governor general of Sudan), and Robert Storrs, Oriental Secretary to the High Commissioner and General Kitchener's intermediary with Hussein ibn Ali al-Hashimi, the Emir of Mecca.[59] Lawrence added his voice to the chorus desiring a landing at Alexandretta, an exposed point in Turkish communications with Sinai and Mesopotamia, but the French killed the plan. He was also cognizant that the government in India actively disliked the idea of having the Arabs revolt at all. They feared it would encourage Muslim nationalists in India to rise up, too, something the Germans were scheming to support in Persia and Afghanistan (see chapter 2).

Lawrence gathered as much data as he could for those who had no idea of the cultural and political complexities of the region. He contributed to the *Turkish Army Handbook*; completed a long analysis of Syrian culture, geography, and politics; and worked on a future free Syria. He dressed poorly on purpose to annoy and cajole the officers around him, causing one to reflect, "Many men of sense and ability were repelled by the impudence, freakishness and frivolity he trailed too provocatively." He was young, shabby, and often out of uniform.[60] But his work stood up. He created the *Intelligence Bulletin*, an uncensored newspaper for generals that allowed him to disseminate his knowledge and ideas far and wide. The intelligence work also gave him vast knowledge beyond that of a temporary lieutenant, and he maintained his interest in new skills by championing aerial photography to improve maps.[61]

By early spring of 1916, British strategy was in disarray. The landing at Gallipoli was a debacle. Cairo was crammed with two general staffs, one under Gen. John Maxwell and the Mesopotamia Expeditionary Force under Lt. Gen. Archibald Murray, now stationed in Egypt. Worse, the Turkish siege of British troops at Kut was racing toward a horrific conclusion of starvation, deprivation, and surrender. Hussein became evasive with British diplomat Ronald Storrs on a future revolt. Against these shifting sands, Lawrence became an expert on Turkish means and methods, often through interrogation of prisoners.[62] The British centralized efforts by creating an "Arab Bureau" under Clayton on February 4,

1916. Lawrence was initially denied as a member but made such an ass of himself in his intelligence position that they asked he be removed. He soon became the leading writer behind the *Arab Bulletin*, which he ran along with the *Intelligence Bulletin*. His reports gave detailed analysis of Syria rooted in his own experience before the war, current knowledge, and deep reading. The goal was to fill the knowledge gap of those who thought all of Arabia was either Turkish or filled with a single type of Arab.

As Kut teetered toward surrender, Lawrence began intelligence fieldwork abroad. In Mesopotamia, he assessed the local Arabs as unlikely to start a revolt and joined Aubrey Herbert (military intelligence) and Col. H. Beach, head of British intelligence on a covert mission. Blindfolded and brought before the Turkish commanding officer, Lawrence held the check book as the senior officers tried to bribe the Turks to allow General Townsend and his men to retreat. Ottoman minister of war Enver Pasha ordered the offer be rejected. Returning to Cairo, Lawrence wrote a scathing report on the situation in Mesopotamia[63] that spared no one, even the high command. Even the sanitized version was damning: intelligence officers relying too much on interpreters "so that many of the finer points are missed. We must send them a linguist or two, who knows the inside of Turkey." Lawrence included recommendations on best practices for map making down with aerial crews and the proper use of irrigation as part of guerrilla warfare.[64]

Before the Arab Revolt began, Lawrence had demonstrated himself as a valuable resource. He added his knowledge to the wealth of data incoming on the Turkish Army, until he was able to discuss their ethnic makeup. Later, when advising in Arabia, Lawrence could pinpoint Turkish units based on their Syrian, Circassian, Anatolian, or Mesopotamian names. "Is this man a God," Abdullah exclaimed, "to know everything?"[65] The *Arab Bulletin* had allowed him a vehicle for two values: he shared his knowledge on Syrian culture, geography, politics, and more and he used it to share his growing ideas on warfare in the Hejaz. Articles such as "Syria: The Raw Materials," published in March 12, 1917, gave a geographic, cultural, and political synopsis that was detailed and destroyed the notion of the ignorant belief that Syria was simply a place full of Arabs—when, in fact, it was a complex network of Arab tribes, Christians,

Druse, and more that have been organized in a series of belts across the country—with uses and abuses of the Turks listed. One such was in the Zionist populated areas, where the Turks "planted along line of Circassian immigrants. They hold their ground only by the sword and the favor of the Turks, to whom they are consequently devoted."[66]

Lawrence was also critical of British policy and blindness regarding the negative impact of their influence as an imperial power.[67] A 1916 report noted that any troops being sent to Rabegh would be disastrous. "We have appropriated too many Moslem countries for them to have any real trust in our disinterestedness, and they are terribly afraid of an English occupation of Hejaz."[68] His memo on this topic reached the War Office and was read by Cabinet members. Clayton was ecstatic, but Wingate was pissed, and his analysis became background noise among many in Cairo until the revolt was launched.

The Arab Revolt finally began on June 5, 1916. Mecca was cleared of Turkish power. An assault on Medina was executed. But the effort stalled. Lawrence was an interim advisor to Abdullah but pushed to meet Feisal, the eldest brother of the Sherif of Mecca who the British worked with to execute the revolt. When Lawrence met Feisal, a partnership was struck. Lawrence coyly shared his belief that the revolt needed to take Damascus, ancient capital and seat of Turkish power in the region. During the turbulent first year, Feisal found Lawrence's knowledge, attitude, and companionship superior to that of any other British officer. Lawrence made himself an indispensable conduit of British support and independent analysis. Indeed, while Lawrence would lead many raids and attacks on rail lines and bridges, his greatest role was as an advisor, working through the influence of others to impact change. He informed his superiors in Cairo not to send troops to Arabia, which Hussein himself decried as dangerous to the revolt's survival. Instead, they should send Arabic-speaking technical advisors, like Major Garland, an engineer whose innovative mines became a staple of the revolt. He was sent back to work with Feisal as an advisor for the rest of the war. It was through Feisal's influence and patronage that Lawrence orchestrated the move that made him legendary. But the strategic foci Lawrence developed came from a military theorist largely ignored by professional soldiers of 1914.

"Bloodless Victories"

Wadi Ais, Arabia, March of 1917. Three months before Aqaba.

Riddled with boils and sick with fever, Capt. T. E. Lawrence reported to Sherif Abdullah Hussein on the recent work of his brother, Feisal, in the taking of the port city of Wejh. Lawrence had been working with Feisal to sustain the Arab Revolt that the Sherif of Mecca, Feisal and Abdullah's father, sanctioned against the Ottoman Turks almost a year ago. "[I]n January, 1917," Lawrence told historian Basil Liddell Hart after the war, "we took all Feisal's tribesmen, turned our backs on Mecca, Rabegh and the Turks, and marched away north two hundred miles to Wejh, thanks to the help of the British Red Sea Fleet, which fed and watered us along the coast, and gave us gun-power and a landing party at our objective."[69] The Turkish advance on Mecca had stopped. Lawrence's operation had cut the Turkish force in half, one at Medina, and the other spread along the Hejaz railway. The immediate threat against Mecca was nullified. "The almost bloodless move to Wejh had pierced no vital organ, won no decisive battle, but it had changed the 40,000 Turks at Medina into a beleaguered garrison although they suffered no actual siege."[70] Arab confidence in Feisal grew, but the revolt had yet to produce a victory that convinced its British detractors that it would not be better placed with British regulars and the Arabs formed into regular units to fight conventional battles against the Turks.

Such an approach, Lawrence knew, was suicide. The Bedouin were raiders and guerrilla fighters who excelled at the operations he had helped organize around Wejh. The value of a single Arab raider was too high for the "cult of the offensive" that infected the generation of 1914. "Bloodless victories were the kind that the Arabs appreciated as an inspiration to further ones," one of Lawrence's famous biographers and enemy of the cult of the offensive, Basil Liddell Hart, noted, "and Lawrence's understanding of this need marked a stage in the evolution of his theory of irregular warfare."[71] Not bad for a young archeologist.

Abdullah was also briefed on plans for raids on the Hejaz railway, the lifeline to the Turkish garrison at Medina. With his report finished, Lawrence retired to his tent and collapsed, all five feet, five and a half inches of him sick with fever, sores, and exhaustion. His career and role in the revolt was poised at a precipice. At GHQ in Cairo, Lawrence was the "subaltern on the staff, without a Sam Browne belt, and always wearing slacks, scorching about between Cairo and Balaq on a Triumph motorcycle, he was an offense to the eyes of his seniors."[72] Yet he was championed by Feisal and Abdullah for his knowledge and support of the Arabs. Lawrence would be able to pinpoint Turkish units based on their Syrian, Circassian, Anatolian, and Mesopotamian names.[73] That respect and knowledge would lead to trust and saliency with Arab leadership as the revolt's future was uncertain and, as Lawrence discovered, seeded with betrayal.

Lawrence knew London had decided to carve the Ottoman lands of Arabia among themselves with the French, making their promises to the Sherif Hussein a nest of lies. The so-called Sykes–Picot Agreement (May 1916) would deny the Arabs the reason for the revolt: a free Arabia independent of rule from Britain and, especially, France. Confidence in the Arabs dropped as rumors of Turkish advances on Prince Feisal's position at the coastal city of Wejh grew. Frustrations mounted as the British tried to organize the Arabs into conventional formations to fight the Turks. Raids were fine when there was no other option, like on the Western Front, but what was needed was decisive battle. And if the Arabs could not form conventional forces, British soldiers would be sent to Arabia to save the revolt. The Emir knew, however, that uniformed British soldiers would be seen as Christian conquerors to the Arabs. He'd only agreed to their use when circumstances were dire. For the British, unless the Arabs changed the way they had fought for 1,000 years, they would be replaced in their own revolt.

In his tent, sick with fever, Lawrence wrestled with these facts and opinions. Forcing Arabs to fight as regulars was suicide, he thought. It was not in their culture or nature. They were raiders, violent when the attack was on their side, and terrified of artillery and airpower. How could you overturn their cultural norms and turn them into Tommies overnight? And large forces of British soldiers would destroy the idea of freedom that gave the revolt its unifying concept and could lead to more chaos and insurgencies against the British. There had to be another way. Suffering from illness, he considered an older author of war than Clausewitz whose ideas on battle offered him solace and a way forward.

"War Is a Science So Obscure and Imperfect..."

Paris, France, circa 1720–1724.

Maurice de Saxe is sick and restless. The city bustles with opulence for aristocrats and their servants. Down the Rue Quincampoix, fortunes are won and lost. Cooks claim to become millionaires overnight at games of chance, and laws restricting the hoarding of spices have people investing in gold and jewels and rich clothing, making them targets for rapine and crime. Through this mix of wealth, power, and corruption cuts the large German frame of the Count of Saxony, off to rest and recover.[74] He cannot pursue his two greatest pleasures, seduction of women at court and defeating his enemy in battle. An illegitimate son of Frederick Augusts of Saxony, later King of Poland, Saxe has been a soldier of fortune for years, fighting for Prince Eugene of Savoy as a twelve-year-old boy and, later, for Peter the Great of Russia against the Swedes in the Great Northern War. His latest foe is the Ottoman Empire, and now he wanders Paris preparing to study mathematics and how to build his reputation enough to command an army of France. Strong enough to bend horseshoes with his bare hands and flamboyant in costume and words, Saxe has recently drained his wife's fortunes before divorcing her and awaits the next chance for glory in bed and battle. But as illness sacks his otherwise robust constitution in Paris, he turns to writing. He drafts a short memoir and pieces of what would become his great work, *Mes Rêveries*, circulated privately through his life and published only after his death in 1750.

"This work was not born from a desire to establish a new system [*système*] of the art of war," Saxe wrote in the final version. "I composed it to amuse and instruct myself."[75] For thirteen nights in Paris he writes up a storm, for which he begs forgiveness: "I was sick; thus it very probably shows the fever I had. This should supply my excuses for the irregularity of the arrangement, as well as for the inelegance of the style. I wrote militarily and to dissipate by boredom."[76] But dismissing works of scholarship was a convention of all aristocrats. They needed to appear bored and amateur. The remnants of chivalric code demanded they not be seen as scholars. Saxe was a soldier, a seducer, and a man of action. Scholars were weak men of reflection remarking on the great deeds of others. So, great men "indulged" in musings of military affairs for amusement and for themselves. Certainly not to influence the future. And yet that is exactly what Saxe accomplished.[77]

In *Mes Rêveries* Saxe disdained the "slavish adherence to custom" which military life cherished.[78] "War is a science so obscure and imperfect that, in general, no rules of conduct can be given in it, which are reducible to absolute certainties; custom and prejudice, confirmed by ignorance, are its sole foundation and support."[79] He defended the advantages of small armies to move quickly and decisively over large ones and believed it was possible for a general to wage war "throughout his career without resorting to battle. Skillful movement and close attention to logistics should bring a commander the desired result without bloodshed." These were not the ramblings of a bookish, armchair general or philosopher, but one of the great captains of his time.[80] Twenty-odd years later, Saxe would drive a crushing defeat on the British at the battle of Fontenoy (1745), among the bloodiest battles of the era. As the cannon died, Saxe led King Louis XV of France through a corpse-strewn battlefield, some men bloated and yellow, others screaming their last words, the agony from cannon, canister shot, musket, and bayonet rending them into human material. Of the 95,000 participants at Fontenoy, 15,000 were dead and wounded. "Sire," Saxe was alleged to have said to the king, "now you see what war really means."[81] And yet, his era was one of restraint on war. The wars of religion in the previous century were horrific, near-genocidal events. Fontenoy was a bloody battle, but it would pale in comparison to the wars of the French Revolution in ferocity, size, and annihilation that lay in the future. Saxe preferred a different approach to battle, one that championed guile as much as force.

Mes Rêveries received mixed reviews, despite Saxe's reputation. In the mid-nineteenth century, after the wars of Napoleon had shattered the wars of the Enlightenment, Saxe had made famous Scottish philosopher and historian Thomas Carlyle dismiss *Mes Rêveries* as a "strange military farrago dictated, as I should think, under opium." Carlyle is credited for the "Great Men" thesis in history, where world events are decided by the actions of powerful figures, such as the most famous man of his lifetime, Gen. Napoleon Bonaparte. Clearly, Saxe was no great man. His ideas were for a simpler age of aristocrats in silk stockings and smaller battles of little account. Napoleon's conquests with hundreds of thousands of soldiers in decisive combat and modern industrial power seemed to nullify Saxe's quaint notions of war without battles.[82] By 1914, Saxe was antiquated in the minds of modern soldiers who shaped the Great War.

But Lawrence hadn't learned of Saxe as a soldier. His introduction to military affairs was both personal and academic. And these drivers would allow him to meld antiquated military theories with his major interest in ancient cultures and peoples of the Levant. It is because he had this empathy and knowledge already "in being" that Lawrence was able to devise a strategy that would reshape the revolt and become the paragon of guerrilla warfare in the twentieth century.

"To Defend Nothing and To Shoot Nothing"

—Wadi Ais, Arabia, March of 1917.

Feverish, Lawrence dissected the difference in the war in Europe and in Arabia. "Ours seemed unlike the ritual of which Foch was priest," he wrote later, commenting on Gen. Ferdinand Foch, who would be made supreme commander of allied forces in Europe and become a symbol for brutal, grinding combat against modern arms.

> *I recalled him, to see a difference in kind between him and us. In his modern war absolute war he called it two nations professing incompatible philosophies put them to the test of force. Philosophically, it was idiotic, for while opinions were arguable, convictions needed shooting to be cured; and the struggle could end only when the supporters of the one immaterial principle had no more means of resistance against the supporters of the other. . . . To me the Foch war seemed only an exterminative variety. One could as explicably call it "murder war."*[83]

As the revolt teetered, Lawrence saw and realized that the object of his own strategy was "to follow the direction of de Saxe and reach victory without battle, by pressing our advantages mathematical and psychological."[84] The last thing the Arab Revolt should do is emulate the waste and destruction of the Western Front. "Battles in Arabia were a mistake," Lawrence noted later,

> *since we profited in them only by the ammunition the enemy fired off. Napoleon had said it was rare to find generals willing to fight battles; but the curse of this war was that so few could do anything else. Saxe had told us that irrational battles were the refuges of fools; rather they seemed to me impositions on the side which believed itself weaker, hazards made unavoidable either by lack of land room or by the need to defend a material property dearer than the lives of soldiers. We had nothing material to lose, so our best line was to defend nothing and to shoot nothing.*[85]

An attack on Medina was foolish, especially since Abdullah was a mediocre military leader. If they could turn Medina into a prison, that would achieve the same end as decisive battle. After orchestrating demolition raids on the Hejaz railway, Prince Feisal recalled him to Wejh. Lawrence shared his strategy with British colleagues Maj. Pierce Charles Joyce and Capt. N. N. E. Bray. Both agreed a concentrated attack on Medina was better than Lawrence's scheme.[86] Besides, who was this captain to discuss changes in strategy?

Instead, Lawrence kept his plan to himself on how best to use Feisal's forces to get the strategic port city of Aqaba. He would organize the Arabs for a march on Aqaba from the eastern desert. Lawrence knew that the guns of Aqaba pointed west at threats from the sea, for it was assumed no force would consider crossing thousands of miles through the burning desert to attack it from the east. Major Clayton, his boss at the Arab Bureau, had thought any assault on Aqaba would induce the Arabs to think it was theirs to do with as they pleased, and given its value to the security of Egypt and the Suez Canal, he wanted it in British hands.

So, in the summer of 1917, Lawrence brought Saxe's ideas to life in the Arabian Desert. From Aqaba, the Arabs would have secure ports for British support as they built the "ladders of the tribes" "Tafileh and the Dead Sea; then Azrak and Deraa, and finally Damascus." He executed this improvised operation without the approval or knowledge of his government. Failure could mean removal from the war. Success could mean the stabilization of the revolt in a victory. Either course offered fatality. The June 5 entry in Lawrence's diary, written a month before the victory at Aqaba, read simply, "Will ride N and chuck it."[87]

Aqaba was the culmination of many facets in Lawrence's arsenal, wedded to the unpopular theorist, and established the victory in which his future successes and controversies were born.

"The Very Book for a Man Interested in Violent Political Revolutions"

As the narrative indicates, Lawrence played a critical role in supporting, shaping, and employing the Arab Revolt. His ideas on doctrine for guerrilla forces allowed a relatively small number of raiders to detain and nullify superior conventional forces of Turks at Medina. His personal goal, of wanting Feisal's forces in Damascus to forestall his government's own agenda in the Middle East, was daring and also treasonous. It was accomplished because of the old adage of preparation meeting opportunity. But that preparation was done without any prewar desire, interest, or investment in soldiering. He demonstrated the value of a subject-matter expert at war. He also showed that a guerrilla force could effectively support much larger conventional operations: Allenby worked with Lawrence to maximize the effort of the Arab Revolt with the British march into the Holy Lands. Through his intelligence work, he educated his colleagues as best he could about the dynamic nature and Arab culture and the unique features of this theater of war.[88] He kept the use of British regulars to a minimum, and thus the great victories at Aqaba and later Deraa were not done with a heavy Western presence. In two years, the Arab Revolt went from an idea, one largely improvised, to a successful irregular warfare effort, backed and advised by the British but executed by a previous nonexistent Arab fighting force. The tragedy remains that British promises for a free Arabia were lies. Yet the legacy of the revolt, as opposed to the bitter diplomacy afterward, was left to Lawrence to proclaim. And while historians can mutter about the relative value of the Arab Revolt in the Great War, and Lawrence's occasional embellishments on his own efforts, none can deny that Lawrence's view and ideas of warfare, born of the revolt, found purchase throughout the globe.

After the war, Lawrence worked for the Foreign Office during the Paris Treaty Conference of 1919. Sir Winston Churchill secured him as an advisor in numerous committees on the future of the people of Arabia (see chapter 7). But disgust at the future Arab world under British and French control was too much to make a career in diplomacy, where his personal sacrifices couldn't find purchase. He retreated from the public eye, first to Oxford, where he wrote his celebrated memoir *Seven Pillars of Wisdom*, and then hid as an enlisted man in the Royal Air Force and the Armoured Corps. Assumed names followed, hiding his identity as he wrote a novel (*The Mint)* of life in the Royal Air Force (RAF) and his own translation of Homer's *The Odyssey*.

Fame found him early. A traveling picture show of Lawrence and Allenby's exploits in the Holy Land became a popular postwar attraction. The image of Lawrence dressed in Arab fashion secured in the popular imagination the unique identity of "Lawrence of Arabia." His friend Donald Graves, a noted writer and poet, wrote a celebratory biography. Films were planned of his life, which he resisted at all quarters, and occurred only twenty-five years after his death. While Lawrence loved and hated his celebrity, his ideas spread.

His article "Evolution of a Revolt" appeared in 1920 and earned fans fast. Basil Liddell Hart, a journalist, expert in women's clothing, and popular military historian, had fought at the Somme. He detested the British way of war on the Western Front but loved Lawrence's ideas. As military editor of the *Britannica*, he asked Lawrence to write the newest entry on guerrilla warfare. Lawrence refused, but he was intrigued and helped Liddell Hart write the entry. Liddell Hart signed it "TEL."[89] Lawrence had written a draft of his wartime memoir, *Seven Pillars of Wisdom*, but it was tragically lost at a railway station in 1919. Lawrence's second attempt, written from memory, emerged in 1926 in a tiny print run. But pressure to write a condensed popular version resulted in the bestselling *Revolt in the Desert*. After his death, *Seven Pillars* was rereleased and has yet to go out of print.

Lawrence's story, ideas, and celebrity spread like a virus. Writers, politicians, and soldiers as well as the general public were fascinated with his work and life. Pioneering thriller writer and politician John Buchan, author of the suspense classic *The Thirty-Nine Steps*, riffed on Lawrence's ideas of guerrilla warfare for his South American adventure novel *The Courts of the Morning* (1929) and became a minor colleague.[90] American literary tough-guy Ernest Hemingway was already the celebrated author of *The Sun Also Rises* and *A Farewell to Arms* when he read *Revolt in the Desert* in 1931, "the very book for a man interested in violent political revolutions."[91] Hemingway then devoured every available work on Lawrence, from his books and articles to a published collection of letters, and used his ideas and theories as part of his great work on the Spanish Civil War, *For Whom the Bell Tolls*. The hero, Robert Jordan, fights like Lawrence and excels at blowing up railways and bridges.[92]

When the Soviet Russian edition of the 1929 *Britannica* was published, the entry "Guerrilla" found fans in the communist brain trust. Revolutionaries and leaders, including Chinese politician and strategist Mao Tse Tung, melded Lawrence's theories with their own ideas of political revolution and war.[93] Vietnamese historian and soldier Gen. Vo Nguyen Giap was a disciple of Lawrence. In a brief respite before the Vietminh went to war with the French in 1946, Giap had a fateful exchange with French general Raul Salan. "My fighting gospel is T. E. Lawrence's *Seven Pillars of Wisdom*," Giap said. "I am never without it."[94] Salan wondered aloud what useful lesson could be taken from a desert revolt in Arabia to the jungles of Southeast Asia, a rhetorical question to point out the foolishness of Giap's admiration. Giap noted, "Is that your assessment of Lawrence?" Salan nodded. "Then you have missed the whole point of Lawrence. He is less about fighting a guerrilla war than leading one. And *leadership*," Giap emphasized, "is applicable in any context: desert or jungle, military or civilian." To the horror of the French and, later, the Americans, Giap would prove an able student of Lawrence.[95]

Biographies of Lawrence soon rushed out from friends and colleagues. After Graves came Liddell Hart's *Lawrence of Arabia* (1934), the angry historian's first bestseller. Lawrence was the "Drake of the Desert," whose ideas on avoiding direct battle inspired Liddell Hart's own theories of modern war, which thrived in Britain and Germany before the Second World War. His ideas on the "indirect approach" to combat, the opposite of the decisive battle that bred stagnation on the Western Front, owed a debt to Lawrence. *Lawrence of Arabia* would be the last biography with the man's input. Lawrence died in a motorcycle accident in 1935.[96]

Challenges to Lawrence's own accounts also thrived after his death. Novelist and veteran Richard Aldington took Lawrence to task in a cynically written biography filled with denunciations of Lawrence's conduct and salacious gossip about Lawrence being a homosexual who solicited servicemen while in the RAF. His death, argued novelist and rumormonger Somerset Maugham, was in fact a suicide to hide his shame. More actual evidence came to light that Lawrence engaged in sadomasochistic practices, including being whipped on the back by a former soldier. Beyond the mysteries of his sexual interest, Lawrence's reputation was also attacked by esteemed Oxford historian Hugh Trevor-Roper in 1977, who cast Lawrence as one of the great "charlatan's and frauds" of the century. For Trevor-Roper, Lawrence's feats were exaggerated by his literary aspirations. The real amazing fact of his war record was that his con worked.[97] Sadly, Trevor-Roper's own reputation was bludgeoned when he claimed to have "authenticated" the so-called Hitler Diaries that emerged in 1983, which were later proven to be a hoax.[98] However, in 1990, Jeremy Wilson's authoritative and "authorized" (by the family) biography of Lawrence offered the first intensive and primary source-rich narrative that investigated Lawrence's life, as much as possible, on documents other than Lawrence's own postwar reflections. Wilson's conclusion, supported by other Lawrence scholars, is that Lawrence's exploits, while dramatically retold, were largely rooted in verity and not imagination. These feats were noted at the time by those around him, including his adversaries and enemies.[99] More importantly, Lawrence's ideas and text continue to inspire the global discussion of military affairs. Gen. David Petraeus, the soldier-scholar whose efforts in Iraq and Afghanistan were informed by his appreciation of Lawrence's ideas and principles, used Lawrence as part of the revived counterinsurgency principles used in the surge. The 2006 U.S. Army COIN manual uses Lawrence's efforts as an advisor in foreign forces.[100] Yet, lost in the ideas was Lawrence's approach. While a soldier may read his works and take his advice, none could walk his path, because it was instrumental that Lawrence was not a soldier.

But Lawrence had contemporary mavericks. His famous and fascinating colleague Gertrude Bell is discussed later in chapter 7, but his peer in Germany has largely fallen into a memory hole. Like Lawrence, he was an eccentric and initiative-driven maverick. And the scheme that led him to war in foreign lands is no less gripping than the Arab Revolt, and even more audacious.

Chapter 2

"The Lone and Hopeless Struggle": Wilhelm Wassmuss and the German Experiment in Islamic Insurgencies, 1914–1918

He rendered stout and remarkable service to his country; if, indeed, they can be measured by the degree of worry and preoccupation which they involved to those concerned with the protection of British subjects and interest in the ostensibly neutral territory of Southern Persia.[1]

—PERCY COX, CHIEF POLITICAL OFFICER IN MESOPOTAMIA

The more tolerant opinion was that he was a crazy fool . . .[2]

—CHRISTOPHER SYKES, *Wassmuss, "The German Lawrence"*

"Treacherous, Forbidding Wasteland"

On May 21, 1916, a month before the Arab Revolt, two agent provocateurs begin a race from Kabul to Berlin.

Traveling north together along a path once taken by Alexander the Great, they came to the hamlet of Dasht-irewat upon the Sarhica Road leading to Tajikistan.[3] Geographer and soldier Capt. Oskar von Niedermayer heads west, above Persia, through the Hindu Kush mountains. "He was a man of forceful personality," one historian noted, "a man whom military discipline was almost instinctive; he was that kind of man who made the German Army almost invincible."[4]

Meanwhile, diplomat, soldier, and explorer Otto Hentig traveled east along the old Silk Road toward Chinese Central Asia. Hentig spoke Persian, had traveled in Asia, and had been, like Niedermayer, yanked from the war in Europe for service in the Middle East.[5] Two long months of snow and suffering follow Hentig's path. Kashgar, the capital, offered the promise of a telegraph, and possible capture.

Niedermayer and Hentig had two goals: survive, and, be the first to inform the Imperial German government that their secret mission to inflame the Muslim peoples of Afghanistan, Persia, and India into *jihad* against Britain and Russia had failed. First to arrive would get the spoil of telling the Kaiser who to blame.

Disguised as a Turcoman with a red-dyed-beard, Niedermayer took his retinue on what appeared to be the less dangerous road through north-western path in Russian Central Asia, avoiding the path this team of insurgents had originally taken through Persia and now cordoned by the British. But his Turkoman escorts were opium addicts who needed constant breaks and soon deserted him. Alone in the wilds, he ran afoul of Russian soldiers in Meshed and like an American cowboy rode his horse out of town, taking the main road south to Tehran.[6] A day's journey from the Persian capital, Niedermayer found his caravan surrounded by brigands. A firefight left horses dead, and Niedermayer was beaten unconscious, robbed, and left for dead.

To the East, Hentig leads his men to Yarkland, the center of an "ancient Buddhist kingdom on the Silk road," and stirs up rebellion with lies of German successes and German troops pouring into Afghanistan to support uprisings against the Russians and British. "Local tribesmen staged a revolt in several districts and murdered a handful of Russian settlers," but the Chinese suppressed them quickly: most insurgents were killed or captured.[7] So it was time to march further into the East. "I shall never forget the marches that followed," Hentig recalled. "It was a black and stormy and cold time, in which we traveled into a foodless, treacherous, forbidding wasteland."[8]

In Persia, reduced to begging shepherds and nomads for support, Niedermayer survived and made his way to Tehran, disguised among British and Russian troops and diplomats and their allies, gathering supplies before pressing east toward the Ottoman Empire's Middle Eastern territories in September 1916. He returned to Berlin before the year ended, winning first place to establish the truth.

For Hentig, Kashgar was "a volatile and unpredictable place for a European," but fearing capture of his small rebellions he rode hard for the capital. He cut a seven-day journey into two nights and a day, evading Chinese and Mongol horsemen before a Chinese official admitted him to the city. But his presence was soon known. Rumors of his looming execution rose in the streets. Hentig's bluffs about German strength in the region soon lost luster. He was let go. By December 24, 1916, he had spent 130 days in Chinese deserts, and pressed for Peking. He'd find passage to the United States only to become an enemy alien as the nation declared war on Germany. Hentig outwitted American officials and British intrigues, returning to Berlin in early 1917.[9]

Niedermayer received a hero's welcome. His epic tale of survival seemingly overshadowed the complete failure of his mission to persuade the Emir of Afghanistan into leading a revolt into India that would ignite the Muslim world against the Allies. But, of course, Hentig was the diplomat, and as such the diplomatic failure was his own. Yet, Hentig had also caused more damage en route, keeping the embers of the mission alive, than had Niedermayer. Hentig later praised the captain for his leadership and endurance[10] but criticized him for taking glory earned by others.[11] Yet another man remained in Persia, continuing his mission as a private crusade to create as much havoc as possible for the British, improvising a rebellion out of willpower, bluff, and bluster.

"He was an impressive man to look at," his biographer noted. "He always wore his hair long and this showed too much advantage of his fine forehead. His eyes were very penetrating . . . . . His features were regular and they had in them an expression of great power."[12] Unlike his compatriots, this man would have to be dragged out of Persia in 1919. His name is Wilhelm Wassmuss, and he would die penniless in Germany in 1931.

Since the end of the First World War, Wassmuss has been derided as a failure and blowhard, his Persian rebellion and the entire scheme of Islamic revolt a terrible mistake. Wassmuss was most notorious for losing diplomatic codes that the British would use to decoding German communiqués, including the infamous Zimmerman Telegram (a false attribution, as we will see). Indeed, he, like Niedermayer and Hentig, failed. But from 1915 to 1918, Wassmuss demonstrated how much havoc a single maverick can make. And his failure raises important questions on why mavericks succeed. Yet despite his failures, he was never a clown to his enemies.

"Once a fortnight the Intelligence Branch of the General Staff issued a map showing the distribution of the enemy's forces in the Eastern theaters of war," noted historian Jules Stewart. "Across the western corner if Persia, in an area several times the size of England, there was written in red ink a single world: 'Wassmuss.'"[13]

"Merciless Diplomat"

Born in Hannover in 1880, Wassmuss passed the Foreign Service examinations in 1906 as Germany continued to build its imperial holdings in Africa and Asia and served in Madagascar. Oil reserves discovered in 1908 had made Persia a target for Anglo/Russian rivalry for the Middle East and Central Asia, the so called "Great Game." For the Persians, Imperial Germany was an ally against the dominant threats of London and Moscow.[14] Wassmuss served as a consular agent in the western province of Bushire for over a year, and was made Persian Gulf Consul in 1909. He left in 1910 to study Persian scholarship for three years, collected documents on ancient East African history, and returned to Bushire in 1913.[15] Among the tribes of the region, especially the Tangistani, Wassmuss proved himself a popular diplomat. He wore their dress and traveled north to the town of Kazerun, establishing himself as colleague and sympathizer with many of the anti-British peoples and leaders, respecting their culture while pursuing his nation's interest. Such prewar expertise and relationships would be the heart of his rebellion.[16]

A short and heavyset man, Wassmuss was an excellent horseman and keen agent whose forceful personality was prone to aggressive forms of persuasion.[17] British geographer, soldier, and civil servant Percy Cox served in Persia at the same time. Wassmuss was "good fellow," Cox recalled, generally liked as a private citizen, but often a merciless diplomat. In disputes he became "troublesome and truculent to deal with, as he was inclined to make up for some lack of tact and diplomatic amenity by an early recourse to threat and bluster."[18] Wassmuss viewed Cox as a professional adversary. He wrote Berlin in December 1913 that Cox "feared every economic influence that Germany might obtain in the Gulf," and that Cox "saw his ambition of making the Gulf an exclusively British sea endangered by every shipload of barley and every tone of oxide exported by the Germans."[19] He despised British influence and the use of British troops against the Tangestani. For Wassmuss, the British were chiefly responsible for the suffering of the Persian people.[20] In August 1914 he handed over the consulate to a Doctor Listermann and returned to Berlin for future war work, where his expertise was noticed by an eccentric archeologist with the Foreign Service who had concocted a bold scheme.[21]

During the Great War, Imperial Germany created a controversial wartime strategy, secondary to their use of conventional arms. They would support and instigate a series of revolutions, rebellions, and insurgencies against the Triple Entente in Europe, Africa, the Middle East, and Central Asia. Unlike the cataclysmic battles of the Great War, Germany had no long-standing tradition in such unconventional warfare.[22] But there was a member of the Foreign Service who had been championing the use of rebellion among the Muslim population of enemy lands for some time.

Baron Max von Oppenheim was an outspoken amateur archeologist who had discovered Tell Halaf, a "rich treasure trove" of artifacts from ancient Syria. His skills and standing led to grudging acceptance by his peers. A young T. E. Lawrence had some disdain for "the little Jew-German millionaire" Oppenheim, a "horrible person" he'd met in Arabia before the war.[23] Oppenheim's travels and knowledge of Egypt and Arabia led him to work led him to the Foreign Service. Being eccentric and half-Jewish, however, barred from the highest echelons of Germany's diplomatic ranks. So, Oppenheim channeled his energies into his chief obsession: the use of religious extremism to serve Germany's interest against their imperial rivals. Powerful elites subscribed to similar views.

The Kaiser viewed the Middle East as rife for exploitation and worked hard to make Germany appear to be a friend of the Muslim peoples, including of the Ottoman Empire (which made their erstwhile ally concerned, given various levels of oppression of the Muslim members of their empire). Field Marshall Helmut von Moltke, the architect of victory for Germany's wars of unification, believed that religious fervor against Britain and Russia might offer Germany influence outside its growing sphere of influence. But Germany had no precedent for creating such havoc in foreign nations. The German Army, a faction of power within the government and culture, had precious little interest in anything but modern industrial warfare against its foes in Europe. While other imperial nations could speak of "small wars" doctrine and traditions of fighting in and among foreign people to crush or create insurgencies, Germany's experience in imperial warfare was localized and brutal.

Under innovative explorer Hermann von Wissmann, Germany had initiated the Schutztruppe, African mercenaries and soldiers who trained under German officers. Wissmann noted the importance of religion and culture awareness in harnessing what would largely be a counterinsurgency force of indigenous people in East Africa, quelling revolts against Germanic rule. He also recognized the need to respect local politics to obtain Germany's aims. His short treatise on imperial warfare was Germany's first colonial warfare doctrine (1903).[24] But as an outsider whose reputation was sullied by accusations of morphine addiction, Wissmann's doctrine was easily manipulated. It initially combined political savvy and even empathy for the African people, all of which was burned out by his conventionally minded replacements who emphasized brutality and conventional force against dehumanized indigenous enemies. The resulting genocides of the Herero and Nama were seen by some as the prelude of later German brutality in the world wars.[25] Beyond using the African theater as training ground for modern war, the German Army had no interest or tradition in creating rebellions in foreign lands.[26] Such things were left to the Foreign Service, where Oppenheim had been writing and pressing for the use of rebellion since the 1890s.

"A Sweeping Programme of Global Insurrection . . ."

The Great War began on July 26, 1914. By Autumn, the German Foreign Office under Foreign Secretary Gottfried von Jagow and Undersecretary Arthur Zimmermann "launched a sweeping programme [*sic*] of global insurrection" that would begin in Poland and reach Persia. By October, Oppenheim completed *Memorandum Concerning the Fermenting of*

Revolutions in Islamic Territories of Our Enemies. It culminated a twenty-year effort to shape German foreign policy toward the use of Islamic insurgency and would become the catalyst for the policy of rebellion in the Middle East. These revolts would be fostered by German, Turkish, and Indian agents already in theater and building the initial acts of defiance. It would require a massive propaganda effort, finances for bribes, and gifts and appreciation for leaders, but not vast numbers of German manpower. An entire section is dedicated to the complex political and military ties required fermenting rebellion in Persia, Afghanistan, and India. If the Emir of Afghanistan could be persuaded by a combined German and Turkish diplomatic mission to move from wartime neutrality to the declaration of *jihad* against Britain and Russia, the Muslims in all enemy territories could be forged into insurgencies and revolts that would drain Allied focus, manpower, and resources away from the European Theater. It might signal the end of their dominance in the region. Rich oil reserves and strategic positioning in the Persian Gulf awaited Germany if she was bold enough to risk it. Compared to the colossal efforts of conventional industrial war in Europe, the cost could be minimal.[27] "For England especially," Oppenheim noted, "the intervention of Islam in the present war is a fearful blow. Let us do everything in our power, let us use all possible means to make it a fatal one!"[28]

Oppenheim's vision was challenged for its audacity and practicality. Orientalist Ernst Jäckh had pursued an independent assessment of such schemes, though strictly in the denizens of Constantinople in mid-December. His report on January 3, 1915, was void of Oppenheim's enthusiasm. "The general impression can be summed up thus: all our undertakings have been set up belatedly and in an improvised manner, for no preparations had been made in peacetime." It was an obvious point. These missions had to be improvised because Germany had no tradition of complex political/military actions in foreign lands that demanded deep cultural, geographic, and religious awareness to achieve strategic aims (see below).[29] Global war, however, made insurgent warfare more viable and interesting. Jäckh's arguments were not as compelling as the mission's potential. Turkey joined the Central Powers against the allies that October, and Oppenheim's ideas were sanctioned by the Kaiser and became part of Imperial German strategy "[O]ur consuls in Turkey and India, agents etc. must inflame the while Mohammedan world to wild revolt against this hateful, lying conscienceless people of hagglers," Kaiser Wilhelm II noted in 1914, "for if we are to be bled to death, at least England shall lose India."[30] In November, Mehmed IV, the wary Sultan of the Ottoman empire, "proclaimed holy war and appealed to the Muslim subjects of the Entente powers to join in a common struggle with the Ottoman Empire." Oppenheim's first condition of success, Turkish support, had been reached. He created the *Nachrictenstelle für den Orient*, "Orient Intelligence Bureau," to become the propaganda and intelligence hub for these missions, filled with German scholars for these regions, including future Chancellor Franz von Papen. Lastly, he also picked the two leaders of the Persian and Afghan mission.

"Overcome by the Spirit of Adventure"

Capt. Oskar von Niedermayer was taken from the battles of the contested Lorraine Forest and sent to Berlin. The General Staff only informed him that he was to join a "combined German-Turkish expedition to Afghanistan, for the purpose of stirring up trouble for the British in India." But the mission's details were at the Ministry of Foreign Affairs. Niedermayer was himself a less conventional mind among the German Army. He had studied geography, geology, and philology at the University of Erlangen and between 1912 and 1914 engaged with privately funded research journey across Persia and Asia.[31] As one historian noted, the "new discipline of geopolitics attracted him, but he retained an independent, critical view of its not infrequent tendency to convert geographic realities into political absolutes."[32] Between 1912 and 1913 he received leave to travel in Persia, joined the Bahai movement, and made many contacts with religious leaders.[33]

He viewed the Foreign Service mandarins who concocted the scheme with interest, but also disdain. From the armchair of hindsight, Niedermayer recalled his view of the mission as "extremely dubious." Few of the twenty-five men already in Constantinople knew anything of Persia; others had no knowledge of the East, and most were soldiers with experience in Africa who had bad habits, attitudes, and zero cultural awareness or cares while traveling in Turkey. "I must, however, admit frankly, that my various scruples were finally overcome by the spirit of adventure which had once more been roused within me."[34] Niedermayer claimed he was given full command of the divided mission, but he refused, "for an enterprise of this kind was far too heavy for me, since I was one of the junior members . . ."[35] for "I was the only one who had an actual knowledge of Persia and India."[36] This was not true. Oppenheim recommended that leadership for the Persian mission be given to Wassmuss. And, in a great irony, Wassmuss had recommended Niedermayer for the Afghan mission.[37] It is unknown if Wassmuss had any hesitations, but he took the mantle of leadership of an untried group of Turkish and German soldiers and diplomats.

Friction was immediate. While in Turkey, the African veterans under Wassmuss made a nuisance of themselves. They disdained the Turkish officers, insulted their culture by smoking and drinking in a Muslim capital, and refused to dress as Turkish officers as part of the mission's necessary disguise: all while the Turks were in overall command of the mission at this stage and still on Turkish soil. Unlike these soldiers, Wassmuss had deep affection and respect for both Turks and the Persians and, bolstering Niedermayer's point, he had a far deeper appreciation of their language, culture, and politics among even the diplomats of the mission. W. Griesinger, who would attempt to raise havoc in Kerman and Baluchistan with Professor Erich Zugmayer (a zoologist who had recently travelled in the region) often referred to the Persians and Afghans as "dirty beasts."[38] Wassmuss tried to reign in the raucous African soldiers, but failed. So he ordered the worst of them back to Germany, thinning the mission's resources but improving their chances. They were gone by the time Niedermayer arrived in Aleppo on December 13, harangued that Wassmuss had left with his "loyalists" without him and clearly trying to establish his dominance of the party. Now Wassmuss had to contend with a senior military leader who also had expertise in Persia and could not be dismissed.[39]

They had met in Persia before the war, where Niedermayer had "formed a high opinion of [Wassmuss's] abilities" while the latter been a consul. Wassmuss was so impressed that he'd made sure Niedermayer would lead the Afghan side of the expedition. But Wassmuss would not relinquish control to a lieutenant. Niedermayer's men found Wassmuss bossy. They debated the best course of action. Wassmuss desired a longer southern route to reach the Afghan border, traveling among the pro-German tribesmen that he had worked with before the war. It was more time, but less risk. Niedermayer refused, wanting a shorter central route that took them to Tehran, which was riddled with British and Russian agents and soldiers. Wassmuss, in turn, became "obstinate" that his route was the soundest. He even wrote Chancellor Bethmann Hollweg that his problem was not with Niedermayer, but Oppenheim, whose "endless committee meetings in Berlin he blamed for the delays in getting the mission's supplies to Constantinople."[40] Meanwhile, Turkish war minister Enver Pasha was now more concerned with the consolidation of Russian troops in North Persia than the Islamic rebellion. He would send Turkish and Kurdish troops into Persia and attacked the Russians at Tabriz on January 15, 1916. He pressed the Germans to hand over command of their mission to Turkish officers.

Both Wassmuss and Niedermayer agreed that such a move would effectively kill the mission. As Wassmuss told Professor Zugmayer, they must not deliver the mission "into the hands of the Turks."[41] But neither Wassmuss nor Niedermayer was willing to serve under the other. Between December 13 and 21, the mission was split into two groups. There is no clear evidence who made the decision, or if it was mutual, or if one man took action when tired of words.[42] However, Zugmayer recorded in his diary that on December 18, 1914, "Wassmuss intends to separate himself from the expedition for some time, work alone in South Persia. He and Niedermayer want to leave soon for Baghdad, the rest of us first to Mosul, then wait for further orders."[43] On December 21, Wassmuss and Niedermayer left for Persia on their own routes. Wassmuss would raise rebellions to help prove to the Emir of Afghanistan that Persia was in Islamic revolt, and then head for Afghanistan. Niedermayer would lead the military half of the mission. Meanwhile, Berlin sent a replacement for Wassmuss in Kabul, Otto von Hentig, himself fresh from fighting as part of the cavalry against the Russians on the Eastern Front.[44]

"I regretted his departure from our small party," Niedermayer noted, "he was the only member of the Expedition, besides myself, who had any personal knowledge of Persia. I certainly could not fail to appreciate the reason for his resolve."[45] Niedermayer's task was mighty and daunting, crossing Persia into Afghanistan with untrained men. But far more deadly was the mission of Wassmuss, who intended to set South West Persia ablaze.

Persia in 1915 was a twilight zone of intrigue, violence, and bluff in the shadow of the Western and Eastern Fronts. For the Germans, it was far more dangerous than Afghanistan. As part of the 1907 Anglo/Russian accord, Britain and Russia were not allowed into Afghanistan, but both had an active diplomatic, military, and intelligence presence in Persia. Russians in the north and the British in the south generated ill will and resentment. Since the war, the Turks had made incursions that soured locals on those affiliated with them. The temperament of the people was in flux for the rest of the war regarding who they hated most. The central government in Tehran was weak, with little authority beyond the city. The Swedish Genderarmie, tasked with security since 1907, was trained in Germany, often corrupt, and sympathetic to Berlin. The discovery of oil in 1908 had established the Persian Gulf as Britain's strategic fuel hub East of Suez, especially since the Royal Navy had switched from coal to oil. These assets were controlled by the government majority in the Anglo-Persian Oil Company. To protect its interest, Britain established deals with the Bakhtiyâri Khans who controlled the region around their oil fields and subsidized their loyalty. But when Wassmuss began his operations, fear grew. Gold might not be enough to assuage local hatred of British troops.[46]

British intelligence soon uncovered more evidence of the German mission in Persia in February 1915. A German agent was caught collecting data on British naval forces; he was bound for Bushire, home of the nearest wireless set. The German consul in Bushire, Dr. Listermann, who had replaced Wassmuss at the start of the war, was caught urging local tribes to attack the poorly defended British residency. The Shah refused British calls to arrest Listermann so, without his approval and despite his diplomatic immunity, Listermann's German Consulate was occupied and he was sent to India. The consulate was raided and within it was found propaganda materials in Pashto, Farsi, and Urdu. Wassmuss's cover was blown. He was among the German agents attempting to incite inciting Pan Islamic revolts in Persia and Afghanistan.[47] British soldiers discovered him in Shustarn, but Wassmuss proved adept at evading capture. He escaped and made it as far as Behbehan Fars before being captured on March 5, 1915, by tribal horsemen paid by the British.

Maj. Gen. Percy Cox, resident and chief political officer to the expeditionary force at Basra, was in charge of his capture but Wassmuss escaped before the British arrived to secure him.[48] What he dropped, however, became legend. Among his abandoned materials was his diplomatic codebook. British made use of the book, and here things become hyperbolic. British intelligence claimed it allowed them to decrypt German diplomatic codes, and was instrumental to the British to intercept the 1917 "Zimmerman Telegram," a secret German cable calling for a military alliance between Germany and Mexico and aimed at the United States.[49] And otherwise astute historians have also claimed Wassmuss never informed his government of the loss of the codebook. Thus, Wassmuss is best remembered for a failure that started a long causal chain leading to the United States' entry into the Great War. But these assertions were contested. Historian Seth McMeekin demonstrated that Wassmuss had informed Berlin of the loss of the codebook as soon as he reached Shiraz. And while the British may have found his book useful, "it cannot have been decisive in deciphering the Zimmerman telegram, which was encrypted with an entirely different cipher."[50] Thus Wassmuss was slandered with a clownish celebrity and his efforts paled in comparison to the incorrect assumptions about the strategic impact of his abandoned codebook. In actuality, he was far more dangerous than a dupe.

His influence was immediate and greatest in Fars, along with other smaller groups in Kermansha, Kerman, and Isfahan.[51] After his March escape, Wassmuss found sanctuary with the Qashqai tribe and Khan Sault-ud-Duala, one of the strongest tribes in Fars.[52] He made his way to Shiraz, and enlisted the aid of the pro-German Gendarmerie and local mujahedeen before heading to Tangistan and Kazerun to organize more support for a rebellion. Niedermayer provided material support until the lines with the south were cut. They reestablished connection through a network of anti-British bandits near Tehran; thus Niedermayer was also able to send Wassmuss news and money before they headed for Afghanistan in July.[53] The arrival of the Wassmuss and company had immediate effects. According to one official history, the "effect of the German propaganda in Arabistan at once became more apparent. Arab cavalry were being encountered daily within ten miles to the northwest of Ahwaz, but our own cavalry were too few in number to be able to cope with them effectually."[54] Wassmuss wanted actions to back words, so he began with bursts of violence and terror by the tribes he knew best.

"THE BATTLE OF BUSHIRE"

First, an Indian cavalryman was shot outside of Bushire.[55] British buildings in Chabar were raided on April 17, 1915, injuring English troops. Wassmuss exaggerated the numbers to spread the fear and influence of the Germans in Persia but they were overshadowed by the British Army's rapid successes against the Turks up the Tigris in Mesopotamia.[56] Still, Wassmuss's presence heightened British fears that Tehran might join the provincial anti-British sentiments and declare war against Britain. Such action threatened a strategic asset: control of British oil in the Persian Gulf.

Wassmuss traveled through Khusistan, controlled by the Bakhtiyâri people, and visited Dizful. His goal was to sow seeds of discontent among the pro-British Khans, men who protected access to facilities of the Anglo-Persian Oil Company. Among possibly hostile Persians, he presented himself as a German alternative and means to help toss off the shackles of British control in the region. Some were intrigued by the opportunity for change.[57] British intelligence took notice.

Cox met with the Bakhtiyâri Khans in May 1915 to thwart Wassmuss. He established a temporary agreement with the Khans. If Persia declared war against the British, and thus the Bakhtiyâri could no longer protect the Anglo-Persian Oil Company, they would provide the company twenty days advance notice and protect the families of the company employees until the British assistance arrived. The main Khans received a thousand pounds each, and in exchange they promised that even if Persia did declare war, their people would answer the call and find a way to make a rebellion ineffectual.[58] Wassmuss still instigated sabotage attacks and the crippling of a pipeline that stopped oil production for several months in 1915.[59]

It remains unclear how much gold Wassmuss had to buy loyalty and support his insurgents as compared to others, including Lawrence, who had, after Aqaba, millions of pounds at his disposal. The "amounts mentioned, during the war and afterwards," Niedermayer recalled, referencing British accounts of the missions, "may certainly be divided by 50 or even by 100, in order to obtain a figure which would be approximately correct. Moreover he would be very astonished to know what great results were often obtained by ridiculously small means. A certain amount of bluff was necessary and, in our position was certainly permissible and essential"[60] Wassmuss's greatest attribute was in convincing others to fight for promises and bought with guile more than gold.

The presence of Wassmuss and other German agents forced the British to prepare more forceful and risky measures. On June 24, 1915, Lt. Gen. Sir John Nixon, commander of British forces in Mesopotamia, was informed by the government of India that he might be called upon to reinforce Bushire at short notice. "Wassmuss, the German agent, was doing his best to induce the local tribes to attack the British residency there."[61] Four days later they made Nixon responsible for the defense of Bushire and instructed him to have a defensive mindset for fear of draining manpower from the campaigns against the Turk. The British garrison was reinforced with two captured 13 pounder Turkish gun, four artillery gunlayers, and instructors. The government of India, with only 15,000 troops and rising fears of domestic insurgencies, said that Nixon's position was ideal. Nixon objected to the new responsibility, 200 miles behind him. He was close enough to do something, but had better things to worry about so he would not squander resources like a young officer with "ambitious tendencies" to make his name against the Germans and Persians.[62] As the British responded to his presence, Wassmuss prepared for violent political action.

The British Residency in Shiraz was under the consul major Frederick O'Connor. It was isolated and lightly defended. On July 12, 1915, before the start of Ramadan, British intelligence noticed 400 tribesman two miles south of the residency. British soldiers were dispatched and faced, according to one source, thousands of Tangistani. Among them was Wassmuss, boosting moral with Koran in hand. The raiders retreated into the hinterland and ended what would be the first "battle of Bushire." Wassmuss's goal was to goad the British into action. It would divert forces away from the Turks and demonstrate to the Persians that the British were not safe.[63]

The British calculated their response. Failure to act would invite more attacks. Abusing Persia's weakness and independence (thin as it was) could also generate volatile opposition. Cox offered a bounty on Wassmuss, dead or alive, though it was revoked: assassinations of foreign diplomats in independent countries, whatever their malfeasances, would make more enemies.[64] Throughout the summer there were also conflicting reports about the loyalty of the Bakhtiyâri, especially from the younger anti-British Khans. Negotiations on loyalty continued.[65] The British asked the Shah to condemn German intrigues and seek retribution for the assault in Bushire. In a fragile balance of power between Great Power intrigue and domestic hatred of foreign influence, he refused. So, the British occupied Bushire with soldiers on August 15, without formal permission from the Shah.

Violence increased. There were punitive actions against the Tangestani base of Dilbar. A brief firefight left sixteen soldiers dead before the Tangistani fled into the interior. The British cut down the palm groves of the village, the chief crop of their limited agriculture, and the town was raised. The cost was sixty to seventy British dead.[66] British violence fed Wassmuss's ranks in Borazjan, his main hub. Ghazanfar al-Saltana and his men were vehemently anti-British and anti-Tehran. They levied illegal taxes, raided caravans, and were happy for Wassmuss to cause ill for their mutual enemies. His men were among the most noted arms merchants (buying and selling) in the Bushire littoral and hinterland.[67] It was estimated that there were 2,000 warriors in the region for Wassmuss to galvanize, most under Zair Khidair of Ahram, capital of Tangestani Country, Bushire.[68] The other bands of German insurgents supported these actions with the murder of a Russian vice consul at Isfahan and expelled the acting governor general. At Yezd, they drove out the British and seized the Imperial Bank of Persia; at Kirman, the British and Russian officials were thrown out and one murdered. The year ended with seven branches of the Imperial Bank of Persia in German hands.

"German Influence Was Paramount in South Persia"

Operationally, the tide turned against the British in the following months. German and Turkish victories grew after the British occupation of Bushire from September to December 1915. There were four raids in Bushire against British and Indian troops, and support grew from reluctant chiefs. British cavalry sent to Mashileh (northeast of Wassmuss's tribal allies) to wipe them out. Morning fog led to a clash in the mist. Eighty British soldiers fell and the tribes escaped while conducting hit-and-run tactics. Each lost similar numbers.[69] Violence against the British permeated Shiraz. O'Connor's men were killed and in September his vice counsel was murdered, as was a mounted messenger. O'Conner discovered that the Genderarmie were active allies of Wassmuss. Given the option to leave, he stayed. In early November, the Tangestani attacked the British Residency and took the eleven members hostage. O'Connor surrendered, and on November 10, he and the men and women were marched on Borazjan.[70]

Wassmuss's conquest in Shiraz preceded the most stunning reversal in the region as the tide against the allies grew. British general Howard Townsend's forces had driven the Turks from Kut earlier, and with relative ease. He was ordered to pursue the Turks to Baghdad, but was repulsed at Ctesiphon by twice as many men as he expected dug into strong defensive positions. By November 24, Townsend decided to retreat to Kut and hold fast for reinforcements.[71] The siege of Kut was prelude to the worst British defeat of the war, and Wassmuss's influence on the operations at Kut before Townsend surrender has been debated for decades. The strange and engaging biography of Wassmuss by Christopher Sykes asserted Wassmuss had diverted 20,000 troops with his guerrilla campaign, troops that may have been used to relieve the soldiers at Kut, but this assertion remains doubtful.[72] Sykes and his editors believed that the British saw Wassmuss as an operational threat, that abandoning Bushire and sending more men and resources solely to Townsend's aid meant that "a great rising against the Allies in South Persia would almost certainly have resulted, the Bakhtiari [*sic*] would have swung their wavering loyalties to the German side, under all this pressure the Sheikh of Mahommerah might have followed suit, and the pipe-line would have been destroyed."[73]

Instead, the British pushed for a formal pact to secure their interests with the Bakhtiyâri. This was signed on December 13, 1915. More Khans signed similar agreements in February 1916.[74] Gen. Sir John Nixon's decision to press the attack to Baghdad was "reinforced" by the need to check German intrigues in Persia. "To regard the capture of Baghdad as impossible would be to give up our best means of countering the German intrigues in Persia and Afghanistan against India and should therefore be dismissed from our calculations," noted Lord Harding, viceroy of India, in a telegraphed message to Austen Chamberlain, secretary of state for India, on November 30, 1915—this was before Kut became synonymous with failure, starvation, and defeat. "Our success hitherto in Mesopotamia has been the main factor which has kept Persia, Afghanistan, and India itself quiet."[75]

British victory in Mesopotamia would be years in the making, first requiring the final defeat of the siege of Kut in April 1916. Gen. Colmar von der Goltz, German commander of Turkish Forces, had drawn up plans for driving the British and Russian power out of Persia, help raise a Persian armed force, and demonstrate to Afghanistan that the tide had turned for a *jihad* into India. Such actions might even counter the British blockade of Germany if it could be done that year. The plan died with von der Goltz that same year.[76] As 1916 began, Wassmuss's efforts in the region had grown from words to deeds and both were as notorious as other German "Angels of Death" in Persia. "German influence was paramount in South Persia," noted Brig. Gen. Percy Sykes, soon to be tasked with containing the Germans. "The Germans looted bank treasuries to the extent of £100,000, apart from the damage done to buildings and in other ways. They also occupied the telegraph offices, and in some cases destroyed instruments; but relatively they did little harm, as they used the line themselves." The British estimated the cadres of agents at roughly 300 Germans and Austrians, 50 Turks and Indian rebels, and perhaps a thousand Persian levies of mixed loyalty.[77] Of the lot, Wassmuss was the "most successful German agent in Persia," being a "stormy petrel" in

Bushire and Fars.[78] The fluid operational environment of 1915 favored Wassmuss and his ilk into 1916, though even he knew the limits. "What I could accomplish here with ammunition and a bit of money!"[79]

Eventually the strategic and tactical events of the year turned against him.

"I Have Eaten Dirt"

Wassmuss continued his recruitment efforts, but his personal influence was only validated by propaganda, promises, diminished gold reserves, and bluster. Their value also degraded when British and Russian military successes played out around him. Support wavered. One tribal leader, tired of Wassmuss, defecated at his home in Ahrem. Others were mesmerized by the lone German diplomat. A Shirazi merchant came under Wassmuss's influence and was played for a fool. Wassmuss had made a dummy telegraph and "spoke" with the Kaiser directly over his fake wireless. Such sham allowed him to con the man out of £10,000 by abusing Persian traditions of hospitality.[80] Clearly things had become desperate. "I have eaten dirt," Wassmuss would say to Sykes in January 1916.[81] These desperate efforts played out while the Turks battered the British into submission at Kut: and in late April 1916 released 12,000 British soldiers who might serve in Persia, making rebellions harder to sell. As Wassmuss caused havoc with little more than willpower, Niedermayer's mission reached Kabul, and Hentig began his efforts to convince the politically astute Emir Habdulla Khan on war.[82] Wassmuss now had to survive, recruit new agents of violence, and bank on the Emir's endorsement to make his promises real. Survival was all he salvaged.

The British response to the assault on Shiraz was the creation of what would be called the South Persian Rifles (SPR). Their commander was the newly appointed Brig. Gen. Sir Percy Sykes, explorer and expert on Persia and, like many of his peers, a vapid self-promoter. His expertise in the region earned him the rank and mission, for his military service was limited to the Boer War. With Indian troops, and no sanction from the Persian government, Sykes landed at Bandar Abbas in March 1916, with the goal to raise 11,000 men to contend with all of the threats in South Persia.[83] They began a counterinsurgency campaign to restore order and reclaim British property until the end of the war. Despite several strange and incompetent actions, Sykes and the SPR became effective in their tasks, buying loyalty and establishing some good will against the more violent tribes.[84] Wassmuss, faced with a direct and concerted effort, was effectively contained.

But what of his influence on the mission to Kabul? The Emir was an expert in playing off Great Powers long before the arrival of Niedermayer and Hentig. He tried the patience of his German guests with protocols and waiting. At long last, they found audience with his eminence. A critical tool in Hentig and Niedermayer's deliberations with the Emir was the effect of Wassmuss's rebellion.

> *The mission held out the hope that Persia would be entering the war, and certainly much that had recently happened there under Prince Reubl and Wassmuss was encouraging. Niedermayer stated the case for an emerging German victory, and pointed out how isolated the Emir might then be if he were still clinging to his British connection.*[85]

The Emir believed that everything needed further study, a diplomatic tactic to buy time to witness results of the Great War and pick a prevailing side. Unfortunately for the mission in Afghanistan, 1916 saw no decisive victories that signaled either opponent's ascendency in any theater of war. The Emir continued to engage in diplomatic talks, negotiations, and the drawing up of a treaty. Meanwhile, British intelligence intercepted rumors that the Germans were considering a coup with the Emir's brother. Allied successes in the Arab Revolt and the Russian victory against the Turks at Erzerum diminished the value of the German promises. The Germans brought no soldiers, no modern equipment, no vast treasure, and yet expected a holy war of blood to be spent solely by the Muslim soldiers of the Emir. The premise of revolution on the cheap, paid mostly by the sacrifice of foreign peoples, and without categorical successes like Aqaba, sunk the mission as much as its improvised nature. In the end, British payments bought the Emir's "neutrality." Cash, not arms, tilted the balance against havoc and bluster.[86] The Mission to Afghanistan collapsed, and on May 21, 1916, Niedermayer and Hentig raced home.[87] The *raison d'être* for Wassmuss being in Persia had vanished. But Wassmuss remained.

After a series of humiliating mutinies, the South Persia Rifles began to establish goodwill by providing a semblance of law and order against various tribes and the abuses of the Genderarmie. Wassmuss's influence and prestige among the Persian tribes atrophied. His promises were no longer compelling, and his presence lost its luster. He asked to lead one tribe into battle, and was refused. His only hope was a reversal of fortunes in the European war, but even the collapse of the Eastern Front to the Russian Revolution in the fall of 1917 was not enough to convince the tribes that Britain was defeated, let alone threatened, in Persia. Pro-British tribes started to threaten Wassmuss directly; battles against the SPR and pro-Wassmuss tribes and others kept on during 1918, but the British increased the number of soldiers in the region. Sykes was joined by Maj. Gen. Charles Dunsterville in wielding 100,000 British and Indian soldiers to quell the unrest.[88] Wassmuss whereabouts in this period, even to his only biographer, remain unknown.[89] Allied victory in the war descended on November 11 with the signing of the armistice, but Wassmuss was still at large.

Given the option of surrendering, Wassmuss attempted to escape to Turkey. He was intercepted by the British but resisted arrest so much that they were forced to drag him from their car. He perpetually escaped confinement like a rogue Harry Houdini, but was finally captured for good and placed under armed guard. Wassmuss was returned to Cologne and imprisoned by the Allied powers in Germany, where he yet again escaped in 1919. But there was nowhere to run in defeated Germany. The war was over, as was his influence. He was released from allied custody in 1921.

The next decade saw Wassmuss attempt to make good the promises he'd made to his Persian colleagues. His efforts as a minor diplomat in the Weimar Republic are not well documented in English, but the glory Niedermayer found and the respect Hentig was given never reached Wassmuss. He eventually returned to Persia in the early 1920s to start a farm and repay his debts to the tribes who had fought for his promises. The venture failed. Wassmuss returned to Germany. Broken, he died penniless in Berlin in April 1931.[90]

Conclusion

The German expedition to Persia and Afghanistan soon became the subject or ridicule, characterized by some historians as a fool's errand to begin with, rife with blunders, incompetence, and ignorance.[91] Max von Oppenheim, the architect for the entire venture, would later say it was a washout or folly.[92] Most of the criticisms echoed Niedermayer's initial concern: there were too few experts, too little money, and much of the plan was to be improvised. Indeed, the "improvised" nature of the plan (for which Oppenheim deserves the most credit) is repeated by historians as a failure of the mission. Yet, the Arab Revolt was largely improvised. Unlike the fastidious prewar work on winning the next war like the German Schlieffen Plan, the Arab Revolt worked.[93]

A more considered explanation for Wassmuss' failure had less to do with improvisation than the relationship of the perceived value of the mission (low cost, grand scheme) and the support for it (minimal). In a desperate time, when Germany's lack of strategic foresight had left her with little recourse after the Marne other than to continue a war they could not win, Germany experienced, for the first time in its young history, the necessity to consider unconventional warfare in foreign lands, working with indigenous peoples, as part of its war effort. Beyond the brutality of imperial warfare in east Africa there was no precedent, but indeed active disdain. There were no means of continued support to feed the tribes arms, gold, and resources. As one historian noted, "the Germans had neither the men, nor the weapons, nor the money, to do more. Two shipments of German cash and gold did reach Persia in 1915. A credit line of 100,000 sterling in paper was wired to the German Consulate in Tehran in May. Another 80,000 Turkish pounds in gold coin arrived by caravan in October, but this was small potatoes."[94]

In effect, it was total victory or nothing: a terrible parallel with the failures of the war in Europe. In a country with no formal or informal tradition of such operations, it's hard to imagine Germany draining gold and resources from the two-front war to support a mission that was heralded for what it could offer with low costs. If Lawrence succeeded despite being part of the "side show of a side show," Wassmuss failed because few wealthy patrons wanted updates from the freak show in Persia.

The Missions to Persia and Afghanistan were likely doomed before they began. As the biographer of Oppenheim noted, "It was drastically underfunded, not well organized, and beset by rivalries."[95] Yet, while the Kaiser and the country would herald Niedermayer for his sacrifice in the face of failure, equally compelling and tragic was the case of Wassmuss. A diplomat with cultural affinity and knowledge organized Germany's first attempt at employing insurgencies in the Middle East against their enemies. This required political, cultural, and military acumen that few Germans possessed (as Niedermayer repeatedly noted). Wassmuss was a rare breed for his age, and his failures are significant, but so were his successes. If we accept that the mission was doomed, what is left is what could be done when facing the impossible. Wassmuss and the other Germans used fear, terror, and violence to sow discord and rancor among their enemies. They forced the British to create a counterinsurgency force that operated without sanction in Persia, a move that might have solidified Wassmuss's revolt and unified many to his cause if not for the lack of external support, one of the essential ingredients in any successful insurgency. His exploits, despite their failure, may have also become doctrine. Maj. Colin Gubbins, father of the SOE, utilized many irregular war campaigns in creating SOE doctrine and approaches, and, according to SOE historian William Mackenzie claimed "it is plain that the doctrine" Gubbins initially wrote had many British influences, but also came "from the German experience of Wassmuss."[96]

That the Mission to Persia and Kabul failed is clear. But the case of Wassmuss is nonetheless instructive. For small cost, a single academic within the diplomatic corps used his unique skill set to create havoc. He worked with a foreign people who despised their imperial overlords and helped engineer a rebellion. If Lawrence is the paradigm, Wassmuss is the outlier as underdog. Historian and Islamic scholar H. A. R. Gibb made this comparison and distinction. "Wassmuss may be compared to Leachman rather than to Lawrence (though how different from both, except for the qualms of conscience which he shared with the latter), but it required another sort of courage to maintain the lone and hopeless struggle in south-western Persia."[97]

Part II

Global War on Ignorance and the Axis: The Special Operations Executive and the Office of Strategic Services

During the Second World War, the demands for intelligence taxed the Western nations as they contended with Axis influence across the globe. German, Italian, and Japanese occupation of foreign nations triggered the Allies to generate innovative ideas and organizations to contend with the unique nature of liberation within foreign nations. Both Britain and the United States had experiences in "small wars" via imperial policing and occupation of their own imperial territories (especially through the Royal and American Marines) and thus had a storehouse of experience and knowledge to draw upon. But these tasks had always been considered second- or third-tier obligations and often necessary evils compared to the focus, demand, and primacy of conventional warfare.[1] Yet, with Axis victories between 1939 and 1942 from France to the Philippines, both nations sought to create means to damage German and Japanese occupation through a variety of nontraditional methods, work that the senior services thought of as secondary to immediate survival or a future liberation campaign.

As Hitler proclaimed the invasion of Britain in the summer of 1940, British prime minister Winston Churchill held a meeting with Hugh Dalton, the minister of economic warfare, who had been given the job the services didn't want: global guerrilla warfare. Churchill was blunt. Britain had no way of direct opposition to Nazi control of Europe. The ascendency of German military was, for the time being, a fact. Dunkirk may have been a miracle of resolve, but recovery would take years. In order to hurt Germany during this period of recovery, Dalton was tasked to create a "Ministry of Ungentlemanly Warfare" whose agents and provocateurs would conduct sabotage, subversion, and havoc. "This form of activity was of the very highest importance," Churchill said. As Dalton left with his clandestine mission in hand, the prime minister remarked, "And now set Europe ablaze." The organization to start this fire was the SOE. Piggybacking on Britain's imperial intelligence services (MI6), the SOE would be the chief vehicle for working with guerillas in foreign lands.[2]

Meanwhile in the United States, a mix of parties across government departments and services in Washington realized the country's vast deficit in global intelligence outside of America's chief areas of imperial interest or control (the Americas, the Caribbean, the Philippines). Despite using its colonial empire to create modern surveillance and intelligence capabilities it later used in the "interior," American agencies had lagged behind the British in intelligence matters abroad. Secretary of State Henry Stimson's famous quip summed up the predicament (and reflected both American exceptionalism and naiveté). "Gentleman do not read each other's mail."[3] President Franklin D. Roosevelt wanted this gap filled, and British intelligence liaison and Canadian spy master William Stephenson (the man known as Intrepid) suggested the creation of a global intelligence organization based on the organizational models of MI6 and SOE.[4] Initially called the Office of the Coordinator of Intelligence (CoI), the Office of Strategic Services (OSS) was created on June 13, 1942, under the leadership of decorated Great War veteran and attorney Brig. William "Wild Bill" Donovan. Despite his Republican association, Donovan was a close advisor to Roosevelt. Presidential influence and approval allowed the OSS its own budget and a mandate for global intelligence gathering and analysis at the discretion of the Joint Chiefs of Staff as well as direct-action roles in theaters or special operations in theaters not assigned to other agencies or services. Donovan often noted that the best OSS candidate was a "PhD who can win a bar fight. We don't just want an officer that can carry a hundred-pound rucksack on his back. We need someone who can think and improvise." Tough, smart, and cunning men and women from all walks of life would join the ranks of researchers, administrators, and agents, including future Nobel Laureate

Ralph Bunche, celebrity chef Julia Child, and father of modern American intelligence culture Sherman Kent, as well as four future directors of the CIA.[5] The OSS held its own secret budget outside of the regular services, allowing theater commanders access to more troops and materials than their due. The price tag was OSS teams who preferred to work with great leniency or outside the normal chain of command.[6]

As new organizations, the SOE and the OSS were seen as rivals and interlopers to the senior services. They and their members had to prove themselves worthy of those around them while operating in some of the most dangerous and distant theaters of the war. Both organizations were thus home to many mavericks, two of whom operated with distinction in the Mediterranean and Southeast Asia.

One was an academic aristocrat.

The other an anthropologist and closeted lesbian.

Neither one was a professional soldier, but both would help reshape regions under foreign occupation.

Chapter 3

"Dishonest Adventurers": Monty Woodhouse and the SOE in Greece during the Second World War

The only bearable war is a war of national liberation.[1]

—C. M. WOODHOUSE, *Something Ventured*

"A Misunderstanding of Orders"

—Spring, 1943.

Adolf Hitler is convinced that Winston Churchill will open a second front on Fortress Europe in the Balkans through Greece, occupied by the Germans in the wake of Italian failure since April 1941. Here Churchill will attempt to drain Axis strength by puncturing the "soft underbelly" of Europe. Greece was a strategic outpost. Possession would allow the Allies to use airpower against Hitler's vital Romanian oil fields, support insurgent forces throughout the Balkans, link Allied shipping to the Russians through the Dardanelles, and possibly shift Turkish neutrality.[2]

That's not all.

For twelve months, Greek guerrillas have evolved from local nuisance to strategic threat. With the aid of British commandos they targeted the Gorgopotamos Bridge in November 1942, crippling German support lines to North Africa. Since then raids, sabotage, and assassinations have increased despite brutal German reprisals on civilians. Along with other clues, the growing guerrilla campaign seems a prelude to invasion. Winter 1942–1943, Hitler orders Lt. Gen. Alexander Löhr, commander of occupation forces, to reinforce his Army Group's half-dozen divisions in preparation for the Allied landings on Crete and the mainland. No longer will they rely on Italian manpower. Ace Panzer and mountain Divisions, air power, and more flood Greece instead of the life-and-death struggle on the Eastern Front.[3]

July 9, 1943, and the con is revealed: Allied forces land on the fascist shores of Sicily in total surprise and begin the Italian campaign. The deception plan known as OPERATION MINCEMEAT has succeeded.

In Greece, sapper Brig. Edward "Eddie" Myers and archeologist Maj. C. M. "Monty" Woodhouse of the SOE have led OPERATION ANIMALS, the harnessing of guerrillas for selling the illusion of MINCEMEAT. It was no small task. The Greek guerrillas were largely divided into leftist (Ethniko Apeleftherotiko Metop [EAM]/ Ellinikós Laïkós Apeleftherotikós Stratós [ELAS]) and rightists (Ethnikos Dimokratikos Ellinikos Syndesmos [EDES]) camps, considered each other enemies, and were heading toward civil war for the future of Greece. Myers and Woodhouse had built a trust with both sides during the harrowing Gorgopotamos Bridge mission and on that success built the campaigns of 1943, leading to the victorious deception. But there was a price: for secrecy, Myers and Woodhouse kept the Greeks out of the con. All believed liberation was coming that year, so rivals guerrillas had fought together instead of at each other. The lie burned trust as the Sicilian campaign began. After ANIMALS, Myers signaled British command in Cairo. He asked when was Greece's turn for liberation.

"Not until early 1944 and possibly later," they replied.

"How was I going to keep ELAS and EDES from each other's throats when they had nothing to do but prepare for further sabotage operations at some indefinite future date?" he wondered. He initiated a formal meeting in Cairo with senior guerrilla leadership and British officials. Woodhouse, a pragmatic cynic, smelled a trap. If you leave Greece, he told his commander, the Foreign Office might not be allow you to return. The "F. O." hated the communist guerrillas and thought little of the S.O.E. But Myers believed he had nothing to hide. He had to try and shift their thinking. They left on August 9.[4]

Myers never returned, finishing his wartime career in North West Europe, far away from Greece. Cairo informed Woodhouse that Myers has been relieved of his command due to a "misunderstanding of orders."

"Colonel Woodhouse" is now in command of the Allied Military Mission (AMM) in Greece.[5] Woodhouse now faced a three-front war: a military front against the Germans, a political/military front between Greeks, and a domestic front against the British Foreign Office, whose chief goal was the return of the despised King George II and denying the country to the communists actually fighting to liberate the country.

Woodhouse was bound for a Greek tragedy. For the next year, this archeologist-turned-commando and guerrilla would manage the contradictory nature of British policy with the actual realities of insurgent warfare in Greece.

Literrae Humaniores

Christopher Montague Woodhouse, son of Lord Terrington and Valerie Philips, was born on May 11, 1917. A gifted student in both the arts and mathematics, "Monty" had desired the life of an academic in the *literrae humaniores*, perhaps with a fellowship at All Souls in Oxford and a life of "lecturing on Plato and Aristotle."[6] Ancient Greek history, philosophy, language, and literature consumed his life from a young age. "The headmistress of my Kindergarten was translating Anna Comnena's *Alexiad*," a Byzantine princess's account of her father's reign, "but I did not appreciate it till years afterwards."[7] He was educated at Winchester College and then New College, Oxford, became his home.[8]

All things Greek enchanted him, including its current history: he supported liberal democratic national leader Eleftherios Venizelos in the 1930s disarmament conference and had some sympathy for nationalists of many stripes. He visited Greece for the first time in 1935, the country reeling from the bloody aftermath of the attempted military coup against the ruling People's Party for fear of royalist sentiments: an event that marred so many of his future wartime allies. Still, he was keen to discover that "living people still spoke Plato's language."[9] He received successive degrees and fellowships from Oxford with top honors, but as some tutors noted, Woodhouse had a streak of enthusiasm that required action. He chose archeology to the armchair existence of an Oxford Don. In 1938, Woodhouse worked in Greece as an archeologist and added Modern Greek to his commanding skill at classical languages.[10]

In 1939, he returned home to enlist. After a stint in the Royal Artillery, the War Office discovered he was among the few British officers with command of Greek and Italian. As the Blitz began over London and the Italians invaded Greece in the fall of 1940, Woodhouse embarked for Crete as an intelligencc officer.[11] Authoritarian Prime Minister August Metaxes had initially declined a British offer of a Commonwealth Expeditionary Force for fear of angering Germany, but when he died in January 29, 1941, it was accepted.

Aboard an armed merchant cruiser a young officer handed Woodhouse a service revolver. Paddy Leigh Fermor was a popular writer of adventure travelogue, a self-reliant man of action and letters who, unlike Woodhouse, wasn't from royal blood. He'd lived among the Greeks and was well acquainted with the shepherds and soldiers as well as politicians.[12] To Woodhouse, "Paddy" was "an avatar of Byron whose quality I was slow to appreciate." They were rivals from the beginning. "This was always the real root of the friction," Fermor noted, "a constant jealous, unarmed struggle as to who had the greater proprietary rights to Greece."[13] Fermor became famous for the SOE caper that kidnapped a German general on Crete. It was a dashing show, ready for a Hollywood film, but devoid of the political intrigue and strategic influence that emerged from the career of his rival. Captain Woodhouse served with the 1st Liaison Military Mission just as the Greek victory against the Italian invasion was routed by the Germans in April 1941.[14]

"W" Force, a 62,000-strong Commonwealth unit, as well as Greek and Yugoslav forces and the Military Mission, arrived at the end of April, but failed to stop the German, Italian, and Bulgarian tide of over a million soldiers. All escaped to Crete, but the Germans viewed the island as a strategic hub to protect Romanian oil reserves and project power toward North Africa. They conquered the island by April 30th. Woodhouse escaped with the remaining British forces to Cairo but the Greeks formed secret organizations to continue the fight. Sabotage, raids and other active and passive resistance against occupation forces began in September. Republican officers, soldiers, and royalists formed the National Republican Greek League (EDES) on September 9, 1941. Communist Greeks, who had a reputation for sage political organization, discipline, and brutality, formed the National Liberation Front (EAM) on September 27, 1941, with its armed faction, ELAS, beginning action in April 1942.[15]

In Palestine, Woodhouse joined the SOE, received commando training, and become adept at hand-to-hand combat and handling explosives. The goal: return to Crete and work with the emergent resistance. But he and his peers in SOE "had a shadow of interest in Balkan politics." Nor was it expected. Yet Greek politics and British hatred for them defined and, in the end, decided the shape of victory.

"I Learned That I Had a Great Deal to Learn"

From 1919 to 1935, Greece endured perpetual changes of government, a dozen coups, and the establishment of a royalist-backed military dictatorship that birthed the authoritarian regime of Prime Minister Mextasas. Refugee crises from the war with the Turks (1919–1922), economic strife, political instability, and the rise of a strong communist party in the 1920s had birthed a range of social and political groups, agendas, and vendettas. Most Greeks supported two wartime goals: national liberation from the Germans, and a plebiscite to deter the return of King George II. Everything else was contested.[16]

Churchill's government was staunchly anti-communist, almost to a fault. Orme Garton Sargent, senior Foreign Office official in Cairo, was often more concerned about Soviet influence than German victory. "Even after Hitler's attack on Russia, [Sargent] was determined to limit the power of the Soviet Union," including local communist organizations and regardless of evidence.[17] Churchill wanted the king and his government-in-exile to return to cripple communist influence, but Greeks viewed the king as a British puppet.[18]

Woodhouse, still ignorant of the complexities of Greek political life, was inserted into Crete in November 1941. It was an ideal "apprenticeship" in clandestine operations and guerrilla warfare against the Germans. SOE members helped troops evade or escape capture, collected intelligence, and assisted the possibility for active resistance, even if successes were minimal.[19] He was then tasked to the mainland, but Crete had hardened Woodhouse. This royal offspring lived on a diet of snails, mountain grass and aikorns, locals introduced him to *kapetanioi* and *pallikaria*, (nationalists and communists) politics. Three times he evaded capture, which all knew meant torture and death.[20] He returned to Palestine in April 1942. "I had learned that I had a great deal to learn." But after teaching Balkan soldiers, he believed professional British officers would need to organize the revolts.[21]

"We Had to Improvise as We Went along"

—Summer 1942.

Gen. Erwin Rommel's mounting victories in North Africa forced the British to think of unorthodox ways to challenge his momentum. The railway between Salonika and Athens was the only one through Greece. German resources followed the rail line, then by sea to Crete, then by air to Tobruk and other bases. Cutting that Grecian vein would cripple Germany's ability to sustain a crushing blow against the British 8th Army in North Africa. Commander-in-chief Gen. Harold Alexander requested a sabotage mission: the first major request for SOE's unique capabilities. At the same time, Prometheus, the SOE agent operating in occupied Athens, suggested utilizing the guerrilla effort. "What was known about the guerrillas was vague," Woodhouse recalled, "but for a start it was important to find out about my companions. All I knew was that I was to be second-in-command."[22]

OPERATION HARLING was commanded by Maj. Edward "Eddie" Myers, a career sapper in his thirties and something of an outsider in the Army—quiet, left-handed, and Jewish. He'd served with his field company on the Egyptian frontier during Italy's invasion of Abyssinia and as part of internal security in Palestine before returning to the Western Desert for the outbreak of the war.[23] Myers found Woodhouse a "most able" subordinate. They picked their team, including engineers Tom Barnes and Arthur Edmonds, from New Zealand, the half-Indian Scot Inder Gill of the Royal Engineers, and others. They trained on the Suez Canal where "[o]ver-confidence led me to make every mistake."[24] The resistance and their operations were still a mystery. "We finally saw the planes in Cairo only a day before we were due to fly."[25] A verbal briefing revealed the plan. They were to be parachuted from three aircraft into the mountains of Roumeli, north of Delphi. "There we would find two different groups of guerrilla and bring them together. How different they were, and how hard to bring together, nobody told us because nobody knew." Together they'd hit rail and telephone lines and destroy one of three river viaducts: the Gorgopotamos, the Asopos, or the Papadia.[26]

Two Greek leaders had men within striking distance of rail lines. Col. Napoleon Zervas was a republican and career soldier who both participated in coups and challenged regimes and was no fan of the king. He commanded the National Republican Greek League (EDES). Aris Veloukhiotis was among the best soldiers in Greece and a dedicated member and leader of the National Liberation Front (EAM) and its field force the Greek Peoples Liberation Army (Ellinikós Laïkós Apeleftherotikós Stratós, or ELAS). But Woodhouse and his crew had "learned nothing about EAM, ELAS, or the Greek Communist Party [(Kommounistikó Kómma Elládas, or KKE) which created EAM] until I encountered them myself a few weeks later." All intelligence on the guerrillas and their locations was false. Myers and Woodhouse "had to improvise as we went along."[27] Woodhouse was to find Zervas, secure his support, and bring as many guerrillas into the operation as possible.

The Foreign Office harbored a different agenda. Sir Orme Sargent told a concerned party in March 1943 that whatever the goal of the SOE mission, the team was to "play up the King and Prime Minister [Emmanouil] Tsouderos." Once the guerrilla bands became organized "under their leadership and under the orders of the Commander-in-Chief, Middle East," Myers was to "move them over as a national movement in favor of the King and the Allies."[28] Tsouderos complained to Foreign Secretary Anthony Eden about the SOE's mission, likely fearing their need to work with the communist groups EAM/ELAS. Tsouderos was assured that "any employee of S.O.E MIDEAST will therefore be dismissed if he is found guilty of expressing sentiment in public which are hostile to the KING and to his present Government."[29]

The mission's initial flight was botched. But on September 30th,[30] high above the Pindus range, three lights flashed in a triangle on the ground. "I sat on the edge of the square hole with my legs dangling out," Woodhouse recalled. "As we passed over the fires for the second time, I jumped almost before the dispatcher could tap my shoulder." Woodhouse landed safely in the moonlight and began his hunt.[31]

In the midnight world and harsh terrain of Greece, Woodhouse, Tom Barnes, and others stalked for guerrillas while avoiding the Italian garrison, aided by local elder Barba Niko who "makes the impossible possible." They headed east to the slops of Giona, closer to the rail lines, with rumor that Aris was close.[32] Niko guarded a cave mouth as men prepared explosives and weapons.[33] With the help of local family, the bridges were examined and on October 29, the target was decided: Gorgopotamos. "The bridge was heavily guarded by Italian troops, manning concrete pillboxes behind barbed wire. We should need an attacking force of at least a hundred men."[34] Twelve against one hundred were suicide odds.

On Halloween, Prometheus's courier arrived: Zervas's was eight miles away to North West in the area of Valtos, near Sakartesi. El Alamein was raging. The clock ticked. Woodhouse had between November 2 and 17 to find Zervas and return.

"Kalos ston Evangelion!"

Fifteen-hour days of walking. Talking with locals. Heading north up the valley of the River Mornos. Five days of climbing cliffs and mountain. Traversing 250 miles on foot while avoiding Italian garrisons. Woodhouse endured and gathered intelligence from locals. A priest presented a letter from ELAS. The priest translated their name as National Popular Liberation Army. "I had not heard the name before," Woodhouse recalled, "and it sounded good."[35]

"I waded across the River Akheloos, wrestling with the current as Herakles", heading toward EDES' camp. Two days later as guerrillas battled Italians at Argyrio "Zervas came out of a hut to meet me, wearing a well-cut tunic and breeches, with no medals or badges of rank, and a brown leather cap. He greeted me with a kiss on both cheeks, which was prickly for both of us. *'Kalos ston Evangelion!'* he said with quiet satisfaction. 'Welcome to the Angel of Good Tidings.'"[36] Zervas accepted the mission and Woodhouse's role as liaison. "From that moment I had an unreasoning confidence that the Gorgopotamos bridge was as good as destroyed."[37]

Returning to Myers, they encountered Aris and his troops at Viniani. Zervas told Woodhouse to avoid the "terrible" communists. He refused. Aris was a "powerful figure in plain khaki, draped with bandoliers . . . radiating self-confidence and power."[38] He agreed to join the mission, and even to allow his men to serve under Zervas command. But only for this job. ELAS were tougher, more disciplined, and determined in outlook than EDES. The rivals walked together, but Woodhouse now knew that each side was pitted against each other for the future of Greece.[39]

November 16. Myers recounted that Woodhouse returned "with General Zervas and 50 rebels, also with ARES and 100 rebels after having covered 250 miles." They now had their team for OP HARLING.[40]

"On a Little Mound, Napoleon Stood . . ."

On November 25, they arrived at the assembly point with six mules carrying their charges. The operation was set for 11 p.m. All orders were now verbal. They descended the last few hundred feet. The explosive party under Barnes was to stay near the command post on the same side of the river, so Myer's could order them to move at the right moment.

The bridge was made of stone and metal piers, and they couldn't destroy the former. The metal piers were in the south end, so Barnes needed to approach from the south side of the river. Myers and the guerrillas argued over the best ground for control of the battle, so Myers separated Barnes. "A narrow plank bridge spanned the river a few hundred yards upstream from the viaduct, and here we parted."[41] Myers was grateful for the "Constant checking and supervision loyally and untiringly carried out by Major Woodhouse as my liaison officer and interpreter." The final group was at the command post with Myers, Zervas, Aris, and Woodhouse and a reserve force as needed. "[W]e were on the north side of the Gorgopotamos, so the river still had to be crossed by the parties operating south of the bridge."[42]

5:30 p.m.: the groups left the forward assembly point and descended Mount Oiti to forming up places. 12 a.m.: telephone lines were cut. 11:15 p.m.: Italian soldiers spotted the cutting party and opened fire. At the north end of the bridge, the first attack failed and the reserves were sent in. Zervas's claimed they were betrayed, and promised only ten minutes of battle before firing the green flare for retreat. But Komninos Pyromaglou, Zervas's second-in-command, had taken the pistol when he led the reserves. Woodhouse chased Pyromaglou and his men to the north end of the bridge. Italian machine gun blasted out of a pill box as Woodhouse secured the gun.[43] Woodhouse returned as Myers ran to the river bank, shouting at Barnes and company to advance, voice nearly drowned by the river.

Chaos reigned until the first explosion attempt on the line north of the bridge failed. An armored train outside Lamia approached. "Every available weapon was engaged to hold it off. Barnes and his team were relatively secure at the foot of the bridge, although firing continued over their heads." Then the sappers were stunned. "The drawings of the bridge given to us in Cairo had shown right-angled girders," Woodhouse recalled, "but they turned out in fact to be U-Shaped." The sappers reworked their plan and tools on the fly and squeezed their explosives into the right shape. Bullets rang overhead for the next half hour, then, silence.

A Very light (flare) burst above: the signal of the end of resistance to the north end of the bridge.

Then, a red Very light shone from the south end. Charges were ready.

Thirty seconds remained to find cover, "but I could not bear to do it. Zervas, Aris and I were on a mound overlooking the north end of the bridge. We stood silent, counting the second. As I looked at Zervas, Browning's couplet flashed through my mind: 'On a little mound, Napoleon/Stood on our storming day.' But my Napoleon was a good deal nearer his target than Browning's."

Explosions filled the night as two spans of the bridge rose in the air and then crashed into the valley. Then, all the lights in Lamia snuffed out: Woodhouse never knew the cause. Aris, Zervas, and Woodhouse joined hands and danced around their mound. More explosives were laid on piers to make them unusable. Myers shouted at Woodhouse to *not* fire the Green flare for twenty minutes, then began to count the Italian dead. Zervas wanted a quick retreat, but Aris and Woodhouse held him firm. Another explosion. The green flare hit the sky. By November 26, the south end of the bridge was in their hands and the demolition party executed their mission.[44] But they were a tad late.

Victory at El Alamein came on November 5, and the battle ended six days later, too early for OP HARLING to be invaluable. But General Alexander was "delighted with this success especially at a time when Axis reinforcements are being rushed to Crete and Southern Greece. Furthermore, of course, railway communications are being relied upon by the Axis owing to their shortage of suitable shipping and the vulnerability of ships in the Aegean and Ionian seas."[45]

Victory encouraged new and bigger plans. "Myers was ordered to return and take charge of organizing a large-scale guerrilla movement, supported by an increase staff of British liaison officers."[46] Woodhouse would continue as his right hand. By the end of December, Myers and Woodhouse began recruiting, and a guerrilla meeting was held with Woodhouse, Zervas, Pyromaglou, Aris, and Tasso Eleftherias. Yet the Foreign Office pressured them in opposite directions. "Nothing should be neglected which might help to promote unity among the resistance groups in Greece" they were told, but at all times they should push for the return of the king. Yet they needed to minimize support for the largest and most effective group, EAM/ELAS, as they were the biggest threat to the king's return. Such orders were rife for interpretation, exceptions, and caveats. It was amazing SOE could actually function within the political demands of the Foreign Office.[47] All the while they were to unite guerrillas that despised each other.[48]

"We Have Been Outlaws for Years"

—Athens, January 27, 1943.

Dressed as a black marketer, Woodhouse sits in the house of his guide Thanas. Outside, Germans and Italians patrol the streets. He had successfully arrived in the capital with the help of Aris and ELAS and awaited Prometheus, their connection with the guerrilla leadership in the capital (including the fabled Six Colonels, career officers who were thought to be power brokers). His mission: gain approval for guerrilla warfare in the mountains.

Prometheus arrived with bad news. Gen. Tsigantes, a wartime hero and liaison with SOE, had been murdered by the secret police. The city's Nazi noose was tightening. The next day they moved to another safehouse. Woodhouse was shocked to find he was hiding in the same building as Prometheus' wireless unit. "We spent an uneasy evening, for I knew how vulnerable the wireless was to direction finding." The next day it was moved, and the Six Colonels failed to show.[49] Woodhouse kept calm, stayed low, knowing his six-foot frame and proximity to the wireless made him a target.[50]

On January 31, Woodhouse met with five members of EAM's Central Committee, who claimed his arrival was an open secret to them. "Your agents have no idea of security," Andreas Tzimas said. "They lack conspiratorial experience, whereas we have all been outlaws for years." He secured their agreement for using guerrillas in the mountains and in the field. A general resistance now seemed possible.[51] The next day, two of the Six Colonels arrived. Neither cared for guerrilla warfare, and Woodhouse wrote them off as useless.[52]

He held another meeting with EAM to fill time, but by 2 a.m. Prometheus was late. News arrived: Prometheus had been captured with the wireless that morning. Torture would give up Woodhouse's position. He had to leave Athens, fast. He asked EAM to help him escape. The two Greek communists Siantos and Tzimas debated in secret. They agreed. But this was not altruism. His capture would compromise them as well. "Communist security was truly professional," Woodhouse recalled, "and for the first time in Athens I felt safe."[53] EAM secured his departure from Athens. He arrived at Mission HQ on February 20 on foot with another negotiation victory. But "the early glory of the guerrilla war had departed."[54]

Myers was frustrated. The Foreign Office pushed contradiction with their goals.[55] "We were to support those guerrilla leaders who supported the king, but there were none. We were also to achieve the maximum effect against the Germans; but that could not be done without ELAS. The more their strength expanded, the harder it became to safeguard the King's position."[56] Myers and Woodhouse accomplished a compromise by getting Zervas to write a telegram of goodwill to the king. Thanks to Woodhouse, Myers also had "an approach from EAM who wished to put themselves under the general control of Zervas," though they'd later renege.[57] The Foreign Office approved Zervas's letter and used it to champion the unity of effort at home that was an illusion abroad.[58] The original communist party of Greece, KKE, the brain trust of EAM, kept up anti-royalist propaganda. They tried to eliminate Zervas's force, but it was too big. Woodhouse worked with Zervas while Myers sought accords with ELAS to create a functioning peace between them "and managed to keep the rivals from each other's throats." But British policy remained obstinate: the king at all costs.[59]

". . . Interesting Reading"

—Spring 1943, the guerrilla effort was being harnessed.
Raids and sabotage increased, though the guerrillas rarely confronted the Italians and Germans directly. Beneath the shadow of occupation, civil war simmered. Still, Myers and Woodhouse constructed the "National Bands" confederation of guerrillas. But who could be trusted and how much? "Colonel MYER's opinion and my own is that Colonel Zervas is now fighting because he likes fighting," Woodhouse reported on March 16. "I believe he puts Greece first, England a close second, and all other interests nowhere. This is true of no other leader known to me." Myers and Woodhouse acknowledged EAM was the communist brain trust of ELAS, but most members joined ELAS for a variety of reasons and were not hard-core ideologues: a common circumstance in many guerrilla and insurgent groups.[60] Rumors mounted of EAM avoiding battle with the Italians. There were "repeated outrages by EAM to provoke the National Bands told to me daily by eye-witnesses and victims too numerous for detailed report." Thieving, fighting, propaganda and more were sowing discord, eating the goodwill of OP HARNESS. Efforts to split EAM from ELAS were considered. Myers and Woodhouse were increasingly aware of EAM's aims, but saw much good in the cohesion of the guerrillas they were recruiting.[61] They convinced Sargent that his desire to split EAM from ELAS would be a prelude to civil war.[62] Meanwhile, the great deception of OP MINCEMEAT was approved, and ANIMALS with it.

Spring 1943 was a season of endless meetings, accusations, backstabs, and thin truces. Myers went to Eastern Greece to consult and reign in ELAS from attacking other guerrillas. Woodhouse updated his commander in mid-May on short- and long-term policy as the guerrillas began to fray. It included saving face, executing the military program, "despite ELAS pre-dominance[,] ensure mobilization maximum forces whether sympathy EAM or not; Forth, to prevent undercurrent opposition to EAM being paralyzed or absorbed by EAM." But the long-term policy of keeping Greece in the British "sphere of influence" under the Monarchy was impossible. A returned king "backed by British bayonet would be disastrous and would lead to clashes whereby all Greeks would be behind EAM." Hope lay with an honest plebiscite, uncorrupted by EAM, and backed by the Allies. It would foster counterforce to EAM and deny EAM anti-British propaganda, and chances of EAM winning or preventing elections would be slim. But at all costs "the King should not return before plebiscite."

When officials in Cairo read Woodhouse's report, they refused to send it on for consideration by the Foreign Office. They were to be enjoyed as merely "interesting reading."[63]

"Animals"

Between May and July 1943, Myers and Woodhouse pushed the guerrillas together for a series of attacks on rail and communication lines, with similar efforts done through the Balkans, to make it appear that South East Europe was ripe for invasion. The Germans even offered amnesty for Greeks who surrendered their weapons. None stepped forward.[64] The Communist and Republican Greeks also refused Myers request to help destroy the Asopos viaduct. Zervas declined, for it was in ELAS country. Sarafis, commander of ELAS, also refused, but destroyed the railway tunnel at Tyrnavos to counter growing British and public criticism that ELAS was avoiding combat with the Germans. Instead, British commandos destroyed the viaduct unaided on June 21, 1943. "We held up German troop movement all over Greece for four weeks between mid-June and June 10," Woodhouse noted, "the day the Allies landed in Italy." The ELAS tunnel operation, in comparison, was fixed in two days and with over a hundred casualties.[65]

Hitler sent six divisions from the Russian Front to the Balkans, "and paid us the compliment of sending Rommel to Salonika as commander-in-chief." Hitler was fooled even deep into the fall of 1944 that Greece would still be invaded (in his mania he'd blame the Italian loss to Greece for the failure of the Eastern Front).[66] The strategic victory of ANIMALS created an operational nightmare, as Myers went to Cairo with the guerrillas, never to return. Myers lamented he had not done enough before his removal to forestall the Greek Civil war, even if such chances were slim. That job fell to Woodhouse.[67] ELAS may have been furious about the deceit, but they were soon compensated.

On September 8, Italy surrendered to the Allies, creating fresh complexities: over 170,000 Italian troops sat in Greece.[68] ELAS coveted Italians arms and the desire for frontier justice was rife. Woodhouse was tasked with securing the weapons of the Pinerolo Division in Larisa under the command of Gen. Adolfo Infante, a man who had destroyed the Greek town of Almiros, executed fifty men as reprisal for partisan attacks, and deported others to concentration camps.[69] Woodhouse had wrestled consent from the guerrillas on securing the division's handover to him, but it was the weapons of the "co-belligerents" they coveted. The Allies now had the greatest cache of firepower in Greece, including 14,000 rifles, mountain artillery, armored cars, and more. ELAS hungered for their weapons and for most of the senior Italian officers to be tried as war criminals.[70] By September 22, Woodhouse feared Sarafis and his crew would disarm the Italians on their own. "This would be unfortunate," he wrote to his superiors "since Greeks cannot *rpt not* use much heavy Italian equipment without training and Italians so far show *no rpt no* reluctance to use them against Germans."[71] Woodhouse now worked alongside American colleagues, as members of the OSS joined what became the AMM in Greece.[72] His initial deputy was paranoid of British and Greek intent, and replaced by Maj. Gerald K. Wines. Older than Woodhouse, he was an excellent observer and quick study of the complexity of Greek politics. Wines worked to mend fences and keep things in line, though Wines colleagues felt he was under the spell of the well-read master of Greek from Oxford.[73]

The AMM had limited communications and only had loose influence over the Peloponnese, Crete, and Eastern Macedonia, which were detached from Woodhouse. "But in the central mass of Greece we had over two hundred officers and other ranks of half a dozen nationalities under a clear chain of command."[74] But his power was through influence, support, and threat. Hitler ordered OPERATION AXIS, the total disarmament of the Italians in Greece. ELAS made out like bandits and forcibly disarmed Italians, making them far more immune to British influence when Woodhouse "starved" them of weapons.[75] Now ELAS prepared to destroy Zervas and EDES, and Woodhouse had no force to challenge them. The communists "hardly concealed their intention to take over the country before the Allies returned." Woodhouse held them back by reducing supplies of much needed ammunition, but ELAS sent the bulk of their forces across the Pindus range and attacked Zervas in his stronghold at Epirus. Excuses bloomed from ELAS: EDES was threatening their troops, Zervas was a traitor and working with the Germans, and the AMM was corrupt. Sarafis even demanded the removal of Woodhouse.[76] Soon reports came that a series of attacks on the National Bands had occurred on that date, and the only organization capable of coordinating such a multisite attack was ELAS. Meanwhile a German advance forced AMM from their HQ at Pertouli. Woodhouse and company dodged German attacks throughout November. As the German threat rose, ELAS's support chilled and accusations of patronage mounted. Woodhouse was clear: no weapons or ammo were to be dropped unless ELAS stopped the civil war. Disdain for Woodhouse grew with each "aid" drop. If Myers had been a symbol of unity, Woodhouse became "the symbol of mutual antagonism." Cairo considered removing AMM from ELAS, but Woodhouse argued against. Their mission remained liberating the country from the Germans. "I went so far as to recommend that, if military operations were really still essential, we should make a settlement with ELAS and leave Zervas unsupported." It was an astonishing offer from the senior officer in the field. And it was utterly rejected by Cairo. Collaborators also rose. Germans formed Security Battalions of Greeks who would fight ELAS out of fear of a communist future and a Nazi present.[77]

"I Come with an Open Mind"

Fighting continued, Greeks against Germans and Greeks against Greeks, through November 1943 until Woodhouse secured a ceasefire in early February 1944. He worked with relentless fortitude to bring EAM and ELAS into some kind of binding agreement, and for his efforts received every possible jab, evasion, interruption, and stall that the communists could bring to bear as their forces, armed with Italian weapons, attacked EDES and other enemies as much as the retreating Germans. Lack of unity aided the Germans. The AMM were in charge of guerrilla attacks on bridges, telegraph lines, and hit-and-run assaults in support of a British Army landing in October 1944. But with success of the Normandy and Eastern Front campaigns making a German retreat now inevitable, EAM and ELAS targeted EDES and prepared for creating a government. In the maelstrom Woodhouse had one goal: focus on the common enemy.

Ceasefire secured, Woodhouse got all sides to agree to a guerrilla meeting at Merokovo to get ELAS back in line. "I come with an open mind, except on three points, which sure all agree," he told them. "Whatever decisions must be unanimous. Whatever decisions must ensure maximum military efficiency. Whatever decision fighting between rebels must never break out again." The guiding principle was "unity of action."

All agreed, and then resumed arguing over politics and the meaning of "unity of action" and the nature of a unified command. Zervas's representative feared EDES absorption into ELAS, and Woodhouse intervened when they began to dispute the need for a single commander. "We should concentrate first on a High Command as agreed in principle and the rest will follow," he said. "A single C in C [commander-in-chief] acceptable to all with a joint staff and appropriate powers would settle points disputed at a lower level by adopting either ELAS or EDES proposal or a compromise." The EKK members objected to a C in C with no government to legitimize him because of the political nature of the war. They were right, and politics was still outside Woodhouse's mandate. The talks fell into deadlock. His old friend Aris visited twice, but did not participate and "avoided me."[78] The good will of HARLING was ashes.

Days rolled. Zervas clashed with ELAS member Pyromaglou over candidates, politics, and the actual need to focus on the Germans.[79] OP NOAH'S ARK, a joint Allied and guerrilla action, marched through planning while EAM blamed "Col. Chris" for the deadlock. Woodhouse had successfully corralled guerrillas since fall 1942, but was now frustrated. Cairo sent few instructions beyond the party line: King good, ELAS bad. EAM were masters of debates that ate time and wore down their opposition so they could leave strong. The only course for Woodhouse, "[a]dopted by eliminations," was continuing the dialog.[80] Then, ELAS threatened to dissolve the National Bands to avoid responsibility for their crimes and previous atrocities.[81] So Woodhouse decided to draft an agreement he knew would die swiftly. But within it was a secret clause that might forestall a bloodbath come war's end. "Request definite and clear reply on all above points," reads his cable from the meeting on the eighteenth. "If you do not *rept not* wish reply on any of the above, please inform me." [82]

"You are handling negotiations extremely well and all yr approaches and answers so far reflect exactly our point of view," Cairo cabled back.[83] "We have great confidence in your handling of the situation." But if a civil war happens, supplies will be cut and ELAS will be publicly denounced.[84]

The meeting moved to Plaka, where Woodhouse made clear that any "accident" happening to Zervas would kill allied aid to ELAS.[85] Even then, Zervas stepped on Woodhouse's last nerve and called the conference "a waste of time" and the civil war inevitable.[86] In a friendless arena, all other avenues explored and exhausted, Woodhouse spent February 28–29 finally crushing blood from a stone by threats. On March 2, the "Plaka Agreement" was signed "by Sarafis [in pencil 'Sam'], Nicolas, Komninos ['Zervas'], Nikolopoulos, Kartalis, Chris, Wines." [87]

The Plaka Agreements included dialog on unity and the need for a single C in C, but produced no "definite solutions, but some armistice terms were agreed to so that the Civil War would not break out again." But there was one success: the secret clause, signed by all the parties, to have British and American units embedded within the guerrilla groups: approval for a "substantial and well-armed presence of Allied troops in Greece before the Germans left, which would help to stabilize the uneasy transition."[88] He lamented that "the negotiations here have been carried out more or less with words and were not based on realities," but the words held.[89]

"Behave Like Guerrillas"

Meanwhile, King George II arrived in Cairo on April 11, proclaiming the future of Greece to be decided by plebiscite after liberation. Six days later, ELAS murdered Col. Demetrios Psarao while Woodhouse awaited him for a meeting at Koutsaina. OPERATION NOAH'S ARK under

Gen. Ronald Scobie was postponed until spring, as the Civil War erupted again.[90] Woodhouse forced another conference at Koutsaina to keep the guerrillas from destroying Plaka. He told EAM this was their "last chance to establish MIDEAST's confidence." ELAS had assassinated allies, turned civil relief into a criminal racket, abused British officers, and hoarded war material. EAM's representative Costa Despotopoulos dismissed all accusations as British lies and propaganda, but admitted the situation was grave. They argued over the reality of British supplies to ELAS, with Woodhouse sharply chastising Despotopoulos for perpetual denials, evasions, and lies about the distribution of arms.[91] "CHRIS replied that no promise had been made and that supplies during the last two months had been far more than expected." Despotopoulos countered that MIDEAST had asked ELAS to redistribute their own fire power, thus current supplies were inadequate. Woodhouse said that reply was made last January, and Despotopoulos denied it. Written proof was provided by Hammond, but Despotopoulos was unshakable. Woodhouse said ELAS refused to put its best troops in target areas. ELAS member Politis responded with "textbook argument against our plans," so Woodhouse countered, "forget textbooks and behave like guerrillas."[92]

After hours of haggling, he suggested boundary lines to eliminate disputed areas.[93] He got the groups to exchange liaison officers and respect Plaka, and boxed ELAS for being accountable for any breakage. "I consider that it is their patriotic duty to accept these proposals. Their rejection will amount a definite sabotage of the Allied work and especially the Allied Missions to this country." Plaka had held a month. Koutsaina patched the holes. To do more, he needed influence from home. But he knew that as soon as he left, his influence would crumble as the guerrilla war continued without him. "Five minutes after leaving Greece," he noted in a May 1944 report, "anyone is out of touch with the reality in Greece and disqualified from speaking for the Greeks."[94]

"The Will of Churchill"

—From April to October, Woodhouse forestalled the inevitable.

EAM/ELAS focused their actions on their internal enemies and preparing to rule. "This state of affairs may well be, as far as I know, an ideal one for Greece," he reported, "that is none of my business. My business is to make them fight the Germans." British troops escorted the new prime-minister-in-exile Georgios Papandreou back home. Woodhouse used the lever of support and public shaming to manage a complex range of affairs: support for OPERATION NOAH'S ARK, the relief effort for the Italians and starved mountain population, and preventing the final reckoning between ELAS and EDES. "This means we are also to some extent tangled up in local politics," he noted to Cairo. "We regret this, but we cannot help it." The mission was now "an isolated foreign colony. We live to a greater extent like normal British units and consequently see less of the rebels and the villagers than we used to."[95] Yet April to July 1944 also saw successful operations against retreating Germans to boast about, until Woodhouse was recalled to discuss the future of Greece, which removed his influence.[96]

At conferences and meetings in Lebanon, Italy, Egypt, and London, Woodhouse found sympathy for his efforts, continued suspicions of ELAS, and limited support to change the established British view. He met with new prime minister George Papandreou. Communists had not yet agreed to join the new government, even if their delegates agreed. "But I knew that Churchill was again contemplating a total breach with EAM, and I urged Papandreou to resist it." ELAS would then seize Athens and the British would find themselves fighting their way out of Greece. "I made the same point to the British Ambassador, Rex Leeper, a subtle and mysterious man who mistakenly supposed that my views must be totally opposed to those of Myers." Leeper, like Sargent, served the "will of Churchill." The king, not communists, mattered, even at the risk of British lives.[97] "I had, of course, been very critical of the EAM leaders," Woodhouse said to British diplomat Harold McMillan, "but I had said that there was no evidence that they were controlled from abroad, though I found their tactics to be quite orthodox." But if they took Athens, they'd never hand it over to Papandreou and join his government."[98]

In London, Greece was a sideshow compared to Western Europe, even for SOE. At SOE, HQ on Baker Street treated him like a "valuable but potentially explosive parcel with a Top Secret label."[99] Scobie would also be given command of all the guerrillas. Woodhouse had repeated Myer's fate. But he was far closer to the corridors of power.

July 15. Chequers Estate. In the drawing room, Woodhouse sat with Mrs. Churchill and Brigadier Armstrong, back from a mission to Yugoslavia. "I looked around and saw a figure in blue denims beside me," Woodhouse noted. "I leaped to my feet, and was surprised to see Churchill down below me. No one had told me how small he was, like Napoleon."[100] Desmond Morton, Churchill's chief adviser on secret operations, had warned Woodhouse that Churchill was "still thinking of denouncing EAM and ELAS as enemies of the western alliance and withdrawing all support from them." Churchill spoiled for a fight.[101] So Woodhouse targeted Churchill's emotions. Such a policy would ensure few AMM members would escape Greece alive. Churchill brooded and then put his hand on Woodhouse's shoulder. "Yes, my boy. I quite understand." "It was the last I ever heard of the proposal to break with EAM."[102] It was also his last move. With Scobie's forces en route, Woodhouse's influence was at an end. He'd managed the impossible in the face of the inevitable, buy his "five minutes" was up.[103]

He returned to Greece to observe more than assist. In September, the British returned to Greek shores with OP NOAH. The Germans fought their way out of the country, though they encountered little resistance from the guerrillas. The National Bands were dead as each group vied for control of the country.[104] Gen. Barker Benfield then sent a large cache of weapons and equipment to ELAS through EDES territory. ELAS then secured abandoned German stores of weapons and ammunition north of Ioannina. These weapons would soon target Zervas, the Germans, and the British into 1946.

"The Guerilla Leaders? What Has It Got to Do with Them?"

As the Germans retreated from Greece, Woodhouse traversed the country, encouraging action with limited results from the guerrillas. British and American troops targeted roads and railway lines through the north and south of the coastal plane, thanks to the secret clause in the Plaka Agreement. It was Woodhouse's last triumph.[105] October 17, on the cruiser Orion, Woodhouse met MacMillan, Scobie, and Leeper near Piaeues. "They did not seem to have anything for me to do, but Scobie's ADC offered me a place in one of the cars which were to take part in the victory parade through Athens the next day." Woodhouse asked to sit with the gucrrillas. The ADC looked shocked.

"The guerrilla leaders? What has it got to do with them?"

Woodhouse ignored the parade and headed north to Grevena. "From there we engaged in a running battle with the rearguard until they crossed the frontier into Yugoslavia just north of Florina. A political decision barred us from pursuing them further, and the Yugoslav Partisans were unfortunately not ready on the frontier to receive them." The Germans hid behind what would be known soon as the Iron Curtain.[106] "I saw the last shot fired across the frontier on 1 November."[107] Woodhouse returned to Athens void of value. He refused a job as a political advisor on General Scobie's staff as "my Greek and British subordinates were being disbanded and relegated to insignificant posts." Scobie's men were told to ignore AMM members as their judgments were untrustworthy.[108]

Early December, 1944. Zervas welcomed Woodhouse to Ioannina, EDES main camp, but the old soldier had "no stomach" for a civil war. ELAS drained reserves from Athens, and with two divisions of men battled EDES from December 18 to 23.[109] Woodhouse and Zervas retreated to toward Preveza where "Antony and Cleopatra once lost an Empire." EDES held the line until Woodhouse secured their escape, but soon lost Art and Ioannia. But the real horror show was Scobie in Athens.

December 3. 200,000 members of EAM marched on Athens, protesting general disarmament, impunity for collaborators that Papandreou championed, and Scobie's order that ELAS be disbanded as the war against the Germans was over. British tanks cordoned off parts of the city, so the protest corralled on Panepistimiou Street. Greek police and soldiers of the provisional government opened fire. All were backed by British soldiers. Thirty-three days of city fighting, terror, and brutality were unleashed on each side, but it ended with Papandreou's British-backed forces in command of the city. The attack on Zervas had drained ELAS's ability to fight, allowing the British to secure Athens. On Corfu on December 31, Woodhouse missed the British coup de grace on ELAS.

Churchill came to Athens to broker a peace, but could not work with EAM, who fought until an armistice was secured in January 1946, their influence crippled. Woodhouse later participated as part of the elections monitoring, but the influence born of the World War did not transfer into the Cold War.[110]

Conclusion

Woodhouse was an archeologist who became a soldier, demonstrated expertise as a commando and guerrilla, mastered negotiating and harnessing a guerrilla warfare effort, and became among the most influential forces in Greece during the Second World War despite disagreeing with his government's strategy of betraying the will of the Greek people for geopolitical gain: one that Britain lost two years after the war. He would continue to parlay these skills in British intelligence circles with MI6, including the countercommunist resistance in Iran (OP. BOOT) and the CIA-backed coup of socialist president Mohammed Mossadegh from power (OP AJAX).[111] He later served in Parliament off and on into the 1970s, continuing to write serious tracts on Greek history and politics and his days in the war.

As a maverick, Woodhouse's assets were legion: robust health, capacity to endure hardship, and near infinite patience for negotiation. His command of Greek and facility with languages allowed him to communicate directly with his guerrillas, as Lawrence and Wassmuss had done in the previous war, without intermediary, making him an asset to Myers in building trust with the Greeks. Language brought him to war in Greece, but what made him flourish was his capacity to learn: a hallmark of successful maverick at war. As Lawrence noted, "Generalship, at least in my case, came of understanding, of hard study and brain work and concentration. Had it come easy to me I should not have done it so well."[112]

Woodhouse was built to learn, though instead of the academia he applied his mind to "the barrack-square, gun-drill, parachuting, guerrilla warfare, sabotage, intelligence, politics, industry and unemployment, in roughly that order." His education wasn't wasted. For Woodhouse "education is not just learning to do some particular thing but learning how to learn, and that knack can be applied in many different ways."[113] He counted this skill as greater to having a specific expertise. Some experts

> *had to start by unlearning everything they thought they knew about the country and the people and the language. Then, having caught up with their colleagues, they had to learn some entirely new psychology. If they wanted to understand the inner workings of the Greek mind, they had to accustom themselves to the delicate nuances of words such as* philotimo *and* aphormi *and* parexigisis.

This happened most with folks with no previous knowledge of the language.

> *They had to understand that the most delicate misunderstanding (*parexigisis*) could be an irremediable blow to self-respect (*philotimo*). This could give the victim a handle (*aphormi*) for bitter resentment: a handle which was at the same time rather satisfying, by reason of the moral obligation toward the injured party under which it placed the offender. The Greek language of motion and psychology is full of words whose contents cannot be fully and accurately rendered into English. Only long experience brings an intuitive understanding of them.*[114]

Woodhouse lived and fought with people far different than his royal blood, and yet had no time for the "the wealthy and cultivated, so many of whom found it hardly more difficult to entertain the British in 1945, than the Germans in 1944, or the Italians in 1943." His lot were "the hunted agent and the condemned saboteur, who found a bond with the life of the guerrilla and the franc-tireur in their common exposure to loneliness and discomfort and danger. The underground cells and secret houses of Athens had both a mystical and physical link with the mountain hiding-places."[115] Class bias informed his sympathy for the "rough and simple" guerrillas. They were "unspeakably poor . . . largely illiterate. . . . They were natural suckers for the clever demagogue and his baited propaganda. They had the vices and virtues of all poverty: the generosity that can deny nothing to the destitute stranger: the avarice that will rob him of everything within its grasp when he turns out to be rich." All were bound by the struggle against the occupiers, for which he had sympathy. "Some succumbed, some turned to the AMM, some to the Red Cross, some to the black market, some joined the security battalions of the Quisling government, some joined the guerillas, some fled to the Middle East: all had to devote their principal energies to find a way to keep alive." [116]

It was for communists, republicans, and the great body of nonaligned Greeks that he forestalled a civil war while fighting the German occupiers and contesting his government's desires for the future of Greece. He was the right man in the right country at the right time, helping shape the strategies of the war in the Balkans and the fate of a nation not his own. "We achieved something," he noted with some bitterness in the aftermath,

> *against a solid body of opinion which ranges from patronizing indifference to fury and contempt. . . . If we were guerrillas, we are now regarded as brigands and cutthroats: if we were Greek officers, we are now regarded as fools who out to have known better: if we were British or American officers, we are now regarded as irresponsible schoolboys playing red Indian at other people's expense: if we were politicians, we were regarded as dishonest adventurers, whose best hope now is to be coldly ignored.*[117]

Chapter 4

"Despite the Handicap of Her Sex": Cora Du Bois, OSS Research and Analysis Chief in Southeast Asia, 1943–1945

By virtue of her high ability, professional knowledge, forceful leadership and devotion to duty, [Cora Du Bois] contributed in a determining degree to the success of 18 major clandestine military operations against the enemy. [That she is] the only woman to whom a position of similar responsibility has been entrusted by the OSS is clear indication of the high quality and value of her work.[1]

—EXCERPT FROM CORA DU BOIS'S 1946 EXCEPTIONAL CIVILIAN AWARD AND SUPPORTING DOCUMENTS

"You Know So Little about This Outpost"

—May 1945, Washington, DC.

Office of Strategic Services (OSS) Director William "Wild Bill" Donovan is reaching the zenith of his influence on the war. In three years, Donovan has led the OSS from idea to global intelligence network, complete with spies and agents (four of whom will become future directors of the CIA), paramilitary and guerrilla units serving from France to China that will be the precursor to modern U.S. Special Forces, and more. But the brain trust of the organization is its Research and Analysis (R&A) Branch, filled with future Nobel Laureates and presidents of academic societies, whose outposts in the field feed the organization's home branch in DC with front-line data so it may service America's global war effort. It was a phenomenal achievement and prelude to the creation of the Central Intelligence Agency in 1947, even if the OSS's reputation was mixed among the mainstays of power in the military and State Department.

They tended to view the OSS's privileged status as a new organization backed by Roosevelt and now Truman with vast discretionary funds with interest and suspicion.

That month, Donovan receives a letter from the OSS R&A outpost in Kandy, Ceylon (Sri Lanka), the hub of the organizations analysis effort as part of SEAC under Lord Louis Mountbatten. After pleasantries, the director of R&A in Kandy went on the attack, telling Donovan that they and other research leaders were "unanimous in their astonishment that you know so little about this outpost."

> *We feel chagrined at the situation because we expend what seems to us a great deal of time trying to tell you about ourselves and at the same time carry more work than can be reasonably expected of even our hard working staff. Do you see our Outpost Letters regularly? Do they tell you want you want to know? How many persons have access regularly to the monthly reports of the IBT [India Burma Theater] Detachments? . . . You may be interested in knowing who some of our local customers and colleagues are. The intelligence and operational needs of the OSS/IBT Mission itself is only a fraction of our work. Many SEAC intelligence and operational Agencies work closely with us. Within the Supreme Allied Command, South East Asia (SACSEA) we have worked closely with P Division, the Director of Intelligence, E Group, PW Division, etc. In Delhi we are closely affiliated with Combined Photo Interpretation Center (CPIC), with SEATIC and with the American Mission. We have done a considerable amount of work for the air arm Eastern Air Command, XX Bomber Command, and 10th Weather. Immediate and valuable tactical services has been given by our R&A staff to the Northern Combat Area Command, to the XVth Corps, and to the XIVth Army. ISTD/SEAC and our staff collaborate closely to our mutual advantage. . . . Needless to say we consider the Home Office one of our important obligations. Unfortunately your program is so centered on China, Japan, and the Pacific that you seem to have little staff or energy to spare for Southern Asia. This is perhaps natural in view of overall American war strategy. But sometimes we wonder just how long range your long range is?*[2]

Donovan, the head of America's first global intelligence service, was being called ignorant by one of his most unlikely hires.

Dr. Cora Du Bois was the only woman to lead an R&A outpost during the Second World War. In less than a year, she had proven herself equal to any man in the field. She was a dedicated leader of an untried research organization that provided valuable real-time tactical data to the British and American troops serving in Southeast Asia, while also funneling strategic analysis back to DC. Du Bois did this against foreign and domestic odds and became a vital member of the State Department when the war ended and America's security interests in Southeast Asia grew. Her wartime experience and successes made her a valuable asset despite gender bias, only to have her stock drop thanks to the communist witch hunts of the early Cold War. Worse, these attacks had little to do with her political beliefs, but her "nature."

"'The Deviants.' The Women, Homosexuals, and Jewish Students"

Born in Brooklyn, New York, on October 26, 1903, Du Bois came from a family of Swiss watchmakers and French entrepreneurs. Her brother was the black sheep, and Cora the star attraction: a brilliant "tom-girl" who liked adventures in the wild and sports as much as school and writing poetry. Her father's early death from lung cancer shattered the family, but it also provided a trust for her future in academia.

Du Bois received her MA from Barnard College in medieval history, but her intellectual curiosity was gripped by the rising field of anthropology. She worked with pioneers such as Ruth Benedict, mentor of anthropology "rock star" Margaret Mead, so celebrated for her field work in Samoa. Benedict had a penchant for working with what one sour colleague called "the deviants the women, homosexuals, and Jewish students."[3] As Du Bois discovered her own sexuality she took solace in writing poetry to express her true "nature," as Oscar Wilde would put it, where her feelings for other woman found relief. She gravitated toward anthropology's more complex view of human culture and, especially, the role of outsiders, individuals and outcasts. At Barnard she wrote out her goals within the world of academia. "I must struggle against the narrowing influence of the academic." She had to stay engaged in many fields. And she had to love what she was doing and avoid the conceit which maintains that reason can motivate and dominate a person. "All that reason can, and should do, is merely temper behavior." Her "interests and enthusiasm [were] omnivorous."[4]

Du Bois earned her doctorate in anthropology in 1932 at UC Berkeley under L. Kroeber and Robert H. Lowie, and conducted field research with a colleague in Northern California among the "vanishing culture" of Native Americans. There was no uniform methodology to fieldwork. Her main piece of instruction was "Be sure you have a good supply of pencils and a note book." So, like the mavericks before, she prepared for the unknown but knew she'd have to improvise, including emotional instability tests she would use when dealing with shamans and other individuals. Du Bois and a colleague spent three months in the bush among the Wintu people, where she focused on "outsiders" or "outcasts." Among her subjects was a shaman who would be called an "epileptic psychotic" in Western eyes, but here was revered and called a "doctor." The unconventional had advantages appreciated by the people and a place in society. Being different was respected.[5]

Du Bois pursued understanding the "psychological characteristics of seemingly aberrant individuals and their fit within society."[6] She would also later study the survivors of the Ghost Dance movement. She entered her field as a maverick of mavericks whose work was exceptionally high caliber. Wanting new experiences, Du Bois also worked at cutting-edge research facilities on the relationship between cultural norms and psychiatry in New York City. Academic curiosity fueled her desire to find connection between different fields of inquiry at a time when anthropology was developing its modern form. She would eventually become best known for "the historical reconstruction of thee movements and her psychological insights into them."[7] "Miss Du Bois is a young woman of superb cultural background, with genuine flair for theoretical problems, which is combined with interest in empirical research," Kroeber noted in a letter of recommendation. "Her PhD examination was unquestionably one of the most brilliant I have ever attended and aroused the admiration of the non-anthropologists of the Committee."[8] Studying culture, the unconventional, psychology as well as history and the negative influence of imperialism lined her work. *The Feather Cult of the Middle Columbia* (1938), and the book *The 1870 Ghost Dance* (1939), examined how specific people became prophets and helped spread their beliefs.[9]

The People of Alors

From 1937 to 1939 she traveled alone to Indonesia to study the native populace of the Alors islands at the village of Atimelang, a mountainous region above the island's northwest coast. There she established rapport with the locals, despised the Dutch's colonial system and ethos, and gathered material for her landmark work, *The People of Alors* (1944). Mead had advised her that "medical work . . . is undoubtedly one of the most fool proof ways of getting to know a community quickly and keeping au courant with what goes on."[10] Du Bois heeded the words of a senior peer and rival.

"Daily I bated infections," she recalled, "dispensed quinine or castor oil or aspirin, and gradually even the woman and children were sufficiently used to my touch to forgive me the size of my body, the whiteness of my skin, and the blue eyes, which looked so frighteningly blind to them. That my nose was long and sharp was, however, to the very end of my stay, a never-ending source of merriment."[11] She researched language, genealogies, conducted a census, and was "pleasantly harassed" by so many tasks.[12] She loved the challenge of the Abui language, the gestures it required, the challenge of translating it to the page (it had no written form), and how much more difficult but satisfying it was than Dutch or Malay. All the while she fought dysentery, countered chicken lice with smoke and Lysol, yaws (skin infection), and tropical ulcers. She loved the struggle, but told her parents that it was not an adventure but research, and studied hard on the nature of their horticulture economy, the role of gender and labor (women did most of everything), death rites, and purchase practices. When she left, some commented on her being a "sky being" or *nala kang* in Abui. Descendents thought she would return. After a fashion, she did.

"The Heartbeat of the Organization"

The intelligence demands of the Second World War brought Du Bois into military affairs and, eventually, back to Asia. The vehicle for this was the OSS. As noted, the OSS's most celebrated members were spies in the field, paramilitary units dropped behind enemy lines like the JEDBURGH teams that were parachuted into France to work with the Resistance, including a young Bernard Fall (see chapter 6). "The shadow world of spies and dark intrigue was a small, albeit interesting, part of OSS," recalled veteran Betty McIntosh, "but the Research and Analysis Branch . . . was the heartbeat of the organization."[13]

R&A would house over 900 members by war's end, a veritable "Who's Who" of future celebrities in policy and academia, including Ralph Bunche (Nobel Peace Prize Laureate), Arthur Schlesinger, Jr. (historian, speech writer for President Kennedy), Sherman Kent (the father of modern intelligence analysis), four presidents of the American Historical Association, and several of the finest émigré and refugee scholars from Hitler's Europe.[14] Along with the DC branch, which was to serve as the hub of strategic analysis, OSS sent R&A units abroad to collect data with OSS units dispatched to the major theaters of war: Western and Central Europe, Africa, Russia, and the Far East (the exception was the Pacific campaign' Gen. Douglas MacArthur despised Donovan and refused to have OSS members involved in his theater). These R&A outposts were initially designed to collect data for Washington DC, to fulfill the task of generating intelligence for the Joint Chiefs of Staff (JCS), including the Joint Army Navy Intelligence Studies (JANIS) reports. But R&A outposts had other clients and customers in the field, mostly for tactical and operational intelligence. These included OSS paramilitary military detachments, the senior services, especially the Army and Air Force, and theater commanders. The pull between these two clients would soon cause Du Bois much grief.[15]

The need for intelligence was so great because American ignorance was so vast. As an official OSS history noted on the challenge of working in Southeast Asia, "the primitive character of the natives in many areas and the absence among them of any deep hatred of the Japanese were as unusual and as formidable difficulties to OSS as the profound

American ignorance of Southeast Asia and the cultural and psychological obstacles to the recruiting, training, and managing of competent and loyal native agents." The same could be said for geographic, economic, political, and social knowledge vital to liberating foreign nations of foreign aggressors.[16]

"Yes, we were picked, one presumed, [because of our] area knowledge," Du Bois recalled.

> *Now I had no general Southeast Asia knowledge, I can assure you. I barely knew Indonesia. My work at Alors certainly did not give me any broad or deep picture of the total heterogeneous Indonesian situation, and I had not been to Thailand and Indochina. I didn't know Burma. I didn't know anything, but we all became labeled experts, which was most erroneous in most cases. But we learned as we went along.*[17]

Echoing Woodhouse, Du Bois found she was capable of learning the job on the fly and was more than equal to the task of growing alongside the increasing demands of the OSS. She knew what she didn't know and was driven to learn about what was then unknown.

Du Bois worked in Washington on the Far East desk under political scientists and Far East expert Dr. Charles B. Fahs. While there, she investigated the Netherlands East Indies and Japanese prison camps, and collected data and analyzed Chinese–Dutch postwar relations, among other things, though her early days in the OSS are spotty due to poor documentation. She was quickly promoted to Chief of the Indonesia Section and Acting Chief of the Political Sub Division under Charles Beard, head of the East Asian Division of the R&A.[18]

"One felt one was really doing something important," she later recalled, "even though one wasn't quite sure what it was." Her first year and a half were spent "slowly building up a small staff, occupying myself with biographical information largely on persons both Western and Asian, who might be good informants for further information for searching out details, and then finally a paper which was the last I wrote, on Japanese prisoners of war in Indonesia."[19] In late 1942, she wrote home in veiled terms. "It is compiling confidential navy sailing directions for the NEI (Netherlands East Indies)" including

> *drawing together all the economic, social, population, geographic, fortification etc. etc. dope on which we can lay our hands—often from secret Dutch, English, and American Intelligence files. It is a stupendous job, but for better or worse is beginning to end-at least my part of it. When I go back on the [regular R&A] job it will no longer be a full-time-all-the-time preoccupation and there will be a few spare hours to apply my notorious organization aptitude [to other endeavors].*[20]

Du Bois was an excellent administrator. Her experiences in academia and in field research provided her the organizational and leadership acumen to execute R&A on intelligence documents. Some was of direct importance. "The first assignment was to find out what we knew about New Guinea. We had to write up secret hydrographic documents of the shorelines of New Guinea at various strategic points. We had access to the Office of Naval Intelligence files. I've never seen anything so barren!" "Newspaper clippings, once in awhile, and copies of British Intelligence. Everything was so clearly dated and incidental that they were of no use. So then the job was to collect people all over the country who had, in some fashion or another, some contact [with New Guinea]. Missionaries, or whoever they might be, who had been along these particular stretches of the New Guinea shore where counter-attacks to invasion were expected. This is where I learned a profound distrust for [some] anthropological observations."[21] This was matched by experiences in the field during the New Guinea campaign (January 1942–August 1945), where American and Australian soldiers were using maps outdated and erroneous to be almost worthless. The 32nd Division's efforts in New Guinea were a nightmare due to rampant illness, Japanese mastery of jungle warfare, and absolutely abysmal maps. R&A became noted for their exceptional work in gathering details to fill in black spots on U.S. maps in the Pacific.[22]

The OSS forced Du Bois to work with everyday people whose capabilities she came to revere. "As I went on in this 'skullduggery' of OSS and ran into lawyers and New York bankers and Washington liquor dealers, all kind of people, I realized how profoundly intelligent people in the real world were. In my stupidity I had assumed that intelligence was the central preserve of the academicians. I learned a great deal during those years, which I brought with me when I returned to the 'groves' and to that extent I became very skeptical of a lot of the theory-spinning that goes on in the academic world, especially in the social sciences."[23]

Du Bois had proven she was a triple threat—excellent at research, administration, and leadership—so when she asked to be transferred abroad, her request was granted. But when offered London she turned it down. "They'll have to think of something better than that. As long as we [OSS] stay out from under the military I can still afford to be picky and choosy. I'll settle for nothing less than the Far East, or Australia at a minimum. The job was really silly, too. A Dutch translator in a British intelligence office. I'd still be on the OSS pay roll, but I don't' see why they have send an American to England to translate Dutch when England must alive with Hollanders. I suspect the gent in England (whom I met here some months ago) was just trying to increase his staff without his budget. I told the OSS so, too."[24] In February 1944, Du Bois was dispatched from DC to Kandy, Ceylon, to work as the chief researcher for the OSS's embryonic R&A Team in the Far East. On the *SS Mariposa* she met another OSS officer and expert administrator, Julia McWilliams, who would later become famous as TV chef Julia Childs. "[S]he is a lovely mad woman you know, when she gets sportive. Every now and then, she couldn't stand the disorder, though she was one of the main constructors of the disorder." She'd often take the mess everyone made "make a great heap in the middle of the floor . . . [and] straighten things out."[25]

"Despite the Handicap of Her Sex"

By the spring of 1944, with the opening of the second front set for summer, the Far East Theater was second fiddle to the European Theater of Operations for people, resources, and attention. And SEAC became a sideshow of a sideshow. Simultaneously, SEAC was also a more complicated theater of operations in terms of cultures, geography, and competitive commands between the British and the Americans for primacy of their respective interest: Britain on its imperial holdings in India,

Singapore, and Burma; America with economic interests China; and both dealing with the Japanese occupation, including of French imperial territories including Indochina. The Quebec Conference of 1943 centralized the efforts somewhat in what was called the China-Burma-India Theater (CBI) with the creation of SEAC. "US interests in the area had been focused on the long supply route that stretched from Calcutta (Kolkata), India, into nationalist China through the jungles and mountains of Assam (northeast India) and Northern Burma. With the establishment of SEAC under a new theater commander, Admiral Mountbatten, and with an integrated Anglo-American staff, the Allies hoped to improve the China/Burma/India war effort."[26] Donovan got OSS expansion as part of SEAC.

But in the China Theater, U.S. Army general Joseph Stilwell, senior U.S. commander in the region and chief of staff for Chinese general Chiang Kai Shek, and Admiral Milton Miles, commander of the OSS in the region did not want to have OSS under British dominance. Donovan's compromise? OSS had the right to gather, "strategic intelligence independently, through its own agents, everywhere in the Theater that US interests required, regardless of whether or not such intelligence was required or requested by SEAC."[27] So they were provided a modicum of independence, and Mountbatten received a small force of specialized American troops for guerrilla activities and R&A personnel. Du Bois was one of them, but how and why she was hired reflects the role of personality and gender biases in the face of such unifying factors as common enemy and active warfare.

By March 1944, the division between China/Burma (CB) Theater and SEAC had been completed. SEAC now needed a specific R&A team led by a "mature research worker with considerable competence in the South East Asia field." The challenging climate and environment meant that any candidate had to be able bodied and tough. According to the first Progress Report of the R&A/OSS, CBI/SEAC, "only Dr. Cora Dubois, a foremost authority on NEI and Malaya, and Lt. Joseph Coolidge, an experienced cartographer, have been processed in Washington and have been assigned priorities."[28]

By May, Du Bois had arrived, and the position of R&A Chief of CBI had been given to Captain Joseph Spencer, a successful geographer of Asia.[29] A driven professional with a deep capacity for organization, Spencer also earned the ire of Lt. Col. Richard K. Heppner, commander of the OSS in the region, who saw him as a cynic with a bad attitude.[30] Heppner, however, was high on Du Bois's efforts and skills. "Dick feels that Cora Dubois is fully capable of heading R&A in SEAC and would much prefer her in that capacity to having Joe Spencer," Col. John Coughlin, a senior OSS officer in Kandy, noted to Dr. William Langer, the Chief of the entire R&A department in Washington "primarily because of certain statements that Spencer is supposed to have made. This personality angle is an important one and must be considered, but it is a consideration that you would have a hard time keeping up to date on from Washington."[31] Spencer would eventually become the R&A chief in China, much to Heppner's annoyance, but both men agreed that Du Bois was first rate and worthy of being Chief in SEAC.[32] Spencer was grateful Du Bois had field experience as well as leadership acumen and organization savvy, compared to the academic being sent in theater "who have had no administrative background. I have had ten years of it and Cora has had enough in our outfit to know the score, to say the very least."[33]

Spencer and Du Bois were challenged by the divergent priorities of their clients: Washington and SEAC. Spencer told Langer, "Both Cora and I lean toward the theater, for we live it day and night, are constantly beset by its needs, whether inside or outside our own shop. But further than this both Dick [Heppner] and I have demanded it." Despite best practices and official doctrine, R&A's priority customers were juggled by necessities and demands of the moment, needs of theater and home division over time, and the changing nature of the war. Under various stresses and duress, Du Bois would become a fierce champion of her outpost. In the summer of 1944, her work was noted to Donovan by one of his staff touring the CBI and SEAC areas. "I understand from every source that she is doing an excellent job and is very highly regarded."[34] By November 1944, things had come to a head, which would see Du Bois rise in prominence. Heppner secured his command of the OSS in China. Lt. Col. John Coughlin was given command of the OSS in India-Burma Theater. But if Spencer left for China, who should remain in Kandy?

"About the only intelligent suggestion we have been able to arrive at is that Cora might remain as chief in the India-Burma Theater, and that Kirk Stone might serve as her right hand person down in Kandy." Heppner noted, "Cora, because of her sex, cannot perform the necessary liaison [in China] and cannot secure access to documents essential to our work."[35] Foreign women were not allowed to serve in the China Theater.[36] Indeed, Du Bois's gender shaped her role in where she would finally land in the Far East. She was made "Acting" Chief of R&A in SEAC "until a suitable officer can be found."[37] When Spencer left for China, Du Bois quickly shone. "Miss Dubois should continue to as head of R. and A, Kandy," Langer told Donovan. "She has done a superb job, despite the handicap of her sex, which alone makes it impossible to name her head of the branch in the China-Burma Theater."[38] A replacement was never found and Du Bois was tasked with massive reorganization and expansion of the research unit with five deputy chiefs and an increasing wartime tempo. "I cannot see anyone on the present IBT R&A staff with the exception of Cora Dubois whom I would want to entrust with this job at the present time," Fahs, told Langer. "Personally I think that for some time yet Cora is needed more urgently here than in Washington and will prove more satisfactory than any other candidate we have for the job."[39] Du Bois resisted any and all attempts to bring her back, and set to make her name in SEAC, not DC.[40] In May 1945, with Cdr. Edmund Taylor out of country, she was made Acting Intelligence Officer, OSS/IBT,[41] and full chief of R&A in May.[42]

"Intelligence on Enemy Occupied Areas"

SEAC originally included Ceylon, Burma, Thailand, Malay Peninsula, Sumatra, and the waters and islands of the Bay of Bengal and Arabian Sea.[43] In January 1944, CBI Theater was divided into two, SEAC and CBI, and Detachment 101, an interrogation unit in New Delhi, went to SEAC. Later, Du Bois's R&A would serve as part of the India/Burma (I/B) Theater.[44]

Du Bois's mission was vast. From R&A Kandy, known as Detachment 404, she directed a regional intelligence gathering and analyzing effort, producing actionable research form a myriad of sources in Southeast

Asia, including public documents, cartography and photography, economic analysis of capture records, caches of enemy documents, POW interrogations, and more. R&A was a boon to SEAC, especially in cartography and targeting data for bombing and SEAC operations being planned for Burma, Malaya, and Indonesia. This included OSS Detachment 101 fighting in Burma, which had its own R&A "City Team," a quick-acting R&A unit that followed the soldiers into Rangoon to "exploit targets for their intelligence value by securing known collaborators, documents, and prisoners from Japanese military, police and intelligence facilities" after the enemy had been defeated or routed under anthropologist Captain David Mandelbaum.[45] Another OSS Detachment 101, not affiliated with the paramilitary arm, operated in New Delhi, primarily concerned with prisoner interrogations. HQ (404) generated reports and memorandum for consumption of OSS R&A Home Office.[46] Kandy's main task would be the increase of the flow of "intelligence on enemy occupied areas to Washington," according to Langer.[47] But the pressure was always on to support theater operations first, regardless of Washington's dictates. By May 1945, Langer included future concerns for the region to Du Bois's mandate and yet, since February, had been poaching money, material, and, most gravely, staff and sending them to China or Washington.[48]

Coughlin was the first to feel Du Bois's anger. "I think I recognize the fact that you are anxious to support China at the expense of the India Burma Theater," he wrote Langer, "that you are likewise anxious to support Miss Dubois and not give her the feeling of being let down."[49] Maj. Edmond Taylor, OSS's chief intelligence officer, was one of Cora's supporters and pushed Langer to have R&A follow Theater needs instead of DC's. Langer relented slightly.[50] Du Bois was astounded that four of her best people were yanked from Detachment 404 to do work on the JANIS reports. These were experts in topographical and area studies in operational areas. When they were done they got shipped to China. To Du Bois, this was an indictment against their work. "It was taken, perhaps quite erroneously, as a sign that OSS/Washington had decided to drastically curtail its support of the SEAC mission," she wrote Langer. "All this came at the very moment that we received strong support for our mission from JCS and State Department. You can well imagine that our bewilderment and distress was considerable." But the implications were clear, as was a change in Washington's conduct. "It also appeared that Washington was abrogating its former policy of consulting with Outpost Chiefs about the shifting of personnel. Involved of course is the JANIS pressure, but also involved was the transfer of the four key men from IBT to China when the job in Washington was done."[51] Apparently it was easier to avoid Du Bois's eye if her men were poached for DC before being told their next job was China.

Du Bois laid out the price tag for ignoring her and the SEAC mission in poaching from her staff. "Since most of the research staff is inexperienced this will involve a good deal of time as Bowers will tell you. To meet this essential obligation I shall have to withdraw from much of the overall intelligence planning for the Detachment and Theater. It will not be possible to take as active a part as I have in the past on either the Operations Committee or the Theater Planning Board." In a thinly veiled jab, Du Bois made her value known. "There is left no-one but Capt. Mandelbaum who can serve as my deputy and he is committed to the Rangoon City Team job which may well be one of our most important opportunities in the area to secure intelligence about Japanese forces which might have direct bearing on the war in the Pacific. With three detachments in IBT to be competently directed and with myself acting in a duel capacity the lack of someone as Deputy Chief is a vital weakness." Air Intelligence was weakened since "we now have no skilled photo-interpreter." These cuts meant the

> *long desired accuracy of our target work will have to be once more abandoned. The safety of operators is in question. In addition the close integration of map work, research and air photography which was beginning to show such excellent promise under Stone's guidance will have be given up. . . . The Battle Order files and map can be maintained with the help of one SI man and one R&A man. This is basically a service to SI [Secret Intelligence], but is deemed by them essential to their work. Papers on military matters, such as the "Organization of the Thai Army" and certain speculative forecasts which have been received with interest in the Theater, will no longer be possible.*

In short, no one had thought of the price tag to Detachment 404. "The whole picture of IBT can be reviewed for you by Lt. Cmdr. Taylor far more adequately than I can. After such a conversation I should deeply appreciate from you a letter giving me the direction of your thinking in Washington and what you expect us to do in terms of the load and direction of work and what personnel can be expected to implement such a directive."[52] It was around this time that Du Bois sent out her pointed letter to Donovan, asking the head of the OSS if he actually "read the reports," coming from her outpost. In May 1945, Langer apologized to Coughlin, "but I think you understood that this decision was not being taken light-heartedly and that it is impossible for me to conduct the work of the branch generally and at the same time take full account of special circumstances in any outposts."[53]

It was clear. All roads led to Washington, even if they crippled active operations in theater, unless that theater was China. Like Lawrence and Woodhouse, Du Bois was a maverick in a sideshow's sideshow. "We feel out here that both China and Washington are not only making many demands on us but that they are being done with a minimum of coordination," she wrote Fahs.[54]

"... There Is No Repudiation for What We Have Done"

In April 1945, a review of the Far East efforts overseas was done. Major R&A achievements in the outposts, Washington noted, were also backed by "extensive basic work carried out in Washington either directly or indirectly in support of the work of the outposts." These include bomb targeting. R&A agents did this for Eighth and Fifteenth Air Force.[55]

"Service to other branches of the OSS has always formed an important and high priority of R&A's mission in the Far East Theater," Du Bois noted to DC. "Far East Division personnel is responsible for the collection of political, economic and geographic intelligence, its evaluation and dissemination through reports. These reports, along with other services such as aid in photo interpretation, interrogation and briefing, have been the main contribution to operations of SI, SO, and MO at Detachments 101, AFU, 202, 303, 404." Their value was noted in other military organizations as well. "Economic and geographic specialists have been assigned to the 14th Air Force and the 20th Bomber Command where they have made available to A2 OSS intelligence collected in other Theaters as well as in Washington, and where they have collaborated in producing target analyses for air operations."[56] The outposts have supplied much basic data, "particularly of a political and economic nature, that has been utilized by R&A/Washington for studies requested by the Joint Chiefs of Staff and the Department of State. Geographic and air intelligence from our air units has been very valuable to the Joint Target Group, servicing the 20th Air Force in Washington." Key programs would stay in place. "There is the possibility of larger-scale operations in China, especially North China, in which case the importance of R&A services to OSS operations would be increased."[57]

By the end of May 1945, Du Bois ran a thriving concern, respected and needed by SEAC. But with the staff decreases, frustrations climaxed as workloads increased and morale sank. R&A's work on Thailand, Burma, and Malaya received increasing recognition from the Theater Command and Gen. T. S. Timberman, American liaison officer to Supreme Allied Command South East Asia (SACSEA). "This increased recognition and awareness of our activities results quite directly in request for additional work. We are therefore in the anomalous positions of more work and less staff with no one apparently concerned about the situation except ourselves. The greatest anomaly is that we quite rightly earn cheers for various jobs, especially the one in Thailand." OSS officers from Ceylon and China had spent the better part of a year infiltrating Thailand to work with a complex network of resistance movements against the Japanese.[58]

> *So apparently there is no repudiation of what we have done. All this brings morale to an all-time low among the people who are genuinely concerned with our mission and have been working for some time to build up an effective plan. The fact that the personnel we have left are increasingly inexperienced in the area or are also-rans does not help. I have reached the point where discouragement and frustration make me toy with asking for a recall.*[59]

Du Bois ended her missive noting that the peace talks in San Francisco in the wake of German defeat were great signs. "With the war still heavy on us out here, it is encouraging to know that peace is being contemplated and planned for somewhere, even though we recognize there is no magical act performed by conjuring up the word."[60]

As Japan became the sole enemy, workloads in SEAC R&A jumped despite the reduced manpower. At the end of May, Du Bois reported the intensity of the workload: "418 hours for 96 pages, Memoranda: 163 hours for 47 pages, Intelligence Objectives (4 major reports) 55 hours and 29 pages, no maps completed, one reproduced, and two in progress (a vaunted telecommunications report for Malaya, Burma, Thailand, French Indo China as well as other work for the Air Intelligence Unit." Target studies were done of Phenom Penh and used by Eastern Air Command, and research on Japanese held railways, using military and POW reports, were of great results for both DC and Theater command.[61] R&A Kandy did this with only twenty-two assigned persons and yet pushed ahead with a vigorous research and publication schedule. As consolation, that month she was made full chief of R&A.[62]

In her own progress report, Dubois reported that the outstanding achievement was R&A's efforts in the final stages of OPERATION JEAN, the conquest of Rangoon. "R&A was represented on all parties in the operation. Documents of military, political and strategic value were collected, classified and microfilmed. Thirty of the local populace were interrogated."[63] Intensive transportation research on Central Thailand and on effects of bombing on traffic in Burma-Thailand Railroad was prized by SEAC. "This report shows clearly that, in order to be effective, the bombing of strategic railroads and bridges must be repeated constantly at intervals given in the report." There were reports on guerrilla movement in Malaya, geographic intelligence studies of long range value, and effects of monsoon season on Burma and Thailand railroad. Her staff also consults and adds to the SI Biographical records section. Report totals for 101/Rangoon, 303, and 404. Totals were 22 reports, 26 memoranda, and 30 interrogations (all in Rangoon) since "Figures for the number of 303 interrogations are not available at this time." Du Bois also noted that she herself and five others of her team were awarded the Emblem for Civilian Services "in recognition of their valuable and faithful service to the United Sates Forces in IBT"[64]

Indeed, Du Bois's R&A Team was actively involved in the Burma campaign. OSS Detachment 101 served as guerrilla and combat troops with British and indigenous forces in the amazing reversal of fortune conducted by Field Marshall William Slim. Detachment 101 was given its own R&A Unit, and individual members of Du Bois's team also served in different capacities, including Lt. Charles Stelle, who served as an R&A officer with Maj. Orde Wingate's long range patrol group and predecessor of modern special forces, the Chindits.[65] "Our participation in the Rangoon affair seems to have been successful to judge from the only OSS summarizing cable received thus far."[66]

"The R&A team did an excellent job despite the confusion of the move into Rangoon for which they were in no way responsible," she later noted. "The plan actually carried out was a far cry from the one sent AFU [Army Film Unit] as a directive. It is our opinion the original plan would have been even more effective since it provided for trained area and language men on the collecting teams. The original plan would have resulted far less bulk and confusion for the HQ people to handle. It would have also been faster."[67] Taylor agreed. The work on Burma, especially the rich document collection done by Mandelbaum and the Rangoon "City Team," was of great value.[68] While the Japanese made away with much of their operational and other sensitive material, "analysis of the catalogue prepared by Capt. Mandelbaum indicated that a large volume of useful material was acquired, notably files of Japanese newspapers, a collection of Japanese publications of all kinds which is probably the richest that US forces have acquired since the beginning of the war, and certain special documents such as the files of a large marine insurance company in Tokyo."[69]

Du Bois's team was pinched in cash and personnel again in June, yet still excelling at their overburden tasks. The budget for OSS in SEAC IB was reduced. Even with the war in Pacific still raging, Du Bois and her cronies were reeling. Burma secured and Rangoon liberated, OSS focus shifted to Thailand and Malaysia. Du Bois divided her team's efforts into long-term strategic analysis and the immediate needs of SEAC, including the creation of another "City Team" for the British invasion of Malaysia, OPERATION ZIPPER.[70] The dropping of the atomic bombs on Hiroshima and Nagasaki ended the war in the Pacific, and soon the OSS. By August 22, Cora disbursed most of her staff, numbering fifty-two, most of whom transferred to China. Others went to Singapore, Bangkok, Saigon, and Batavia to do postwar collections and analysis for the State Department. She sent them off with this message:

> *You will be judged, quite correctly, as representatives of the United States. Your behavior both professionally and personally will be under constant scrutiny and criticism both by Europeans and Asiatics. I have not the slightest question concerning the integrity and good breeding of any member of the R&A group. I hope that you make felt your influence and example.*[71]

"Tactics of Our Enemies"

After the war, Du Bois worked for the State Department, becoming a sage voice on the growing trouble in Indochina. But as anti-communist paranoia spread, some of her close friends and even lovers became targets of whisper campaigns and investigations. Work conditions also worsened. The State Department never gave her the freedom and respect that the OSS had, and the Cold War's paranoia began to infect the zeitgeist. "So much happens so fast in this racket that it seems impossible to keep my friends posted," she wrote to Robert Lowie in 1948. "At the moment I am more than a little distressed by the stench of fear which pervades the bureaucracy. If it were a decent honest fear of the world as it is shaping itself, I would welcome it. Instead it is the nasty crawling fear born of blackmail and bullying in a red-smear era. . . . I so deplore the ease with which we adopt the tactics of our enemies."[72] By 1950, she had left government service for good.[73]

Du Bois was offered the chance to head the anthropology department at UC Berkeley. There was one snag: Since 1942, the university had required a loyalty oath. She refused to take it unless the anti-communist clause was cut. As she wrote to UC Berkeley President Robert G. Sproul, "However futile gestures against such means may sometimes be, not to make them is the beginning of personal and social degradation. In all conscience, I cannot feel that I would be loyal to our country if I abet the adoption of methods used by ideological systems antipathetic to those of our democracy."[74] Berkeley's loss was Harvard's gain. She was the second Zimurray Chair at Radcliffe College, the first woman tenured in Harvard's Anthropology Department, and the second woman tenured in the Faculty of Arts and Science. Later she became president of the American Anthropological Association and the first female president of the Association of Asian Studies. All the while, she was creating a rich body of work within her field and training legions of excellent graduate students.

The Cold War forced Du Bois out of government service just when Southeast Asia grew from peripheral to core interest in the United States. And as we shall see, her voice could have been added to other mavericks whose experiences in Southeast Asia made them valuable, but whose ideas on warfare made them outcasts. In Cora Du Bois the United States witnessed the ascent of talent, dedication, and service over bias and prejudice, a woman who had both physical and moral courage to serve abroad in wartime and who overcame the stigma against her gender and orientation to become a leading figure in intelligence analysis at the dawn of America's rise as a global power. It's instructive that she was forced out of government service just when her expertise was needed most.

Part III

Mavericks of Vietnam

I had never visited Indochina, nor did I understand or appreciate its history, language, culture, or values. Worse, our government lacked experts for us to consult to compensate for our ignorance.[1]

—ROBERT MCNAMARA, SECRETARY OF DEFENSE (1961–1968)

EVEN IGNORING DU BOIS, the United States had experts on Vietnam in the 1950s. Refusing to utilize them to their greatest extent was a choice. When McNamara said "our government lacked experts for us to consult to compensate for our ignorance," he lied. Three were mavericks.

One was a child soldier, fighting for survival in the streets of a foreign nation against an occupying force whose brutality orphaned him and his sister; he channeled his fecund mind to be become adept at guerrilla warfare, hiding in plain sight amid despised collaborators and in direct action against the genocidal enemy.

One was an archeologist, who had roamed the plains with the Navajo, excavated ancient civilizations from Alaska to New Mexico, and dressed like a lost frontiersmen from a bygone America; his capacity for hardship, to silently hunt a starved and bitter enemy, and respect and lead soldiers of indigenous peoples not his own was matched by bravery in combat, making him famous in the jungle warfare of Southeast Asia.

One was an advertising executive who hated guns, loved Thomas Paine, and had an aptitude for the art of social psychology, the power of appearances, and a knack for helping people find solutions that were very often rooted in his own dynamic imagination; he parlayed his talents into the United States' first global intelligence and special forces organization, where his unconventional intellect focused on people and culture, not body counts, when he considered counterinsurgency.

None were career soldiers. If not for the Second World War, each would have pursued careers in academia or private business instead of military affairs. Two were mavericks within the system, the other an exalted outsider. Each took a unique path to influencing Vietnam from within and from without until their efforts all come to a stunning halt in 1967: one would die in the field; another, so disgusted with the war effort, chose exile from the United States; and one became the "father" of South Vietnam whose many enemies curtailed his influence after two decades of American success and influence in Southeast Asia.

Chapter 5

Expert in Exile: Bernard Fall and Speaking Truth to Power in Vietnam

"... This Is Bernard Fall on the Street without Joy"

—February 21, 1967, South Vietnam.

Dr. Bernard Fall and U.S. Marines are trucked out from Phu Bai to Lai Ha, a jumping off point for OP CHINOOK II. Here he stands on the *La Rue Sans Joie*, the "Street without Joy," where he'd stood ten years before conducting his doctoral research in the field, following the French Army against the Vietminh.[1] Now it is home to the 802nd Vietcong Battalion.

"*Charlie Company picked up two Viet Cong suspects . . .*" he says into his tape recorder. "*Yesterday evening also we captured two of them: a little girl about twenty—strapping girl—and a boy about sixteen, in the village. By the time the Vietnamese had left us they were already beating them and, of course, it's no small wonder no civilians stay behind except a few old women.*"

Fall is perhaps the greatest authority on war in Vietnam, yet has never been consulted by three administrations.

"*We have been walking now for two and a half days in a virtual desert. . . . Charlie Company already exploded a mine with a trip wire and apparently one fellow is hurt.*"

Why?

"*Afternoon of the third day. Still on the street. . . . But Charlie Company has fallen very badly behind; now there's a big hole in our left flank and there's some people running away from us.*"

Fall tells the truth, no matter the consequences.

He'd watched, fought, and challenged Nazi Germany's attempts to create a Third Reich and then lie about its abominations, including the murder of Fall's parents, to save itself from justice. For Fall, you had to speak truth to power or stand in the ranks of the butchers. You must have the courage of your convictions no matter who is in power.

"This is Bernard Fall on the Street without Joy."

"Doctors Are Never on the Front Line"

—Vienna, 1938.

He was only twelve, a brilliant and confident student who dreamed of war, adventure, and being a mighty general, when German tanks roared into the capital. But Berthold Fall's father Leo, an émigré from Silesia, Poland, had fought in the Great War and escaped being one of a million casualties of the Austro-Hungarian Empire. Now a pacifist, Leo had secured a safe, middle-class life running a woman's clothing shop in the capital with his wife, Anna, a trilingual émigré from the same city. Berthold hid his military books from Leo, his sister Lisette noticed, because his destiny was to be a doctor. "[W] hen there's a war," Leo argued, "the doctors are never on the front line."[2]

That spring, Berthold was hunted by "Patriotic Youth Groups," early devotees of the racist militancy in the air who had been given free rein by public and state. He was beaten in the streets.[3] The family's business was taken by the government. In Nice, France, the Fall's hoped to escape more Nazi horrors.[4]

"Renegade Aristocrats . . . Unorthodox Professional Soldiers, and Jews"

Germany defeated France in June 1940. Nice was in the so-called *zone-libre* or Free-Zone under the control of the Vichy Government, but occupied by Benito Mussolini's Italian Army. Hardly benevolent, the Italians were initially less racist and thuggish in their occupation policies in France.[5] By 1942, however, Vichy's racism was "interchangeable" with the Germans.[6] Anti-Semitic laws restricted the rights of Jews in France, the only occupied power enact such laws without German direction.[7] A French paramilitary police force, the *Milicie*, hunted down resisters and undesirables.[8] Once a model of tolerance, Nice became the French heart of the Holocaust. Leo went into hiding, but was eventually captured, tortured, and killed by the Gestapo. Anna would die in Auschwitz. Hiding under false identities, Fall and his sister fended for themselves.[9] But Berthold fought back undercover.

The *Compagnons de France* was a patriot "Youth Group" created by the Vichy government. Dressed in military uniforms, 100,000 strong, these *Compagnons* sang the song of the Petain regime's right wing "Nationalist Revolution" and focused on physical education, skills, and service.[10] Fall excelled at the role of a proud, energetic French youth. It gave him access to resources, freedom of movement, and a chance to build up his strength to fight back. "With all my bookish air. I nevertheless enjoy a good tough scrape," he said later, "just to prove to myself that I'm no sissy. I guess that I've been trying to prove a point to myself ever since my parents died."[11]

The French "Resistance" was stronger in the south, an area outside direct German control until the Italian surrender of 1943. There was an eclectic mix of "renegade aristocrats, bourgeoisie collectivists, Christian democrats, unorthodox professional soldiers, and Jews." [12] Fall joined Jewish resistance groups that rescued orphaned children, worked with commando squads, and built the skill set of an urban guerrilla hiding in plain sight. He also learned the calculus of terror: killing Germans lead to brutal reprisals, but one multiplied the value of terror if you targeted collaborators.[13] You saved lives, since the collaborators were not often armed, and "there would be another five thousand Frenchmen who wouldn't give the time of day to the German Army henceforth." With that math, "Terrorism . . . becomes a strategic weapon."[14] In Cannes, he even attended Jules Ferry School thanks to his membership in the *Compagnons*. "I play the genius," he wrote to his girlfriend. He also created a new identity. His forged ID now said "Bernard Roger Fall." The boy beaten on the streets of Vienna was gone.[15]

"The Endless Tunnel"

The summer of 1944 he joined the maquis in the Alps.[16] Assigned to the *2e Bureau of the Forces Francaises de l'Interieur* (FFI), he was sent to Upper Savoy, where his skiing skills would be put to good use. Fall was immediately "on the Wanted list . . . I was in a real *maquis*. a combat outfit. There was no such thing as living at home like a solid citizen and then go[ing] out and shoot a few Germans . . ." The route ahead was "the endless tunnel." There would be liberation with the Allies "or you'd just die—you landed in a concentration camp for extermination."[17]

Over the next year, Fall worked with JEDBURGH parachute advisory teams of the OSS who supported the Resistance,[18] sabotaged railways and controlling bridges, [19] and saw combat against the Germans at the village of Chindrieux[20] and during the liberation of Aiguebelle.[21] He fought with the FFI until they were integrated into the French Army in August, and served in this capacity until the end of the war.[22] In 1945, Fall was eighteen and had earned *la Médaille de la France* from his adopted nation.[23] But he was not done fighting.

"Common Points Existed between Nazi Ideology and Krupp Traditions"

—August 14, 1947, Nuremberg, Germany.

Alfried Felix Alwyn Krupp von Bohlen und Halbach was brought from incarceration and sat before twenty-one-year old Bernard Fall. Krupp was forty, wide of forehead, and long faced. Master of his family's web of weapon manufacturing empire that, as Fall had discovered, spread across the globe, including into occupied Europe. Now? Charges mounted regarding Krupp's war crimes. Gustav, Alfried's father, had been the prime mover of the Krupp Empire, but his mental faculties had degenerated so much by 1943 that Alfried had assumed command. At the Nuremberg War Crimes Trials, Gustuv was found unfit to stand trial. All eyes were on Alfried. Fall recorded his affidavit.[24]

Yes, Krupp told Fall, he voluntarily sponsored members of the *Schutzstaffel* (SS) in the early 1930s, joined and promoted Nazi organizations before the war, and participated at Nuremberg Party meetings in 1937 and 1938. But he was no ardent Nazi. In fact, he and his global arms empire were victims. In 1943, after the battle of Stalingrad, Krupp did not think there was much chance of victory. Why, then, did he appeal to his workers to keep up production? Krupp was only concerned for "the moral of the worker" after the horror of Allied bombing in Germany. The backsliding continued. "[Krupp] stated that he could not do otherwise than follow the German leaders." While Krupp agreed that "several common points existed between Nazi ideology and Krupp traditions," differences could not be made public out of fear for safety.[25] Such would be the defense of most of the elite in the

Third Reich. There was no choice. They had no knowledge. They were just following orders.[26]

Krupp was lying, and Fall knew it. At Nuremberg, the young guerrilla forged the conviction of speaking truth to power against the nation that butchered his family.

Two months before meeting Krupp, Fall rode a degenerating jeep from Nuremberg to Essen, the heart of Krupp's industrial "octopus" whose tentacles reached out from Germany.[27] Fall had been a translator for the Nuremberg War Crimes Tribunal in 1946, but his superiors at Trial Team III recognized his drive and intelligence. The next year, he was made a research analyst. Through June and July 1947, Fall screened and then analyzed caches of documents and witness statements, conducted interrogations, and document raids on Krupp buildings in Essen and Northern Germany. His goal? Amass evidence of Krupp's guilt in a series of war crimes.[28]

The trip to Essen only confirmed the truth of two years of research at Nuremberg. Krupp birthed an empire of enslaved foreigners and Jews to feed Nazi's war needs. Reading through Krupp's personal files and correspondences, hunting for documents in Germany and Britain where evidence was shipped, Fall reconstructed the world of Krupp, an industrial hell forged in blood and iron. At Essen, rape, slave labor, and other tortures were wedded to industrial efficiency. There were even abortion clinics built into the factories to keep raped women from having pregnancies comprise their value as labor for war production. Krupp also had facilities within the death camps of Auschwitz where Fall's mother was murdered, an initiative started by Krupp himself.[29]

"The Cage"

In Essen, witnesses spoke to Fall of "the cage," the Locomotive factory (LoWa) with a concentration camp surrounded by barbed wire. It also employed death camp inmates. Fall hurried, but the Germans had already started to dismantle "the Cage" into pieces to hide the truth of their complicity. A surprise raid, Fall told his superiors, would catch them in the act and grab their documents before they could be destroyed.[30] The Krupp managers and workers at the Fredrick-Alfred Foundry (FAH) were "arrogant, argued, wants to see your papers, your orders, would even call Mr. Lupton [Fall's boss] in order to identify you, etc."[31] The Germans defied the investigation, trying to rewrite history to save themselves from accountability. Against this enemy, Fall showed cunning, independence, and command of a vast range of issues and subjects of legal, political, and military value. H. Russell Thayer, chief prosecutor for the Krupp Trial Team at the Nuremburg War Crimes Trials in U.S.-occupied Germany, set the research agenda, but "my work on technical projects is performed independently"[32] The Krupp trial dragged into 1948. Before the final verdict, Fall asked a colleague if she'd be going to witness the "final judgment. It'll be lousy anyway."[33] At the trial, Alfried Krupp refused to testify.[34]

"What of the Torture Chambers. . ."

On July 31, 1948, the International Military Tribunal rendered their verdict. Krupp and his cronies were found guilty and convicted of war crimes for which they had profited, supported, and initiated. Alfried was sentenced to twelve years in prison and was forced to "forfeiture of all your property, both real and personal."[35] Fall wrote in his diary, "Victory for us. Krupp condemned."[36] And it was no small victory for Fall. He'd contributed significant work to the "trial of the century," and the picture that emerged during the trial was horrific.[37] Within the crucible of Nuremberg, Fall's view on the importance of research galvanized with his sense of justice. Here, he learned to speak truth to power against the vilest regime in human history. That pride for contributing to such a monumental effort soon became outrage.

In 1951, U.S. High Commissioner John J. McCloy commuted the sentences for Krupp and many Nazi officials. The German leaders in the occupied Western sectors of the country had pressed the Americans to pardons many war criminals in exchange for support in defending Western Europe against and increasingly belligerent Soviet Union. The Cold War reversed what had been a clear case of justice.[38] Fall made his outrage known.

"Without battling an eyelash," Fall wrote in an early article, "the Krupp works used the poor wretches from the concentration camps for the heaviest jobs that were to be found. The whole town of Essen—Krupp's hometown—saw every day the rag-clad column of five hundred Czech concentration camp inmates, all girls from fifteen to twenty, march to their assigned place of work at Krupp's: twelve hours without food and without protective clothing in the armor plate rolling mill."[39] "Were those girls quickly executed at Bergen-Belsen? And what of the torture chambers in the cellar of the Main Administration building?"[40] The reversal at Nuremberg hardened Fall's resolve. Even victories against evil regimes could rewrite the past and absolve the guilty of their crimes if it served a political need. Countering such manipulations of justice would fuel his desire to speak truth to power.

After a series of jobs, the tough, smart, and angry researcher put his energies toward education.[41] In December 1950 after excelling at an American school in Germany, Fall won a Fulbright Scholarship given to international scholars who sought graduate work in the United States. In October 1951, he arrived in the United States and set up shop at Syracuse University's Maxwell School of Citizenship, New York.[42]

"The Hitler Regime Cannot Be Entirely Held Responsible. . ."

A year after he arrived, Fall was in command of his life. He fell in love with a beautiful artist Dorothy Winer, whom he would later marry, and finished his MA thesis. "Illegal Rearmament under the Weimar Republic." Fall utilized his expertise regarding Krupp's role and built a scathing indictment of the how German military, political, and industrial leaders worked against international sanctions. His contacts at Nuremberg also provided access to documents, including, ones unavailable in English, giving his work an edge.[43] German politicians, soldiers, and industrialists were responsible for the illegal rearmament of the country in the 1920s and 1930s, including Krupp.[44] A vibrant writing style infused the work. When discussing the grooming of Nazi military leadership in the late 1920s, Fall noted that they all had "glittering careers which, for many of them, ended either on the gallows of Allied Military Tribunals or the butcherhooks of the Gestapo's Torture chambers."[45]

Yet, Fall also found blame in the Allies. Most chastised was the Allied Control Commission (ACC), whom Fall painted as "utterly helpless to enforce their decisions or even efficiently carry out their assignments."[46] Hypocrisy was also rife. It was "a sad joke on the Allied Powers, which professed to see nothing and hear nothing," and yet "the authoritative 'Jane's All the World's Aircraft' for the year 1929 listed Heinkel Fighters and Bombers—five years before the Nazi regime openly admitted possessing any war planes at all."[47] "Reading the preceding study, one must gain the impression that the Hitler regime cannot be entirely held responsible for Germany's illegal rearmament and the ensuring one of having unleashed World War II. This impression is correct." Among the guilty parties were "the Allied Powers" and the Treaty of Versailles.[48]

But the present compelled him more than the past. Dr. Amry Vandenbosch, a Great War veteran who served with the OSS in Asia, taught a compelling class on colonialism.[49] He championed Fall's interest in Indochina where many of Fall's wartime colleagues were serving.[50] Fall was armed with unique assets for analyzing the French war against the Vietminh guerrillas in Indochina: he understood guerrilla warfare, occupation policies, was fluent in French, and hungry to make his name. So in 1952, he started his "bad love affair" with Vietnam.

"This Is Not a Military War . . ."

By 1953, French forces in Indochina believed they were on the cusp of victory against Ho Chi Minh's forces, a mix of conventional and guerrilla troops with deep inroads into the peasantry, wielded by a mix of pragmatism, nationalism, and peasant communism, and welded together by vast disdain for the imperial French forces. Since the end of the Second World War and the end of brief Japanese occupation, Ho Chi Minh and his forces contended against the French with mixed conventional and guerrilla successes. By 1949, Communist Chinese victory infused them with support over their northern border, but an overconfident Gen. Võ Nguyên Giáp switched to conventional battle against dominant French firepower in 1951 and found failure. For the next two years he recovered and tried new tactics against an increasingly innovative but still conventionally minded French, who wanted to bring an unpopular war to an end sooner than later. In May 1953, French commander general Henry Navarre predicted they were close to the end.[51]

From May to October 1953, Fall conducted intensive research across most of Indochina (Vietnam, Laos, and Cambodia) and got closer to the violence than almost any other journalist in the region in seven years of war.[52] He visited refugee camps, training camps, flew with the U.S. Military Assistance program officers, and famously rode in Flying Boxcar C-119 that dropped its load by tilting the nose and opening the back ramp like a "garage door." He watched fighters strafe jungles and dodge flak, how the Vietminh disguised themselves as women. "This is not a military war," one officer noted, "it isn't even a political war. It's strictly a social war. As long as we don't destroy the mandarin class and abolish excessive tenancy rents and give every farmer his plot of land, this country is going to [go] Communist as soon as we turn our back."[53] This truth, Fall discovered, was ignored by many.[54]

Fall studied French operations in the Red River Delta, one of the major theaters of the war in the north. With 900 forts and 2,200 bunkers, one officer noted, "We are going to deny the Communists access to the eight million people in the Delta and the three million tons of rice, and we will eventually starve them out and deny them access to the population." When asked about communists inside the Delta, he indicated five small blotches on the map. The proof? "[W]hen we go there we get shot at; that's how we know."[55]

Fall didn't buy the argument and wanted it tested. His Vietnamese friends at Hanoi University laughed: communist rebels controlled the Delta and lied to the French. Fall deduced that his friends were right by examining tax records and teacher positions for the region and found a black hole: no one was paying taxes, and there appeared to be no teachers, which seemed highly unlikely in such a political war. Mapping his metrics, the Communists likely controlled 70 percent of the Delta inside the French Battle line. France held Hanoi, Haiphong, and large garrisons, but the countryside was Vietminh.[56]

"Re your recommendation that I stay out of trouble—well," he wrote to Dorothy, "I guess I should but it is intellectually dishonest to write about a thing (in non-fiction) that one does experience directly. If I came to Indochina it was to collect first-hand knowledge and actually seeing it makes you understand the how and why of a few things."[57] In the north he studied communist government.[58] In Hanoi he studied the morale and dedication of the Vietminh that would later astound the United States. And Fall stayed closed to French military operations.

July 28, Central Vietnam. The French High Command commenced OPERATION CAMARGUE, the cleanup of Road 1 up the Annam coast, called the "Street without Joy" because of high casualty rates.[59] "A force equipped with tanks and artillery was landed from the sea," Fall wrote, "and two parachute battalions were dropped from Dakota aircraft and linked up with ground forces moving north from Hué."[60] The scene was impressive. "Using a total of more than thirty battalions, including the equivalent of two armored regiments and two artillery regiments, the operation against the 'Street without Joy' was certainly one as formidable ever carried out in the Indochinese theater of operations. Yet the enemy, on the other side, amounted to a maximum of one weak infantry regiment."[61]

But the terrain was harsh for the French. One hundred meters in from the coast were dunes from 15 to 60 feet high, hard to climb and ending in ditches and precipice. And in the dune zones were fishing villages, followed by 800-meter-deep zone "covered with small pagodas or tombs and temples, which offer excellent protection to any defender." After that was the "Street without Joy" itself, a fringed system of interlocking small villages separated one from the other by often less than 200 to 300 yards. Each was a labyrinth of bushes, hedges, and bamboo. Vietminh Regiment 95 had spent two years fortifying their position. "It was impossible to knock down in a single thrust," he wrote later. But it was the heart of Vietminh power in the region.[62]

". . . And Caught Nothing"

Fall watched the initial wave of the amphibious assault. Despite the vehicles limitations in armor and movement "it was an impressive sight as the 160 vehicles of the 3d Amphibious approached the central Annam coast." Infantry unused to amphibious assaults followed. There was almost no enemy resistance when they passed the dunes and villagers of Tan An and Mu Thuy. Other units came from the south and north. The north was sealed, but too many vehicles bogged down.

Next, the hard task of sweeping villages began, followed by K-9 units. "Each village was first surrounded and sealed off by troops. Then heavily armed infantry moved in and searched the houses while mine detectors and bloodhound teams probed in bamboo bushes and palm tree stands for hidden entrances to underground caches in the midst of the sullen and silent population"[63] Battles to clear sectors continued. Then stopped. A shell hit an ammunition depot. Tremendous explosions followed.

Human waves of Vietminh troops emerged to stop the coming tanks and buy the Vietminh time to retreat and reclaim the night.[64] Communist fled through gaps in the net south of Van Trinh Canal. Some firefights and mortar fights erupted. A Vietnamese Parachute Troop was ordered dropped during wild winds at Lang Bao to seal of the Vietminh from lagoon or shore.[65] Some were strangled in trees, crashed into bogs, and equipment went wild.[66] OP CAMARGUE was a success, of "appearances" more "than of reality."

"A trap ten times the size of the force to be trapped, had shut and had caught nothing."[67]

"... *I'm Not Un-American*"

OP CAMARGUE proved it was impossible to seal off an air tight pocket in a swamp, as long as a battalion had to hold more than 1500 yards of ground. As soon as the infantry moved slowly, guerrillas escaped under cover of night. None of these flushing-out ops or sealed off ops could work unless one had a force ration of 15:1 or even 20:1 to make up for enemy knowledge of terrain and in-play defenses and organizations. The French also had almost no intelligence of value on the areas, while the Vietminh could know quickly what French intentions were with their vehicles.[68] Yet it was promoted as a success.

Fall headed to Saigon in the south. The war seemed distant but the disparity of wealth was obvious and painful. He met with the president, worked with the high commissioner to access research materials, and joined the Minister of Information Dr. Lê Văn Hoạch at Tay Ninh, the capital of Cao Dai, and the political religious sect of Vietnam that was a power unto themselves. Fall journeyed 3,400 feet to the Sacred Mountain and then beyond it the Cathedray of Tay Ninh, the Holy See, to meet Cao Dai's Pope.[69]

Not content with visiting the powerful, he also "went two hundred miles behind commie lines with a small pocket of two battalions one of our last toe-holds up country, among the T'ai tribes," and interviewed commandos who had "become irreplaceable because of his specialized knowledge."[70] He witnessed discussion of "Revolutionary Warfare," as the French called Vietminh efforts, where politics and economics dominated the dialogue on strategy. He'd later note "[a]ll this differs radically from the American emphasis on guerrilla techniques alone and the almost total discounting of the primacy of political factors in revolutionary warfare operations."[71] Fall also visited Cambodia before preparing his return. Despite rankling some U.S. official in Vietnam who didn't invite him to a fourth of July celebration, Fall got his visa renewed and set off home December 8th. "I'm too happy for words to know I'm *not Un American.*" [72]

Fall left as plans were laid for a French strongpoint at Diem Ben Phu to launch a decisive retaking what had been lost in 1952. While in Indochina, Fall published an article critiquing the French decision. With such long lines of support, such a strategy was dangerous. "It cannot be denied that a certain 'Maginot Line' or 'wall psychology' spirit had developed in the French High Command."[73] Less than a year later, Fall's critique was realized with communist victory at Dien Bien Phu, May 7, 1954.

". . . Certain Sentences Are Insulting Both in Intention and in Style"

In December 1954, Fall submitted his doctoral thesis, a three-volume one-thousand-page-plus opus, "Political Development of Viet-Nam, VJ-Day to the Geneva Cease-Fire." It covered the political, economic, and military experiences of the chief forces in Vietnam as the French began their withdrawal: the Vietminh, the French-backed Regimes, and the International Influences of the USSR and the United States. It argued that the Vietminh were indeed a government, not a movement; that French innovations in revolutionary warfare were crippled by a failure to realize a strategy that offered a true political and social alternative to the Vietminh; and that many international actors, including the United States, could play a vital role in the country.[74]

His thesis supervisor was Polish diplomat Wladyslaw Wszebor Kulski. What was initially warm regards turned into mutual irritation later as Kulski found Fall's brash attitudes unfitting a student and Fall found Kulski's revision notes petty and overfocused on Soviet influence on the Vietminh. Kulski found some paragraphs "reflect a highly emotional mood," he wrote to Fall. "Certain sentences are insulting both in intention and in style. I seriously wonder if it is proper for a foreign student at an American university to talk in these terms about American policy." Perhaps they could be written "in a courteous manner."[75] Fall's wife assumed he complied, but one wonders how harsh Fall was before the final draft.[76]

Fall's thesis was a tour de force that demonstrated his intellectual acumen and command of a range of topics already mentioned, but it also put emphasis on the role of economics and the geography of food and the nature of political ideology in the Vietminh and the politico-military structure of the party. The political aspects of the war were as essential as the military capabilities, such as the means and success of taxes and finances, agrarian policy and waging war in a "rice economy," and how realism trumped communist ideology.[77] It portrayed the Democratic Republic of Vietnam as a totalitarian state, complete with "auto critiques," "brain-washing," "show trials," "one-party rule," and "supremacy of a political party over the governmental machinery."[78] But Vietminh popularity was not just brainwashing. Good people fought for a cause that they believed in: ending French rule.[79]

Volume II covered the Bao Dai Regime. It included and the challenge of backing French imperialism, countering Vietminh uses of terror, the challenge of the multiple ethnic minorities of the south and its impact on violence through Southeast Asia, the role of political cults, Buddhism and Catholicism in national life, innovation of population movement to provide aid and shelter called *Groupes Administratifs Mobiles Operationnels* (GAMO)[80] and the complexity, novelty, and ill use of "pacification" campaigns. Faithful to their habitual tactics, "all French and Vietnamese troops retire into their forts at nightfall and leave the small farmer and the untrained and badly-armed militiaman at the complete mercy of the night-fighting Viet-Minh. The ensuring moral climate among the population is, hence, perfectly understandable."[81]

Volume III covered external influences, most notably that of the Americans. Fall wished "to bring some light to this particularly interesting aspect of the Viet-Nam problem and it can be candidly stated that no other research activity in connection with this work has met with such total non-cooperation on the part of the authorities concerned."[82] President Roosevelt's desire for an international trusteeship was covered, as was the abandonment of this policy by Truman, replacing it with U.S. aid for the French war effort. Like Ho, the Americans were now in the role of crusader. But crusaders, above everything, required faith, faith in one's cause and in one's deeds. "In Viet-Nam, the West has shown a lack of both."[83]

This was Fall being "courteous."

". . . Politics Be Damned"

Between 1954 and 1958, Fall was married and started a family, worked as a consultant for a series of private and government agencies, and earned a reputation as an authority on the war in Vietnam. The Institute of Pacific Relations offered Fall the chance to return to Vietnam and report on the emerging divided country and the American advisory and support effort. Fall arrived in Saigon on June 18, 1957, and worked with French contacts, members of Diem's government, and the National Assembly. "I am once more in my favorite hunting ground that is, so to say, political research."[84]

The Americans were nice as ever and "want to go home, p.d.q. No colonialists they."[85] He met Ngo Dinh Nhu, brother of President Diem and the chief advisor, "a very intelligent man. I rather not say more here." French report Francois Sully became a friend. His cynical nature and critical mind matched Fall's.[86] Gene and Ann Gregory, publishers of *Times of Vietnam*, were also friends and allies with access to Diem, but whispered criticism of Fall's work. "I want you to know this so that you can take proper action with U.S. authorities in case anything at all befalls me here," he wrote to his wife.[87] Rumors rose from Ann that Bernard was a French agent. That accusation would later haunt him.[88]

He accessed French files on the death marches after Dien Bien Phu.[89] It was "the most harrowing thing I've seen since Dachau. . . . And it is kept secret for fear it'd upset the delicate apple cart in certain situations. Like hell—I'm gonna get some of this out and politics be damned."[90] Fall spoke at the Saigon Rotary Club in early August and impressed critical members of the United States, Vietnam, and even China in the audience. "You know me—I kept things relaxed and, I think, fairly interesting. I did not knock the US (on the contrary) but did not skirt witch-hunting or racial discrimination either." He visited Cambodia, the 17th parallel, and Laos.[91] While abroad he was offered a job in Cambodia with the U.S. government to teach at the Public Administration School in Phom Penh from 1958 to 1960. He had punched his own ticket, and the rewards arrived.[92]

Back home, Fall told Dorothy how Diem was presented as in charge and in good shape against the North. Fall didn't buy it. The South Vietnamese government ignored the data on the killing of village officials, blaming the bandits to avoid the harder reality of communist victories. He'd talked with the minister of interior about the troubles, and the minister agreed. So, why not tell the president? "Nobody can tell the President we are in trouble. He believes we are doing fine." Then did the Americans know? Probably not.[93] The minister also challenged Fall's data. Vietcong guerrillas controlled only one-fifth of what Bernard had calculated. In June of 1956, Diem also ended elected village chiefs and village councils, a mainstay of strong local government and legitimacy. Instead he replaced them with appointed councils. All these moves were to centralize his power.[94] Politically, South Vietnam was being lost just as U.S. government interest in his expertise grew. With the Cambodian job pending, he began work on his report, *The International Position of South Vietnam*. It was finished in December 1957 and presented in Lahore, Pakistan, the following year.[95]

"A Perfectly Orwellian Job . . ."

In another three-volume effort,[96] Fall's work argued the ceasefire would not hold and a war was coming from the ashes of French defeat between the North and the South. "The peace which prevails in Viet-Nam at present is probably due to the fact that . . . war at the present time does not fit into the plans of the major powers standing behind both of the two Vietnamese regimes."[97] South Vietnam was little more than "a provisional refuge area until such time as it can be reunited with the northern zone." Temporary structures, however, could endure.[98]

America's interest in the former sideshow was the "most enormous Santa Claus act of all time."[99] The United States was state building South Vietnam, with Diem as the pillar of a strategy to end French influence. Working through Diem were prominent officials as well as organization like the Military Assistance Advisory Group (MAAG), and the Temporary Equipment Recovery Mission (TERM).[100] U.S. aid supported nearly the whole South Vietnamese Army, about 80 percent of the total national budget, and nearly 92 percent of total imports. Current practices, however, appeared wasteful and with limited influence on Saigon fiscal policy.

Fall singled out one American as most praiseworthy, Col. Edward Lansdale, a "reserve officer on duty with the Central Intelligence Agency." Fall credited Lansdale for splitting up the various political sect leaders "through cajolery, threats, and corruption, and thus must be credited with saving the nationalist government of South Viet-Nam almost single-handedly in the spring of 1955." Buying loyalty or noninterference was also part of Lansdale's strategies.[101] "From his office in the presidential residence, he directed the planning of the 1955 political and military operations which eventually led to almost total control of the territory of South Viet-Nam by the legitimate government."[102] Their paths would cross in the future, mostly in lectures and workshops for USAID. Lansdale and Bohannan respected Fall, but considered him an outsider to their own schemes.

Yet American influence had to be viewed through the "brutal fact" of economic and military dependence, which made everything harder. Every U.S. idea accepted made South Vietnam look like a puppet to other Asians ("which it is not, politically") and the United States like economic imperialists.[103] American materials from jeeps to clothing were flooding the streets, but with only 2,500 staff who were not, as a people, embedded in Vietnam. Americans also "do not readily take to native food, both out of taste for fear of contamination; they do not use native taxi or pedicabs as much as the French used to, and they have little liking for local beer or French liquor."[104] The legal position of MAAG personnel was troubling: they wore civilian clothes, were not subject to disciplinary measures of a military unit (because it was small and not unit-focused), and Vietnamese courts couldn't try them. Street justice seemed more fair to some Vietnamese against occasional American abuses.[105] Diem was also far from pliant and gave his "fair share of headaches" to the Americans. Compounding this was ignorance of the "true conditions" of the country. Histories written on Vietnam for incoming officials barely detailed Ho Chi Minh compared to Diem and was littered with errors and vital omissions. It was "difficult for an American who arrives in Viet-Nam armed with such information to understand the intricacies of the present situation."[106] After presenting his findings in Lahore, Fall returned to the United States, looking forward to his future work in Cambodia with the U.S. government.[107]

"Fall Has Been [a] Consistent and Vocal Critic [of] U.S. Policy . . ."

On May 26, 1958, a confidential State Department telegram was sent to the U.S. embassies in Saigon and Phnom Penh. It is stamped "DULLES," after the hard-line secretary of state for President Eisenhower, John Foster Dulles.

Thomas Eliot, official of the International Cooperation Agency (predecessor to the USAID program) in Cambodia, and Ambassador Joseph Mendenhall in South Vietnam receive it. Eliot, along with Alvin Roseman, another ICA official and a member of the U.S. Operations Missions in Cambodia, had selected Fall for two contracts in Cambodia: to advise the U.S. ambassador in the newly independent Cambodia and teach Public Service and International Relations at Cambodia's Royal School of Administration. The telegram noted the following: "Fall has been [a] consistent and vocal critic [of] U.S. policy and in recent months has made public statements extremely critical [of the] U.S. aid program Vietnam." His conduct had been so egregious that members of the Vietnamese Embassy and "American Friends [in] Vietnam" were actively looking to "offset" the influence of this "self-styled expert on Vietnam in U.S."[108]

No specifics of Fall's critique are mentioned. Nor is there a word on their validity. The telegram "question[s] whether Fall should be employed in above capacity by US Government at present time. Desire your comments. Reply priority."[109]

For Eliot and Roseman, the State Department's about-face was a complete shock. Fall already obtained his security clearance and was preparing to leave. There was no replacement. And Roseman and Carl W. Strom, ambassador to Cambodia, pressed the State Department that he was the man for the job.

But Fall was informed that he himself had ruined the opportunity. He had given an "unfavorable" speech about the Government in Saigon on April 1, 1958, at the Association of Asian Studies in New York. On May 29, the ICA director of Far Eastern Affairs, Frederick H. Bunting, killed the job offers.[110] Fall protested. His critiques were based on an "honest-opinion" and not an anti-Vietnamese bias. A flurry of calls and memos followed. But the jobs were gone.

Worse followed.

In 1958, FBI agents initiated a surveillance of Fall's life. They coerced Fall's friends for information. They broke into his house and bugged his phone, and later listened to his private conversations. They tracked his and his wife's movements, opened their mail, and inserted themselves as students in his classes at Howard University. Director of the FBI, J. Edgar Hoover, would press attorney general Robert F. Kennedy to maintain surveillance of them during the early 1960s. Kennedy agreed.[111] Hoover believed that Fall's expertise put him in "an excellent position to influence US thinking regarding Vietnam."[112] He might have been a spy or communist. By 1966, the investigations found nothing.

Fall would have limited roles in U.S. government work, but he would be denied any senior position of influence as an advisor to the U.S. government and officially blocked from South Vietnam.

But that did not stop him from trying.

"I Could See I Was Really Hated . . ."

Fall began a research and publishing offensive. A voracious writer, he sold his next monograph to Stackpole Publishing for what would become his first major literary success, *Street without Joy: The Indochina War, 1946–1956*. Securing support from the South East Asia Treaty Organization (SEATO), Fall would travel to Laos and Thailand in the summer of 1959, but not South Vietnam. He'd use the experience to write a report for SEATO entitled "Problems of Communist Subversion and Infiltration in Certain Territories in the SEATO Area."[113] He even snuck into South Vietnam. "I could see that I was really hated . . . and all that just for having said the truth as honestly as I saw it."[114] A similar trip to Laos had him continuing a detailed analysis of how government corruption, economics, and insurgencies functioned.[115]

Despite exile, his opinion was desired. He advised Senator William Fulbright that despite increased American involvement the war was headed south. "Yet persons who voice such fears have come under sharpest attack," he noted because some officials refused to see the truth of beautiful theories "destroyed by harsh facts."[116] Fall secured work as teacher at Howard University in Washington DC and was appointed the Ralph Bunche Chair in International Relations in 1958. While denied access to Vietnam, many of Howard's students did field work in various provinces for the USAID program, and one suspects that via them, he kept himself in the loop through unofficial channels.[117]

"Café Strategist"

Street without Joy, his analysis of French failure in Indochina, was published in April 1961 and praised in the *New York Times* for providing an immensely readable account of the "new" kind of warfare being waged in Southeast Asia. But the book didn't make a dent on the Kennedy administration. President Kennedy was himself fascinated with Special Forces and counterinsurgency, and under his influence there would grow more interest and infusion of capital into studying U.S. and international experiences, including the French colonel David Galula, a French Army officer and friend and colleague of Fall, who wrote two major works on counterinsurgency based on his experiences in China and Algeria. He, far more than Fall, was allowed into serious discussions with U.S. counterinsurgency leaders, including with Lansdale and Bohannan.[118] But Galula wasn't tarred by the FBI. In 1961, Fall returned to Cambodia on a grant from the Rockefeller Foundation for research on "emergent problems of foreign policy, diplomatic analysis and history." He befriended the deposed king, Prince Norodom Sihanouk, and taught at the Cambodian Royal School of Administration. In 1962, his opus, *The Two Viet-Nams*, rooted in his doctoral thesis and bolstered by current research, was published by Praeger.

The literary offensive continued. His "anonymous" article, "The War in Vietnam: We Have Not Been Told the Whole Truth," critiqued not only the U.S. policy in Vietnam but also the complicity of journalists who refused to challenge the government's line. Publisher I. F. Stone, a former friend, labeled Fall a "phony . . . café strategist." Fall's counterpunch was to travel to North Vietnam for the first Western in-depth interview with Ho Chi Minh, published the *Saturday Evening Post* on November 24, 1962. It was the first major interview with the adversary of the United States.[119]

The *Post* article made him less friends in Washington, DC, even with those that agreed with him. All the while, the FBI hounded him. His friendship became a stain that insiders of the beltway could not afford to endure[120] The FBI even attempted to block Fall from speaking to the U.S. Special Forces School, and the Defense Intelligence Agency advised the Bureau in April 1964 that it was issuing instructions to U.S. military services that "*Fall was not to be used for briefing or lectures before Defense groups or at defense schools.*"[121] Some senior officers realized his utility and ignored these instructions, forcing them to be made into orders: none were made and Fall returned to the military lecture circuit. But Fall's public allies remained few.[122] Instead of a government insider, Fall became a public intellectual, his opinion and articles wanted by numerous TV and media outlets as U.S. involvement in Vietnam increased. In the wake of the Army's assassination of Diem in 1963, he was allowed to return to Vietnam as a journalist writing for the *New Republic*, the *New York Times*, and the *New Yorker Times Magazine*.[123]

He returned on August 15, and was soon in the Mekong Delta with controversial advisor John Paul Vann, a critic of the war effort and innovative force in unconventional war.[124] They drove all across the province with Colts, carbines, and a handful of grenades, "enjoying the whole goddamn dare."[125] The bombing campaign against the North disgusted him as brutal and strategically useless. "Blitz in Vietnam" was as unrestrained in its critique, but clear. "The incredible thing about Vietnam is that the worst is yet to come."[126]

"Shadows Are Lengthening . . ."

Fall's opinion was cultivated by dissenting voices on the war. These ranged from Edward Kennedy and George McGovern, Robert Kromer, Daniel Ellsberg, and more. Army chief of the general staff Harold K. Johnson met Fall for lunch in April 1965. The war Fall spoke of sounded nothing like the one he was hearing about from his own troops. Johnson formed a small team of talented midlevel officers and assigned them the task of developing "new sources of action to be taken in South Vietnam by the United States and its allies." Assembling in July, the team produced the "Program for the Pacification and Long-Term Development of Vietnam" (PROVN) report in March 1966. PROVN was a controversial program, and Fall had no active role in it but was the catalyst for a deeper analysis of the war.[127]

Fall's influence never reached the senior operators of the government. When a government colleague went to bat for him, National Security Advisor McGeorge Bundy's responded, "Well, I'm not sure we need that. We've got people who understand that part of the world." Fall briefly met with Assistant Secretary of State Eugene Rostow. "Rostow listened, but he didn't *hear* me." Fall recalled.[128] Secretary of Defense McNamara never spoke with Fall. Given his disdain for Lansdale, perhaps it was for the best. "I have at no time whatever been consulted by, or been in contact with, the White House in regard to any matter whatever concerning Vietnam," Fall noted in 1966. "The White House has its own vast source of information on Vietnam, which thus far have excluded me."[129]

But his work and reputation grew. 1966 saw *Hell in a Very Small Place: The Siege of Dien Bien Phu* published. Fall then won a Guggenheim fellowship for a study on the Viet Cong.[130] For this, he would be allowed back between June 1966 and September 1967.[131]

Conclusion

Street without Joy, February 21, 1967.

"*First in the afternoon about four thirty*," Fall says into his tape recorder, "*shadows are lengthening and we've reached one of our phase lines after the firefight and it smells bad—meaning it's a little bit suspicious. Could be an amb—*"[132]

On patrol along a dike with Marines, Fall detonated a "Bouncing Betty" land mine. He died instantly, the tape recorder miraculously intact. The man who knew the true face of warfare in Vietnam died with many fans, his arguments validated both during and after his lifetime, his work championed from diverse cadres of experts from Noam Chomsky to Colin Powell. Fall's life as an outsider of war is both inspiring and cautionary about speaking truth to power, a calling for which he spent and gave his life. He refused to soften his intellectual rigor to placate political notions. This was done not out of naiveté but out of conviction. And, in the distance of time, Fall's work is even more prescient. His career as both maverick and outsider is instructive on how power refuses to listen to advice as much as the quality of the advice itself.

Chapter 6

The Ad Man and the Wolf: The Victories and Defeats of Edward Lansdale and Charles Bohannan in Southeast Asia, 1945–1968

—January 29, 1954, Washington, DC, the office of deputy secretary of defense Roger M. Kyes.

U.S. Air Force colonel and CIA agent Edward Lansdale attends the President's Special Committee on Indochina. United States fears of a communist-nationalist Vietminh victory over the French in the Tonkin Delta are high, and Allan Dulles, director of the CIA, wonders if they should send Lansdale to work in Indochina. Dulles turned to Lansdale and said, "We're going to send you over there."[1] The goal is to add Lansdale to a team of liaison officers serving under the command of French commander general Henri Navarre.[2]

"Not to help the French!" Lansdale says. He has little to no regard for how Navarre and other French strategist are conducting their campaign against Ho Chi Minh's Vietminh forces, and losing. He especially dislikes their treatment of the Vietnamese people as second-class citizens in their own country.

"No," Dulles said, "I [only] want you to do what you did in the Philippines."[3]

What Lansdale had done in the Philippines was nothing less than America's first major success in counterinsurgency after the Second World War. What was more astounding was that his strategy was improvised. But to make it work, he needed the assistance of a fellow maverick in uniform. One who was asked to stay in the Philippines as advisor to Lansdale's chief supporter and fellow strategist, President Ramon Magsaysay, but couldn't help visiting his old boss in Indochina.

April 29, 1955. The French defeat at Diem Bien Phu on May 7, 1954, has brought U.S. aid and soldiers as Vietnam becomes divided between a communist North and noncommunist South under provisional president Ngô Đình Diệm. A referendum on the south's future government is set for October, and amidst the mire of interests, influences, agents, and threats is Lansdale, "alone in Saigon. I had tried to resolve the differences between the sect forces [religious and criminal organizations] and the Diem government. Instead, the government forces and the Binh Xuyen sect were fighting in the city streets of Saigon, with the Binh Xuyen radio broadcasting appeals that I be brought in for torture, so that my dead body could be floated down the Canal de Dervivation." Despite the threats, Lansdale wants the sects to be massaged into government service, turning an adversary into a resource. Two major players in the Binh Xuyen wanted to meet one of Lansdale's team on a street corner. He sent Maj. Lou Conein, unconventional warfare expert with a hand in the underground, armed with some back up.

Mortar fire soon hit their house on Rue Tabard. They were "only shakily . . . obeying me to stay there behind the house walls, which I assured them were thick enough to stop mortal shells."[4] While street fighting continued, Lansdale works on pacification strategy for Central Vietnam at his house on Duy Tan. Suddenly, he receives a surprise visitor. Without a knock, a man enters his office with armed guards.

Col. Jean Leroy was "leader of a Catholic guerrilla group called the Unités Mobiles de Défense de Chrétienté."[5] He is an ally of Lee Van "Bay" Vien, leader of the Binh Xuyen forces attacking Diem's in Saigon. Lansdale tells Leroy to have his men wait outside. They leave. Leroy tells Lansdale he is to come with him immediately. That meant kidnapping, torture, and death. "I knew Jean Leroy well," Lansdale noted, "we had been through a lot together the past year. So, I told him that I wasn't going with him and his troops, and pleaded him to get his troops out of the neighborhood quickly: the army would kill them if caught in this army zone." By his window drapes, Lansdale has hidden some grenades; mimicking a man's daring defense of his home he'd witnessed that year.[6] Leroy begins to argue, Lansdale edging toward the drapes.

"Just as Leroy was turning to leave," Lansdale recalled, "to my astonishment Boh came through the door, accompanied by a Marine Corps officer (John "Demi" Gates), reporting for duty with me in Saigon." Maj. Charles T. R. Bohannan had been Lansdale's right-hand man in the Philippines. An archeologist who had served in the liberation campaigns of New Guinea and the Philippines, "Boh" is considered a talented "eccentric" frontiersman, quiet and seemingly always in the know. Tough, smart, and taking special glee in being underestimated, he'd left Manila to check up on his boss.

Bohannan knows a dirty trick is in play, so he teases Lansdale about the armed men out front. He says he "didn't realize [Lansdale] needed bodyguards to protect him now." Lansdale introduces him to Leroy and says that he and his troops were just leaving. Realizing the kidnap plan has turned into a confrontation with three men, including the rangy six-foot-one combat soldier Bohannan, Leory leaves. Outside, mortar fire rattles in the street. Moments later, Conein rushes in, dazed. He'd gone to meet the Binh Xuyen and a mortar shell had hit a taxi right in front of him. Inside it was a Vietnamese family with children, blown to pieces. The contacts were another hit job. Conein, the daring career soldier and adventurer, is in shock. Lansdale pours him a stiff scotch. "Then I asked Boh to get Conein and the new Marine, Gates, over to the Taberd House, upon which would he please take command there, since the men were green?"

Why has Bohannan showed up? According to Lansdale, Boh just "figured there was some good fighting in Saigon he was missing," so he got on the PanAm flight from Manila to see for himself. "You couldn't have picked a better time," Lansdale tells him, "because I need your calm way with a lot of things here, starting with a handful of newcomers." Conein is drunk and stunned, muttering to himself about the horror of a little girl turned into human scrap before his eyes. They get the men in the car, and Bohannan turns to his boss and says, "I'll take care of it." Taberd Street is a war zone, filled with burning and upturned cars, including against the door. But Bohannan takes command near Conein's residence, "calmly talking over the situation with the residents, giving them tasks for defense. Other American officials in Saigon had asked my advice on the safety of their families. With Boh's help we set-up a radio and patrol network for the Americans. He agreed to take it on as a responsibility. So that's how Boh went over to Vietnam in 1955 on his own to see what the fuss was all about. It was the gladdest I ever was to see Boh."[7]

Together, Lansdale and Bohannan would shape the fate of two nations with strategy that emphasized guile, psychology, political accountability, and cultural acumen more than firepower and casualty statistics. Victory in the Philippines brought them to Vietnam. Their victories here muted by adversaries in the U.S. Army and Defense Department as much as the Vietminh and Vietcong, but the price would be the same: failure and the near destruction of a powerful friendship.

"Men Who Fought as Guerrillas . . ."

—February 6, 1908, Detroit, Michigan.

Edward Geary Lansdale was born to a middle-class family of shopkeepers and professionals. His father was a successful automobile executive, his mother a car enthusiast and Christian Scientist who believed in the power of mind over matter. "Ed" was raised to believe he had the talent and means to succeed at anything if he could just figure out what it was he wanted to do.[8] He worked numerous service jobs as a young man and demonstrated a knack for listening well to others, being quiet yet giving a positive impression. He worked well with the wealthy and also the working class, though the uneducated were harder for him to read and relate.[9] He enjoyed Reserve Officer Training Corps (ROTC) but was a lousy shot, never had a fetish for weapons, and was later evaluated as "sane thinker possessed of balanced judgment. Better equipped by temperament for cerebrations than action." He studied at UCLA before dropping out due to his inability to handle foreign languages. Instead, he became adept at communicating through image, idea, gesture, and body language. During the Depression he pursued journalism in New York while working odd jobs he hated, held on to ROTC despite the Army teaching men to fight "yesterday's wars," and searched for work that would keep his antic mind and need for hands-on involvement on point.[10] A family connection brought him to San Francisco, and working in advertising, Lansdale found his medium.

—1928, the American West.

Dr. Charles D. Bohannan gave his fourteen-year old son a gun and some money. "If you run out of food or ammunition," Dr. Bohannan said, "come home."[11] Young Charles Ted Rutledge Bohannan spent months in the wild. He would work in New Mexico or Colorado as his family searched for climes suited to his mother's ill health. Like other amateur grave robbers and treasure hunters of the era, he earned a living collecting rare snakes and Native arrowheads and selling them to locals or the Smithsonian. Born in Kentucky in 1914, Boh called the West home. Fiercely independent, he became a marksman, hunter, and cartographer, following the footsteps of Clyde Kluckholn, author of *To the Foot of the Rainbow* and popular ethnographic scholar, who had roamed with Navajo and other Natives in Utah, New Mexico, and Colorado.[12] In the West, Boh labored as an amateur archeologist, learning about lost peoples, ancient cultures, and those who called them kin. When the sun fell, Spanish, Mexican, Native, and White workers spun tales by the fire, and Boh picked up smatterings of courtly Spanish, Quebec French, German, and Native dialects. The Navajo and Apache nations impressed him—skilled hunters, warriors, doctors, and scientists, they endured hardships that made white men sick. Their oral folklore was magic.[13] Boh suffered the bias of white superiority, but he and his family respected the indigenous people. Skill meant more than education, which didn't always equate with intelligence. "I had known so many highly intelligent people who could barely write their own name," he recalled at the end of his life. "I had known PhDs who probably needed assistance in dressing themselves." He learned this in the West and South-West and also earned an informal education in warfare. The Natives and other men of the West Boh worked with were not career soldiers, West Point or Annapolis graduates, nor were they cogs in large industrial armies. Instead, they'd learned guerrilla tactics from the examples of Crazy Horse, Red Cloud, and Geronimo, "men who had fought as guerrilla or as regulars in. our Indian Wars on the High Plains. men from both sides. to the men who rode with

Pancho Villa in Mexico." These had been wars of hit and run, of vanishing in darkness, where mastery of terrain, guile, and endurance challenged numbers and superior technology. They went shirtless to blend into the wild, used improvised weapons, and often reused cartridge shells.[14] Boh would later find Filipino guerrillas were similarly armed and conditioned.[15] The virtue that shaped all was personal courage.[16] He served a stint in the National Guards before studying geology at George Washington University, serving on digs in Alaska, New Mexico, and Colorado and impressing the leading men his field with his endurance and capacity for work, meticulous notes, and analysis. He was also memorable for his eccentric frontier attitudes, dress, and penchant for swears, practical jokes, and quiet manner housed in a tough frame. Among the earliest champions of his work was renowned anthropologist and Aleš Hrdlička, first curator of the Smithsonian Institution National Museum of Natural History.[17] Digging up the dead seemed a good career, and when he graduated in 1938, he returned to Kentucky to direct a massive dig at the Folsom deposits at Harding Village. Once it was done, he was off to Harvard for a PhD in anthropology.[18]

"Hero of the Week"

—1941, San Francisco.

The Leon Livingston Ad Agency was a regional powerhouse, and a hotbed for talent, including Emerson Foote, who started as a copywriter there in the 1930s before cofounding million-dollar agency Foote, Cone & Belding Communications Inc.[19] After four years of success with a smaller firm, Ad-Man Ed Lansdale met Livingston at a party and convinced the founder to have Lansdale join the firm as an executive officer at the Mills Building on Montgomery Street. Clients included Wells Fargo Bank, the Union Trust Company, Morris Plan, Nestlé's Nescafe instant coffee, Italian Swiss Colony wines, and Levi Strauss. After accruing a series of skills in media management and production, Lansdale studied local cultures to target ads but also utilized universal symbols and slogans for mass appeal. Among his favorite subjects was heroism. At an earlier job, Lansdale had created an in-store magazine that often asked, "Who's the 'HERO OF THE WEEK'?" turning employees into celebrities. Another of his advertisements for grocer Wellman, Peck and Company rang, "America loves its heroes. You do. Your customers do. And, so do we! In fact, we have known of so many unsung acts of valor in California, that we have decided they shall no longer go unrecognized." Hero scouts would search for the company's "unsung heroes," and lucky winners would get a "specifically designed Wellman Valor Award medal."[20] By the forties, Levi Straus was a major account at Livingston's. They sold farm clothing, primarily in the West. Livingston and Lansdale met with their board of directors in 1941. Keep doing billboard posters, Livingston argued, and stay the course they'd been following.

"No," Lansdale said, to Livingston's horror. "Don't do that. Put your money into salespeople to get in and hit all the major eastern outlets and have them lined up before you launch any major advertising campaign." It would take weeks. There would be no serious money on ads. But the payoff would be greater. Strauss loved the idea.

On the streets of San Francisco, Livingston yelled at Lansdale for keeping his plan secret and sabotaging him in front of their client. Ed held firm. He'd believed every word and stood behind this strategy. Straus latter took both men's ideas, initiating Levi's move as a national brand, and Lansdale's skin was saved. It was a powerful lesson. Victory made up for his unconventional ways.[21]

When Germany invaded Poland, Lansdale had unsuccessfully tried to reinstate his commission.[22] After Pearl Harbor, he told Livingston he was getting his commission reactivated. "If you want to fight someplace, go join the Russian army," Livingston said. "They have better-looking uniforms," then fired him. Jobless again, with his military future uncertain, Lansdale joined the local Office of Civil Defense, lying about the quality of his Spanish and French. He pushed for his reinstated commission to be a public relations officer or in intelligence. While DC ramped up for the war effort through 1942, Lansdale took his medical exam. It found "a moderate enlargement [of the] thyroid gland caused by colloid goiter." By army standards, his health was impaired, and registration changed: "deferred by reason of a physical impairment."[23] Lansdale was no coward. He appealed to the surgeon general of the army for a health waiver. By February 1943, they relented and gave special order #54, reappointing him as first lieutenant; he was made captain later that month. Thanks to a bureaucratic error, he never went through basic training.[24]

The San Francisco field office of Army Military Intelligence Service (MIS) would be his home "for limited service only." But his paperwork lagged. Still jobless, Lansdale pressed friends who had connections in Washington to free him as a hostage of bureaucratic fortune. The OSS took interest.[25] For the next two years, Lansdale served two masters as he worked in intelligence gathering of foreign nationals and developed psychological warfare pamphlets. He excelled in this kind of research and intelligence gathering, combining human and cultural knowledge with personal experience. While he may have been naïve on "complex forces that might motivate another culture," his harshest academic critic noted that "Lansdale's culture-based approach was strikingly in contrast to the standard contemporary American depiction of the Japanese as subhumans and even insectlike."[26] He worked with Indonesian sailors, Spanish refugees, academic experts at Stanford, and vetted foreign agents for work with the OSS (one of the most controversial programs). Lansdale needed an interpreter, but excelled at reading body language and assessing motivation, including vetting possible agents for guerrilla work in Spain.[27] But Lansdale hungered to get in the Pacific campaign in some fashion. By war's end, he'd serve briefly in the Philippines before the atomic bombs ended the war with Japan. By now, Lansdale realized that in war, his skills with people, with culture, with media, and his genuine interest in the struggles of the Filipinos who had endured Japanese occupation had led him to opportunities far greater than his Levi's ads.

"Old Betsy Failed Me Just Once"

—February 1945, the Philippines.

Feces abounded; the Japanese who retreated northeast of Manila had no time for latrines. Everywhere lay "decomposing human bodies covered with flies and emanating a paralyzing stink." The U.S. Army's 32nd Division marched the snaking path of the Caraballo Mountains known as Villa Verde Trail. Caves gaped along the mountainside like angry maws. These simple holes or complex networks hid Japanese soldiers who refused to surrender. They had to be ferreted out and killed. "Old Lobo" was tasked to do just that.[28]

"Old Lobo" was Bohannan, a nickname he gave himself when radio operators kept butchering his last name. He took his Intelligence and Reconnaissance (I&R) platoon, a mix of American regulars, Filipino and American guerrillas, and indigenous headhunters, to a "rest area" where an infantry company bivouacked in an abandoned Japanese cave on the mountainside. The Japanese blocked the trail ahead—twenty soldiers with a light machine gun, tommy guns and hand grenades, TNT, and rifles.

"I'm going to clean those buzzards out," Old Lobo told his unit.

He crawled close and silent to the Japanese position. Six of his men followed, including a Filipino guerrilla named Felix Jabillo who served with Old Lobo since Leyte. To the horror of many Americans, Old Lobo wore no boots in the fetid jungle. As a kid, he'd learned to walk barefoot and silent from the Navajo he'd worked with on excavations. To the Filipino guerrillas, Old Lobo walked as they had for almost four years and more. He also ate as they did, squatted where they squatted, and always led the way into danger. Despite being six-foot-two, with red hair and glasses, the Filipinos saw a man who respected them, coming to toss off the Japanese. Some would call him brother. Others believed him charmed.

Crawling back, Old Lobo grabbed two squads of rifles and reported to his men. The Japanese were, in fact, held up in eight caves over, under, and alongside the Villa Verde Trail.[29] With six scouts and twenty-four soldiers, Old Lobo went on the offensive, but not guns blazing.

He crawled into the first cave. Alone.

His men waited.

This was abnormal. Caves were taken by digging trenches, like in the Great War, and pushing "sandbags ahead . . . until [soldiers] drew close enough to throw dynamite into the caves and bury the inmates alive."[30] Or it was done by suppressing fire from a .50-caliber, .7mm, tank or artillery fire, followed by an assault team charging with grenades, flame throwers, and TNT to kill the enemy and seal the cave.[31] Who prowled inside to kill them at close range?

The men waited.

Minutes later, Old Lobo ran out. An explosion followed. He turned on his heels, ran back into the cave. Journalist John Carlisle covered the

32nd Division in the field and reported the "men saw him wrestling with a Jap officer. With his old-style Colt .45, Lobo killed the Jap."[32]

"Old Betsy failed me just once," Charles Bohannan recalled. Betsy was his Colt. She had misfired. "The Jap threw a hand grenade at me."[33]

A series of sharp and deadly assaults followed. The caves were finished. Eighteen enemy dead at point blank range, twenty five others buried alive with demolition charges. Bohannan proved stealth and courage could save time and bullets—if one had the guts to do things the hard way.[34]

The men revered their eccentric archeologist, who'd "spent a month within the Jap lines in the Leyte campaign." He was a tight purse in paying his officer's mess dues, yet "he gave a Filipino guerrilla a wrist watch costing 30 pesos ($25)!"[35] That guerrilla was Jabillo. On Leyte, Jabillo had seen Bohannan survive a dozen "scraps," barely injured. Half-jokingly, he said Old Lobo carried an *anting-anting*: an amulet with Latin inscriptions, believed to keep its owner safe from harm by combining Filipino folklore and Christian, as well as Freemason, symbols. Bohannan knew the power of symbols and superstition in Native and now Filipino culture. But if the men thought he was "protected" they'd assume he wasn't sharing mortal risk when they went out to fight, so while he respected the culture, he tried to end talk of his "invulnerability" that dogged him on the Villa Verde Trail.

Bohannan had served on radar rig in Australia at war's start, but his hankering for action got him into combat in New Guinea at "bloody Buna" with the 32nd Division. He'd been fighting ever since, including Officer Candidacy School in Brisbane, which he called an "unmitigated pain in the ass."[36] He was decorated at Aitap, smuggled into Leyte, and worked with Filipino, American, and Igorot guerrillas against the Japanese before Betsy failed on the Villa Verde Trail. On that trail in July, El Lobo conducted another clearing operation. But a botched start led to an early firefight and El Lobo's luck ran out: he was shot so badly that when he returned to the regiment's HQ, he was "bleeding like a sieve."[37]

He recovered stateside as the war ended, healed up enough to join the Counter Intelligence Corps to hunt for Japanese War criminals on the home islands, only to be punted back to the Philippines given his intensive knowledge and contacts with all the guerrilla groups, many of whom needed vetting for compensation for their war service. When not separating real guerrillas from opportunists, Bohannan did investigative works on threats to the U.S. interest in the newly independent Philippines. Foremost were the Huk, the communist-led guerrilla group, who refused to fight under U.S. command. They had links to Chinese and Russian spies and agents, were tough, refused to be disarmed, and their members were denied political office, including their Supremo Luis Taruc, a former tailor whom Bohannan had some sympathy for. The Huk and its senior leadership were the chief threat to the new government, who chose to ignore them. But Bohannan found someone who was also sympathetic to his concerns, though at first he didn't know it.[38]

"A Carnival Built in Hell"

In Manila, the fall of 1946, Capt. Charles T. R. Bohannan, Counter Intelligence Corps (CIC), was having a shit day. Yet again, his junk army jeep had broken down, this time near Malacañang Palace, workplace of President Manuel Roxas, the first president of the newly independent Philippines who, as far as Bohannan was concerned, was a war criminal.

"I must go to the G-2."

The voice came from behind. Bohannan took out all six-foot-two of his tough, rangy body from the hood, and turned.

It was a sharp-looking Air Force major, almost as tall as Boh, with dashing good looks like Douglas Fairbanks. Boh said, "Oh?" and then went back to fixing the car, ignoring his superior as if he was a lost tourist.

Shocked, the major insisted to his subordinate that he "must go to the G-2," his tone more imperious than before.

"Oh?" Bohannan repeated, and kept working.

Maj. Edward G. Lansdale, officer and covert agent for the CIA's predecessor agency, had to make a choice. Negotiate or escalate. Friend or foe.

At war's end, he'd become an intelligence analyst for the Armed Forces Western Pacific (AFWESPAC) in the Philippines, managing and investigating almost 300 people of Asian, German, and other backgrounds who had been prisoners of war, untangling fact from fiction.[39] He had also investigated the Ryukus islands, between Okinawa and Japan, where a Japanese soldier had starved and abused the population. Infuriated with the soldier's inhumanity and defiance, Lansdale had dared him, in front of the suffering people, to make a move for a gun he had hidden. The soldier chose surrender, and Lansdale dodged a bullet: his own pistol was so poorly holstered that if he'd had to quick draw, he'd be a dead man.[40]

Lansdale reassessed the "shade tree mechanic" who refused his superior. Here was a guy who clearly didn't give a damn about rank and wasn't going to be persuaded by escalating an argument into a screaming match. Lansdale didn't need a foe. He needed a friend. And making friends was his gift. His voice softened. He said he just arrived in the Philippines, and it was critical he get to the G-2, as they were awaiting him. "Do you have any suggestions on how I could get there?"

Bohannan pulled his head out again. "Well, since you put it *that* way. If you'll just wait a minute or two until I get this monstrosity fixed, I'll be glad to take you there myself."[41]

The storm had passed and now both men chatted. From the start, Lansdale listened to Bohannan instead of dismissing him as some weird combat soldier who'd gone native and rude. Lansdale's capacity to listen to people of all kinds was a trademark of his success. Another was sharing his own ideas in a manner that created agreement. Bohannan soon realized Lansdale was no ordinary senior officer, either. He held most of them in high contempt. Lansdale could communicate with anybody, even when he didn't know the language, a feat he admired and did not have. So Bohannan listened, too. Common ground emerged. They liked Kipling and Forrester novels and Sherlock Holmes, science fiction, comic books, and classics of literature and devoured and debated history and philosophy. If it weren't for the titanic changes of the Second World War and the American occupation of the Philippines, Ed and Boh would have never had crossed paths.

When Lansdale and Bohannan met in 1946, Manila was a city of ruin. The Japanese had fought a campaign of horrors on the inhabitants and the returning U.S. soldiers, and the American use of artillery destroyed most structures. Almost 100,000 civilians were estimated as killed. Shanty towns, crime, and violence ruled. "To one observer who had loved the old city, the new Manila looked like a carnival built in hell."[42]

Lansdale got to know the inhabitants of Hell's Carnival and most of Luzon, often with Boh as his go-to man. He traveled to barrios and cities on his own, became fast friends with journalists, politicians, workers, and business leaders. He even met with guerrillas, and barely escaped a run in with bandits. Complaints and data rolled in about landlords with private militias (usually ex-guerrillas), abusive Filipino and American soldiers, and more. Bohannan filled him in on communist spies in the Russian brothels who preyed on U.S. soldiers, as well "imposter" guerrillas trying to get U.S. benefits for phantom war service. Lansdale may have worn a uniform, but he had also retained membership in the Office of Policy Coordination (OPC), an embryonic intelligence organization that would become part of the CIA in 1947. Working both jobs, Lansdale realized most intelligence reports received at United States and Filipino bases were watered down truths, if not outright lies. He and Bohannan both knew that the real problems were vast, deadly, and being ignored, and they did their best to work with or beside the Joint Military Assistance Group (JUSMAG)'s advisory capacity to the Filipino government. The biggest threat was a rogue guerrilla group who called the government, police, and military corrupt and abusive. The problem? They were right.[43]

"The Huk"

The Hukbong Bayan Laban sa mga Hapon (People's Army against the Japanese), were commonly referred to as the Hukbalahap or Huk. Their supporters and members, like many rural poor, were disgruntled peasants, abused by years of crooked land holding laws from Spanish and American rule which bred an elite class of landlords. Huk leadership came from the urban professional class, most prominently the Socialist and Communist parties of the Philippines. While fighting for peasants' rights, the Socialists and Communist Party merged in November 1938, but the party soon became dominated by communist party apparatus. When the Japanese invaded in 1941, Luis Taruc became their military "Supremo."

The Huk were dispersed largely on Luzon, and controlled other regions of the Philippines. With scraps of Maoist theory and training by Chinese guerrillas, they took the fight to the Japanese in raids, assassinations, and kidnappings. They learned fast and even participated in some of the conventional battles at the end of the war, including the battle of Manila. Like the EAS/ELAM guerrillas in Greece, the Huk earned a reputation as aggressive, offensive oriented troops and claimed to have killed 20,000 Japanese, Ganap (Filipino collaborators), spies, etc. They had a reputation for keeping crime down and were the real authority in their region.[44] Despite platitudes about respecting the "people" as water and the guerrillas as "the fish" that swims through them,[45] Huk abuses were also rife. They "liquidated" collaborators, fought Filipino and American guerrillas, and even, on occasion, the U.S. Army.

During the fighting on the Villa Verde Trail in 1945, Bohannan and his guerrillas had prepared an ambush for the Japanese "when we were hit in the back by the Hukbalahap, the Communist guerrillas. They didn't do much damage, but had I needed any further persuasion about the real nature of this Huk Movement, that alone would have provided it."[46] When the war ended, the Huk refused to surrender their weapons, and some were disarmed and killed by U.S. and Filipino forces.[47] They took to the jungles of Luzon, and began raids on Military Police, sowing informants and supporters in the barrios to feed them and provide intelligence through the "bamboo telegraph." The wartime brutality did not end in peace. Kidnappings, murder, arson, and rapes continued, as did forced recruitment.

The Roxas government dismissed the Huk as bandits, leaving them to the Military Police Command (MPC). The MPC were a joke. Armed with Billy clubs, whistles, and a few old carbines, they were "pitted against experienced Huk guerrillas, who were armed with the heaviest infantry armament available, including bazookas," recalled Captain Napoleon Valeriano of the Police Constabulary (which later replaced the MPC). The Huk walked all over and through the MPC's 11,000 officers and men. America had supported the Philippines' rush to independence from American control, removing thousands of liberation troops and replacing them with advisors. Nor had they provided JUSMAG Cdr. Maj. Gen. Leland Hobbs latitude in conducting intelligence missions. All the advisors, mostly U.S. Army officers, "were prohibited from visiting

Philippine military units and bases and very little firsthand information on the country's deteriorating situation."[48] By 1948, the military was given the task of dealing with the Huk. Massive sweep operations began. Brutal interrogations of the rural poor were the norm. And all the troops stayed on base instead of in the dangerous barrios.[49]

The government's nonstrategy backfired. The Huk avoided direct battle. Brutalized peasants swelled the Huk ranks. Those who hated the Huk and helped soldiers were defenseless when the MPC soldiers returned to their bases and left their collaborators ripe for Huk retributions. Valeriano, a former guerrilla and innovative soldier, pushed for a hunter-killer group to hunt the Huk, and received some support for his own dreaded Nenita Unit. Lansdale recognized "Val's" courage and imagination, but disdained the unit's brutality. Still, unlike the rest of the Armed Forces of the Philippines (AFP), Val wanted to take the fight to the guerrillas, and he became fast friends with Lansdale and Bohannan.[50] Lansdale and Boh supported Val's other ideas, including using smaller, mobile forces called Battalion Combat Teams (BCTs), designed for endurance and patrolling, units that lived with the people and shared the risk of Huk retribution. Force X was a team of 16th PC soldiers who were trained and disguised as Huks and used to infiltrate their southern bases. They gathered valuable evidence before they were unmasked and then fought a pitched battle before escaping.[51]

As ingenious as Val and his colleagues were, Lansdale knew these military measures would not win the war alone. Lansdale considered Thomas Paine among his most prominent influences on his thinking, and Paine's focus on injustice and brutality on the part of British forces influenced Lansdale's view of strategy as the politics of "people" over the enemy.[52] The people either feared or supported the Huk because the government could not prove itself legitimate or effective in protecting them. In short, when the Huk told the peasants the government was corrupt, selfish, and would not protect them or help them, they weren't wrong. For all Roxas talk of a "mailed fist" to quash the guerrillas, the AFP used brutal and outdated Japanese methods for fighting guerrillas: strategies the Huk knew better than the AFP. Large "sweeps" rarely worked, and their harsh treatment of the peasantry turned more people into sympathizers. All the while, Huk support grew. Collaborators were rife. It was so bad that "the anti-Communist political opponents of the administration did not rally to it when they realized the extent of the danger," Bohannan recalled, "rather, they felt, and said, let the Huk throw out the government and then we will throw out the Huk."[53]

Lansdale knew the problem was political and economic as well as military. Trust of the government had been lost. "Land for the Landless" and "Equal Justice for All" were popular Huk messages and validated by the government's own misconduct or unfair laws. The hearts and minds of the people, Lansdale realized, was where the war was to be won. Without their support, there could be no longstanding victory. And that's where psychological warfare took root.[54]

While back in Washington in 1947, Lansdale became intrigued with psychological warfare (psywar), operations and tactics designed to use ideas and media to influence enemies. The similarity to advertising was stunning. He organized a seminar with experts, which likely included academic, veteran, and CIA spook Paul Linebarger, best known as the science fiction author Cordwainer Smith, whose book *Psychological Warfare* had condensed his own war time experience on the subject into a powerful tool kit that both Lansdale and Bohannan championed. Psywar was a weapon Lansdale could handle with aplomb. It was a tool of political reform, a tool to separate supporters from the Huk, a vehicle for change in strategy. In modern parlance, it was the art of winning the "hearts and minds" of people, something sorely lacking in the Philippines. President Elpidio Quirno's 1949 "dirty election" was corrupt to everyone and much of his government ignored the Huk's swelling of influence in central Luzon, now nicknamed "Huklandia," where guerrillas roamed without fear. Raids, assassinations, and assorted brutality mounted.[55] The government and Americans ignored lessons from their own history of fighting insurgents that had, as Lansdale and Bohannan understood, the safety and support of the people as the goal.[56]

1950 was a dark year for the West. The Soviets had an atomic weapon. Mao's forces had defeated the nationalists and ruled China. Troubles worsened between the newly divided Korea before all out war when the Communist North invaded the South. And, in the Philippines, the Huk's

Politburo "Out" (the party's governing body in the field, the Polibturo "In" was hidden in Manila) declared a "revolutionary state" had emerged. It was time for open war and revolution. Massive coordinated attacks on villages and cities erupted in a hail of bullets and brutal Huk victories. Manila was now threatened.[57]

Lansdale had gathered data, made contacts, and experienced enough to know Manila needed a better strategy. In Washington, he cultivated his allies in the State and Defense Departments. He did not want U.S. forces. The Filipinos had to fight this insurgency themselves. America could only provide guidance and assistance, but together they could turn the tide with large-scale military reform, especially in the broken intelligence system. Psychological warfare could help shift opinion of the government from foe to friend. But none of this mattered if there wasn't political change, too. He secured himself a position as intelligence advisor to President Quirino. But Quirino was a Roxas disciple and had mismanaged the war with the Huk. Lansdale found someone dynamic, different, who would better fit into his plans.[58]

"Our Guy Magsaysay"

Ramon Magsaysay was a member of the House of Representatives and the Armed Service Committee, who had been assigned to Washington to head up the Filipino Committee on Guerrilla Affairs to secure veterans rights. A former bus driver and mechanic, Magsaysay was a decorated guerrilla leader during the war. Big, brave, and cunning with an aggressive but friendly disposition, Magsaysay had little interest, inclination, or patience for bureaucracy or red tape. But he got stuff done. For Lawrence, it was Feisal. For Lansdale, it was Magsaysay. Quirino thought him a lightweight, "only good for killing Huk," but could not deny American pressure to have Magsaysay join his cabinet. In exchange for continued aid, Magsaysay was made secretary of defense in 1950. The skies in Asia darkened. The Korean War broke out, threatening world war between East and West. The Huk, bolstered by the success of the communists in the Korean, fought on with pitched battles, aiming for Manila.

At U.S. military barracks, Magsaysay lived with Lansdale and Bohannan, bouncing ideas off each other on how to defeat the Huk.

Bohannan recalled just how close things were. They were together "all the time; spending virtually (this is literally true) a minimum of 20 hours a day with Filipinos who had something to do with, or contribute to, the solution of the problem; . . . poking their noses into everything, and trying to get it all working in the same direction, whether it be the press, or the army, or the business community, or politicians from the President down to ward-heelers, or any of the dozen churches in the country." They never let Magsaysay alone "except when he went to bed with his wife," until he was indoctrinated and supported their plan. Everyone around them saw that Lansdale and Bohannan were committed, dedicated, and never asked "anyone to do anything unless he believed it was right and in the interest of his country, but making unlimited (at times shameless) demands on him to do what was right."[59]

Change took root and reforms stuck, as Lansdale had hoped. Magsaysay's surprise inspections uncovered corruption and increased discipline. Promotions rose for men like Valeriano and those who took the fight to the Huk and not the peasants. Scout Rangers were created for harassing the Huk behind their lines, much like Bohannan's I&R platoon had done. Magsaysay hammered into his soldiers that they were saviors of the people, not brigands, and got discipline enforced. The armed forces had to be seen as heroes, or it would not matter how many Huk they killed. A psychological warfare branch opened to promote the army. From 1950 onward, the AFP learned hard and well how to fight an insurgency, and repulsed the Huk in the field.

But Lansdale knew that economic ruin and political corruption was at the root of most peasant grievances and fuel for the legitimacy of the Huk. If you could make the Huk's claims empty, deny them their message, and provide a counter-message, the Huk would be seen as brutes. Poisoning the "sea" for the guerrillas through championing Magsaysay was Lansdale's forte.[60] The three of them brainstormed ideas that ranged from the gothic to the saintly. Magsaysay was most interested in political action and peasant relief. He established an office of "Civic Action," a term coined by Lansdale, which used military resources and manpower to do civil reconstruction, medical work, and other means of civilian support. Lansdale made sure their good work got maximum publicity.[61] None of these actions were easy. But they worked. The AFP Civic Actions began "building over 4,000 schools, repairing roads and bridges, digging wells, distributing food and medical supplies, and performing other public works. Troops carried 'candy for kids,' military lawyers represented indigent farmers in court, and Filipino and U.S. soldiers observed polling places to ensure fair elections."[62] Both Lansdale and Bohannan were interested in Filipino folklore and culture, and Bohannan was an expert on indigenous folklore, especially the Navajo. They used superstitions to plant fear of supporting the Huk. Papers were dropped with the "evil eye" painted on them around those who spoke to the Huk. A dead Huk soldier was pricked in the neck and drained of blood, and then left for all to see. Rumors spread that the Aswang, Filipino vampires, preyed on guerrillas and their supporters.[63]

Magsaysay was especially attuned to the suffering of peasants in the barrios, those who saw the Huk as an alternative to corrupt government. Cruel laws kept landlords oligarchs in the Philippines rich, and their private militias of ex-guerrillas often abused their charges. For ten cents, peasants could send a one-page letter to one of Magsaysay's chief intelligence advisors about the Huk, corrupt politicians or soldiers, or anything else. The officer would verify the legitimacy of the claims and take action with Magsaysay's approval against the abusers. Peasants were granted access to military lawyers to file grievances and challenge corrupt and abusive landlords. And, in darker sectors, civil liberties were suspended for suspected guerrillas, so jails did not become revolving doors for the Huk.[64]

The most ingenious Civic Action program was called Economic Development Corporation (EDCOR). Magsaysay, Lansdale, and Bohannan all agreed that many in the Huk ranks had real grievances, and not all were hardliners or bastards. There had to be a way to detach them, return them to civilian life, and deprive the Huk of numbers. According to Lansdale's biographer, "someone" recalled the Roman practice of colons, of raising legions for military service that were given grants of land in remote or troubled areas where they could govern. They became the authority of the region and worked with the locals to defeat criminal conduct. Bohannan was likely the inspiration. Magsaysay was not well educated in ancient history, and Lansdale, while very well read, was not a details-oriented reader. He saw the big picture. Bohannan was schooled in ancient civilizations and a deep reader of military history.[65]

Magsaysay had done minor efforts in rehabilitation, but together they created the EDCOR concept that Lansdale saw as the heart of their work. Huks were offered their own land in a remote area and under military authority, if they surrendered. While EDCOR failed in the long run (not all Huks could be resettled, and many poor farmers took the offer to get out of hard times), it was initially novel, successful, and enticing. It denied the Huk the legitimacy of their message of abuse and unfair land practices. While only hundreds of Huks were resettled out of a hard line of 10,000–15,000, word spread that the government was making good on promises. They weren't just brutalizing the people, or the Huk. Filipinos saw a decline in abuse by soldiers and victories against the Huk in battle. Collaborators were dragged into the open forced to switch sides. Perceptions changed, just as Lansdale had wanted.[66] Then, he upped the ante.

He convinced Magsaysay to run for president in 1953 to wipe clean the stain of the "dirty" election of Quirino and have much greater command of the war effort. Lansdale had backing and support from the CIA and brought in American political experts to help engineer a relatively "clean" election.[67] Magsaysay's run turned politics into a hornet's nest, and controversy remains over Lansdale's influence over Magsaysay. When Magsaysay disagreed, though, he let it be known. During one of these bull sessions, Bohannan thought one of his ideas stupid, then ducked as Magsaysay threw a haymaker.[68] In a similar almost unbelievable squabble on a plane, Magsaysay refused to use one of Lansdale's lectures. Tempers flared, Magsaysay and Lansdale drew up fists, and this time Lansdale scored a knockout. Quirino's daughter witnessed it and said it was clear who was calling the shots. Lansdale said they fought as brothers do and nothing more, and the two made up quickly. Still, Lansdale's role in the Magsaysay's victory earned him the nickname General Landslide. Magsaysay's 1953 victory ushered in renewed hope for many Filipinos, and the Huk were on the run.[69] But the Huk also helped seed their own destruction, and thanks to Bohannan, they caught them.

In 1950, the Huk's Politburo "In," senior members hiding in Manila, was discovered, in part thanks to many of Bohannan's grassroots spies.

One was a janitor who discovered Huk documents in the trash of their headquarters. When their HQ was raided, the AFP had an intelligence harvest of codes, locations, and people. They pressed the attack for the next four years, driving the Huk deeper and deeper into the harsh northeastern jungles of Luzon. Food and support thinned to shreds. Bohannan coordinated military and intelligence efforts with key men like Valeriano and many others. Support for the Huk dissipated. Surrenders grew. Taruc had realized the "revolutionary state" had been a mistake. The Politburo rewarded his critique by removing him from authority. Taruc surrendered after tense negotiations in 1954. The Huk rebellion was no longer a threat, just a nuisance. Magsaysay's presidency was popular and secure. In Washington, Lansdale was the man who pulled it off. Bohannan had done his best to stay in Ed's shadow, but Lansdale told a promotion board that Boh had "accomplished one of the key positions for the Unites States in the defeat of a Communist armed force by a national army, and in surrender, capture, or death of Communist leaders, in an Asian country." He'd also made huge contributions to the political stability of the country. "Much of his service since his last promotion has been accomplished under physical risk. His calm devotion to duty has had a beneficial effect on ever-increasing number of Americans and Asians."[70]

But Lansdale became the symbol of American unconventional warfare. Quiet, empathetic, but tough and ruthless if he needed to be, he could travel the corridors of power or the back roads of a foreign country and appreciate the challenges the people faced (though through a particularly idealized lens of a positivist American). CIA agent and friend Jonathan Dickson told Lansdale's biographer, Cecil Currey, "[Lansdale] is something like. Lawrence of Arabia he is the closest thing we have, right." Currey agreed but said, "Lawrence just did it once, but Lansdale did it in two different countries."[71] He'd find, though, it was a success not easy to replicate in Vietnam, especially without Boh.

"The Quiet and Ugly Americans"

In Washington, 1954, Col. Edward Lansdale met with Secretary of State John Foster Dulles. Eisenhower's chief foreign policy strategist wanted

Lansdale to join an advisory team heading to Indochina. Lansdale was told to "[H]elp the Vietnamese as much as I helped the Filipinos."[72]

The French had been fighting a guerrilla war against the Vietminh under Ho Chi Minh and General Giap for almost a decade. Lansdale had briefly seen the French war earlier that year and loathed their imperial conduct, doctrine, and mistreatment of the Vietnamese. There was little hope for the country so long as the French were in charge. The feeling was mutual. French generals thought Lansdale's ideas on counterinsurgency were weak and eccentric. They seemed unimpressed with the fact that they worked. Lansdale also found evidence of General Salan, commander of French Forces, financing their efforts through the opium trade. "We don't want you to open this keg of worms," he was told my officials in Washington, "so drop your investigation."[73] By the time Lansdale returned in 1954, the French had suffered the decisive defeat at Dien Bien Phu. At the Geneva Conference that year, the fate of the country was decided. There would be a division: a communist North under Ho Chi Minh and a "democratic" South under the Emperor Boa Dai. Free movement between the two would be allowed for nearly a year. All the while, Vietminh guerrillas ruled the night and the villages. In the south were also powerful mystic sects, power brokers under the French, who controlled much of the vice trade. They were authorities unto themselves. Chief among them were the Hoa, Cao Dai, and the Bin Xuyen, "a social organization number tens of thousands in the Saigon-Cholon metropolitan area," Lansdale noted, "whose leaders had won control of the criminal underworld."[74] They were a power unto themselves, especially in Saigon, filling the void of the French with money and influence that Lansdale worked to co-opt as South Vietnam emerged as a country.[75]

Corruption and instability ran in a thousand directions. Vietnam was more chaotic than the "carnival built in hell" of the postwar Philippines. But Lansdale's mission was the same: help the Vietnamese help themselves with American ideas and support. And again, he demonstrated a difference in dealing with the Vietnamese. Daniel Ellsberg, a protégé of Lansdale in the 1960s, noted, "What I saw him do with the Vietnamese-and I learned from him-was to listen to them instead of lecturing or talking down to them, as most Americans did. He treated them respectfully, as though they were adults worthy of his attention."[76] The U.S. investment in Vietnam began with the French and was growing in the new South Vietnamese government. The MAAG and CIA resources were in play when Lansdale arrived. But he was given the authority to create his own establishment, the Saigon Military Mission (SMM) as his hub. It was an independent but complimentary unit.[77]

The SMM's chief goal was to "to help the Diem government use the army to win the loyalty and co-operation of the rural population, particularly in areas formerly controlled by the Viet Minh, and to ferret out and destroy the Viet Minh underground network."[78] "Civic Action" teams were created to link the urban elite with the rural populace and build bridges of trust through construction, services, and engineering programs. Civic Action was Lansdale's use of EDCOR and other nonmilitary stratagems in the Philippines, added to initial efforts at similar experiments done by the French called *Groupes Administratifs Mobiles Operationnels* (GAMO). Building provincial infrastructure with competent and dedicated civil servants would be a key in proving Diem's legitimacy.[79] Within his fiefdom, Lansdale gathered experts and advisors to create strategies and tactics of psywar, pacification and civic action, training, and counterguerrilla warfare for the new regime. In short, he was building a COIN program, as he had in the Philippines, which targeted the links of people to the insurgents, while at the same time taking on the task of "nation building." There were also "black propaganda" efforts to instill fear of the Democractic Republic of Vietnam's (DRV's) growing malice. Maps with nuclear blast radiuses were found in many refugee quarters and rumors that the Vietminh would provoke a nuclear attack spread "conceivably, an example of Colonel Lansdale's handiwork."[80]

Lansdale backed his hopes of political reform on Ngo Dinh Diem, the prime minister. Diem was a respected but divisive former governor. An effective administrator, Diem was also elitist and Catholic in a country of Buddhists who viewed Catholicism as the religion of the oppressor. Diem was cagey and elitist, unlike the populist Magsaysay. Getting the people to love him was an uphill battle. One great asset was how much he loathed and despised the Vietminh. They'd kidnapped him once, and murdered his youngest brother. He would have no problem in making them a priority.[81]

But the Vietminh were only the sharpest problem. President Boa Dai ruled in absentia on the French Riviera and picked Diem to run South Vietnam under almost impossible conditions. He was creating a new country out of imperial control and popular desire for a united Vietnam. The economy was shattered, starvation and poverty rampant, and dangers shifted on every urban street corner. And the Americans were viewed as replacements for the French. In this sea of violence and strife, Lansdale befriended the struggling prime minister and became his advisor. He hoped Diem could be groomed to become like his "brother" Magsaysay.[82]

But Diem already had a brother. Nhu was a corrupt, messianic power broker in the new South Vietnamese government. His private militia enjoyed abusing and executing their enemies. Nhu was Diem's greatest advisor, but Lansdale pressed hard to be listened to about winning the people as well as fighting the guerrillas. Being only one voice in Diem's ear meant mixed results.[83] The original SMM was a mix of old and new faces, but Bohannan was not among them. He was needed in Manila to advise Magsaysay and give Lansdale access to a friendly nation's experiences and resources. Among the new recruits was Rufus Philips, an exceptionally bright CIA agent that Lansdale recognized as talented. Lansdale planned to modernize and professionalize the Vietnamese Army by having them train in the Philippines, so Philips headed off to Manila to meet "Boh" in 1955. Instead of finding a U.S. Army major in formal dress, he got the usual Bohannan surprise. After an "imperious rap," Philips opened his door. Bohannan blew in, wearing sandals and a khaki jacket, muttering, "I knew they would send me some goddamn, green shave-tail over here to do a man's job. Son, do you know what you're supposed to be doing?"[84] "Back then," Philips recalled, "the severity and formality of his manner made me feel like a junior recruit. Apparently, I had gone up a degree in his estimation, for now he gave me a thin smile and told me that when President Magsaysay had heard I was coming he had insisted I stay in the tea house at Malacañang Palace and share Christmas breakfast with Magsaysay's family. In response to my astonishment, Bohannan said simply, 'You're one of Ed's People.'"[85]

After Bohannan's surprise visit on Lansdale in 1955, the two partners worked with the SMM toward giving South Vietnam a fighting chance for survival. Bohannan's major contribution was organizing and training two major projects in conjuncture with groups in the Philippines. Both fit Lansdale's strategy on psywar and Civic Action. Operation Brotherhood (OB) was the brain child of Lansdale and one of his Filipino colleagues, businessman Oscar Arellano. OB was a expeditionary medical program of volunteer Filipino doctors, nurses, and medical staff sent to administer to the sick and wounded in Vietnam. It was not a government operation but made of citizens and came under the Junior Chamber of Commerce. The purpose was to provide medical services to the many rural poor in Vietnam and proselytize the message of goodwill Filipinos had for the Americans who they had worked with to defeat the Huk. Bohannan knew the value of medical aid to build trust, from first aid to surgical teams, and of having Asians seeing other Asians succeed. OB was largely a success, treating 700,000 Vietnamese, and knowledge of its good work spread to almost three million.[86]

But OB, and its training facilities, also acted as a cover for a sharper project called Freedom Company. South Vietnam was desperately weak in military training, from weapons and vehicle maintenance to anything like counterguerrilla warfare theory. The members of Freedom Company were led by former guerrilla Frisco "Johnny" San Juan, who organized a bunch of ex-Hunter ROTC guerillas to join. These men had fought the Japanese and the Huk. They were trained to mentor the South Vietnamese Army. Bohannan believed in the value of different cultures working together, but the similar challenges facing the Vietnamese made using ex-Huk fighters a natural fit. It would be far more valuable successful Asians to assist other Asians instead of "Lord of Manner" advising by Caucasians. All the men were interviewed and assessed by Bohannan at his home north of Manila. Family members recalled how he knew every man, his skills, his family, by heart when he picked the team. He never wrote anything down.[87] In contrast, Conein's efforts with the inserting covert teams of Filipinos and Vietnamese in North Vietnam, while daring and inventive, were tipped off and did only minor damage.[88]

Lansdale worked with Diem on how to relate to his people and create trust through civic action and other trust-building campaigns to make Diem the countersymbol to the Vietminh. Lansdale was convinced that one must have a better message than the enemy. One must challenge the cause of the insurgent, destroy its validity, and that meant gaining legitimacy in the eyes of the people. This included military reform, and integrating all the disparate pieces of armed services and police forces and paramilitary bodies into a unified front. Lansdale pushed and got most of these initiatives up and running. Former sect members were included as part of the South Vietnamese Army, giving them much needed muscle, reputation, and intelligence assets. Lansdale denied ever paying them off, though it emerged later that their loyalty was bought with CIA funds.[89] Money was and remains a lever of influence with insurgents of all kinds, from Arabia to Vietnam to Iraq.

Lansdale's greatest feat was both engineering and preparing for the mass migration from North Vietnam during the "open" period of travel between the north and south as each political entity solidified. While many migrated because they'd been pro-French and feared reprisal from Ho's forces, thousands of others listened to the whispers Lansdale planted about Vietminh abuses, brutality, and corruption. Lansdale's team "began an accelerated program to prepare the South Vietnamese" for the incoming migration, and "helped the South Vietnamese to set up a civil affairs organization, to create specialized task forces, and to draft appropriate directives."[90] All the while, he fought a rear guard action to limit Nhu's influence on Diem and abuses abroad. He did not always win. Lansdale hoped to make the 1958 election the milestone of Diem's legitimacy and argued against ballot stuffing. He knew Diem would win, but if the election victory was ridiculous, no one would believe it. Diem would be just another lying politician out for power. He needed to be a victor of the people. Diem ignored him, won by over 90 percent, and no one bought it. For better or worse, Diem would not be Magsaysay Mark-II, a comparison Diem despised and shirked from. He thought Magsaysay a weak-minded puppet of the Americans. Defiance of Lansdale was proof that he was his own man, even if the ideas he rejected were for valid and necessary.[91] Lansdale was convinced South Vietnam could be saved, but championing Civic Action was a tough sell. This included curtailing abusive conduct by Vietnamese and American soldiers. "Civic action was essentially the brotherly behavior of troops along lines taught by Mao and Giap to their troops," Lansdale said. "Admittedly the Americans never succeeded in teaching this to the Vietnamese Army. Up to the very end of the Vietnam War the army was still stealing from the population. We sure tried though."[92]

Bohannan left South Vietnam in 1956, Lansdale in 1958. Both were adamant that the experience in the Philippines had proved American advisors and historical lessons of COIN from the Philippines and elsewhere could help Asians find stability and success against an insurgency. Even in the wake of Magsaysay's tragic death in a plane crash in 1957, the Philippines was not on a precipice of revolution. Diem's regime was new, shaky, and confronted with a myriad of challenges. The Vietminh had created a shadow government. The rogue sects still vied for greater power in the emergent state. Religious tension between Buddhists and Catholics rose. As bad, the sadistic influence of Nhu and his militia made enemies of the people. But South Vietnam was holding. Lansdale was hopeful the work he, his team, and other U.S. advisors in MAAG and the CIA had done would help Diem save his country. "Can these techniques be used where Americans in general do not have such prestige as in the Philippines?" Bohannan asked in an unpublished report. "Yes. Proved by some of the same men in Vietnam in 1954–1956."[93] Lansdale concurred. "All we have to do is remember the lessons we learned in the recent past."[94] According to the foremost writer on Vietnam in English in 1957, Lansdale "must be credited with saving the nationalist government of South Viet-Nam almost single-handedly in the spring of 1955." Bernard Fall was not easy to impress.[95]

The stability Lansdale bought, however, eroded after his departure. From 1959 to 1963, the United States poured advisors and resources and infrastructure into Vietnam. Rufus Philips stayed on for years working on Lansdale's ideas of civic action, especially in the rural areas. But Diem's shaky rule, the quality of the Communist guerrillas, and the volatile challenges at every turn made every gain temporary.[96]

"Sensitive Understanding and Wisdom"

Lansdale's star was high, but emanated friction with illumination. He became a brigadier and Pentagon insider as deputy assistant secretary for special operations and eventually assistant secretary of defense for special operations. He had his champions, but Secretary of Defense Robert McNamara was not among them. In a famous anecdote, McNamara summoned Lansdale for a briefing on the war in Vietnam. Lansdale grabbed a handful of Vietcong guerrilla weapons and "dumped the weapons on McNamara's polished desk" in January 1961. These weapons, used by people in black pajamas and tattered sandals or going barefoot, are facing U.S. trained and equipped South Vietnamese forces. "Yet the enemy is licking our side. Always keep in mind about Vietnam that the struggle goes far beyond the material things of life." Ideas, ideals, and harnessing the will of the people (what Lansdale called the "X" Factor in People's Wars) were what mattered most. McNamara was unimpressed with the qualitative response and would pursue a far more quantitative war.[97]

And yet, Lansdale's celebrity grew. Most of his time was spent debating, challenging, and working on anti-Castro initiatives in the wake of the 1958 Communist victory in Cuba. Lansdale's criticism and focus on people and ideas rather than harder action dropped his popularity with the CIA. Then his name became a pop culture gag. Two novels, Graham Green's *The Quiet American* (1955) and Eugene Burdick and William Lederer's *The Ugly American* (1958), were accused of using Lansdale as a character who emphasized either American arrogance or strained virtues and naivity in Asia. Lansdale despised the spotlight and preferred to keep on with his work.

But his heart was in Vietnam. As the Kennedy administration took control of the war, reports showed it degrading. Diem was pushed around by American advisors, and Nhu's influence becomes toxic while the Vietminh successes mounted. Lansdale raised hackles with reports about the trouble in Vietnam that reached President Kennedy, ("You know," Kennedy said to an aid after being aghast at Lansdale's report, "Eisenhower never uttered a word about Vietnam.")[98] But Kennedy's key advisors like McNamara and Gen. Maxwell Taylor soon lost interest in the unorthodox Lansdale, preferring more conventional, quantitative, and quasi-scientific approaches to war with metrics they understood.[99] The CIA also felt he'd either gone soft or strange and his influence within the agency waned while in Washington. These were modern and conventional soldiers and strategists who wanted metrics and systems of war and victory, not talk of immeasurable like "the feelings of the people," or why ragtag soldiers with rusty French carbines and punji stakes had a chance against the ferocious firepower and limitless resources of the U.S. military. They froze him out of any major work in Vietnam and countered Kennedy's own suggestion on making him ambassador in Saigon. Alone in the wilderness of DC, working on a variety of unconventional warfare projects for the CIA and Defense Department, Lansdale watched from afar as Vietnam crumbled, working on a variety of unconventional warfare schemes like OPERATION MONGOOSE, a complex covert operation that followed the Bay of Pigs fiasco and followed through the Cuban Missile Crisis that failed to overthrow the Castro regime through internal revolt (1961–1962). It's best known for its assassination ploys on Castro, including exploding cigars.[100] Controversial and a fail, OP MONGOOSE sullied Lansdale's reputation. He watched as Vietnam, too, seemed to crumble under circumstances he'd seen before. The French had picked the wrong way to fight a people's war, he thought, and the United States would do the same damn thing. Despite best intentions, the United States would lose.[101]

Bohannan, meanwhile, was still looking for fights. He was stationed at Fort Riley as a Battalion commander in the 1st Infantry Division ("the Big Red One.") In short order, he became "grossly unpopular" for calling the unit garbage, barking at their company commander to get their police units "up to the standards of a second-rate National Guard Division," and for fighting against "the popular and asinine idea" of turning I&R Platoons, the kind he'd led in the jungles of the Philippines, into a "miniature armored task force" so it could fight and die on an atomic battlefield: one of Maxwell Taylor's pet projects.[102] He was then sent to Headquarters Special Troop, where he stayed until retirement in 1961. Lansdale selected him to participate in the 1958 U.S. Special Advisory mission to Colombia, where he made a distinct contribution on plans to help the government counter bandit and guerrilla threats.[103]

Lansdale also pressed him to write a book on their Huk experiences as an aid to those in Vietnam. Bohannan, with Valeriano's aid, wrote *Counter Guerrilla Operations: The Philippine Experience* in 1961, an eclectic and detailed examination of the success against the Huk. They also rallied national and international experts to help U.S. advisors understand counterinsurgency, something the U.S. Army had deep experience with and yet perpetually disdained and tried to forget.[104] In September 1960 Lansdale pressed in a memorandum for more decisive action to stabilize "the deteriorating situation in Vietnam." Correcting the ruining state of Diem's government was critical, but the immediate need was to counter the growing success of the Vietcong guerrilla. MAAG needed to shift focus from training to "on-the-spot advice and assistance in the conduct of tactical operations against the Vietnam." MAAG needed to be "staffed . . . with officers skilled in the conduct of counter-guerrilla operations and who are capable of operating in the field." Clearly, Vietnam needed a new equivalent of Ed and Boh.[105] He spent January 2–14, 1961, in Vietnam to conduct an evaluation of the situation. Close to the action, he saw the Vietcong were closer to victory "than I realized reading the reports received in Washington." MAAG was ineffective and would remain so "unless the US system of their operations is changed sufficiently to free these Americans to do the job that needs doing, and unless they do it with sensitive understanding and wisdom." Diem was still the only choice as president. A coup attempt in November had failed, but "I believe there will be another attempt to get rid of him soon, unless the US makes it clear that we are backing him as the elected top man . . . the communists will be more alert to exploit the next coup At present, most Vietnamese oppositionists believe that the US would look favorably upon a successful coup." Lansdale's perceptions would be tragically prophetic.

He told Ambassador Dubrow that he had no immediate suggestions.

> *The situation in Vietnam is not black and white, but a most complex one in all shades of gray. Many Americans and Vietnamese expected me to come up with some sort of miracle, to turn Ngo Dinh Diem into an Americanized modern version of an ancient Vietnamese leader Le*

> *Loi. However, the task requires more than a gimmick or some simple answer. It will take a lot of hard work and follow-through. In 12 days, all I could do was learn as much as I could and to 'plant a seed or two' with Ngo Dinh Diem and other Vietnamese leaders who know that I speak out of a deep affection for the free Vietnamese.*

His initial recommendations were to view Vietnam as an emergency and "combat area" of the Cold War, get experts with support to manage the problems, and make sure they were a "hard core of experienced Americans who know and really like Asia and Asians." MAAG officers needed to get in the field and actually see conditions. In a separate memo, he also called for Dubrow's removal due to fatigue and lack of trust between him and the Diem regime. A new ambassador with senior skill and savvy in conducting "political operations" was needed. "This must not be a 'clever' type who is out to gain reputation as a 'manipulator' or word-smith who is more concerned about the way his reports will look in Washington than in implementing US policy in Vietnam."[106] Lansdale was building a case for a job only he could do, as well as a program of improving conditions in Vietnam. Yet, when Kennedy asked for Lansdale to become ambassador, he turned it down in an act of humility he hoped would secure the offer. It failed. Kennedy would pick someone else for the role Lansdale had groomed for himself.[107]

It was a mixed success, blocked by politics and growing resentment of Lansdale's influence. In April 1961, Lansdale was made government-wide coordinator and manager of the country's "first major test in the new art of counterinsurgency" under Deputy Secretary of Defense Gilpatrick's Vietnam Task Force. Lansdale would serve as his executive officer. Despite President Kennedy's support, the task force was removed from Defense and placed into the State Department. The revised May 3rd draft of its report "eliminated the special role laid out for Lansdale, shifted the chairmanship of the continuing Task Force to State, and blurred, without wholly eliminating, the Defense-drafted recommendations for sending US combat units to Vietnam and for public US commitments to save South Vietnam from Communism." He initially had W. W. Rostov's support to be Kennedy's "first-rate, fulltime backstop man in Washington to Vietnam Affairs" but by the end of the month. Even before State took over the Task Force program, Gilpatrick had wanted Lansdale sent to Vietnam "to consult for with Vietnamese and US leaders and make further recommendations for action; but [Secretary of Defense] McNamara made Lansdale's mission contingent upon an invitation from the US Ambassador in Saigon an invitation that never came." Disdain for Lansdale's maverick approach and significant influence led to a perpetual block on his efforts to return to Vietnam. Despite detailed memorandums on supporting Diem's regime, focusing on political and economic action and increased boots-on-the-ground advisory efforts by sympathetic and experienced American experts (though he saw the use of training missions a means to get U.S. forces on site if needed), Lansdale's voice was losing purchase within the halls of government, where he contended with growing adversaries such as McNamara, Rostow, Under Secretary of State George Ball, and others.[108]

Lansdale put words to actions in trying to improve the cadres of available counterguerrilla and counterinsurgent groups. The most famous was organized by the RAND Corporation in 1962, which included experts from Britain, France, as well as the United States. Bohannan spent most of his time arguing with Captain David Galula, the modern champion of COIN theory in the United States who served and/or observed in COIN campaigns in China, Indochina, Algeria, Greece, and the Philippines. Boh believed Galula was one of the best minds on COIN, though second place to Lansdale and perhaps himself. After all, unlike Galula or any French senior officer, Ed and Boh had actually defeated an insurgency. For Boh, the distinction between Galula and himself was the primacy of politics in COIN.[109]

In 1962, skies darkened in Saigon. Rufus Philips made a frantic call to Bohannan to return. Support for Diem had dropped. Violence rose. Retired and restless, Boh dropped what he was doing, joined USAID as an advisor, and then hightailed it to Saigon. Together, Bohannan and Philips worked hard and fast on a surrender and resettlement program for guerrillas known as Chieu Hoi ("Open Arms") in 1963, based on the principles of EDCOR in the Philippines. Five thousand defections occurred in the first three months.[110] Sapping strength for the guerrillas and increasing goodwill to the government was a positive step. Diem grudgingly supported it, his hate for the Vietcong almost too strong to contemplate such measures. But surrender programs were not enough. Support for Diem rotted. The Vietcong (the communist guerrillas in the south) mounted victories bloody numbers. Government violence against Buddhists enraged much of the population, and images of Buddhist torching themselves shot across the globe.[111]

From South Vietnam, Philips pleaded with the Defense Department for Lansdale's return. "There is no other American, regardless of position or rank, who can evoke the same response from the president or in whom he has any comparable degree or confidence," he argued in a memorandum. "Our attempts to influence the situation through normal channels seems unsuccessful. General Lansdale, as many of us can attest, has repeatedly demonstrated his ability to cause President Diem to act in accordance with high U.S. policy, when all other appeals . . . were unavailing. I most emphatically recommended his immediate assignment."[112]

No dice. In November 1963, the "Generals Coup" removed Diem and Nhu from power, an overthrow exercised with complete U.S. knowledge and assurance that they would not intervene, thanks in large measure to the new Ambassador Henry Cabot Lodge Jr.[113] Lansdale claimed he had refused to support the coup, and this soured his reputation further with McNamara.[114] What happened next, however, shook each country. Once in custody, Diem and his brother were executed. American policy makers were horrified with a fait accompli. The South Vietnamese Army and its U.S. advisors now had to create a government, an economy, and maintain law and order while fighting a very effective communist guerrilla force and the North Vietnamese Army. It had never been done before.[115]

Lansdale was furious. He had never believed a coup would make things better[116] and worked with Bohannan and Philips to spread the word that change was needed in Vietnam if any victory was possible. But they all believed victory *was* possible. They campaigned, wrote letters, twisted arms, and exerted influence until, finally, Lansdale was asked by the Johnson administration to return to Saigon at the behest of the U.S. Embassy and Ambassador Lodge in 1965. Bohannan, Philips, Conein, and much of the old team followed. But this was not Manila in 1950. Nor was it Saigon in 1955. After surveying the military and political situation in 1965, Lansdale was depressed. "I don't believe this government can win the hearts and the minds of the people," he confessed. Strictly in the role of advisor, retired from the Air Force, his influence in this era was minimal.[117] But he would not give up. And in the heat of fighting the system one last time, the friendship of Ed and Boh cracked.

"Bo Worries Me . . ."

Early in 1965, Philips was convalescing in the United States and received a troublesome letter from Lansdale. "Bo worries me considerably," Lansdale wrote. "Apparently, he tried to set up his own control net within the team. I had a straight talk with him, without mentioning that particular action and he swore he was 100% loyal. But most of the old team members are really down on him. Luigi [Leo Conein] says Bo offered money, a car, etc., if he would report to Bo instead of me. Val stopped him from mis-instructing the guards to obey his orders only, not mine. Similar things with others. Damn! I feel perhaps Bo was only trying to operate in his own old fashion, and was clumsy. Hope so."[118] But it wasn't just the team that Bohannan tested. He'd also begun to annoy the senior political and military leadership. William Holbrook at the embassy and General Westmoreland, commander of the Military Advisory and Assistance Command-Vietnam (MAACV), had had enough of this strange retired soldier who never wore a uniform and was seen barefoot in official meetings, sitting in a corner as if hiding from the world. For years, Lansdale had defended Bohannan, his unconventional attire and attitude. But something had changed with El Lobo.[119]

Lansdale's biographer claimed "Boh's" ideas on what needed to be done "would have loused up everything." But those ideas are still in the shadows. A brilliant young soldier and writer, Daniel Ellsberg, who was part of Lansdale's team, claimed Valeriano told him that Boh had "made a bid that undercut Lansdale in some way so he would be regarded as head of the team. It was regarded as a betrayal by Ed and Bohannan [was] out. A couple of times [after that] Bohannan got missions out to Vietnam and would come to visit but the relations were very strained." Lou Conein, who never met a fact he could not spice up with fiction, said

Bohannan was tired of talk and wanted "nuke the goddamn bastards."[120] Rufus Philips mentioned it was a scheme involving a rebellion of some kind, some kind of action to get things moving in the team's way, and that Bohannan was exhausted with the red tape of Washington politics and dogmatic thinking.[121] Many of these men, by this time, had very tense friendships and personal foibles that may have colored their thinking of whatever it was Bohannan had done or not done.

What is clear is that Lansdale was back in Vietnam, under enormous pressure and stress, and his partner of the last twenty years was no longer solving as many problems as he was creating for his boss. Lansdale asked Bohannan to leave the team in 1966. Bohannan agreed and returned to Manila, where he would live the rest of his days. He was still contracted to USAID for lectures and more, but it was never the same. After three wars, one bandit rebellion, and more brushes with death than he ever expected to survive, Bohannan was out of the fight. A young protégé once noted most veterans of the era pined for the return to civilian life. Not Boh. War had become his natural habitat. But a quarter-century of warfare had been, perhaps too long. It was time for a break.[122] Bohannan's wars were over. As was his friendship with Lansdale, until a far bigger betrayal brought them back together.[123]

Lansdale held in for three more years, struggling to make an effective counterinsurgency strategy. But his ideas had little sticking power with almost no unity of command and the growing reliance on U.S. conventional firepower to solve problems.[124] He tried to act as a coordinating body between the agencies of American influence and the differing goals emerging on Vietnam. But he was blocked from political influence in Saigon by the empires of State and the CIA, and found his efforts stymied by U.S. officials who would rather dictate than cooperate with local leadership. In other words, they chose the opposite strategy of what Lansdale championed in COIN.[125]

He was also less feisty. "Maybe Ed's trouble is he's not enough a son of a bitch," wondered Leonard Unger, Lansdale's superior in the State Department. "Maybe if Ed beat his fist on the table and raised more hell, he would get some things done. But that's not his way, to raise that kind of hell." [126] No, that was always Bohannan's job (though always as

"Johnny Behind the Door"). The combination of the quiet, sage advisor and the calm, mad soldier had created a much better dynamic at convincing people of the rightness of their course. Despite making valuable contributions, Lansdale returned to the United States after the Tet Offensive and the radical militarization of the war effort, unable to work his magic a third time.

"LET THERE BE NO REGRETS"

While letters had trickled between them, Ed and Boh reunited in the wake of Daniel Ellsberg's leaking of *The Pentagon Paper* in 1971. Lansdale tried fence-mending with Ellsberg,[127] who he'd help train in Vietnam during his last ride. He even wrote his memoirs *In the Midst of Wars* as a means to a psywar counterpunch to the Pentagon Papers, a work that said little of U.S. involvement and championed the efforts of Filipino and Vietnamese leaders in their struggles. While important, it was most noted for its omissions that the Pentagon Papers filled.

Boh offered Ed a different suggestion. "If someone told me in advance that he was going to do what Ellsberg did, and asked the penalty, I would say: Pull out, slowly, sequentially, fingernails, toenails, teeth, testes, then boil the remains slowly in oil; although perhaps the old Cherokee stunt of parboiling until the skin slips off, then let the customer go howling off through the woods might be as appropriate. . ." When his anger cooled he noted, "However much [Ellsberg], or anyone else, including you or I, may disagree with the conduct of the war in Vietnam, and with the incredible meatheadedness of some of those responsible (and I suspect we both feel pretty strongly about these things) to commit such a colossal breach of trust, and thereby endanger the lives and reputations of so many people, too. dammit, words fail me. is, to put it simply, unforgivable."[128]

Letters filled the distance until 1981, when Bohannan revealed that he had esophageal cancer and not long to go. A lifetime of Bull Durham and Filipino peasant tobacco had done what Imperial Japan, the Huk, FARC, and the Vietminh never could. As he approached the "Wild Blue Yonder," he told his old boss and partner he was content, as only he could. "I've had a good life, far better and longer than I ever expected or deserved. On the other hand I have been so disappointed by what has happened, what it's done and not done (and the Philippines the same) that on the whole I am glad that I will be saddened no longer by observing them going to hell. So, let there be no other regrets."[129] El Lobo died in 1982.

Dorothy Bohannan lamented that Boh never received credit for his efforts. But he was never one for the spotlight, preferring to operate in Lansdale's shadow. Lansdale tried for years to get Boh his due in medals and commendations, but found opposition.[130] "The powers that be may not have seen fit to give Bohannan any credits," Dorothy recounted, "but the Filipinos have done so in their own way. The number of families who respect and treasure his memory are astounding. Families wanting bits of his ashes to put in their sanctuaries; the friends who come back again and again to say they will never forget. Maybe this is more worthwhile than all the medals the United States could ever hand out. Too many have been awarded to those unworthy; too many have been desecrated."[131]

Lansdale carried on without his old partner, helping historian Cecil Currey write a biography, a valuable book that filled in the missing pages of his important but didactic memoirs. He died in 1987 and was buried in Arlington National Cemetery, with full honors. His passing was noted by newspapers and magazines, discussing his incredible life and controversial contributions. Many called him America's "Lawrence of Arabia."

But all analogy is fudge, as Lawrence said. Here, a partnership between two mavericks, one senior and the other junior, had made the difference. None of their successes could have been possible without Lansdale's acumen with people, psychological warfare, and empathy for foreign cultures. But success, especially against the Huk, was steeled by Bohannan's unorthodox mind for warfare, direct experience in fighting alongside Filipinos against the Japanese, and knowledge of human culture. While amazing apart, together they brought out the best in each other. Dorothy Bohannan loved Ed and believed in him and his mission. But her husband was a pillar of their victories, too. "Ed was a gentle person, severe in a way, but a gentle sort of a person," contemplative and caring. "And Bo was a military man, a fighting man. He was a guy who enjoyed being back in the bush. He enjoyed the discomforts, believe it or not, of camping and all that sort of thing." Ed was always the leader, no question. Few could imagine Boh being able to work in the Pentagon or in senior staff meetings or with the president of the United States. He could be charming and brilliant, but he was never a diplomat. One of Lansdale's greatest victories was seeing past the unorthodox personality and recognizing Bohannan's deep potential as a partner. "[M]y husband," Dorothy noted, "was a brilliant guy. His mind also went along the same lines as Ed's. [they] worked together so beautifully because Ed had Bo to back him up in the military way," as well as "in the mental way. They approached their ideas in the same way. They both had the same target, the same ambitions, they knew how to draw out people, and it was a perfect team."[132]

Lawrence of Arabia became a legend in two years of unconventional warfare and genius. The Ad Man and the Wolf spent twenty years fighting insurgencies and changed the fate of two nations, even if only one was a success. Sometimes, it would seem, mavericks are at their best when they stick together.

Part IV
Mavericks after Vietnam

At war's end, the U.S. Army was not interested in looking backward. Vietnam, nation-building, counterinsurgency, massive use of NGOs, innovations, successes and failures in America's long war effort, none of these subjects had "career success" branded on them for young officers.[1] After the "bitter peace" of the Paris Peace Accords and U.S. withdrawal from Vietnam in 1975, counterinsurgency and nation-building became stained with failure and bad goals within professional circles. The future of U.S. armed forces would focus on technical excellence and lethality than anything resembling the social sciences or cultural awareness. The knowledge gap would be filled with modern marvels.

Between 1975 and 1989, the U.S. Army re-created itself. It focused its doctrine and force structure to meet enemies unlike those in Vietnam, largely the armed forces of nation-states in the Middle East, or perhaps South America. The CIA would remain in the covert and guerrilla warfare business, but the U.S. Army sought to fight wars against the armed forces of modern nation states armed with high-tech, Soviet-supplied missiles and air power demonstrated by Egyptian forces in the 1973 Arab/Israeli War. As future-war theorists in both the Soviet Union and the United States pondered what nonnuclear warfare might look like between them or medium-sized powers, a belief emerged that modern information and weapon technology was increasing the lethality of weapons and the pace at which information could be gathered, analyzed, and executed. Those who had a modern, flexible, and well-armed command and control system could feasibly not only make decisions quicker but also execute their attacks to disable their rival's technical infrastructure and paralyze their means of gathering information and making decisions. This state would expose their forces to predatory and decisive attacks.

The reorientation of the U.S. Army to what would become AirLand Battle Doctrine was the result of many influential and aggressive military and political champions. The creation of new Training and Doctrine Command (TRADOC) under Gen. William DePuy took a lion's share of the effort. DePuy was a Vietnam veteran, but not a student of counterinsurgency, nor was that what the Defense Department considered a priority. High-intensity air and ground combat operations with proper doctrine, technology, and organization mattered. Iterations of DePuy's 1976 Field Manual 100-5 Operations would continue to refine the army's approach to future war. They faced resistance and challenges for expensive training and equipment, but all followed DePuy's lead.[2]

As the U.S. Army rebuilt its ethos, reputation, and mission, analysts in the mid-1980s began to refer to the "Military Technical Revolution." This phenomenon was brought on by information and weapons technologies. If one harnessed their doctrine, organization, and technology to optimize their value, one could outpace, outfight, and outstrike their enemy to such a degree that one might cripple their ability to direct battle. Such a revolution was no small task. It required ingenuity, support, and innovation in an army that was suffering from the wounds and stigma of the first major U.S. military defeat (minus the end of the Confederacy) since the War of 1812. By the end of the 1980s, the U.S. Army, working with the USAF, was poised for fighting the kind of war it wanted to fight: high-tempo conventional operations against the armed forces of a modern nation-state. When Saddam Hussein's Iraqi Army invaded Kuwait in 1990, President George H. W. Bush organized an international coalition to liberate Kuwait. Hussein's men were battle-hardened veterans of the Iran/Iraq war and armed with Soviet-purchased materials ranging from SCUD missile launchers poised at Israel and Saudi Arabia to a modern ground force. Public fears and media pronouncements about getting "bogged down" and memories of failure in Vietnam fostered the image of the U.S. military as ineffective and liable to butcher more than it saved.

The First Gulf War (1990–1991) demolished the ghost of Vietnam with stunning precision strikes, special forces, modern tanks, and unmatched victories against the Iraqis and with almost no casualties on the American side. It was so one-sided an affair that theorists, pundits, academics, and others now viewed the modern U.S. armed forces as having been transformed by a "Revolution in Military Affairs" (RMA). Small, quick, technically sage, precise, and lethal armed forces could achieve what mass armies had in a previous generation. But one of the requirements, less discussed, for these RMA victories was choosing the kind of war you wanted to fight: a luxury not always afforded to Great Powers. If an RMA victory wasn't possible, it wasn't attempted. This view was rooted in what was known as the Powell Doctrine, named after General and former national security advisor Collin Powell, who espoused a doctrine for using U.S. forces only if certain requirements were answered first. They were categorically designed to avoid anything akin to a Vietnam War, with requirements for clear, defined war aims.[3]

For a decade, the United States fought only where it would dominate. Cruise missiles acted as a lever of compliance with Hussein's violations of no-fly zones and other requirements from the end of the Gulf War. But in chaotic, complex, and ethnically diverse regions, the United States chose to limit their footprint. President Bill Clinton resisted calls for large ground troops in the violent disintegration of Yugoslavia (1990–1995). U.S. troops supported UN and NATO missions, and air power contributed in sorties against transgressing Serbian and Croatian forces, but these failed to stem the tide of brutality targeted on civilians by Croatian and Serbian forces. The brutal ethnic cleansing at Srebrenica in 1995, as 8000 Bosnian Muslims were butchered or driven out of home and into graves by Serbian forces, was one result of limited involvement. If Europe's southern region was not worthy of decisive U.S. intervention, Africa became a stage for U.S. failure of any meaningful intervention at all. During a humanitarian mission in the failed state of Somalia in 1993, U.S. forces lost eighteen soldiers to criminal militias, gangs, and insurgent groups vying for power in Mogadishu. Retreat and containment followed.[4] The United States, along with the rest of the world, chose not to bolster UN forces in Rwanda to stop the genocide of Tutsi civilians by the Hutu government during the Rwandan civil war in 1994.[5] Each conflict posed challenges the RMA-style forces were not well equipped to face: paramilitary forces, complex ethnic environments, urban warfare, corrupt governments and their militias, and brutality against civilian populace. Precision-guided munitions harnessing satellite imaging technology could target any number of possible enemy combatants, but it could not help establish local governance with legitimacy to provide an alternative to falling in line with strongmen, dictators, and criminal syndicates.[6] Yet the U.S. military continued to tout its expensive, decisive, and pronounced ability to project force across the globe, unmatched in this capability by any other major power. They remained a threat to regional powers like Iraq should they decide to violate another nation's sovereignty. They were, sadly, useless to prevent the attacks against the United States orchestrated by terrorist groups on September 11, 2001.

From that intelligence failure emerged wars where two mavericks filled in the knowledge gap on culture, politics, economics, and more. In this regard they followed in the footsteps of another maverick of the Great War, one who shaped the region as much as Lawrence, and who did so against the tide of oppression against her gender.

Chapter 7

Prelude: Gertrude Bell and War in a "Devil's Cauldron"

No other woman of recent time has combined her qualities-her taste of arduous and dangerous adventure and art, her distinguished literary gift, her sympathy for all sorts and conditions of men, her political insight and appreciation of human values, her masculine vigour, hard common sense and practical efficiency-all tempered by feminine char, an a most romantic spirit.[1]

—DAVID HOGARTH ON GERTRUDE BELL, 1926

—KINGDOM of Iraq, 1926.
"She could play a man's part in the action . . ." King Fiesal of Iraq noted. "She ventured alone and disguised into the remotest districts. . . . Death held no fear for her. Her personal safety was her last consideration." Faisal even claimed Miss Maj. Gertrude Bell, political officer, oriental secretary, and one of the chief architects of the his nation, had led tribesmen in an attack on the Turks and had escaped Ottoman captivity after a kidnapping.[2] His ascension was the apex of Bell's career, and as new officers came to work the mandate of Iraq Bell focused on archeology, earning much admiration for her desire to maintain the great artifacts of Mesopotamia. But by 1926, Bell was exhausted. Her family fortune had dwindled. The work was dull with the exception of establishing the first National Museum of Iraq. And the region's notorious climate competed with compulsive chain smoking to devour her nerves.

July 12, 1926. Gertrude Bell dies by her own hand, by accident or suicide, and leaves the world to wonder how a woman of her era helped birth a nation in Mesopotamia whose troubles echo today.

"Brilliant Constellation"

Gertrude Margaret Lowthian Bell (1868–1926)[3] was the queen maverick of the Great War, though her greatest impact came in the rubble of peace. Among the greatest students of Oxford, this heir to an industrial iron works fortune in Britain was not only a poet but one who chose the "strenuous life" of explorer, mountaineer, archeologist, and writer of foreign cultures long before the Guns of August in 1914. Her childhood of privilege brought some of the greatest minds of the day to her wealthy home, from Charles Darwin to Charles Dickens.[4] Driven, engaging, and social, Bell spoke Arabic, Persian, German, and French. She would take seven expeditions of the Middle East and Turkey in her lifetime, continuing a period tradition of women of privilege bucking the bourgeoisie standards and leading lives of toil and adventure. She had no time for the "idle women" of her wartime male colleagues, who took "no sort of interest in what's going on, know no Arabic, and see no Arabs. They create an exclusive (it's also very second rate) English society quite cut off from the life of the town." Bell preferred to be in the field where, before 1914, she worked as Hogarth, Lawrence, and others had done, as an informal spy for the British government in the Middle East.[5] The Great War's mammoth need for global intelligence brought Bell to formal government service.

In the early days of the war Bell served with the Red Cross in the Wounded and Missing Enquiry Department, researching the whereabouts of the missing and the dead for soldiers' families. She despised its disorganized manner and attitude, so she modernized the system of information gathering, storage, and analysis in short order. She was made head of the department but kept researching on her own and saw firsthand what modern industrial warfare did to the men of her generation. "Sometimes we recover lost ground and find all our wounded carefully bound up and laid in a shelter, sometimes we find them all bayoneted. But day by day it becomes a blacker weight upon the mind." This was only December 27, 1914.[6] Archeologist David Hogarth defied British convention and secured her a position at the Arab Bureau in Cairo. His influence, however, was not enough. Her knowledge of Arab tribes was not only vast, but fresh; her last expedition to Hayyil in North-West Arabia was only eighteen months old. Her life before the war had given her a strategic value in a theater needing the freshest intelligence as the Arab Revolt became a reality.

She was given the honorary title of Major Miss Bell and found herself in a community of smart and often eccentric figures, including T. E. Lawrence. Bell and Lawrence had met on archeological digs before the war (1911) and shared a fun though sharp professional rivalry, Bell the elder and commanding presence, Lawrence the young contrarian. While sometimes heated, their relationship had mutual respect for recognizable genius. This respect kept them colleagues in troublemaking within the British military and political establishment (her earliest comment on him was "he'll make a traveler.")[7] Lawrence nicknamed them the "The Intrusives." Bell labeled the gang of the Arab Bureau a "brilliant constellation."[8]

Her command of Arab culture, social groupings, and history made her one of the integral minds behind the Arab Revolt, especially regarding the divisions between two of powerful rival forces, the Wahhabis of Ibn Saud and the Hashemite of Faisal. As one biographer noted, "Her knowledge of Arab methods of warfare was a novel addition to the collective determination of the bureau to find the way ahead. . . . Gertrude would have discussed funding insurrections, cutting railway links, hijacking supplies, fostering terrorism, and provoking guerrilla warfare." Lawrence was among the greatest customers of her ideas, reports, and analysis, and later admitted how indebted he was to her.[9]

In March 1916 Maj. Gilbert Clayton ordered Bell to Basra, Mesopotamia, to be advisor to Sir Percy Cox, among the most powerful British agents in the Middle East. Her official title was "Liaison Officer, Correspondent to Cairo," but like Lawrence the title was simply a key to influence across a wide range of affairs, including cartography, political strategy, and monitoring the work of other British agents. She tried to counter what she viewed as reactionary instead of considered Arab policy coming from London, and played the political games of influence and control between the two centers of British power in the region, Cairo (represented by the Arab Bureau) and India (established in Cox's authority). She was deft at both, but with open eyes. "Politically, too, we rushed into the business with our usual disregard for a comprehensive political scheme," she noted from Basra. "The coordinating of Arabian politics and the creation of our Arabian policy should have been done at home—it could only have been done successfully at home. There was no one to do it, no one who had ever thought of it, and was left to our people in Egypt to thrash it out, in the face of strenuous opposition from India and London, some sort of wild scheme, which will, I am persuaded, ultimately form the basis of our relations with the Arabs."[10] For better and worse, it was improvised.

She navigated political intrigues between power brokers by avoiding the official bureaucracy and emphasizing personal diplomacy. She excelled with both Arabs and British elites, even if she ran into the patronizing world of male privilege and misogyny (one rival in archeology, Sir Mark Sykes, referred to her as a "silly chattering windbag of conceited, gushing, flat-chested, man-woman, globe-trotting, rump-wagging, blithering ass!")[11] Yet she knew her strategic value was knowledge and understanding of the people Cox and company were trying to harness against the Turk. The knowledge gap gave her saliency which could not be ignored. She championed structure and "water tight compartments" for administering aid and receiving intelligence to harness a unified policy. While she admired and soon adored Cox, Bell was a Cairo stalwart who believed the Arab Bureau and senior officers were of higher grade than the lot in Mesopotamia, largely administered by officials trained in India. There was no equivalent "brilliant constellation" in Mesopotamia, which she and Lawrence viewed as a third-rate operation compared to the revolt. But perhaps through the agency of Bureau agents things could be made right. "We have had great talks and made vast schemes for the government of the universe," she wrote to Lawrence in 1916.[12]

Her contribution as representative of the Arab Bureau in Mesopotamia was substantive and situated between intelligence gathering and analysis on the one hand, and diplomacy on the other. Indian officials disdained her expertise and Cairo outlook. They read and censored her mail despite her prominence and importance. Yet she chugged on. "Her familiarities with the local vernacular provided a new dimension to political intelligence there," one biographer noted. "The eloquent reports and memoranda that flowed from her hand were scrupulously to the point and seldom ventured into the realm of political polemic."[13] She enjoyed and protected her "free hand" in writing and recasting intelligence reports and from Basra she felt she could "keep an eye on all the developments in the Near East."[14] Though she suffered from the romanticizing of the "noble Arabs" and their feudal life as antidote for a "modern" Europe her privilege disdained (Arabia being viewed as a "utopia of Aristocrats" in one author's phrase to Bell, Lawrence, and others), Bell had immersed herself deeply amidst the Arabs and her judgment was vital; she was the only woman who could claim, in the vernacular of the era, to know the "Arab mind," a pejorative term for cultural appreciation from a white elitist stance.[15] "I do know these people," she said. "I have been in contact with them in a way which is possible for no official, and it is this intimacy and friendship which makes me useful now."[16]

In March 1917, she was given the title oriental secretary and sent to Baghdad to work with Cox as the Ottoman armies retreated. Creating a country out of the province was the promise that united many Mesopotamian Arabs with the British against the Ottomans. But nation-building where there was no nation was as complex as it was compelling. Bell herself wanted to play "a decisive hand in [the] final disposition. I shall be able to do that. I shall indeed, with the knowledge I'm gaining. It's so intimate. . . . What does anything else matter when the job is such a big one. It's the making of a new world."[17] The end of the Great War and the collapse of the Ottoman Empire birthed that new world. Bell was one of the midwives.

"The Credit of European Civilization Is Gone . . ."

British lies had led the Arabs to believe that the wartime revolt would secure for them an independent Arabia free of imperial rule (Ottoman or otherwise). These lies haunted Lawrence as he sought to put Feisal's family in the strongest position at Damascus, knowing that the Sykes-Picot agreement would divide the Ottoman Empire between victorious France and Britain. In the outrage and tumultuous actions that followed the reveal of the agreement, Bell's hand would help shape the future of the region and rename part of it Iraq.

April 1920. The San Remo Conference of the Supreme Allied Powers puts Mesopotamia under British mandate to ostensibly lead it toward independence. By May, resistance against British rule was organized with peaceful protests. Repression and armed revolt followed in May. Leachman's murder caused a surge of violence that forced the issue. Bell found his death unsurprising, considering how much he was hated (Leachman found Bell conceited, she found him vulgar).[18] Cox was briefly replaced by A. T. Wilson as civil commissioner, an administrator whose imperial bearing and low opinion of the Arabs led to increased use of violence on dissent. Wilson's tenure made many enemies of many Arabs and Bell. She was demoted and the office of the Arab Bureau in Mesopotamia closed. Under Wilson she wrote "The Political Future of Iraq," in which she championed reconciliation among former foes. She also argued against postwar British domination. "Give them [the Arab governments] responsibility and make them settle their own affairs and they'll do it every time and a thousand times better than we can."[19] Wilson ignored her arguments and kept the pressure on the insurgents instead.[20] Among his best agents was Colonel Leachman, who enjoyed the brutality of the work. In one instance he and his forces targeted a suspected insurgent with "burned ten miles of huts, drove in all the cattle, destroyed everything we could see, and incidentally slew a few Arabs who got in the way."[21] The result was a resurgence of violence and hatred that would kill Leachman in August and threaten the future of the country.[22] "We're near to a complete collapse of society," she wrote on September 5, 1920, "the end of the Roman empire is a very close historical parallel. . . . The credit of European civilization is gone. . . . How can we, who have managed our own affairs so badly, claim to teach others to manage their better?"[23] The worsening insurgency ended Wilson's career, and Cox returned to lead in the effort to stabilize the country. But the violence rolled on.

In this maelstrom, Bell's efforts were diplomatic and analytic. Bell wanted Arab self-determination, as American President Woodrow Wilson championed, but Feisal's ejection from Syria by the French crippled faith in British promises. Bell worked overtime to correct British views on the country they were creating with a collection of essays for incoming British officers called "The Arabs of Mesopotamia." Her encyclopedic knowledge of the people, the cultures, and geography guided the influx of War Office civil servants. The topics ranged from agricultural history, factions, and ethnic divisions and diversity, and more.[24] She met with the vast range of Arab leaders to give credence to British claims and rebuild trust; her reputation held currency as it had been built before the war. "Who was there," a biographer noted, "other than Gertrude, who would recognize and be recognized by so many of them, who could extend the traditional courtesies and interview them in their own language or dialect. Who knew the difference between mujtahid, Sunni cleric, mufti, makhtar, or mutawalli?" She also established her authority on the future of Iraq in a series of writings. In nine months she produced an opus on state building in wartime, *Review of the Civil Administration of Mesopotamia*, which dealt with reconstruction, revenue, public health, education, legal and humanitarian considerations, and the role of oil in the future political economy of the country.[25] After the difficult consultation period with the various groups in Iraq, she was tasked to write "Self-Determination in Mesopotamia" for the Paris Peace Conference, outlining the volume of difficulties they faced. It also established the importance of the British mandate to remain, as many (British and Arab) debated its value and purpose.[26]

The Cairo Conference of March 1921, led by Winston Churchill, was set to resolve these issues and stabilize the region. Bell and Lawrence were two of his special advisors. Bell knew that the map of Iraq was problematic, with unfortunate divisions of peoples. Like the Treaty of Versailles, it was plagued with harshness and short-term solutions or compromises. Many future historians and policy makers would look at Bell and her colleagues' work as setting up future horrors with ill-conceived territorial and ethnic divisions. Bell was aware of compromises and contradictions of the task, riddled with wartime bargains, real-time insurgencies, and future unrest. For this reason, she labeled the region from the Levant to the Indian frontier the "Devil's Cauldron."[27]

One pillar of stability for Bell and Lawrence was Feisal. Denied a throne in Damascus by the French, Feisal was the closest match to a valid authority in the eyes of many peoples in Mesopotamia and elsewhere. He would need to be made King. Bell did extensive research to assess the acceptability of this strategy from the peoples of Iraq.[28] Churchill agreed to the appointment, but there still had to be structures of government and validation of his authority from the people. Bell spent the lion's share of her effort over the next two years with the goal to make Feisal a legitimate king. She was instrumental in getting the most respected man in the country, the elderly naqib of Baghdad, to back a provisional government. She initiated the work on a fair and representative voting system in a country that had never known such political discourse. She took into account the rivalries and feuds as well as indigenous structures and claims of the diverse peoples of the region.[29] Meanwhile, the death toll of the revolt grew, though British statistics on causalities hid how many were civilian versus insurgent targets.[30]

Cox would not establish government with so much chaos, and Bell, while hating the bombings, knew that the embryonic government could not fight them on their own. She was also no pacifist. She found the use of air power necessary, and against reviled enemies justified. She was proud of "our power to strike back" the Ikhwan tribe, among the tougher and more active tribes whose use of terror struck fear in many, who "with their horrible fanatical appeal to a medieval faith, rouse in me the blackest hatred." There was no moral calculus when dealing with those "notorious for . . . cruelty and . . . inhuman injustices."[31] Yet, the appeal of this technique also fed the insurgencies against British interest. Bell always preferred diplomacy and reconciliation, even among former enemies, making her even more of an outlier.[32] The novelty and lethality of air power killed Arabs and enthusiasm for the revolt, though not completely. With the rebels quelled, Bell continued her efforts on tribal representation in a government with Feisal as ruler after the Iraqi Council declared him king. Feisal was affirmed by 300 notables Bell and others contacted with paperwork. But local victory was followed by challenge. The high commissioner still desired to be the ultimate authority in the country, which Feisal refused. Cox found a compromise in having Feisal agree to a new treaty as a means to dodge the British mandate. Feisal agreed, though refused to sign it, and he was crowned King of Iraq on August 23, 1921. She participated in the early diplomatic efforts to help break another swell of violence, including the famous episode where Feisal, sick with fever, had refused Cox's desire to engage the rebels. Then he fell unconscious. Without Feisal's approval, Cox ordered the crushing of the insurgency. With Feisal's hands clean, the king of Iraq signed the Treaty of Alliance between Great Britain and Iraq, guaranteeing British military occupation and advisory role, for twenty years on October 22, 1922. At important functions, Bell was often set at King Feisal's side.

"DEATH HELD NO FEAR FOR HER"

On July 12, 1926, Bell was found dead from an overdose of Dial, diallylbarbituric acid, also known as allobarbital, a barbiturate derivative later discontinued in part for its frequent use in suicides.[33] She was given a military funeral at the behest of the Iraqi government and buried at a cemetery outside of Baghdad, her coffin draped with the flags of Britain and Iraq. Crowds gathered to watch her funeral march and, despite the plague of problems of this new country, she had fans of her efforts even into the Baathist period.

CONCLUSION

Bell's hand on the creation of Iraq is well established and remains controversial. Her desire for a free Iraq for the Arabs having as much control of the country as possible within the confines of the borders drawn up may have been her Faustian bargain for the failure to have independence at all, but she pursued that goal relentlessly to the end of her days. That she could have reached a position of authority as a "kingmaker" or "shaper of nations" (which we now call nation-building) was extraordinary, and she was in many ways Lawrence's twin as a maverick of the Great War. Two factors help explain why she could translate her phenomenal energy, skill, knowledge, and talent into the successes that mounted. According to one biographer, "Her lifelong creed was to seek out and engage with the opposition in order to understand their point of view. This was regarded with the deepest suspicion by some of her colonialist colleagues, who knew that her Baghdad house was frequented by dangerous nationalist subversive to the British administration."[34] Second was an attribute noted by her stepmother Florence at the time of her death. "In truth the real basis of Gertrude's nature was her capacity for deep emotion. Great joys came into her life, and also great sorrows. How could it be otherwise, with a temperament so avid of experience. Her ardent and magnetic personality drew the loves of others to hers as she passed along."[35]

Emotional depth and the capacity to sit and reconcile with the enemy. Between 2002 and 2010, two women with these capacities would rise in the rubble of two invasions, two failed postwar policies, and two resurgent terrorist movements in two nations within the "Devil's Cauldron." If Lansdale and Bohannan were America's Lawrences, Sarah Chayes and Emma Sky were modern-day Gertrude Bells.

CHAPTER 8

Warlords, Commanders, and the Truth: Sarah Chayes in Afghanistan, 2002–2010

"KILL ME. BUT DON'T PUT ME IN THE SUN"

—Summer 2003, Kandahar, Governor's Palace.

9 A.M. Sarah Chayes, an American woman dressed as an Afghan man, sits before Governor Gul Agha Shirzai and his associate Khalid Pashtoon. Chayes has been a thorn in Shirzai's side for almost two years, ever since the Americans returned him to power when they ousted the Taliban. Chayes runs a nonprofit civic rights organization working on reconstruction after the bombing. She sleeps with a Kalashnikov by her bed, because even with the backing and protection of the Karzai family, including the president's brother, her reputation for challenging corruption has made her a target. Chayes has heard that Gul Agha has asked President Karzai to get rid of the meddlesome woman, even threatening to resign, but to no avail. The day before, he found her outside his home visiting other government agents. He barreled from his black car to demand, "Are you doing aid work or politics?" Chayes, ever cool and firm, suggested a private meeting the next morning.

She brings a Karzai aid, Abdullah the "Engineer," to help translate and act as presence.

And here they were. Two adversaries who had been trying to counter each other's influence over the rebuilding of the city: him backed by the U.S. government and his own truck company, her with "national" Afghan backing and grassroots support for the locals who despise the malfeasance of the governor and his cronies. Gul Agha fires questions: What's your job? Why are you attacking me? What are you doing, humanitarian work or politics?

"Well, that was a good one," Chayes responds. "I asked it myself just about every day."[1]

Did she have a vendetta against him?

No, she replies. She had a vendetta against "a system, a certain way of governing." That way was corruption. And it doesn't matter which province. Gul Agha and Pashtoon say she's spreading rumors that the latter worked for both the United States and Pakistan.

Gul Agha fiercely denies it. His father was the "Lion of Afghanistan" and the family was adversaries of Pakistani influence.

"Then why does the ISI run the one Internet café in town," she says, "which your friend here Khalid Pashtoon recently inaugurated."

Gul Agha feigns ignorance before brushing off the café as of no consequences. "Besides, if you can't twist their arm, kiss their hand."

Chayes parries the dodge by attacking his vanity. Surely it was sad that the son of the Lion of Afghanistan "should have to kiss *anyone's* hand."

He reverses the charge of his asking for her removal, making Karzai the bad guy who is demanding Chayes leave. Then he makes a threat. People do not like what she is doing. And there could be no stopping them.

Chayes, schooled on Afghan politics by Abdullah, responds with name drops of power. "I'm not working for the Americans, but when General McNeill or Colonel Campbell asks me what's going on in Kandahar, I can't tell a lie. I have to describe things exactly as I see them."

Gul Agha softens, claiming hurt feelings about insults she had said about him blowing his nose in his turban, an insult Chayes never gave. He offers his aid with any problems she has, just don't write more articles that make him look bad, and come to him first. Then he offers another proverb. "Kill me. But don't put me out in the sun."

"Better dead than exposed," Chayes notes later. "It was a notion that cut to the core of the worst cultural clash I confronted in this land I had adopted: its utterly incomprehensible relationship with the truth. Words were not all important, it seemed, since people lied so systematically. And yet words were terribly important, since they outlasted deeds; so the battles that counted were about getting the last word."

Like Fall, Chayes has a lodestar she'd followed since her days as a reporter for NPR. "To me, words were precious and weighty-but only in their power to communicate the truth."

Truth kept her in Afghanistan for nearly a decade. Chayes transformed into a civil rights and business leader, living in the heart of Taliban country. She became an advisor to the International Security and Assistance Force and special advisor to the Chairman of the Joint Chiefs of Staff. American refusal to admit the truth finally led her to abandon a role in a strategy she viewed as bound for defeat.[2]

"I Didn't Want to Go Back to . . . Bourgeois Reporting"

Born in 1962, Chayes was one of the children of Abram Chayes and Antonia Handler Chayes, career lawyers with deep inroads into Washington's power elite. Abram had been part of President Kennedy's Executive Committee (EXCOM) during the Cuban Missile Crisis. Handler had been the Under Secretary for the Air Force in the Carter administration. Service was championed and her father instilled a sense of justice that stayed with her into her adult life. "But I think I may even have focused on the question of justice more intensively than him," she'd recall after being soured on government service.[3]

After graduating from the Philips Academy (1980), Chayes wrote a BA thesis at Harvard (1984) *magna cum laude*, and then served in the Peace Corps in Morocco for two years, a country she had visited with her childhood friend and future author Sebastian Junger.[4] Here she learned of the dynamics of a multicultural region, including the complex world of Islam in North Africa. When one of Admiral Mullen's executive officers, an Air Force lieutenant colonel, asked on a bike ride how to build "Sarah Chayeses" into the system, Chayes reflected it was probably impossible. To perform the function she did, advisors needed to not want anything the system was offering, such as promotion. Outsiders have a freedom of movement denied those whose careers may adversely impacted by harsh and unwelcome critique. The Peace Corps, she thought, was a good place to learn the type of approach she brought to the job, because of the experience of being embedded within another culture.[5]

She later graduated with an MA in History and Middle Eastern Studies, focusing on Medieval Islamic history, though she chose not to write a thesis. A woman of action and critical thought, Chayes worked as a reporter and journalist for National Public Radio as Paris correspondent (1996–2002). In 1999, she won Foreign Press Club and the Sigma Delta Chi award as part of a team covering the war in Kosovo.[6] After experiencing the warzone of the Balkans, especially among the Muslim populations of Kosovo and Albania, a return to restaurant reviews and the exploits of consumer culture seemed trite. "I don't want to spend my life entertaining upper-middle-class Americans with the foibles of upper-middle-class Europeans."[7] She thought little of the foreign press efforts during Operation Allied Force (OAF) in Kosovo. "The foreign press corps in Kosovo didn't do our job; we sat on the border."[8] She considered humanitarian work but became cynical of the humanitarian-industrial-complex that did a lot of grandstanding in Kosovo but produced little relief.[9] "I didn't want to go back to Paris and do bourgeois reporting," Chayes said.[10] The war in Afghanistan was her ticket out.

"Was 'Pro-Taliban' Necessarily Synonymous with 'Pro-Bin Laden?'"

In Fall 2001, a U.S.-led coalition attacked Afghanistan, then in the hands of the Taliban, an extremist Islamic political and terrorist group originating in Pakistan during the 1980s. The Taliban had provided safe haven for al Qaeda, an Islamic terrorist organization led by Saudi mujahedeen (holy warrior) Osama Bin Laden. The terrorist attacks of 9/11 were largely orchestrated by al Qaeda and their supporters. Their haven in Afghanistan was the primary target for U.S. retribution through Operation Enduring Freedom (OEF). In short order, coalition special forces worked with Afghan guerrilla groups, particularly the loose coalition of tribes known as the Northern Alliance, and used overwhelming air and firepower superiority to destroy the Taliban's limited air defense system, overrun their key strongholds, and force both Taliban and al Qaeda forces out of the major cities, including Kabul. The enemy retreated to Kandahar, the first major stronghold of Taliban power in the 1990s and one of the major provincial capitals in Afghan history. The Battle of Tora Bora and the initiation of OPERATION ANACONDA saw Special Forces and conventional forces drive the enemy out of Kandahar and toward the Pakistani border. Many were killed, but senior leaders, including bin Laden, found protection in Pakistan's northwestern regions, many run semiautonomously by local tribes whose regional focus makes them wary allies of both Taliban and al Qaeda.[11]

No one could dispute the overwhelming display of power in knocking out the Taliban's defenses in short order by early 2002. Few argued against the return of Hamid Karzai to the country to lead in the establishment of a new Afghan government. But if the United States had an intensive plan for the future stability of Afghanistan after defeating those who had ruled since 1996, it was hard to see it on the ground. And the initial moves seemed fraught with horrors.

Chayes arrived in Quetta, Pakistan, bordering Afghanistan. Here Taliban and war refuges flooded the border to escape U.S. bombing and capture. "It was from Quetta that the Taliban . . . had set off in 1994 to capture Kandahar to the widespread indifference internationally." Kandahar, the ancient capital of Afghanistan, was the main base to thrust out against the rest of the country.[12] In Quetta, Chayes was in her element. She recalled journalists in Albania during the Kosovo War who would get shaken down by bandits because they rode in rented four-by-fours that would get "stripped to the bone." Chayes paid seven dollars to ride with the locals in vans to the border of Kosovo. This delighted the male passengers, "who would teach me Albanian and make me drive the torturous mountain roads when they discovered that I – a woman! - had a license."[13] She had fasted for Ramadan during her time in the PeaceCorps during Morocco. It never occurred to her that, out of cultural respect, she shouldn't have done it then, which shocked members of the Taliban press conference in Afghanistan on November 22, 2001.[14]

In Quetta, the United States hunted for supporters while the CIA headed to the Northern Alliance. Here they found Karzai as well as Shirzai, warlord of the South and former governor of Kandahar. The United States used both in a pincer move, south and north. Karzai was friends with Zabit Akrem, future police chief of Kandahar and a friend of Chayes, who was murdered in 2005. Akrem was asked to raise fighters, but with no coordination, just money. Shirzai was asked to help. Akrem did not like Shirzai and distrusted him, but agreed. Shirzai claimed in public that he had 5,000 men and would refuse a postwar job.[15] Chayes found sources close to Shirzai who claimed their leader and his cadre recounted "events not as they had actually happened, but as Shirzai and his American advisers wish they had."[16]

Shirzai was a prominent politician of the Barakzai tribe and warlord of Kandahar after the Soviet occupation. His reign was stained with corruption and graft, institutionalized rape of boys and women, murder, and other war crimes. It was the horrors of his rule that made people sympathetic to the Taliban's extremist views of justice and retribution. Few in Kandahar wished for a return of the brutality of Sharia law, but the lawless evil of Shirzai seemed worse. Now? Shirzai was returning, backed by the United States, to rule where he'd been thrown away.[17] Debate continues on the following moves, but Chayes's sources indicated that Shirzai ignored initial orders to take Kandahar airport first while Karzai headed to Kabul. Instead, perhaps on American initiative, his men and U.S. forces took Kandahar.[18] Many Taliban escaped. Some were bribed to leave. But Shirzai cemented his position.[19] Chayes wrote about the conflicting stories on the conquering of Kandahar, but the story was quashed by NPR.[20]

The media wanted specific tales: battles stories, U.S. victories, and Taliban evil. The more complex truth Chayes and friends uncovered was not needed. Instead, a story line was given and they were asked to substantiate with facts. CNN correspondents were given primers on how to frame stories on Afghan suffering. "A BBC reporter told me in our Quetta hotel the weekend before Kabul fell how he had had to browbeat his desk editors to persuade them that Kandahar was still standing."[21] Her editor at NPR was also questioning her judgment as being less than critical on the Taliban regarding sources, which the editor began to view in the binary terms of pro or anti-Taliban. But that wasn't the truth out on the road from Quetta to Kandahar, "was 'pro-Taliban' necessarily synonymous with 'pro-bin Laden'? I had learned that it was not."[22] Indeed, the new governor was just as profound an enemy. Shirzai chastised Mullah Naqib, a local elder and rival for control of Kandahar. Tribal tensions between the peoples grew.[23] Two tribes who did most of the roadblock violence and extortion in the 1990s were the Popalzai, moderately loyal to Karzai's father, and the Alokozais, under Naqib. Both admitted their people got out of their control.[24] The Taliban, who Americans could only see as evil, had earned gratitude from the people of Kandahar. "They rid the countryside of the vultures that were picking the very marrow from its shattered bones."[25] But who in the wake of 9/11 could stomach such a story?

Chayes ignored the hotels and stayed in the field with a family of Achekzais in their private home. While experiencing the segregation of male and female tasks, Chayes had dressed in men's clothes for comfort and utility since the war began, and her strange garb was generally accepted (if not approved) given her outsider status. Yet she lived among the Afghan people, surviving in the wake and rubble of U.S. air attacks against the Taliban. There was no electricity or running water. She sent her stories via satellite from a small writing desk. She lived and ate with the family, segregated by sex, learning the ropes of Pashtu culture from the ground up. Mahmad Anwar, a colleague from the border, checked up on her with his own fighters, but she was otherwise left alone in the former hotbed of Taliban and terrorist country, learning etiquette on greetings, meals, and personal relations like Lawrence had done among the Arabs.[26]

Shirzai may have assumed command as governor, but Naqib's Alokozais were in charge of the security apparatus. This was Karzai's attempt at balancing power. Chayes faced down Zabit Akram, head of the police department, who attempted to eject her from the private home. Her defiance and local support provided her legitimacy and Akram became a friend and confident until his murder in 2005. The fact that she had the courage to stay where no Western journalists dared was also seen as impressive. But she was sick of her stories being massaged or quashed. She needed a new vocation. Disillusionment with journalism helped spark her immersion in Afghanistan with deeds, not words.

"A LITTLE GIRL WITH RIVULETS OF DRIED BLOOD . . ."

Recovering in the United States to consider her career options, Chayes met Aziz Karzai, brother of the president, over dinner at a fundraiser.

They discussed corruption, growing up with warlords, and aid money issues in Kandahar, primarily in rebuilding the bombed cities. He asked if she would come back to help them rebuild. She said yes. Together with Qayum, Karzai's older brother, they founded Afghans for Civil Society (ACS) in Boston: part policy center, part humanitarian organization. "We are trying to have an impact on a policy level as well as on a concrete level," Chayes said in 2002. "That's what makes us totally unconventional." She quit NPR, began the PR task of fund raising on the East coast, and returned to Afghanistan in March 2002, landing at Kabul. "The devastation that stared sullenly out at our passing car for blocks and blocks surpassed anything I had imagined."[27] Her letters home from June and July showed Chayes adapting to the culture and norms of social, political life in war-traumatized Afghanistan. She also saw the true face of modern warfare.

Collateral damage from U.S. precision-guided munitions had hit a wedding in a village in Dehraout, poisoning President Karzi's diplomatic efforts to raise local troops against the remaining Taliban in Kandahar. Chayes surveyed the damage before hunting for aid. Among the causalities was "a little girl with rivulets of dried blood caked on her legs, and traces of eyeliner still showing from the wedding she had been attending when the sky had opened." Few organizations offered more than excuses to aid the victims. Chayes negotiated the politics of aid between provinces, organizations, NGOs, hospitals, and more.[28]

In full combat gear, Chayes worked alongside her Afghan team to begin rebuilding after the bombing. The threats now weren't from U.S. precision-guided munitions (PGMs) or Taliban assassins, but against indigenous bias against the incursion of Westerners and the criminal militias turned "security forces" of Gul Agha Shirzai. The governor also controlled access to almost all the building materials for the city and province and ran one of the trucking companies. She built alliances with U.S. Civil Affairs Troops[29] and initially lived in a compound that contained an office and living quarters, as well as animals in the backyard.[30] Immediately, Chayes publicly discussed Shirzai corruption, graft, and abuse, past and present. For her, such exposure was necessary for understanding the rise of the Taliban in Afghanistan. "The warlords are the bad guys, and the Americans don't seem to take that on," Chayes told a Peace Corps reporter. "There is no lack of religious extremists hanging around in the woodwork waiting for this experiment to fail."[31] She would soon sleep with an AK-47 by her mattress.

Corruption plagued their efforts at every turn. In Akokolacha the year before, al Qaeda conducted a final holding action against U.S. bombs in the village, near Kandahar airport. Ten out of thirty houses were destroyed. Everyone lied about the size of their houses, hoping for extra aid money. Chayes's fund-raising efforts secured private donations of $18,000. It wasn't enough. Indeed, money alone, like military force alone, would not provide a strong foundation. Support of the local people had to be gained for any traction. So Chayes, with a rudimentary command of Pashto, spoke to the village elders by holding shuras (council meetings), focused on immediate repairs. They rebuilt mosques and elders house, and had to give everyone the same style place because there was no other way to be fair with all the lies about everyone's old houses.[32]

The rampant dishonesty was infuriating at first. But these people had been suffering PTSD from thirty years of violence, instability, corruption, and abuse. Precious few remembered the relative normalcy and modern world of Afghanistan before the Soviet invasion. There was no longer a through line of peace or stability to bank on. Life was conflict and chaos. Truth could not be trusted and banking on the future was foolish. One had to grab everything they could up front, by hook or by crook, or be left behind.

Shirzai's nephew and brother opened a gravel plant that destroyed the local quarry's business and made the warlord aristocracy the only game in town. U.S. contracts came fast. Supporting competition caused threats to emerge from the governor's security teams. And with it fear of detention.[33] Local fears were true: get rid of the Taliban and the monstrous "Noble Flower" returned.[34] His operators wore U.S. uniform. His abuses were seen as sanctioned by American officials. His rule was a whim of the United States. After being denied rebuilding materials, Chayes got an official to come with them to look elsewhere for more stones. Only after none could be found was the old quarry owner allowed to sell them. After which he was promptly jailed and Gul Agha's jails were the stuff of nightmares. Chayes cajoled local and international support to have him freed.[35] Here, among the people of Kandahar resisting oppression, the truth had given her both purpose and direction. She had no interest in a safe life. She would not run. "I feel like my destiny is bound up with the destiny of this place. . . . And in contrast to other places I'd been, notably the Balkans, I felt strongly there were a few people acting in the true interests of their country. I felt I just had to throw my lot in with them."[36]

"Opposing Power with Power"

In 2003, with American eyes and interest focused on Iraq, resurgent elements of the Taliban leaked back into Afghanistan. The NATO-led International Security Force (ISAF) was created in 2001 out of a series of international actors and agencies to help train a national Afghan army, rebuild government institutions, and also conduct military and security operations. OEF continued direct action against the Taliban.[37] Yet as Iraq became America's focal point, these forces were run with less robust support than the original operations of 2001. "There wasn't a lot of thought by the folks who wanted to oust the Taliban about what would come afterwards," Chayes said at the time, "and there still isn't a lot of thought. So long as there's a skin-deep layer of stability, that's all basically we're caring about."[38]

Between 2003 and 2006, Taliban influence, presence, and violence would grow from their safe haven in Pakistan and back to Kandahar, taking advantage of the divided attention of the coalition fighting almost three wars without unity of command. OEF fought the Taliban. ISAF handled internal security and supported governance under NATO starting August 2003. Regional Command (RC) South was established in Kandahar, largely run by the Canadian Forces in 2003–2009. Their provincial reconstruction teams worked on civil infrastructure and governance, with a range of successes among the wary Afghans.[39] The United States focused its efforts on the prelude, war, and postwar abandonment of Iraq.[40]

Even with a resurgent Taliban, Chayes was protected through her connection with Karzai and U.S. fiscal support. It counted more than guards. "For the moment, I enjoy that kind of deterrence."[41]

On the street, in the village, threats were closer than Taliban safe havens like Quetta. "It is the militiamen loyal to regional power-brokers, or warlords, who break into people's houses, who kidnap people, or rape or torture them for ransom, who shake down taxi and truck drivers, and so forth. These people are in uniform, and ostensibly represent the new regime." It made some nostalgic for the Taliban.[42]

In this haven of shifting loyalties and predation, Chayes and ACS worked against graft in reconstruction, taxes, and banking; worked on women's rights; and received independently gathered aid from international actors to push for change in Kandahar and Kabul.[43] She also made mistakes, including whom to trust.

Afghans who were more "western" turned out to be the most corrupt: the kind of people regular Afghans would not deal with. Among her most important allies was "a balding, dour-faced Karzai retainer named, Abdullah," Karzai's half-brother who claimed to be an engineer and who worked with other NGOs. Initially Abdullah seemed trustworthy and accountable as a partner. When Chayes had to leave Afghanistan for a funding run, she found he'd ignored almost all of the accounting practices she had established, and substituted his own. She later heard "painful stories of suppliers who had never been paid, projects unfinished, people without schools and money missing. On top of being duped she had been made "an accessory to fraud."[44] Abdullah cultivated fear. He viewed Kandaharis as murderers and thieves, and never left Chayes alone in a room with officials. "I lost touch with the people I was purporting to serve"[45] and had "provided fodder to the extremists arguments I had come to help Afghan rebuke."[46] But she kept learning.

From 2002 to 2003, Chayes worked independent of any senior U.S. government. Her security was her own concern. She lived as Afghans lived, with Afghans, in the Spartan style that she'd had her whole life. She earned trust by sharing dangers and thus proving she wasn't there simply for a day or a week, but invested on what could be built, and sustained, against the odds, to break the cycle of uncertainty that had permeated all facets of society since the late 1970s. This bought saliency as she lived and learned from Afghans and fought corruption.[47] She was also critical of her own government. She challenged aid programs that seemed shortsighted, done for optics of success but seemed absent of a strategy for the future of Afghanistan's, "small projects that won't be much of a loss if they fail, but that by the same token don't make much of a difference to the people." These were projects she and her people could handle. The crippled hydroelectric dam in Kajak, Helmand Province, was too complex, political, and expensive, though generating electricity would increase self-sufficiency in two crippled provinces. Yet only ISAF and American aid organizations had the means to make it work.[48] "If you don't help us," a man shouted at her once, "we don't want you here."[49] And all training foci seemed to be on the Afghan National Army, not governance, though the Provincial Reconstruction Teams (PRTs) in Kandahar disagreed.[50]

After homes were built and the systemic corruption studies were completed, ACS secured more work ranging from a dairy co-op to advocacy work on women's right.[51] By 2004, Chayes had secured a contract to detail her experience in the book that would become *The Punishment of Virtue: Inside Afghanistan after the Taliban*. She took a sabbatical from the ACS work to write of her experiences. It was published in 2006 to rave reviews for its in-depth analysis of what was clearly a losing war effort.

But her adversaries changed. In 2003, President Karzai decreed that governors could no longer hold military posts. Gul Aga Shirzai was removed from Kandahar. Chayes and others believed his vast range of human rights abuses and corruption had finally caught up with him but it was merely a shift of chairs, not the start of accountability. He held different positions, and grew over the next five years to be an important ally of Karzai.[52] The new governor, however, was his chief advisor and fellow tribe member, Pashtun. Sherzai's power was intact. Only the face had changed.[53] The president's move showed his true intent. He wasn't interested in fighting corruption, either.

"Presiding over the Gang Rape of His Country"

By 2005, Chayes was fed up. She'd confronted Shirzai for years, lost friends to violence, and watched as the Taliban and Pakistani agents returned. ISAF and its Provincial Reconstruction Teams attempted to keep the peace but were starved of support and interest. The final straw was realizing the Karzai family's depths of corruption, "How self-serving those brothers were." After Shirzai's "removal," she couldn't in good conscience work for them directly anymore. Anger against their corruption, malfeasance, and denial of warlord brutality boiled. "He's presiding over the gang rape of his country," she told the press.[54] Instead, she'd work with the people.

Gathering resources ranging from private donations to support from Oprah Winfrey, Chayes opened her own small soap and skincare business known as Arghand Cooperative in Kandahar. She became fluent in Pashto and experienced corruption from the ends of private business. A bank official demanded bribes from one of Chayes' employees for the final deposit required for registering the cooperative.[55] When Chayes heard, she came to the bank herself, offered to pay, but demanded receipt for the bribed price. The official laughed, but Chayes wouldn't budge. She escalated to the manager where she gave the same line. "Suddenly I was seated crossed-legged atop the man' s desk." She wouldn't budge until they signed for the money. The bank eventually succumbed. "We had won. We had obtained an administrative service without giving into corruption."[56] But she wasn't a local. She was a privileged Western woman who'd succeeded to push the system. These victories were never, ever complete, Chayes knew. Yet, she again pushed forward.

In different ways, working with Western aid agencies was just as frustrating. The Canadian government had an increased presence in Kandahar as part of RC South, and Chayes tried to secure funding from the Canadian International Development Agency (CIDA) to support her co-op. As she wrote to the U.S. Senate Committee on Foreign Affairs, "I'm in the process for applying for some money from CIDA, I looked at the application form, and I have a MA [from Harvard] and I can't read the thing."[57] That said, CIDA funded both solar panels and salaries for Arghand.[58] It was while working in soap against corruption that NATO called on her in 2007. A colleague asked her to participate with them as a civilian subject-matter expert. Later, she admitted her frustrations got the best of her tone. Her hard-earned knowledge emerged from the same kind of ignorance of Afghanistan that now stared at her from the eyes of incoming NATO soldiers. "I forgot what the fog was like. I lost patience, because time was passing and the grace period Afghans had accrued us was running out. I couldn't contain my shrill frustration as I watched successive Western officials make precisely the mistakes I had made, and their predecessors had made."[59]

NATO had increasing interest in Chayes and her expertise in the region. Nicholas Williams, deputy NATO senior civilian representative, invited her to meet senior officials. She visited ISAF HQ in Kabul once a month. Early in 2009, she was asked to see ISAF commander General David McKiernan. It was just the two of them. Both loved Afghanistan and Chayes thought highly of the quiet general whose career was hurt by not being a "yes-man" to Secretary of Defense Donald Rumsfeld. McKiernan was removed from command, Chayes believed, because COIN was now being thought of as the solutions to problem in Iraq and Afghanistan. McKiernan was considered too old school, conservative, and conventional compared to stars of COIN like Gen. David Petraeus, commander of the "surge" in Iraq. But Chayes recalled that McKiernan had established the troop requirement of the additional 30,000 troops his successor, McChrystal, would view as necessary for the "surge." Deploying and maintaining them would lie with McChrystal under the Obama administration, since it was ignored by Bush.[60] Chayes missed McKiernan but hoped that with Obama in the White House, she could do good through the U.S. government. She hadn't thought that of President Bush. A year before she'd noted, "Osama bin Laden and certain members of our government are actually on the same team. Because … they want to split the world apart, into two poles that are enemies. I'm on that other team."[61]

While in Washington, she also met Chairman Joint Chiefs of Staff Admiral Mike Mullen. She brushed off his concerns about her security. "I call mothers," he responded. "I don't want to have to call your mother." She offered a security suggestion. "Next time you see President Karzai, and next time you're in Pakistan to visit the chief of the army staff, General Kayani, let it slip that I'm a friend of yours. That will reduce the threat to me about seventy percent."[62] It also established good will: Chayes, who had spoken truth to power against her own government for seven years, would soon become Mullen's special advisor in Afghanistan and elsewhere.

"McChrystal Got Captured by Corrupt Intermediaries" —March 2009.

Tough winter operations against the Taliban by British, American, Danish, Canadian, and Afghan forces achieved mix results in direct combat and state building, though Taliban casualties and failures made their claims of success harder to believe. As Canadian, U.S., and Afghan forces prepared for clearing operations to place government presence and resource,[63] congressional leaders visited Afghanistan. Chayes offered to introduce them to tribal leaders, an ad hoc council to speak for the people. The military and state department and RC South resisted it as unsafe for a big group. And Afghan elders refused to be searched. "I soon discovered . . . RC-South command had not invited any delegation of Afghan elders on base yet . . ." The search issue was just another dodge. The congressional delegation insisted on the meeting, with Chayes as interpreter. "You want the truth? There is no government here," she told them. "They don't even control their official buildings."[64]

The new ISAF commander was Gen. Stanley McChrystal. If Petraeus was the master of COIN, McChrystal was like the star graduate student. COIN did not come naturally to McChrystal, the commander of Special Forces in Iraq, but he had studied up, and seemed determined to apply its precepts. Still, there was always a gap between his somewhat ambivalent execution and Chayes' understanding of what it would take to win the war. McChrystal overemphasized the value of good relations with Karzai, which Chayes found counterproductive given the corruption and abuses his government perpetrated. How do you "win the people" if you champion someone who allows his officials to prey upon the population almost as viciously as the Taliban did? Chayes was of limited interest to McChrystal. In 1,000 hours on the ground, he had not yet looked at her and her team's papers and work on the growing importance of government legitimacy as integral to any successful COIN strategy. He appreciated COIN, but still saw it in tactical terms, as something to be executed by platoons on the village level.[65]

McChrystal was an "emaciated bundle of torques nerves," but she liked him and his team's energy even if she "had underestimated the accompanying arrogance."[66] McChrystal was keen. He wanted the brigade and battalion levels to switch the focus from government to populace, and examine how the political environment needed to change. But dropping government support or focus also spiked anxiety. Chayes worked with Andrew Exum, an Iraq and Afghan war veteran and unconventional warfare expert from the COIN-championing think tank the Center for a New American Security, providing intelligence on the continuing infiltration of the Taliban into Kandahar who, thanks to the corruption and hording of aid and support of Ahmed Wali Karzai and others, now controlled a ring around the city in four districts from which to cause havoc. But Chayes' focus was not on the front line of security, but the roots that made it strong.[67]

She sent him an anti-corruption strategy she'd been working on for years. Seven months later it was still meeting fierce resistance from the Afghan government and international officials. But she learned about the creativity of corruption "and all the reasons that can be dreamed up for ignoring it."[68] Under his command she tried to make meeting with the tribal elders. McChrystal talked her down the day they were to meet on his tour. There was a conflict with the governor regarding these tribal elders. But McChrystal's team had allowed her list of elders into the hands or RC South, who reviewed it with the governor, a crony of Karzai. The event was canceled. "McChrystal got captured by corrupt intermediaries, whose abuse was driving Afghans into the arms of the very extremist insurgents his soldiers were fighting."[69]

Chayes trucked on, trying to learn the language of the army and speak in PowerPoint on corruption within the context of COIN. Since the surge in Iraq, COIN was all the rage, but at least it shifted focus to the population and the role of legitimate authority as integral parts of strategy. It was hoped COIN would offer more than the preferred lever of influence of counterterrorism (CT), operations against enemy targets. She argued that most Afghanis were "fence sitters" who were not actively extremist and could be separated from the die-hards, a point made by Col. David Kilcullen, an Australian COIN expert and advisor to Petraeus.[70] The regular Afghans needed to be the target. ISAF had to "win the people." Yet working with Karzai reduced ISAF's legitimacy. It had been the same in the Philippines, the same in Vietnam. Unless you had political actors whom the people could trust, you would always be seen as tools of the abusers.

Yet, Karzai's regime was "easy" for Americans to work with, another sign of a problem. "Not only did most officials, unlike the vast majority of Afghans, speak English, they picked up our vocabulary, our technical terms, our acronyms, the latest fashion in interagency jargon for whatever it was we were trying to accomplish." Regular Afghans required more from Americans. Not the corrupt officials.[71] "Time and again US officials are blindsided by major developments in countries where they work. Too often they are insensible to the perspective and aspirations of populations. Focused on levers to pull, on people who 'get things done,' they overlook or help enable networks that are bent on power and private enrichment and are structured to maximize both, at the expense of the citizenry." Even when it goes against national interest.[72] As a U.S. official in Kabul told her in January 2003, "We work with governments. And lots of them aren't savory."[73]

"Corruption . . . Was a Force Multiplier for the Enemy"

—Late spring, 2009, Kabul.

There was forward traction. An "Anti-Corruption" post was created and led by Dutch lieutenant colonel Piet Boering. Chayes and others worked on governance, accountability, and trying to make the next round of Afghan elections legitimate instead of a farce. They included historical lessons from wars like Vietnam. Other officers balked at becoming involved in local and international politics, unwilling to admit that politics and law were COIN as much as CT or direct action missions. They tossed those jobs at the feet of diplomats, aid groups, or the United Nations. But for Chayes, the aim of the mission had the wrong target. "Our security mandate was understood to mean protecting Afghans from violence perpetrated by insurgents only—not from violence *perpetuated by the government*."[74]

Soldiers were dealing with Afghan population more than officials. Many did so with Human Terrain Teams (HTT), academics providing cultural awareness to the military.[75] "Why not add a few queries about electoral intimidation to their standard questionnaires? What about allocating some of the flight time for all those satellites and drones and blimps floating above military instillations to observing polling places?"

And soldiers dealt with most of the Afghan officials. Soldiers made sense as the front line in the anti-corruption strategy. "In Afghanistan, forty-year-old battalion commanders were closeted with provincial governors every week. Troops were training the Afghan army and police." To view them as unpolitical was willful blindness.[76] She worked with ISAF intelligence chief Gen. Michael Flynn who was interested and supportive. In late 2009 they argued that for the surge to work, they needed to oust Ahmed Wali Karzai, whose influence through a "web of business interests as well as a long running relationship with the CIA" had kept the United States from assailing his abuses.[77] When she asked about satellite monitoring, Flynn said such assets only tracked insurgents, not political actors. She, Boering, and others soldiered on with recommendations on anti-corruption practices to help the election. But the party line was "security trumped governance," and their efforts went unheeded.

Yet, one group in ISAF was interested in the anti-corruption work. "It was the civilian assessors who had been called in from universities and Washington think tanks to analyze the Afghanistan campaign." Their assessment was later leaked to the *Washington Post*, and poisoned the Obama administration's relation to the military, but Chayes and Boering worked with these outside experts. By June 2009 the anti-corruption post had made arguments and proposal projects on corruption in policy and military jargon. "In plain English: why would a farmer stick out his neck to keep the Taliban out of his village if the government was just as bad? If, because of corruption, an ex-policeman . . . was threatening to turn a blind eye to a man planting an IED, others were going further. Corruption, in army-speak, was a force multiplier for the enemy."[78]

Chayes also discovered compelling evidence that aid infusion could worsen problems by increasing corruption. "Development resources passed through the corrupt system not only reinforced that system by helping to fund it but also inflamed the feeling of injustice that were driving people toward the insurgency."[79] Thus one of the pillars of counterinsurgency, building trust through aid, was cracked. The crack was systemic. A colleague introduced Chayes to a theoretical model to help explain the damage. "Ultimatum Games" are experiments that "allocate a sum of money to one player, with instructions to divide it with another. If the recipient accepts the offer, the deal goes through. If she rejects it, both players get nothing. Economists had presumed that a recipient, acting rationally, would accept any amount greater than zero. In fact, in experiment after experiment—even with stakes as high as a month's salary—roughly half of recipients rejected offers lower than 20 percent of the total sum."[80] Chayes argued it was the same with aid money that's skimmed and skimmed into a corrupt system. It helped explain why development projects kept getting attacked, as being part of a corrupt system as much as a target for extremist behavior.

She also challenged "corruption is normal" arguments from colleagues, since corruption served the insurgency. The 2009 election was so fraud-ridden that everyone decried it. It also fed Taliban ranks. Corrupt elections tell the populace that the government is their enemy. Afghans lost faith in a "political process that only seemed to strengthen power brokers and maintain the status quo" as one Taliban detainee put it.[81] Her team's recommendation revealed the need to repair massive ignorance. "Despite the thousands of intelligence professional spread throughout the country, not to speak of the hundreds of diplomats and development practitioners, the international community knew almost nothing useful about the government officials or local contractors we were dealing with." All eyes were on the Taliban, not the government.[82] The team put a full spectrum list of anti-corruption policies into a fragmentary operations order (FRAGO) for soldiers. And the order was, in fact, issued.[83] The FRAGO was shaped into actions that could be issued by battalion, brigade level task force, and the RC commands.[84]

Soldiers and others resisted the FRAGO. It demanded a two-front war against both the Taliban and the government they were allied with to fight the Taliban. It raised risks to soldier's lives. Others refused to strain relations with a corrupt government who were favored by Washington, DC. The internal contradictions of corruptions and COIN would be exposed.[85]

"The CIA Was Paying One of My Prime Targets"

Still, hope remained. In July 2009, Acting Ambassador Tony Wayne met senior officials and there was an inkling of convergence of interest among the various partners. These included the British criminal investigation unit (Major Crimes Task Force [MCTF]), supported by the FBI, DEA, and the Treasury "Threat Finance Cell," who created their own "Sensitive Investigation Unit." Dialog continued on how to target corruptions, and Chayes contended against a push for targets that didn't impact change but looked good on ledgers (minor officials and daily graft). "Such a formulation profoundly misunderstood the character, impact, and structure of acute corruption."[86] They had to avoid binary thinking about corruption, for it wasn't a case of either-or, but across a spectrum of depth that exerted influence. New metrics were needed. They utilized a bottom-up model that was used for gathering intelligence and targeting insurgents created by an Anti-Corruption Task Force. It examined such variables as public outcry, political backlash, and the relationship of insurgencies and crime.

Given the political, military, and economic range of interest, cooperation met resistance from a variety of actors it needed to work, but Chayes quickly identified the greatest counterpressure came from the CIA: the agency that had brought Gul Aga Shirzai back to Kandahar. They blocked her as an uninvited "regional affairs officer" from coming into their room. "The CIA was paying one of my prime targets—I had seen it with my own eyes—Karzai's younger half-brother Ahmed Wali, who pulled the strings to most of southern Afghanistan, who stole land, imprisoned people for ransom, appointed key public officials, ran vast drug trafficking networks and private militias, and wielded ISAF like a weapon against people who stood up to him. The inhabitants of three provinces hated him." But the CIA backed him as a government operator. In the end, the CIA's influence and goals served a strategy that Chayes would soon find, like Woodhouse near the end of Greek liberation, to be contradictory and thus impossible.[87]

"The Strike Force Was Purportedly Trying to Spring a Friend Out of Jail"

Chayes also worked with Steve Foster, a Scotland Yard detective, one of the men behind the Afghan police investigation unit the MCTF. And it was here that the shadow influences in Afghanistan began to unveil themselves. An investigation led to a border cop tied to the drug trade being arrested for trafficking. Hanif Atmar was a long-time government official, minister of interior and former minister of education and rural development. "One of the international community's darlings." He'd tried to fire the detention facility workers where the cop was held. "I had to mull that one over to let the implications sink in. The Afghan minister of interior had nearly relieved a senior officer for doing his job: for providing temporary detention, at the behest of the U.S. and U.K. officials and his own superior, of a duly arrested suspect, who happened to be a border police officer."[88] In the wake of the case, MCTF had agreed to let Atmar know of impending arrests within his jurisdiction. Thus, they had to provide corrupt official details of their work against the system that he supported. MCTF then caught another border official when $100,000 went missing. Bank records and wire taps caught three men. The lead suspect was named Sayfullah.

Weeks before, a Provincial Police chief, Matiullah Qatih, had been assassinated by his own Kandahar Strike Force. These men had trained and lived with the CIA. This was a commando assault. "The strike force was purportedly trying to spring a friend out of jail. The beleaguered provincial prosecutor had called Police Chief Mutiallah, who had to drive over and walked into the ambush." Chayes disputed the details: the jailed man wasn't at the location. The phone call seemed a setup. Everyone blamed the CIA, and Chayes recalled that Ahmed Wali Karzai had provided the details of every member of the Kandahar Strike Force to the CIA. They were his men. "The potential implication—the move this murder might represent on one of several chessboards—outpaced the ability of dull-witted international officials, myself included, to keep up."[89]

Sayfullah was a local chief of the Afghan Border Police. A nobody. And yet he'd been arrested. Foster was told he was no great shakes, so the arrest continued. Interior Minister Atmar, when informed, delayed the arrest with request for detailed review. ISAF's intelligence chief Flynn visited Atmar regarding his action and informed him it would be good for him to not stand in the way. But Atmar wanted no handcuffs for him. On October 19, 2009, Sayfullah was invited to Kabul for a conference, quietly escorted out of the building, and arrested. They'd secured another small victory.

Days later, Hakim Angar, the police official who became Sayfullah's replacement, called Chayes. He was on a plane to the new job when Atmar's deputy ordered him off the plane. The appointment was suspended. Chayes spent three months investigating that aborted appointment. Flynn confronted Atmar over his actions. In January 2010, McChrystal was going to talk about removing Atmar from his position with Karzai. Angar's position remained in limbo.

Then the search warrant for Sayfullah's office had been canceled. Atmar had talked to Karzai, who talked to Ahmed Wali, who warned of "tribal unrest" if the search warrant was executed. Karzai told Atmar to kill the warrant. The reason was to "save lives" in the wake of unrest, but it was bogus. Karzai and others just said the right words to the international officials. The case stressed the actual political system, and the system had moved with lightning speed. But why?

"Vertically Integrated Criminal Syndicate"

Working with Col. Chris Kolenda,[90] one of McChrystal's chief officers in his strategic assessment of Afghanistan and among the most successful American COIN practitioners in Afghanistan, Chayes and others discovered a shadow structure of power and influence of the Afghan government that first appeared to be counterintuitive. History and tradition had led them to view the government system as being one of patronage that spread downward, from Karzai to his subordinates and sectors of influence. In diagramming it, Kolenda discovered the reverse. In the triangle of power, money wasn't flowing down from a master patron. It flowed up. "Money, Kolenda argued, was moving up the chain of command in today's Afghanistan, in the form of gifts, kickbacks, levies paid to superiors, and the purchase of positions."[91]

That diagram gave shape and form to what Chayes had experienced and studied for years. "I've been perfecting that diagram for years, adapting it to fit different countries. I've confirmed the behavior it predicts in hundreds of conversations with Afghans and people living under other kleptocracies." The crux is the money flowing upward. Karzai was not dispensing patronage to buy off rivals. "If anything . . . the reverse was true. Subordinate officials were paying off Karzai or his apparatus.

What the top of the system provided in return was, first, unfettered permission to extract resources for personal gain, and second, protection from repercussions." That model explained Atmar's behavior and Karzai's' response. "The whole system depended on faithful discharge, by senior officials, of their duty to protect their subordinates." Like a crime syndicate, these ties held strong regardless of the power of the subordinates under duress. "If Karzai failed to uphold his end of the bargain, the whole edifice would collapse."[92] Chayes called this system a "Vertically Integrated Criminal Syndicate." Governance was not its function. It existed to perpetuate itself via support and indulgence. The Afghan government was "not incapable. It was performing its core function with admirable efficiency—bringing power to bear where it counted. And it was assiduously protecting its own. Governing—the exercise that attracted so much international attention—was really just a front activity."[93]

"I'm Not Willing to Die for This Any More"[94]

Invigorated by this structural reveal, there was hope of unwinding Afghanistan from this model and push for legitimacy and accountability within a functioning system of governance. Chayes premiered her case on the Afghan Government as a vertically integrated criminal syndicate in Germany at the Marshall Center in January 2010. Her model resonated with people from various nations suffering under corrupt regimes, which she would later investigate for her second monograph, *Thieves of State*. But there had been another changing of the guard.

In July, McChrystal resigned his command in the wake of an article in *Rolling Stone* magazine that revealed the cocky, disrespectful, and nasty attitudes of McChrystal and his senior officers toward other officials and President Obama.[95] Gen. David Petraeus, at CENTCOM until McChrystal's removal, took the job. Chayes already knew Petraeus. She'd corresponded with him on corruption and he had even called the Karzai government a "criminal syndicate" during a White House policy debate the last fall. He seemed a likely champion of their work. Chayes had left ISAF work in February 2010, but was on loan to Petraeus while working as Special Advisor to Admiral Mullen. Petraeus was her last big hope.[96]

Chayes and this group became Petraeus' "Directed Telescopes," a group of "aides or trusted advisers, often junior officers, to focus on issues beyond his sight, thus helping the commander expand his knowledge of the battlefield."[97] Chayes was part of the academic wing of the directed telescopes of experts and think tank types. It included Fred Kagan, American Enterprise Institute, and his wife, Kim, who ran the Institute for the Study of War, and among the most influential academics in Petraeus' Headquarters. There were also four "Junior Scopes," RAs in their twenties who were "perhaps the most productive members of the team."[98] And in June, the team thought they'd caught their big break.

Chayes and a team of experts built a Governance Campaign Plan for Petraeus. After a revision, Petraeus read their plan. "As we discussed some of the minor revision in his office a few days later, I heard Petraeus murmur something under his breath. '*This* is the revision of the field manual.'" He was referring to *his* field manual, *Counterinsurgency Field Manual 3-24*, which was created to forestall the collapse of Iraq three-years after the invasion. Chayes had found a champion for their work, one with even more influence than the Karzais or McChrystal.[99]

On June 25, 2010, Muhammad Zia Salehi, administrative assistant at Afghan NSC, was arrested for selling his influence for gifts. But he was likely the bagman for "a vast palace slush fund that President Karzai's closest intimates controlled and used to buy alliances, votes, or silence." These revelations come under Kirk Meyer, DEA agent who worked with Chayes at the Anti-Corruption Task Force. Corruption was only the third priority of the Threat Finance cell and the special Afghan police unit it mentored, the Sensitive Investigation Unit (SIU), under terrorist funding and drug money.[100]

SIU had dug into a Kabul-based money operation used by extremists. They raided the *hawala* (remote system of money transfer) office in downtown Kabul. Cash was being funneled from it to the Kabul bank. The hole was nearly a billion deep, "the result of $100,000 Master Cards handed out to select officials, directors' fat expense accounts, binges for government tenders, and the kind of 'non-reimbursable loans' that were then so common in Tunisia." The cards were the impetus, but Meyer and his crew were under pressure for a watertight corruption case and this was it. Salehi was the tip of the spear.[101]

Karzai had him released, went on TV, invented a commando raid that abused Salehi, and clearly established to the other members of his syndicate that they were being protected. Not an ounce of Karzai's statements was true.[102] The U.S. officials backed Karzai's version. Petraeus gathered resources and support from the coalition and local forces to make the police units and their funding independent. "Karzai backed off"[103] until he could attack through the judiciary to weaken the police's independence on grounds of "sovereignty." Lawyers in the Salehi case were demoted and removed. The deputy attorney general who had supported the arrest and warrants was fired, accused of being a spy, and fled to Iran. The U.S. government's response was of no consequence. Indeed, many within ISAF and Washington still thought of corruption as a necessary evil for doing business.[104]

Still, Chayes and the Directed Telescopes believed in their boss. Petraeus was about to have a "commander's conference" to meet his senior commanders and establish the next iteration of his mission.

Kabul, August 14, 2010. Chayes and the crew worked on their slides, ready to present what Petraeus viewed as integral to his COIN strategy. "To our appalled shock, as Petraeus worked through his presentation the next day, he dwelled not on our slides—which signaled a new approach that was countercultural in the military and would require patient explanation—but rather on slides telling the officers to do what they already knew how to do best: kill the enemy. Pausing to expand on the contents, Petraeus even argued against some of our slides."[105]

And that was it. "I remember the sentence audibly going through my mind: 'I'm not willing to die for this anymore.'" Nor to have anyone die for it. Convinced no serious anti-corruption effort was now being contemplated, Chayes left Kabul on September 3 to serve Mullen as a special advisor in Washington, DC. She continued diverse research on corruption and the nature of thieving states in Libya, Nigeria, and elsewhere, and pushed her arguments into the political halls of Congress and Secretary of State Hillary R. Clinton, but they fell on increasingly deaf ears. She would not return on government dime to serve in Afghanistan for a strategy she saw as futile. She now works for the Carnegie Endowment for International Peace as senior fellow in the Democracy and Rule of Law Program, continuing the fight outside of government.

Conclusion

For nearly a decade, Sarah Chayes contributed to the rebuilding of Afghanistan. She did so as a political agent of the Afghan government, a private business owner, and advisor to ISAF. Each one of these means ran into the face of resistance from a common denominator, government corruption. Without government legitimacy, talk of COIN was merely that, and Chayes argued against the increasing reliance on CT and targeting high-profile Taliban members as the chief metric of success (a new spin on the Body Bag statistics of the Vietnam War, and almost as limited in what this evidence proved). That she was able to survive, let alone succeed, in any of these ventures was a testament to her capacity to learn, to understand, and to risk her own life among the Afghan people. It was this expertise that made her valuable in a war where ignorance was rife, and it was her conviction that allowed this currency not to devalue as she criticizes warlords, presidents, and rockstar generals. Like Bernard Fall, she spoke truth to power in print and at personal risk, living in the warzone she researched. Unlike Fall, her obstinacy in the face of power didn't deny her a place within the war, but earned her a seat at the table. Initially provided for by patrons, Chayes refused to bow down when evidence piled higher and deeper that all of them were part of the problem. When they refused to be part of the solution, choosing corrupt systems instead of meaningful change, she removed herself from working from within their domain. Like Woodhouse in 1945 and Lansdale in 1968, she had reached the limit of where truth, expertise, conviction, and connections could influence events from a maverick outsider. It remains to be seen if working outside the system will produce different results.

Chapter 9

British Pacifist versus American Pride: Emma Sky in Iraq, 2003–2010

"You Made Me a Better General"

—March 7, 2010, Baghdad, Iraq.[1]

Emma Sky watches the Iraqi election. It is the culmination of a seven-year Odyssey. She opposed the war that toppled Saddam Hussein, yet was now political advisor (POLAD) to senior American commander Lt. Gen. Raymond T. Odierno, commanding general of Multi-National Forces Iraq. Creating a legitimate election in the wake of the U.S. "surge" to curb internecine violence had been their driving goal for the past year.

The nonsectarian Iraqiya Party (Iraqi National Movement, or INM) had done well, winning 91 of the 325 seats in the Council of Representatives. Second was the State of Law Coalition, run by incumbent President Nouri Maliki, who claimed fraud and conspiracy and demanded recounts. Fear of a dictatorship coincided with American desire to decouple themselves from Iraq. Sky was ordered to broker a deal between Maliki and the incoming Ayad Allawi of the INM and smaller parties,[2] while Odierno came into direct conflict with U.S. ambassador Christopher Hill over the election results. "He told me that Iraq is not ready of democracy," Sky recalled Odierno saying, "that Iraq needs a Shia strongman. And Maliki is our man." The election proved the opposite, but the State Department wasn't interested. Sky had much preferred Ambassador Ryan Crocker, who had helped unify political-military efforts. But with Hill, the armed forces and the State Department have two different objectives in a country resisting civil war.[3]

The INM press Maliki to step down, but he is recalcitrant. Among his biggest supporters are President Obama and Vice President Joseph Biden.

Maliki is "their guy" despite his divisive conduct and accusations. When Hill is replaced by the able Jim Jeffery in August it is too late. "By coming out in support of Maliki the US had lost its ability to broker an agreement among Iraqi's leader." Leaving Iraq now is more important than leaving Iraq viable. It is an inversion of the Bush doctrine: strike and have no plan beyond leaving.[4] And Sky has reached her limit. "I was running on empty. It was as if everything I had ever learned, every experience of my life, had been in preparation for serving in Iraq during this tumultuous period. But by the end there was nothing left. I was exhausted."[5]

Sky's enemies are legion. She is an adversary for many U.S. military officials and the State Department. Her greatest champion is Odierno, who had once been deemed part of the intellectually deficient and culturally illiterate soldiers that compounded the failure after the invasion.[6] Yet Odierno emerges second only to Gen. David Petraeus for engineering the U.S. Army's first COIN strategy since Vietnam and with successes. It required a skill Odierno didn't have: cultural knowledge, conflict management, and diplomacy. Sky has them all, but also refused to bend to his unwavering American pride.

"You made me a better general." Odierno said before she left.

How she did so speaks to the value of mavericks of war.

"I Never Felt Limited By Gender"

Emma Sky was born in a working-class home in London, 1968. She was raised by a single mother whose work as a live-in housekeeper at the Ashfold boarding school afforded them the chance to have Emma attend. She fit in well with the adventurous boys and the writings of explorer-adventurers in foreign land like Thor Heyerdahl, J. H. Speke, and Richard Burton. "I never felt limited by gender," she recalled. "I played for the school's junior soccer team, going by the name of Fred Blogs during matches so the opposition would not know I was a girl."[7] She also endured Northern Irish boarding schools "which felt like a prison," before returning to England and attending The Old Ride as the only girl. "It was a *Lord of the Flies* experience, dealing with nasty boys who did not want a girl 'contaminating' their school." She endured chauvinism, aced her classes, and won a scholarship at thirteen to the Deal Close school in

Cheltenham where she was a jock, army cadet, and excellent student who rebelled against its evangelical Christian doctrine. After Kibbutz in Israel, she returned a self-professed "humanist."[8]

Thanks to support for low-income families, she attended the alma mater of Lawrence, Bell, and Woodhouse. At Oxford, she focused on "Oriental Studies" as the first Intifada broke out in December 1987. Leonard Cheshire, Victoria Cross winner, philanthropist, and conflict management expert, inspired Sky with a talk of life in service and not in wealth.[9] "I had taken Edmund Burke's maxim as my own. All it takes for evil to triumph is for good men to do nothing." In her second year she studied at the University of Alexandria, Egypt, and worked in the West Bank for a Palestinian NGO dealing with food independence. "I experienced life under occupation, carrying an onion to bite on when tear gassed and learning how to get around Israeli checkpoints. I came to understand the insecurity of Palestinian's lives and their yearning for justice."[10]

Despite hardships at home, Sky took her degree and headed for North Africa and Egypt again, doing journalism before crossing the Sinai to Jerusalem where she lived for two years.[11] In 1993, as the Arab/Israeli Peace Process was brightest, she worked for a committee involved with the Middle East Peace Process, visited Palestinian refugee camps, and worked in reconciliation. Moving to Jerusalem Sky worked for the British Council members involved with Palestinian Authority's public services. She created and managed projects in civil service, government and law, and human rights, and built bridges between Palestinians and Israelis. On November 4, 1995, Prime Minister Yitzhak Rabin was assassinated, and "[a]ll the progress of the Oslo Accords was lost." She remained working in the Middle East for the better part of the decade.[12]

Sky returned to the United Kingdom in 2001 as the tragedy of 9/11 instigated the race to war in Afghanistan (2001) and Iraq (2003). She opposed the Iraq war and its stupidity, but she was concerned about the power vacuum in such an ethnically diverse state. When the British Foreign Office asked for volunteers to do three-month terms, she took her skills in Arabic, conflict resolution, and postconflict development and joined the Coalition Provisional Authority (CPA).[13]

The CPA was the American-led organization created to run Iraq after the fall of Saddam Hussein and his Baathist party. They were to initiate the transition to a new Iraqi-run state government. CPA was a mix of chaos, expertise, and naiveté headquartered in the Green Zone of Baghdad and filled with old guard diplomats and experts, business professionals tied to the Republican party, government employees, and grad students, all under the auspices of Ambassador Lewis Paul Bremer III. CPA's mandate was to examine the country as fifteen provinces plus Kurdistan. Each province had a senior civilian who coordinated their efforts and administered the province with U.S. military, Iraqis, and local leadership.[14] Sky arrived in Basra, but no one was expecting her. Heading to Baghdad on her own, she was told by CPA there was greater need in the province of Kirkuk. With no immediate job description, "I interpreted what my role should be."[15]

". . . I Will Take You to the Hague"

Col. William Mayville, U.S. commander of the 173rd Airborne Brigade of the 4th Infantry Division (4ID), worked out of the old Baathist governor's office. He was "sometimes a quiet and thoughtful introvert, other times bouncing with energy and enthusiasm, other times furious." He was dismissive of CPA and its chaotic mess, but had little knowledge of the region he was now in charge of. His unit had only come to Kirkuk when Turkey denied America rights to the area. "We focused in on Kirkuk because of the oil," he told reporters in December 2003, "and because of the concern of the Kurds what would happen if the Kurds were seen to be taking Kirkuk, and what would that mean to our allies and friends to the north." The complexity of the region was studied at the last minute.[16]

Sky survived a rocket attack on her accommodations. Unlike Bremer, whose security team followed him into bathrooms, she "had no bodyguards to protect me when I was away from the house, nor armoured cars to transport me, even though regulations stated that I should only go out in one."[17] Mayville promised her the attackers would be hunted, but Sky countered they weren't attacking her. "They were attacking the symbols of foreign occupation, and they deserve to be given a trial if arrested." She showed him the Fourth Geneva Convention on her laptop. "From my years working in the Palestinian territories, I regarded the Convention as the legal framework for the conduct of any occupying army. . . . If I find you in violation of any of the articles, I will take you to the Hague."[18] From such friction are friends and enemies made.

Sky's knowledge, initiative, and capacity to build bridges and gather intelligence were soon put to work. "She seemed in control of everything in her domain," Fred Kaplan argued, "reaching out to all the sectarian groups; coordinating the brigade's civil-affairs soldiers with AID officials and nonprofit volunteers, and, all the while speaking to any and all military officers, of whatever rank, with brutal frankness."[19] Knowledge and frankness bought her salience with Mayville. She could do what he couldn't. So, he shared what he knew. The major strife was between the Kurds and the Arabs. Kurds made the majority of the population, but Hussein's regime "Arabized" the region and displaced Kurds from power. Many returned for reclamation, and abandoned weapons from the Iraqi Army–fed violence. Coalition forces restored order by April 17, and public sector workers returned within a week as top Baathist officials vanished. Kurds backed political parties to establish control of Erbi and Sulaymaniah. Arabs and former officials feared the retaliation of "Kurdification."[20] On May 17, coalition forces suppressed an attack by Arabs on Kurdish sectors of town and Colonel Mayville established a thirty-member provincial Council to mitigate the violence.[21] Sky worked side by side with Mayville and met with community leaders, touring villages while traveling in SUVs and Humvee convoys that never made her feel safe. "Our presence on the roads was obtrusive. We looked like, and were, an occupying army."[22] She also filled in blanks for Mayville about Arab culture and history, even if her specific knowledge of Iraq was general.[23] This included notes on Hussein's abuse of and gassing of the Kurds, Kurdish uprisings done at the behest of a U.S. Army that then decided to not invade Iraq in 1991 that Hussein violently repressed, of the power of oil in the region, and how two Kurdish parties, the Kurdistan Democratic Party (KDP) and Patriotic Union of Kurdistan (PUK), had waged a civil war until the U.S. invasion.[24] Displacement of peoples fueled violence and division, but "the coalition policy was for displaced people to stay put while we developed a legal framework to deal with competing property claims." Managing the space in-between was improvised. Coalition forces had not been trained for these kinds of cultural and political outreaches, making Sky invaluable.[25] She worked on claims for "land, water, oil, minority rights, citizenships, identity and allegiance." No one would budge. All had past grievances. "And the CPA had not developed a strategy to address past conflict, manage current conflict and prevent future conflict, nor did it have the political legitimacy to do so." So an interim solution was needed. To do that, she'd need to master her military environment.[26]

Sky worked at the Tactical Operations Center and learned to speak military, receiving fragmentary orders (FRAGOS) and collecting data, all while the Orwellian American Forces Network blasted commercials and programming on fitness, insurance, and how the army was looking after your every need. Sky and Mayville gathered intelligence in the field. Her ability to work among Kurdish and Arab concerns, especially regarding property and land claims, helped the U.S. forces appear just.[27] Conversely, she tried to understand how American soldiers, or "the American Tribe," operated in Iraq.

"I Could Well Understand Why Iraqis Were Shooting at Us"

"What do we need to be loved?" one soldier asked her.

"I said that after the First Gulf War of 1990–1991 a decade of sanctions with its devastating effects on the health, education, and the economy, and the humiliating defeat of the Second Gulf War, I could well understand why Iraqis were shooting at us." Americans soldiers were invaders who had killed civilians. Expecting love was ridiculous.

"Who are you going to believe, a West Point graduate or a lying Arab?" another officer barked at a meeting when Sky disagreed with him. She challenged the morally and politically simplistic and dangerous binary thinking "Good Guys" (pro-American or Kurd) and "Bad Guys" (anti-American or Arab). Reality was more nuanced. "I wanted to understand who we were fighting and what they wanted. I tried to argue that how we treated people would affect how they reacted to us. But the military did not do nuance. . . . And they were sure they were always right."[28]

Arrogance and ignorance was something Sky fought to change over the course of her time in Iraq, but contempt was rife for Arabs and others in "man dresses" giving "man kisses to each other," living in "mud huts." Respect was to be bought and culture was for aid agencies or State. This racist, homophobic, and simplistic attitude made no sense to anyone working in aid organizations, conflict resolution, or foreign affairs. While Secretary of Defense Donald Rumsfeld and others preached for years that anything resembling nation-building was nonmilitary business, the failures of the Iraq war had proved otherwise.[29]

Sky was seconded to CPA for Kirkuk, but she was a British volunteer "with no money and very few staff, and was reliant on the army for my basic 'life support.'" Clearly, postwar planning had not been done. The military was now working overtime despite its security focus to do work on priority project for the provinces.[30] "Tank commander were working on economic development, paratroopers on governance, civil affairs officers on education."[31] The CPA agenda was a fantasy. The "Government in a box" concept of experts deployed with ready-made systems "was a mythical, not magical concept." Sky would have no support beyond the military. She worked with Mayville to start finding nonmilitary metrics for success, empowering Iraqis to take over tasks.[32]

Sky soon became POLAD to Mayville when officials visited. They operated almost as an island in the sea, with little instruction or contact from Baghdad or London, and her rancor against U.S. soldiers eased as shared experiences built trust. Kirkuk is where she met Major General Odierno, commander of the 4ID, based in Tikrit, Hussein's old hometown. The 4ID had been aggressive in their operations and occupation of Tikrit, ignoring much of the outreach with the local populace done by the outgoing Marines. Odierno, a massive soldier with the frame of a professional wrestler, was on record thinking there was no insurgency in the region, dismissing evidence a guerrilla operation as criminal conduct, and demonstrating little knowledge of how insurgencies start or function.[33] He was surprised to find an anti-war advocate advising one of his subordinates.[34] Odierno asked Sky why there was still instability in Kirkuk when most of the Baathists had been killed or had fled. "Kirkuk sits on top of 40 per cent of the Iraq's oil reserves," she said, "6.7 percent of the world's." This is why Hussein tried to ethnically cleanse the region and make it Arab. She briefed him on this "state-building challenge" and Odierno took to the confident, capable, and frank Sky.[35]

Sky met with leaders of Arab, Kurd, and Turkmen groups and discussed with Mayville how Kirkuk's situation might be stabilized if their "special status" was recognized. But her papers on this policy were never read in Baghdad, and, when she managed to steal time with Bremer and pushed him on the topic, she earned a trip to Baghdad to make her case. It went nowhere.[36] Even into the maelstrom of 2006, the U.S. government refused to broker any move to make Kirkuk "special" for fear it would be a powder keg for a civil war.[37]

Governance was also thorny. CPA Order Number 1, May 2003, established that the top four ranks of the Baathist party would never be allowed to hold power in government. But since Hussein had made membership mandatory for government work and public sector jobs such as teaching, there was an instant power vacuum. Many Baathists were branded die-hard Hussein followers, even secondary school teachers.[38] When 540 teachers from Hawja were expelled for these reasons, Sheikh Wasfi of the Provincial Council told Sky in September 2003 that Sunnis were taking up arms. The coalition had no strategy for what to do with thousands of civil servants and soldiers of Saddam's regime who were now unemployed: they were instant fuel for an insurgency.[39] Sky's reports to CPA HQ in Baghdad did nothing. "They did not feel the devastating impact of this order on people's lives." Odierno saw the rift that de-Baathification held in Kirkuk, so he issued an amnesty for all level-four Baath party members in his three provinces. Teachers and doctors returned to schools and hospitals. Baghdad CPA refused to fund it, so the military bankrolled until the funds dried.[40] Sky also met Gen. Ricardo Sanchez, the humorless commander of U.S. forces in Iraq. "What's the corruption like?" he asked, assuming Arab graft as a norm.

"Sir, the American soldiers aren't too bad." Someone had to explain that Sky was kidding. Despite his interest in civil infrastructure, Sanchez was tone deaf to the deeper issues, including the political nature of violence in the country.[41] Sky could have left, but she had her contract extended and immersed herself in Kirkuk. Investigating police corruption, she met with Abdel-Fatah Mousawi, a prominent Shia Arab from Najaf and follower of Muqtada al-Sadr, a powerful religious and political leader south of Baghdad. Sadr had not been included in the Iraqi Governing Council and saw the Coalition as an enemy to his own ambitions and his Shia followers. In October 2003, Sky and Mayville meet Mousawi. War between Arab and Coalition-backed Kurds was imminent, he believed.[42] Mayville pressed for time to diversify leadership and root out corruption and created a bridge to the Shia as orders grew for the arrest of Sadrists. But Sky wanted contact with Mousawi. "We took the decision that it was better to try to work with him for as long as we could." After their initial meeting he chose to work through a colleague.

Sky and, in turn, the U.S. military would learn more about Mousawi and Muqtada, and his militia Jaysh al-Mahdi (JAM), as powerful factions. She researched the relationships between unemployment, security, and basic needs, while confronting American arrogance: Dr. Ismail Abud, director of the Employment Office and vocal critic of the Provincial Government, was forced to wear an American flag, as a member of the public sector, which made him a target for accusations of corruption and being an American toady.[43] Ignorance continued on issues of wealth and power. She had to correct Paul Wolfowitz, a chief instigator of the war in Iraq as deputy of defense, who visited Kirkuk in October 2003. He couldn't understand why the oil wealth of the province wasn't fueling state building. He had ignored lack of modern infrastructure and investment, Sky noted, "[a]nd insurgents kept blowing up the pipelines."[44]

"The Kurds Are Seeking to Redress Thirty-Five Years of Ethnic Cleansing in the Coalition's Time Frame"

Washington accelerated the timetable for a new Iraqi government. The entire creation of the political process for a free, democratic, and independent Iraq was to be done within seven months. Kirkuk became a battleground between Arab and Kurd. Sky worked with Arab leaders held captive by Kurdish factions, settled land disputes, informed Bremer that the capture of Saddam by Odierno's forces had not decreased the violence, and prepared for the departure in December 2003.[45] Demonstrations grew through the month; some were cover for political action for various factions, including the KDP. Sky argued for freedom of demonstrations despite the growing violence.[46] In early 2004, U.S. soldiers returned to the streets for added security. Mayville warned Kurdish leaders against fueling a civil war, and Sky deduced that the plethora of civil society organizations were fronts for political action by the Kurds, some of which were harboring RPGs.[47] "The Kurds are seeking to redress thirty-five years of ethnic cleansing in the Coalition's time frame," she told Bremer during a visit. "But the Kurdish drive to make Kirkuk part of Iraqi Kurdistan is rejected by Arabs and Turkmen-and leading them to seek allies in Turkey and Syria." A strategic framework to open dialog on mutual security and peace was needed. Sky outlined the rise of Kurdish power and argued for multiethnic plurality for all the displaced, and the Coalition needed to be viewed as legitimate. Bremer agreed, then had Sky seconded to his governance team in Baghdad within the CPA Green Zone.[48]

"We Had Invaded Iraq, Rid It of Saddam and Promised the Iraqi People a Better Future."

In February 2004, Sky entered the Green Zone. She attended meetings at the al Rashid Hotel, where the Governing Council met and many of the new government agencies worked. Senior operators with great influence worked here, but were least interested in Sky.[49] So she built her own network of intelligence and information outside of the governance team. These included veteran U.S. diplomats Ron Schilcher, Chris Ross, and Ron Neumann. "All three had spent a large part of their careers in the Middle East, loved the cultures and had a strong affinity for the people." Schilcher was in charge of the Office of Provincial Outreach, and focused on Sunni and tribal outreach alongside British diplomat David Richmond.[50] He was her conduit about what happened in the rest of the country while she'd focused on Kirkuk. "He described how de-Baathification, the dissolving of the military and the closure of state-owned enterprises had left hundreds of thousands of Iraqis jobless and angry." This led to large cordon operations against "military-age" men, and increasing resentment against the United States. "Ron was constantly battling with the US military to get detained Iraqis released."[51] Ross was a retired U.S. ambassador and executive director of NGO Search for

Common Ground. Sky pushed Kirkuk for special treatment. "We had a moral duty: we had invaded Iraq, rid it of Saddam and promised the Iraqi people a better future." If civil war erupted, the values of these actions would die. Sky's drive helped inspire him to find a way to make Kirkuk's special status stick.

The interim constitution was called the Transitional Administrative Law (TAL). Kirkuk was central to the discussion. Article 58 included issue of Arabization and the need to resettle, compensate, and support those who had now been displaced. "But there were no Arabs on the Governing Council who were sensitive how this might be perceived in Kirkuk." While the TAL was signed, outrage by the disposed Arabs followed. Muqtada al-Sadr was an instant enemy of the TAL. While the CPA tried to assuage the public, violence rose through the country.[52]

"... The Coalition Did Not Understand Who It Was Fighting"

—February, 2004.

The 82nd Airborne pulled back from patrolling Fallujah. Responsibility lay with the new Iraqi Security forces. As violence increased through March, including the death and mutilation of four Blackwater employees, U.S. Marines sent a cordon of troops, tanks, and artillery around the city to root out the estimated 2,000 insurgents, many of the Sadrists. When the Marines went in, the Iraqi security forces deserted. The Siege of Fallujah was a bloody nightmare. Twenty-seven Marines died, and close to 200 Sadrists, mujahedeen, Baathist, and other factions died. Fear rose and attacks on the Green Zone increased. But who was responsible?[53]

"I was becoming increasingly alarmed that the Coalition did not understand who it was fighting," Sky wrote to Mayville. "There were elements in Iraq that had not been here a year ago. Local resistance to the occupation was combating with Islamist militants. And many Iraqis who had looked to us in gratitude for liberating them from Saddam now wanted us gone as soon as possible." Most of the coalition viewed the enemy as Arab or criminals. Such thinking fed enemy ranks. When U.S. forces mistakenly bombed a wedding party, killing over forty civilians, the military spokesman glibly commented that "even bad guys have weddings."[54]

Sky took new British commander Gen. John McColl on tour of the north. In Ebril, he asked, "Do you think we are facing massive strategic failure?" Her answer was an "obvious" yes. Yet CPA wasn't interested in inconvenient truths, thus new strategy was irrelevant. The goal was the handover of government to the Iraqis on June 30.[55] Bremer established an "outreach strategy" to bring different communities into the Green Zone while pushing President Bush's plan for Iraq to become a democracy by January 2005, with government legitimacy established and rule of law in place.

It was a pipe dream (the Founding Fathers of the United States took four years to work the Bill of Rights into the Constitution). Borders were weak and undefended, there was little internal security, and starvation existed in some quarters. "An environment of violence had been created. Democracy couldn't exist in such an environment of be developed under such conditions in a matter of days."[56] Bremer remained positive to the point of delusion. The Iraqis now had "freedom," which made the generals look mystified. Sky realized the United States had no real plans, just hopes and assumptions. "Only 150,000 US troops had been deployed to Iraq because Rumsfeld had insisted on the minimum and wanted to downscale immediately, to avoid the US military becoming involved in 'Nation building.'" In April 2004, the Abu Ghraib prison abuse scandal fueled hatred for the American Forces. Sky visited the facilities after their supposed reformation, but a year later was shocked to see detainees in tents—no real shelter, gripping the fences, and yelling about the injustice and lack of rights.[57] It was more fuel for the insurgents about abusive, imperial Americans.

Time draining, Sky forestalled violence in Kirkuk with diplomatic outreach and dialogues with Sunnis, and even visited the volatile Sunni Triangle northwest of Baghdad as assassinations and violence strained relations between factions. But even with Bremer's backing, pluralistic initiatives like the "Kirkuk Foundation" failed to establish itself as a viable option.[58]

Her words echo Fall's critique on on early U.S. involvement in Vietnam. "I had been part of a modern-day Crusade of ideologues and idealists . . . people who believed they could bring liberal democracy to

Iraq and hence to the Middle East." Cultural ignorance and idealism had made Americans resistant to realism as she left Iraq and the country continued to collapse.[59]

"... This Is the Greatest Strategic Failure Since the Foundation of the United States"

Post Iraq, Sky worked a variety of jobs: a conflict management task force in the United Kingdom, POLAD to American general William Kip Ward in Africa, a developmental advisor to Italian and then British Forces in Afghanistan, and for a NGO focused on historical urban areas.[60] But in August 2006, Sky received an email from General Odierno to become his political officer (POLAD) in Iraq at Multi National Force-Iraq (MNF-I). She agreed, with classic British understatement. "I did not want to miss the opportunity to help him make the situation in Iraq a little less worse."[61]

In January 2007, Sky returned as the "Surge" strategy for Iraq went from contested idea to policy. While not part of these dialogues, Sky rode the crest of the return of counterinsurgency practices within the U.S. military despite many adversaries in the White House, the Pentagon, and Bush's inner circle. Under the command of Gen. David Petraeus, who spearheaded the creation of the first U.S. Army counterinsurgency field manual since Vietnam, U.S. forces sent an additional 20,000 troops to embark on a mix of nation-building efforts, increased operations against enemy forces as well as attempting to win the "hearts and minds" of the Iraqi people and several factions of influence and power against the most dangerous and radical insurgents. Given the violence around the capital, the initial surge focused on Baghdad.[62] Sky shadowed Odierno, going everywhere he went, attending meetings, and offering a different perspective. Many saw her as an interloper.

Iraq had witnessed skyrocketing violence among the population, an embryonic civil war with international players like Iran as key members, and little faith in the "independent" government. Prime Minister Nuri al-Maliki was thought by President Bush to be the best chance of holding Iraq together as U.S. strategy shifted from negligence to the surge. Odierno, despite senior rank and career success, was not a natural for the political and civilian focus of the crash-COIN program. Sky's expertise gave him credibility and insight. She was a conduit of intelligence, political troubleshooting on civil/military relationship, and understanding of the cultural environment in which they were fighting (she spoke Arabic). If he didn't have the skills for COIN's "winning the population," Sky did.[63]

Sky attended Battle Update Assessments (BUA), which connected the MNF-I with corps and divisions. The lingo, alphabet soup, and volume of information being pushed at division level were daunting, but data divorced from any human aspect was of little value to Sky. She culled media, interrogation reports, and Friday sermons from mosques, which the coalition recorded and translated. Still, she was seated behind the chief of staff, closer to the inner circle than she had been in Bremer's group. And she was no less blunt.

"Sir," she said on one occasion, "this is the greatest strategic failure since the foundation of the United States."

"What are we going to do about?" he responded. "We're not leaving it like this."

But Odierno had been part of the problem. He was among the most accomplished soldiers of his generation, but without depth of education or experience beyond the army. "He had total faith in America, in the government, in the system." Odierno refused to imagine a world where his government would lie. The weapons of mass destruction (WMD) fiasco wasn't malice, just a mistake.

Thankfully, working with Sky had awoken him to potentials beyond force-oriented idealism. She was a subordinate, but her job was to speak truth to power *at him*. She became, in her words, "his 'conscience.'"[64] And he and his men needed it. The door-kicking and mass arrests that had tarnished his reputation as commander of 4ID were actions that fueled the insurgency.[65] At a BUA, an officer reported that there were five killed in action (KIA) in Diyala. And an improvised explosive device (IED) emplacer was killed. "The atmospherics were positive," noted the officer, meaning the operation played well with the locals.

"Who were the other four people killed?" Odierno asked.

"Four children, sir, who were in the vicinity."

Silence. Sky later asked, "Sir, I noted the briefer said that the atmospherics were good. Do you think they were fat children, or they were doing badly at school?" Black humor was rife, but Sky made it clear that dead children helped create fresh enemies at ration of 1:4. How was this good atmospherics?[66]

Sky challenged assumptions made about "ancient hatreds" between Sunni and Shia. There had been periods of peace and understanding within these communities. The universal hatred of the Baath party had made the state the supreme evil, and much of that evil lay in its corruption. But since the Baath party had been in power since the late sixties, there was no civil service class to inherit the throne. It was a free-for-all of old grievances. By 2006, Shia Islamists won the majority of the elections and formed alliances with the PUK and KDP. The current political system favored the large parties. "Secular and liberal parties had neither funds nor militias to promote their vision of a nonsectarian Iraq. The majority of Sunnis boycotted the elections." By December 2005, "the Shia and Kurds had already 'captured' the state."[67] Insurgency became civil war. Iran backed the Shia and foreign jihadist who looked for the next fight in the holy war. Al Qaeda in Iraq was born in this cauldron and perpetrated much of the atrocities. Shia militias who had fought against Iraq during the war with Iran joined the security forces. Sunnis fled into their own insurgent groups. Again, the need was reconciliation as much as CT.[68]

In January 2007, Sky wrote an assessment for Odierno that mirrored her critiques of U.S. visions of the enemy in Kirkuk: end binary identities of enemies and friends and focus on motivation, connections with security forces, and the depth of corruption. A strategy of outreach was needed. "With the majority of the violence caused by sectarian conflict, our effort should focus on protecting the population, suppressing the violent actors and brokering agreements between different groups."[69]

"The New Religion Was Counterinsurgency"

Sky served on Odierno's initiative group to define the nature of these threats and how to respond, along with four colonels, Derek Harvey, Mike Meese, Robert Taylor, and Gary Volesky. "We redefined 'success' in a much more modest way as "sustainable stability" and identified *drivers of instability,* namely sectarian violence, al Qaeda in Iraq (AQI), Sunni insurgency, Shia extremists, Kurdish expansionism, Shia-on-Shia violence, external subversion, criminality and weak state institutions."[70] Risks included being used by one faction to "cleanse" another as communities fought each other, and the government was also considered "part of the problem."[71] This matched with the incoming commander of the Multi-National Force—Iraq, Gen. David Petraeus, on February 10, 2007. "The new religion was Counter Insurgency," and it concurred with Sky's own judgment that the target wasn't the enemy, it was the populace.[72] Odierno briefed Petraeus on the situation, using his favorite PowerPoint slide: "the gap slide."

"Coalition forces were needed to displace the armed groups and fill in the 'gap' [vacuum of power, order, and stability] until the Iraqi government had developed the capacity to do so." The surge bought time and legitimacy for this to occur.[73] Petraeus agreed. The initiative group was disbanded, operations planned, and troops moved out to live and work with the Iraqis, sharing the burden and risk while keeping Iraqi security forces accountable. Sky's work validated Odierno and the Americans as she interacted with Iraqi officials and citizens, a step toward legitimacy.[74]

Sky worked on the critical tome Baghdad Security Plan, named *Fard al-Qanun* or Operation Imposing Law. She also worked with Gen. Abud Qanbar, selected by Maliki for the Baghdad Operations Command (BOC), in charge of all Iraqi army, police, and security forces. Others in the BOC included Hussel al-Awadi, the head of national police, and Gen. Ali Ghaidan, head of Iraqi ground forces. Sky watched meetings with the BOC. They agreed at a Ministerial Committee for National Security that after military operations were run in the major neighborhoods the focus would be on essential services. The insurgents had knocked out all the lights in the capital, making night deadly. Hospitals were also potential death traps since the Sadrists ran the Ministry of Health, and reports of JAM killing Sunnis grew. When Sky's contract was closing, Odierno had the British agree to a one-year extension.[75]

Sky rode with new Ambassador to Iraq Ryan Crocker among the populace since he wanted to see how the troops lived among the people, conducting foot patrols, and worked with people on the street to gather data and asses grievances.[76] As the surge ran through April, 117 Coalition members died. Violence was still high. Working with those who were perpetrating it, instead of solely seeing them as enemies, required a paradigm shift. The major ray of hope was the Anbar "Awakening" in 2006, where Sunni insurgents under Sheikh Sitar Abu Risha turned their sights on al Qaeda in Iraq and stopped fighting with the coalition. That enemies could be allies seemed an opportunity too good to pass up, even if it was inconceivable months before when there were only good guys and bad guys. Now there were intelligence officers who understood the complexity and diversity of Iraqi militias and other groups. Under Col. Jerry Tait, this team of primarily women intelligence officers targeted the differences that could help separate insurgents, separating potential partners from diehards. Lt. Col. Nycki Brooks had a "much more sophisticated understanding of Iraqis and what moved them" than other senior officers."[77] Among Odierno's other assets was the British deputy to Petraeus, Gen. Graeme Lamb, known as "Lambo," a commander of the Special Air Service (SAS) and veteran of Northern Ireland. Tough, smart, and unconventional, he was not soft on enemies. But when arguments arose about refusing to deal with those with blood on their hands, "Lambo pointed out that he and others had very bloody hands." Lambo "would never have survived in the US military culture of political correctness." Smart, rude, and crude, he was also relentless in changing the American view of the war. Reconciliation could stop the insurgents from fighting. There had to be options besides join or die; that was the mantra of the enemy. Persuasion and coercion needed to work in tandem.

These were soldiers Sky could work with.

"It Was Difficult to Convince Her of the Coalition's Incompetence"

Thanks to the surge, fighting the coalition was now less cost-effective and many Sunnis who had been insurgents now wanted to work with the United States. And the coalition still needed data on who they were and their motivations. Some groups were in the thousands. Others were a tribe. "A number of US commanders on the ground where following the example set by Col. Sean MacFarland in Anbar, doing deals with previously hostile Sunnis."[78] The Sunni Awakening gave the surge somewhere to go, find purchase, and reduce violence against the coalition and rout

out al Qaeda. Loyalty would be bought, as it had been with guerrillas and insurgents for centuries. But there was resistance from Maliki, who feared them becoming part of the security force. This included the Concerned Local Citizen (CLC) groups: Sunnis who had been abandoned by the regime, enemies of the minority Shia in his government, some with ties to insurgent groups and Iran.[79] Indeed, evidence of Shia militias working for or within the Maliki government began to grow. And the Shia insurgents propagated the narrative that the coalition worked exclusively with Sunnis. Dealing with Maliki's chief of Staff, Sky argued that JAM's murder of coalition member had to stop. The Shia were not the enemy but the Sadrists had to stop attacking the coalition.

Sky also worked through the Iraqi government. Maliki was out of reach, so she cultivated other influences. Dr. Basima Jadiri, a Shia woman who was military adviser to the prime minister, was considered a sectarian agent by U.S. intelligence. Some accused her of operating most militias and death squads. Sky thought this absurd.[80] She met Basima and found a tough, intelligent ally in a male- and military-dominated world. She also met Gen. Abu Mohamad, director of intelligence at the Office of the Commander-in-Chief (OCINC). Basima believed that Maliki had the "stature of Nelson Mandela" and believed in his leadership, and both were suspicious of American intent. Sky tried to explain the influence of neocon thinking on U.S. strategy and the invasion. "Basima started at me incredulously. 'How can a country such as America, a country that can put a man on the moon, not know what it is doing? How can the US not have had a plan for Iraq after removing Saddam?' It was difficult to convince her of the Coalition's incompetence." But admitting that it existed likely bought her another ounce of trust.[81] OCINC also had a faction in opposition to Basima, under Lt. Gen. Farouq al-Araji, who maintained preeminence in advising Maliki."[82]

The three promoted and extended reconciliation among Shia and Sunni toward common purpose as well as common enemy. They tried to rehire soldiers and find them work in civilian jobs. Sky acted as a new broker, since according to OCINC, the Coalition hated them and thus the information flow on their work was stymied. They actually believed that the Coalition was hostile to reconciliation. Sky broke the block. Information was shared, in part because she was anti-war and not American. But it was still a challenge to win her trust. Sky knew she was an agent of influence and could get things done. But Sky fought on many fronts.

"I was continually up against US officers who remained antagonistic towards the prime minister's advisers and argued that we should push ahead our deals with the Sunni groups regardless of the Iraqi government." Sky countered that if they supported Sunnis fighting al Qaeda "while ignoring the concerns of the Iraqi government, we would fuel Maliki's paranoia that we were seeking to overthrow him; we would create more militias; and we would weaken the state by creating alternative power centers."[83] Even Odierno accused Sky of "going native," of being a pessimistic sympathizer with the Iraqis with her work in OCINC. After being dressed down by her boss she realized she may have let him believe that she, his most trusted advisor, had abandoned him.

Changing his mind required solutions. She wrote a note on requiring understanding of the motivations of all these actors and to co-opt Sunnis into stakeholders in the new Iraqi forces. But such tasks must be backed by a political process or the security forces could become dominated by one party or group. "We needed our senior leaders to push the Iraqi government toward national dialogue. And we needed to set a time limit for these groups to be incorporated into the Iraqi security forces or be disbanded." Odierno agreed. This became part of the complex Coalition effort to harness the "Sunni Awakening."

Sky worked with Basima, Lamb, and others building bridges to Maliki on this initiative through new cells and committees.[84] Sky gathered intelligence to make up her own assessment, worked with people the military disdained, and managed to find via them partners. These would help ideas that men like Lamb had initiated to be part of a broader, legitimized strategy. When Petraeus and Crocker were meeting with Maliki to push for reconciliation with the Sunni, Odierno told Sky to meet one more time with OCINC to get them to accept a series of Sunni recruits. Basima was aggravated and didn't want to talk. Sky discovered that they had in fact agreed to 1,700-plus members. But they had not pressed the Maliki on it, nor told him of their choices. Sky told her and Abu

Mohamad that Petraeus and Crocker were en route to meet Maliki, and believed that he'd rejected the idea of the group. They don't think he can or will reconcile with the Sunnis. They need to have this information, of a fait accompli, now. Basima called the Maliki and Sky called Petraeus. Next morning at the BUA, thousands of soldiers listening, Petraeus said that he'd had a great meeting with Maliki and congratulated him on his discussion to reconcile with the Abu Azzam and his men.

"Ray," Petraeus said, "your POLAD saved the day."

Odierno joked "She is an insurgent!" The room laughed.[85]

"JIHAD SHOWED WHAT WAS POSSIBLE AT A LOCAL LEVEL WHEN WE ALL WORKED TOGETHER"

By August 2007, fatalities had dropped: 131 in May, 108 in June, and 89 in July. Local Sunni men held checkpoints where there had been no security. Violent acts against religious icons and materials did not spark massive rebuttals that increased the violence. With the Sunni forces largely focused on al Qaeda, the greatest threat became Shia militias via explosively formed penetrators (EFPs, bombs). Many had infiltrated Iraqi security forces and targeted enemies within.[86] Sunni areas were "cleansed" by Shia-led units in the national police. Ousting that police chief, and support and training by Italian carabinieri, helped staunch some of the excess corruption.[87] While the Anbar Awakening and Sunni outreach helped mitigate violence, the Iraqi government had "failed to meet most of the eighteen benchmarks established by the White House to measure Progress in Iraq." Petraeus argued with Congress that the weak point was the Maliki government's commitment to reconciliation, and former insurgents had to be part of the solution. Sky and company now had public endorsement for their approach. "When I went around to see Basima and Abu Mohamad they told me they had been following the news closely and were genuinely surprised at the level of recognition of their work." Petraeus and Crocker had bought time for the surge to have sustainable results. Not soon after al Qaeda assassinated Sheikh Sitar of the Abu Risha, whose shift in alliances had led to successes in the Anbar Awakening.[88] Such targeting meant reconciliation not only worked, it was feared by their enemies.

Then, the same month, Sadr announced the suspension of activities from the JAM due to a rise in Shia–Shia attacks, especially in the city of Karbala. This action was done as Coalition initiatives, including a PR campaign that demonstrated the guilt of the JAM in a series of atrocities marked against Shia Arabs, made it clear it was not Sunni or Coalition members responsible.[89] With blame rising against internecine violence, Muqtada al-Sadr said anyone one conducting attacks was not the real JAM. Internal fighting among Shia bought the Coalition an "in" with the Sadrists. Sky knew, however, that reconciliation with Shia militias would be more challenging. "The Sunnis and the Coalition had come together to fight against al-Qaeda. Former Sunni insurgents now took shelter behind the Coalition and saw common cause with us against Iran. The Coalition felt that the Shia should be grateful for their liberation from Saddam: instead, Shia militia attacked our troops and bases"[90]

Petraeus appointed Sky to be his representative with Safa al-Sheigh, head of Maliki's Implementation and Follow up Committee on National Reconciliation (IFCNR). Their goal was to co-opt the Shia. Safa was essentially the superior of Dr. Basima and Gen. Abu Mohamad, a devout Shia who joined the Dawa party (whose ideological founder was Mohamad Baqir al-Sadr, Muqtada al-Sadr's father-in-law). Safa provided insight into Maliki's personality and opinion of the Coalition and now had access to men of Sadr City. According to Petraeus' executive officer Col. Peter R. Mansoor, the IFCNR were not easy to work with, and their sectarian outlook made "compromise with the Sunni groups tricky, but its formation was nevertheless a step in the right direction."[91]

They met with Maliki about reducing violence in Sadr City, but attacks continued from Iranian-made EFPs and Iranian-supplied 240mm rockets. The Green Zone was no longer the target. Camp Victory was. Odierno knew these were criminal elements, not JAM, that could not be ignored. Maliki argued proportional force, and using more Iraqis than coalition members in the raids. Instead, Special Forces raided into Sadr City on October 20. Under fire, they'd called in helicopters. The results played out in Camp Victory and the streets. "The US military claimed forty-nine gunmen were killed. But Iraqi television showed footage of dead women and children." Outrage rose about abusive Americans on the heels of Blackwater security members opening fire in Nissour Square and killing seventeen Iraqis. Maliki was livid and threatened to refuse signing the strategic partnership declaration and more.[92]

Sky worked with Safa on reconciliation among Shia faction, taking the lead in talking with the enemy and, frankly, providing some distance between the U.S. military and the militias. She also saw the trust U.S. soldiers had built with local communities by living with them outside the protective fortifications of the Green Zone. And some new commanders were proving apt at working with Iraqis. Sky built connections between Lt. Col. Patrick Frank, commander of the 28th Infantry Battalion (the Black Lions) in western Baghdad's dangerous Bayaa, Jihad, and Ammal neighborhoods, and Safa and Basima. By September, Frank was working through intermediaries and gathering intelligence against criminal elements and established mutual ceasefires with the Sadrists. He was able to generate monthly meetings with Sunni and Shia leaders and hosted by coalition forces.[93] Shia detainees were released by Odierno. The sands were shifting and new opportunities emerged. Frank and Basima engineered a good working relationship, all "charm and chocolate." Sky worked with Safa on the origin of these attacks to have them stop. If they didn't, the Coalition would hunt them down. Safa then told her about Sadrist leader Abu Abli who was prepared to meet with Lt Col. Franks to help neutralize the attacks. They did not trust the coalition, Safa noted, but they trusted Franks.[94] "While many US officers tried to bulldoze their way past her, he treated her with respect. In the absence of progress at national level on reconciliation, we were brokering local agreements. We had come a long way."[95] But there were still threats and power brokers, like the Islamic Supreme Council of Iraq, who had its own militia, the Badr, who conducted attacks and claimed to be JAM to sow dissent. Sadrist were at war with the ISC, between Arab and Iranian *hawza*. Progress was not stability, let alone peace.[96]

Sky worked with Frank to reconcile Shia Clerics and senior JAM members in West Baghdad, Abu Miriam. The Iraqi Bagdad Division was against it, but Odierno backed Frank. Miriam had a price of $10,000 on his head from the Coalition. Sky worked a meeting with Frank and Abu Miriram. Was he "willing to return to Jihad and to contribute to rebuilding the religious shrines and repairing community relations," Sky asked. "He said he very much wanted to do so."[97] Soon, attacks against Camp Victory dropped as cooperation with the Shia community increased. Sky emphasized that Frank took the lead, though he found her support integral. "I had helped connect Lieutenant Colonel Frank with the Iraqi government. Jihad showed what was possible at a local level when we all worked together."[98]

There were growing successes in reconciliation. American and Iraqi forces and agencies coordinated the inclusion of Sunnis into CLC units, the neighborhood security force that was later rebranded as the "Sons of Iraq" (SOI). They were put to work by the Iraqi government but Maliki was paranoid about the CLC as the enemy within his own palace.[99] Coalition's support for them made it worse. Abu Mohamad warned her about Maliki's growing CLC paranoia, much of it fostered by General Farouq. Odierno believed Maliki was largely sectarian himself, and willing to believe such things.[100] Sky also watched as poor wording and sectarian fears crippled the signing of the Strategic Partnership Declaration. Yet, reconciliation by interest, diplomacy, and money bought time, loyalty, and reduction in violence. December 2007 saw a decrease to 25 soldiers lost and 963 Iraqis killed, down from a monthly total of 3,000 before the surge. The Sunnis had found they stood stronger with the United States against the Shia. The decrease in violence bought time for political change, which was just as hard, if not harder, with Maliki's growing paranoia.

As POLAD, Sky made reconciliation the focus of Odierno's revised commander's intent, changing it from its original focus on military operations. "He had presented my version at the planner's meeting the night before. Gen. John Anderson, the chief of staff, had turned to me, mimicking the slitting of my throat and a bullet through my heart." Clearly, the COIN school had not infected everyone.[101] But Odierno backed her play. His speech included Sky's contribution and role. "Emma has been extremely annoying, but worth the pain." She'd advised him on politics, culture, and strategy. If he ever called, she'd return.[102]

"I Did Not Believe There Was an Overall Strategy . . ."

Petraeus called first, and Sky returned to help Basima with integrating the SOI into the Iraqi Forces, May to June 2008. When Petraeus left to replace outgoing Admiral Fallon as CENTCOM commander, Odierno took his spot at MNF-1. Sky returned in September with no end date in mind. She initially worked with Maj. Joel Rayburn, Petraeus's aide, and soon discovered that Basima and Abu Mohamad were being investigated by Maliki's government, their reconciliation committee stalled. Farouq was the chief instigator. Safa told her of the influx of troops into Sadr city, which the Sadrists were using as a pretext to war with Bardr. The deep breath brought by the surge had expired.

Sky pushed for the Iraqi national elections to be as legitimate as possible. Sky gathered intelligence with Rayburn by meeting with Ayatollah Hussel al-Sadr, uncle of Muqtada. They were joined by Middle East experts Avli Nasr and Peter Bergen. Sadr's followers were the downtrodden and the criminal. "If they had jobs," Ayatollah Hussel al-Sadr noted, "many would get back on the right track." He had talked with over 600 sheikhs from different tribes and groupings at a conference on what could be done. He said his Council would be part of the elections, promoting "non-sectarian" and nonethnic division, but unity.[103] Sky and Rayburn went to Anbar to speak with sheikhs interested in partnering with the United States, who viewed the Americans as better to deal with because the government was Shia-infested and lazy. But there was a growing chorus that Sky heard: Iraqis didn't want sectarian division and violence but a united Iraq.

Petraeus tasked Sky with examining how to define success, in part because he felt he hadn't answered it well when Senator Obama asked him. She reviewed the Joint Campaign Plan. "After I had read the multitude of documents, I sent him a paper explaining that, actually, I did not believe there was an overall strategy which explained why we were not good at defining when the job would be done and the troops could go home. We had development pragmatic tactics in-country to bring down the violence, but there was no overarching strategy at a level above us to which our Joint Campaign Plan contributed."[104] She had just told the most important general in U.S. history since the Vietnam War that he *didn't* have a strategy. He explained the process and structure behind the joint plan and then politely suggested that "military leaders were somewhat sensitive to being told they did not have a strategy, particularly when they had worked rather hard on one!"

"But it was not Petraeus I was criticizing." Or Crocker, the ambassador, whom she saw as a machine of work and a superior realist to Bremer. Unlike CPA, Petraeus and Crocker had unified command between civilian and military, avoided duplication and other problems that had plagued the CPA.[105] Sky had less time for Washington. "They assumed that once the violence dropped, the Iraqi elite would take forward national reconciliation and state building." But since those were the same politicians who instigated the violence to serve their interest, it had not happened. "There seemed to be little chance the Iraqi parliament would pass the specific legislation which Washington had identified as indicators of success."[106]

"I Hate You—So Does Everyone Else"

In September 2008, Odierno returned and the dominant issue for her last years in Iraq was the Status of Force Agreement (SOFA) between the United States and Iraq. Negotiations had stalled. U.S. forces were set to leave in December 2008, and they needed a new legal framework for them to stay and build on the surge. Sky observed how well Crocker worked on the SOFA dialogues. "A master diplomat, he was a good listener and displayed sound judgment. And he often thought out loud, giving us insights into this knowledge of Iraqi history, and why Iraqi politicians were so fearful. It was a revelation to me the way the personality of a leader can shape a whole organization, which became very clear after he was gone and relations broke down."

Sky reshaped the narrative and strategy from counterinsurgency toward Iraqis sovereignty "The greatest threat to Iraq's stability was now the legitimacy and capability of government, rather than attacks by insurgents." She became the target of disdain for some on Odierno's staff who resented her influence. "Stop sending emails directly to General O or I will destroy you," one said. Another accused her of parking her tanks on his lawn. Another grumbled that General Odierno needed Sky more than him, "I was tempted to reply that this was because he was acting like a Neanderthal, but suggested that we were both needed but in different ways and fulfilled different roles." His response?

"I hate you—so does everyone else."[107]

The school-yard misogyny from professional soldiers had far deeper consequences. An anti-American demonstration at Checkpoint 2 nearly became a riot between Iraqis and U.S. forces. Mahmoud Mashhadani, speaker of the Iraqi Parliament, was to work on the SOFA. His son claimed that a U.S. soldier had called his sister a whore, and now the delegation and crowd were at near blows. Sky found the soldier, who claimed he had not said "whore." He had called her a "bitch." The translation done by Iraqi entourage had turned bitch into prostitute. "A thoughtless insult to a young woman had almost jeopardized the legal future of the US troops in Iraq."[108] Yet most soldiers around her found it funny.

SOFA was finally approved, after much wrangling, in November 2008.[109]

"We're Just One Checkpoint Incident Away from a Civil War Here"

Maliki won the election and Iraq began to change into a modern dictatorship as Sky traveled through the country with Safa. She spent the rest of her year in Iraq doing her best to build networks and connections, trust and support, and contacts and outreach with Iraqis on the SOMA, in meetings with Odierno and Maliki, and was even charged with getting Maliki to his first visit with President Obama despite a serious or obstacles. On June 30, 2009, Iraqis took control of the security of their cities. The result in the north was increasing pressure from the Kurds to expand their influence against that of Maliki's government. Odierno sent Sky to work with the commanders in the north to mitigate the problem, and to establish his legitimacy via her presence and reputation in Kirkuk. She took Lt. Col D. J. Jones as her support. Sky tempered his enthusiasm with realism on how deep these wounds were, and that the best they could do was diffuse tension to let them make political decisions. "D. J. soon proved to have the intellect and the temperament for the role." Deputy Brig. Gen. Bob Brown's assessment was, "We're just one checkpoint incident away from a civil war here."[110] They established a ministerial committee with Odierno as chair and senior Iraqi and Kurdish officials.[111] The first meeting at Camp Victory was in August 2009. "I had recommended to General O that he use the initial meeting to get everyone to agree to a set of principles that would guide the work of the group. If we went straight into tactical arrangements, they would contest ever detail."[112] Odierno agreed and six principles were agreed to. The dialogue brokered a deal, with the United States training Kurdish Regional Government forces. This led the Peshmerga (Kurdish militia) to become a single force that had more centralized control. Maliki also agreed to integrating two Kurdish brigades into the Joint Security Architecture in the disputed territories.[113]

Sky worked with the Kurds over disputes on election processes and other grievances. Indeed, among Sky's greatest attributes was her ability to listen and not disdain or judge. She was no fool, she didn't blindly believe every sob story, but she took her role as mediator and node between the Iraqis, the Arabs, the Kurds, and U.S. forces seriously. In the mountains of Kurdistan, she brokered a deal about KDP politburo member Kemal Kirkuki's refusal to budge on negotiations with the Iraqis because of how fiercely he fought for Kurdish rights as a brutalized minority. She managed to work through White House official Molly Phee via satellite link and told her that "the only person who could get him to budge was Masoud Barzani, President of Iraqi Kurdistan himself, and that would require assurances from President Obama."

"The next day, the White House issued a statement saying Obama had spoken to Barzani and had expressed his support for implementation Article 140 of the Constitution which referred to 'normalizing' the situation in the disputed territories—and for the constitutional review which the Sunni Arab nationalists were demanding." The law passed and "Obama's involvement had made the difference."[114] Sky mitigated tensions over Kurdish guerrillas attacking the governor, of Arabs kidnapped and working via the Asayish (Kurdish intelligence) had them returned. None knew why they were being detailed. Once proof of life was had, an exchange for Kurdish detainees was brokered without resort to door-kicking or raids.[115] "We had prevented war breaking out between Arabs and Kurds, had stopped Turkey from invading, and put relations between the Kurds and the US military back on track. Just another day in Iraq."[116]

Odierno had a slide and lecture in which he argued the value of continued joint U.S. and Iraqi cooperation. "I thought he was overly optimistic about the US role in Iraq and the region, but there was no alternative vision coming from anywhere else within the US government."[117] Things worsened when Crocker retired from service in Iraq. He was replaced by Chris Hill, a seasoned diplomat but with no regional experience. For Sky, Hill sunk what gains had been made by his ignorance. He surrounded himself with people who served the White House but thought little of Iraq. They disdained foreigners, tried to Americanize their quarters even worse than the Green Zone, and Sky was seen as a foreign national and possibly a threat. Now Sky had something in common with all U.S. serving personnel. "For the military, the greatest threat to the mission had become the US embassy."[118]

Conclusion

Sky's days in Iraq were up in September 2010. Exhausted, she required connection with the rest of the world and sought to parlay what she'd learned into a broader context. She taught at Oxford, King's College, and Yale University before becoming director of the Yale World Fellows. Her instructive memoir, *The Unravelling*, offered a unique perspective on the postinvasion failures and recoveries of the U.S. Armed Forces in Iraq. Sky works hard in her memoir to credit others, especially Odierno, but it is evident that her role as his "conscience" was just one arrow in the quiver. She was a diplomat who went where soldiers refused to go. She worked with those whom the soldiers disdained. She built bridges and stood in stark contrast to emblems of American power and violence, a diminutive but tough five-foot-five against Odierno's six-foot-plus hulking frame who protested a war she eventually shaped. She could provide legitimacy to those who had none. While many disagreed with the surge, Sky's role speaking truth to power and having the courage to talk to enemies gave credence to the reconciliation strategies in play. On the surge as a whole, Sky noted that the successes were notable. They found the means to prevent escalation of a civil war and the power of reconciliation. But their good works have, as her title states, unraveled. "I think Iraq really brought an end to a sense of international community, and to the idea of

Pax Americana. I think the symptom of that is the inability to deal with the Syrian crisis."[119] Indeed, as more literature emerges about the Anbar Awakening and the rise of ISIS, Sky's efforts may have forestalled the collapse of Iraq, but they cannot be seen as being part of a decisive victory. Perhaps none was possible.[120]

Conclusion

"Don't make him a hero in your book."

These were Lawrence's words to a friend writing about his contemporary Gerard Leachman, whose murder near Fallujah in 1920 started a bloody revolt in Iraq. Leachman's disdain for Arabs, his racist attitudes and preference for "slaughter" over diplomacy, and his inability to tolerate differences in opinion to his own may have made him a successful imperial soldier in the Great War, but it also got him shot in the back. In comparison, Lawrence became a controversial legend. His success in the Arab Revolt and his writings on guerrilla warfare helped shape both the modern Middle East and the nature of insurgent and counterinsurgent warfare that the west has found itself ever since. His death, while dramatic, was an accident.

Lawrence set the standard for a maverick of war, the unconventional expert involved in military affairs that brings knowledge and skills to a military that needs them. As the preceding pages have shown, many people have walked in the invisible footprints Lawrence laid down at Aqaba (though they ran side by side with Gertrude Bell). Now, each maverick fought their own wars in unique times, geography, and historical and cultural contexts. Many had distinct limitations or qualifications on their successes (including how long they could last). And historical case studies must not be seen as ready-made lessons learned. But as the modern saying goes, history does not repeat itself, but if often rhymes. There are many points of mutual consideration in the experience of these mavericks to help understand why some succeeded and others failed. Below are some patterns, echoes, and warnings.

Validated By Success

What transformed Lawrence from an eccentric intelligence officer to an influential operator was the success of Aqaba, a success borne of fatal conditions and done without authorization. Successfully demonstrating one's value to superiors among the Arabs and the British officers bought him saliency for the rest of the revolt. But the success needs to be calibrated by its relationship to the end goal. Aqaba provided the means to support deeper operations in the Levant. Wassmuss's success in the battle of Bushire, his greatest military victory, failed to be demonstrable enough to convince Persian tribes to believe German propaganda on the need for a regional *jihad* against the British. Nor did it secure more funds or support from Berlin (who viewed his mission's greatest value in its ratio of audacity to cost). Woodhouse secured saliency with the Gorgopotomus Bridge demolition with a united guerrilla front, though that saliency was eaten by both the British government and the guerrillas: London with its strategic demand for the return of a Royalist King no one wanted and the communist guerrillas for having their trust betrayed when OP ANIMALS did not produce liberation. The Plaka Agreements recovered Woodhouse more credit with an increasingly impossible strategic goal of starving the communists of support while pursuing liberation of the Germans.

But success wasn't limited to the battlefield; it could be exercised in politics, research, civic rights, and diplomacy. Bell's work in nation-building was instrumental to the establishment of a stable, if troubled, Iraqi kingdom. Du Bois's work supported battles in Burma, including bomb targeting, but was plagued by having two masters for her efforts in South East Asia Command and R&A headquarters in Washington. Lansdale and Bohannan cultivated support for those disenfranchised with Manila's failing efforts against the Huk, including doctrinal and training reform. But their major victory was political: establishing Magsaysay as the legitimate alternative for people to rally. Without this "win" and Magsaysay's own drive to change a failed strategy, the successes that mounted from 1950 onward are hard to imagine. Lansdale also scored initial political victories in helping forge alliances that created South Vietnam, and Bohannan's work with the Chieu Hoi Surrender Program was heralded. But neither could mount a big enough victory to save the post-Diem regime. Fall, as an outsider to the U.S. power structure and a soldier of a foreign army, scored successes within the world of analysis. Frontline data as well as his own analytic mind gave his work credence as his fears of

French and then U.S. strategies played out in real time. Chayes's victories in Afghanistan were initially more existential: she existed in opposition to the corruption of the governor of Kandahar and, in the process, accrued trust, allies, experience, and more. Similarly, Sky's victory was through presence and accountability and building relationships due to her unique status with a U.S.-led occupation army and presence. Success had many colors, but almost all were against the grain of opposition (internal and external).

Backed By Senior Operators

Mavericks must have allies within traditional structures who can negotiate the corridors of power that bristle in the face of outside judgment. Lawrence, Lansdale, Bohannan, Bell, Chayes, and Sky were excellent in this regard. They built trust and support from both indigenous leadership and their own national or international patrons. Wassmuss was abandoned by his government, despite being the only part of the mission to keep fighting until after the end of the war. Woodhouse had support from Myers, but saw the precedent written on the wall when his superior was exiled for challenging the will of Churchill. He had the hardest time negotiating the demands on the ground and the competing interests of his government and the will of the communist guerrillas toward liberation from German domination. Du Bois was perpetually gutted in staff and funds, and if not for her expertise would have been brought back to Washington instead of Kandy. Fall had many fans among soldiers, politicians, and diplomats, but none were willing to back him as an advisor in the way that Gen. Ray Odierno backed Emma Sky in Iraq. What limited his influenced maximized hers.

Fiscal and Other Support

By far the wildest variant, funds for each maverick varied wildly. Success cultivated support. Lawrence after Aqaba could have access to thousands of pounds in gold to buy support and supplies.[1] Bell worked the resources of the major operators in the British India sphere that funded her work in Mesopotamia. Lansdale and Bohannan established Magsaysay as part of economic and political negotiations between the United States and the

Philippines. And, in the case of Lansdale, support often came in the form of funds from the CIA as well as the army and State (though records on this funding are still confidential). Wassmuss remains the outlier, the value of fighting global jihad being its relative inexpensive nature, and, after 1916, support for the venture ended completely. Woodhouse could use levers of support against the Greek guerrillas to cut through communist obstinacy and game-playing, though his influence was compromised when the Italian surrender provided the communists a means to arm themselves independent of British will. Du Bois rallied research efforts with dwindling resources as China became the greater focus of U.S. efforts. Fall took pains to show his objectivity in his funding, proudly noting that the work he was doing in his major trips to Vietnam were not at the behest of a government patron, but even with his resourcefulness his means of participating in the dialog of Vietnam was boxed in within his work. Chayes had a mix of support, from Karzai's family to ISAF, but fought for an ideal as much as the means to influence anti-corruption policy. Sky's access to resources was vast through MNF-1, though much less so under CPA.

Knowledge of Global Peoples before Major Conflict

Most mavericks had either excellent or working knowledge of the foreign cultures, geography, and people in which they found themselves. Or, they had the capacity to learn greatly about them when the time came. This gave them strategic value in filling the "knowledge gap." Lawrence, Bell, Wassmuss, Woodhouse, Du Bois, Bohannan, Chayes, and Sky had spent serious time among foreign peoples, understood their language, and many of their cultural norms held within that region. Lawrence and Bohannan were archeologists who had lived and worked among different peoples (Arabs and Native Americans), and Du Bois as an anthropologist was also experienced working among foreign culture. Bohannan learned as much as he could about Filipino culture during his combat service during the Second World War. Lansdale studied Filipino culture, folklore, and history in great measure to understand the people and their struggle. Fall had no major interest in Vietnam until his doctoral work, but was relentless in becoming an expert in their political economy, ethnicities, and culture before French defeat in Indochina.

Empathy for Foreign Cultures

In most cases, mavericks had a genuine affinity for the foreign people they served (unlike Leachman, Westmoreland, Sanchez, and others). While most suffered the biases of their age about gender and Western superiority, and some like Lawrence and Bell held idealized notions of the Arabs that bordered on romantic exoticism, mavericks separated themselves by actually caring for these "others" even while in pursuit of national objectives. Wassmuss's view of the Persians is hard to ascertain, though he was held in regard by many of them. Fall's affinity for the Vietnamese people was rigorously seen through his own sense of objective analysis that he unleashed on all his subjects of study, but he certainly viewed them as a people suffering under colonial rule. Harder to gauge is empathy as merely a "tactic." Priya Satia has argued that many British imperialists of the Great War used their love of exotic cultures and desire for mastery of the esoteric to generate a kind of "empathy" for Arabs and other peoples of the Levant that was, to paraphrase Sky, transactional or needs-based. It was a tactic of spy craft.[2] Lawrence clearly maintained the lie of Arab independence during the revolt. He was also willing to die in putting Feisal in Damascus so that the Arabs could negotiate from a position of strength. His action speaks not only to the uniqueness of his nature but the depth of this empathy for their plight, and his sense of guilt for his betrayal. Fall returned to Vietnam to influence a war he'd watch descend into failure, only to find death. Bohannan was sickened with the U.S. failure in Vietnam and refused to return, and would die among the Filipinos whom he had twice liberated. Du Bois returned to anthropological study but not at the behest of the state. Wassmuss died penniless trying to repay the Persians who believed in his promises of gold and victory. Chayes and Sky continue to globe-trot in hopes of shifting Western perceptions on war and corruption and support the peoples of Afghanistan and Iraq.

Trust Built by Shared Risk

All of the mavericks were willing to expose themselves to harm on a continual basis, though the degree of danger varied. Du Bois, for instance, may have been at risk in Kandy but never took to field research like the

Rangoon City Team. Legal restrictions denied women to serve in some theaters, like China, at all. She was by far the most safe from enemy action. Every other maverick found themselves in the line of fire and often without large conventional forces as immediate support. Indeed, most mavericks lived among the people and shared the risk-built trust that these foreigners meant what they said about support, liberation, and more. Proximity to harm fed them better intelligence from personal sources and countered the accusations of their adversaries, from ELAS in Greece to Arabs of Kirkuk, that these men and women from foreign lands were willing to sacrifice themselves for others. Bernard Fall, and perhaps Gertrude Bell, paid the ultimate price for it.

National Support for Irregular/Unconventional Warfare

Some mavericks have benefited and been compromised by their nation's views of unconventional warfare and its role as a tool of the state. Conventional warfare does not require detailed cultural analysis of the people in which wars are fought. Primacy is placed on geography and enemy, where it is hoped most battles will be waged. But as we've seen, war in the twentieth century has been global and in most instances unconventional, creating a spat of terms to explain its complexity and variety (irregular warfare, counterinsurgency small wars, counterguerrilla warfare, pacification, imperial policing, operations other than war, hybrid warfare, etc.). In these forms of warfare, there is greater need for appreciating the people of a foreign nation. And, within this dialog is a spectrum of appreciation of other cultures that ranges from the racist to the empathetic. Here, Britain has had a much denser experience due to its imperial history and development of incentives and support for both big and small wars, in part due to the smaller role of the army and greater need for expeditionary forces in a global empire. They have also been more tolerant of "eccentrics" within the world of military conformity. Historian and critic of Western imperialism Edward Said noted, "There were no French Lawrences or Sykes or Bells."[3] Germany, as we've seen, had no grand tradition in irregular war and its only major work on unconventional warfare before the Great War was co-opted by the dominant paradigm of total warfare and brutality. Thus, Wassmuss was not doctrinally supported.

The British maintain a richer tradition of unconventional warfare, but could produce many more Leachmans as Lawrence's. Yet, Bohannan and Lansdale both noted that the British always maintained a higher tolerance for eccentric experts in their armed forces than the United States.[4] Despite revolutionary origins, the U.S. experience with unconventional warfare was a mix of forgotten successes and well-documented failures, with the notable exception of the Marine Corps's "small wars" of the interwar period.[5] The OSS was created in small part to fill in this gap. It's notable that Douglas MacArthur denied them a place in his liberation campaign, where Bohannan served in the largest guerrilla campaign of the American war effort. He and Lansdale, however, took lessons from America's successes against Native Americans and in the Philippine–American War and welded it to a political and psychological strategy that worked.[6] Because this was done through advising instead of U.S. Arms and soldiers, it found itself far more appealing to U.S. Authorities. They ran into resistance when dealing with a much more conventionally minded Westmorland. Fall, as the outsider, contended with this bias against counterinsurgency by being sought out by the minority opinion of dissent on the United States' waging of the Vietnam War. But lack of a greater professional support meant a minority voice was drowned by conventional wisdom. Bias against warfare that required cultural acumen hardened after the failure of Vietnam, plaguing the war efforts and shortsighted strategic outlook of both the Operation Enduring Freedom and Operation Iraqi Freedom, creating the knowledge gap that Chayes and Sky filled.

Indeed, one truth of this research is that American disdain for unconventional warfare in favor of high-tempo, technically savvy, and lethal small professional forces has made the need for mavericks even greater. The limits of what Chayes and Sky could achieve, however, is the counterpunch to their value. Chayes had neither the influence nor the means to challenge dominant CIA culture and preferences within Afghanistan, despite having patrons as powerful as COIN champion Gen. David Petraeus. Sky may have been Lieutenant Odierno's "conscience," but as a foreign national her work was even more suspect in the eyes of her detractors than Chayes.

Use of Violence

Indeed, Sky is the only clear pacifist among the mavericks. Bell disliked strategic bombing, unless the enemy was particularly brutal. Du Bois had no problem with interrogations of enemy prisoners. Chayes slept with an AK-47 near her bed. Yet none saw violence as the sole or chief tool to influence operations. Lawrence understood the need for violence, and used it, but still revered Saxe's "war without battles" most of all. Woodhouse was adept at diplomacy and demolition, and had a strong tactical sense, but as a guerrilla leader he was fighting at a disadvantage against conventional foes for most of the war. Lansdale preferred psychological and political means to violence, but knew its necessity; Bohannan, one of only two combat soldiers of this group, excelled in tough operations during the Pacific campaign, but preferred guile to force. Fall survived the Second World War, a master of guerrilla warfare, and brought his expertise on foreign occupation to see to the war in Vietnam, guerilla or otherwise. Wassmuss, denied other means to instill rebellion, fell into the need for demonstrations of violence to make his claims good.

Capacity to Learn after Mastering Their Own Field

The best of the mavericks demonstrated this ability by walking into a military environment and foreign culture and excelling. Lawrence took every opportunity to learn about modern weapons and ancient cultures. Indeed, his ability to learn new things was essential to his concept of generalship.

> *[G]eneralship, at least in my case, came of understanding, of hard study and brain work and concentration. Had it come easy to me I should not have done it so well. If [Liddell Hart's biography of Lawrence] could persuade some of our new soldiers to read and mark and learn things outside drill manuals and tactical diagrams, it would do a good work. I feel a fundamental crippling incuriousness about our own officers. Too much body and too little head. The perfect general would know everything in heaven and earth.*[7]

Bell was a career learner of foreign peoples and applied it to government work. Woodhouse claimed his ability to learn, more than his knowledge of Greek, allowed him to rise to prominence in the SOE. Du Bois turned her skills as a researcher and administrator into a leadership position in a volatile theater. Lansdale and Bohannan were relentless in learning as much as they could about Filipino and Vietnamese culture, history, and geography. Bohannan, who had greater academic depth, partnered with Lansdale's ability to shape political and psychological messaging to foreign peoples (though through a very American lens).[8] Chayes and Sky had to learn how to operate among diverse cultures, including Iraqi, Afghani, and American military "tribes," all with their own systems of power and influence. Fall maintained a high capacity for learning until his death: his childhood as a soldier made it clear that knowledge meant survival. Wassmuss remains a mystery, as detailed knowledge of his life and career remains spotty in the West.

Threshold for Improvisation

But Wassmuss, like the other mavericks, was willing to attempt what no one had done before. Many contemporaries and historians have viewed the lack of planning of his mission as proof of its future doom, if not hilarity: while traveling through neutral Romania, the early parties of the mission were stopped for inspection. Their equipment was labeled circus gear, and when the Romanians didn't buy the act, the mission was delayed and the early covert agents viewed as "clowns."[9] And yet, with no tradition of starting uprisings, Wassmuss had no choice but to improvise. Aqaba was improvised. The Plaka Agreements were improvised. The Rangoon City Team was improvised. Applying the research techniques of Nuremberg to the French war in Indochina was improvised. "Our Guy Magsaysay" was improvised. Creating Arghand was improvised. Bringing reconciliation into U.S. occupation policies was improvised. Detailed planning is of course critical and necessary in military operations. But the capacity to consider alternative and attempt the novel distinguishes mavericks from their conventional colleagues and helps give them their strength. This does not, however, mean that improvisation always works. Every single maverick suffered failures or took chances on strange ideas that didn't pan out. But those failures are part of the learning process, just as surely as trying a new weapons system in the field is fraught with the potential for failure. Improvisation to break through the conventional and conformist mentality and approaches of the armed forces is paramount to a maverick's value.

CAREER IMMUNITY

The need to improvise and take risks is in part protected by a maverick's status. Many are not beholden to a government contract or a professional career within the armed forces. Wassmuss here remains the outlier and his doom was sealed when he failed in his mission and returned not to academia or the private sector, but a Foreign Office that despised him. Every other maverick had a career to fall back on (in Fall's case, it was his career in academia that kept him relevant while being exiled from government influence). While working for or within military structures, many mavericks felt far freer to buck the system and take chances because they were not afraid to ruin a military career. Chayes and Sky had no problem telling senior military officials how and why they were wrong or ignorant, in part because being outside their chain of command meant that they were harder to "correct" or discipline. Both had no problem returning to the civilian world they had emerged. Lawrence, Du Bois, Woodhouse, Bohannan, and Lansdale all came to war with an already professional skill set that they then applied to their environment, and careers to fall back on if they ended government service. Most mavericks were willing to risk their lives *and careers* for their ideas and operations and against resistance from various sectors of influence knowing they didn't need the armed forces as much as they needed them at this juncture and time.

SPEAKING TRUTH TO POWER

Career immunity allowed many mavericks to speak truth to power. And speaking truth to power was necessary. Mavericks were valued because of their skills. But unlike technology, mavericks speak back and tell you why something doesn't work and suggest how it can. Telling the armed forces how and why to change is difficult and despite acknowledging their own "knowledge gap," most militaries are utterly resistant to changing how they function, especially on the advice of outsiders,[10] even if the outsiders are correct.

How you spoke truth to power also mattered. Fall crucified himself on integrity. He had to tell objective truths as he saw it, triggering an FBI investigation that tarred his ability to influence a war he knew better than most. Lawrence had champions but he also annoyed many and made discrete enemies who disliked not only his ideas but his indifferent nature toward military decorum. Lansdale was a master at building alliances and persuading opposition toward his own point of view, but his lack of interest in conventional solutions and avoiding red tape made him enemies that included the secretary of defense. Bohannan's quiet but more eccentric matter made him enemies, too. Almost as soon as she landed in Kandahar, Chayes took her arguments on corruption and abuse to the press. She used the court of public opinion to hold U.S. and Afghan officials accountable for knowingly working within the "kleptocracy" she studied as the root of resistance to legitimacy in the Afghan government. Sky was a perennial nuisance to U.S. soldiers. She refused to remain silent on their ignorance and the price of that ignorance as she tried to compensate for it in the realm of reconciliation.

Helping Others as a Calling

A repeated theme with many mavericks is a sense of obligation to help a foreign people overcome opposition or hardship. These took the form of liberation (Lawrence, Bell, Woodhouse, Du Bois, Bohannon), combating insurgencies (Bohannan, Lansdale), and invasion, liberation, and nation-building (Chayes, Sky). Fall's ruthless objectivity allowed him to see the Vietminh's struggle against French and then American imperialism as rational and not nearly as ideological as his Cold War compatriots feared, but he rarely offered an opinion on what was a best-case scenario and rather what would likely happen: unification under Northern hegemony. No communist himself, Fall was more interested in how revolution and imperialism operated than in championing the French or American cause over the indigenous peoples of Vietnam. Most mavericks felt a sense of destiny tied up with the people whom war had brought together. Words like "calling" and "destiny" or "duty" and "responsibility" were instilled in almost every campaign. A sense of duty matched or exceeded domestic nationalism or permeated deep in many mavericks.

Writing

Almost all mavericks undertook the intellectual rigor of putting their careers and efforts into print. Only Wassmuss and Du Bois kept generally quiet (though Du Bois was active as an anti-war lecturer). Lawrence's work is the most celebrated. *Seven Pillars of Wisdom* remains necessary reading on Westerners among foreign people in war. Bell was an established writer before the war, and her wartime writings are still key documents (for good or ill) on the history of nation-building. She died, however, without writing an opus of her wartime efforts. Woodhouse wrote a series of works on the political and military campaigns of Greece before, during, and after his era with the SOE, including *The Apple of Discord*, *The Struggle for Greece*, and his memoir, *Something Ventured*. Bohannan wrote reports, papers, and articles before constructing a compelling view of the defeat o of the Huk with colleague Napoleon Valeriano, *Counter-Guerrilla Warfare: The Philippine's Experience*. It covered legal, political, historical, and other facets that demonstrated his command of unconventional warfare theory and his own innovative mind for such operations. Oddly, this American success story was not included as part of *Counterinsurgency FM 3-24*. Lansdale's *In the Midst of Wars: An American's Mission to South East Asia* was a less candid affair and meant as a counterpunch to the release of the *Pentagon Papers*. While valuable in putting men like Magsaysay and Diem at the forefront of events, it is just as noted for all that he left out (including the role of himself and Bohannan). Fall's denial into the realms of influence in Washington fueled his rich production of work, including dozens of articles and lectures to his three major monographs, *Street without Joy: Indochina at War, 1946–1954*; *The Two Viet-Nams: A Political and Military Analysis*; and *Hell in a Very Small Place: The Siege of Diem Bien Phu*. Chayes wrote from the field while working in Kandahar, producing the scathing and insightful *The Punishment of Virtue: Inside Afghanistan after the Taliban*, then detailed her career with ISAF and as special advisor to the Chairman of the Joint Chiefs of Staff in *Thieves of State: Why Corruption Threatens Global Security*. Emma Sky's long-awaited memoir *The Unraveling: High Hopes and Missed Opportunities in Iraq* laid bare much of the cultural deficits in U.S. military thinking and the benefit of filling ignorance with expertise.

The act of writing creates empathy for the reader, and not just for the subject. Even if the intents of all these work are laced with the normal biases and objectives of men and women hoping to shape policy and their own legacies through the lens of their version of the "truth," they speak of the importance to serve others. But that limitation doesn't dilute the fact that the majority of mavericks value the need to communicate ideas beyond their golden years and careers.

Gerard Leachman held few of these traits. Indeed, cultural knowledge never bred cultural empathy in him. He remained a cunning and brutal imperial soldier until his murder in Fallujah in 1920. He would have no doubt cheered the return to Iraq of British soldiers and the invasion of Afghanistan, and probably laughed at the horrors of Abu Ghraib as part and parcel of one's duty to an empire. He was the kind of soldier whose contempt for foreigners feeds, breeds, and explodes insurgencies. His tradition is impossible to snuff out, as racism and xenophobia plague our human condition in peace and at home; the creation of enemies as an inhuman "other" is how modern conventional soldiers are taught to kill.[11] But the excesses, abuses, and worse can be limited by codes of conduct and strict rules of engagement. And the best means to combat ignorance and its malfeasance in warfare is through the expertise of mavericks of war.

From Lawrence to Chayes, from Greece to Burma, across a one-hundred-year span, mavericks of war have proved valuable contributors to modern warfare. They fill gaps of knowledge and ignorance. They challenge conventional wisdom. They are willing to risk their lives among foreign peoples for mutual gain. They speak truth to power.

Today, the United States maintains the most technologically advanced and lethal armed forces in the world and yet, despite these assets, finds itself with a mixed record of failures and recovered successes in the wars it has prosecuted since 9/11. Much ink has been spilled on the failures of U.S. strategic thinking as it faces the growing challenges of globalized communities. But an equally powerful argument is being made on the core failures being rooted in cultural ignorance.[12] The current national security picture is rife with challenges in which ignorance must be labeled as a dangerous and crippling hazard to strategy and operations, a truth that needs repeating as current political actors refuse to view the past, present, and future of U.S. power in objective and historical terms. Blinded by zealotry, many of them seek to view the world as a clash of cultures.

Mavericks know different. Success in a global context requires deeper understanding as much as greater lethality. But if past is prologue, then ignorance and willful blindness to how insurgencies and unconventional threats operate from abroad will mean that mavericks will be needed in an ever growing supply to fill the knowledge gap and offer alternatives to the brutality of power. It is hoped that as the world deals with hybrid warfare with Russia and China, regional insurgencies with global reach, and a nuclear armed North Korea, the tradition of Lawrence and Chayes will drown out the Leachmans. Greater knowledge and empathy will trump ignorance. In a letter to his friend and biographer Liddell Hart, Lawrence asked the following, a fitting remark to end on. "So please, if you see me that way and agree with be, do use me as a text to preach for more study of books and history, a greater seriousness in military art. With 2,000 years of examples behind us we have no excuse, when fighting, for not fighting well."[13]

Notes

Introduction: Leachman's Ghost

1 Rory McCarthy, "Saddam Makes an Exhibition of Himself," *The Guardian*, January 10, 2003, https://www.theguardian.com/world/2003/jan/10/worlddispatch.iraq.
2 See Priya Satia, *Spies in Arabia: The Great War and the Cultural Foundations of Britain's Covert Empire in the Middle East* (Oxford: Oxford University Press, 2009), 1–23; Karl E. Meyer and Shareen Blair Brysac, *Kingmakers: The Invention of the Modern Middle East* (New York: W. W. Norton, 2008), 158–77.
3 H. FV. F. Winstone, *Leachman: O. C. Desert* (London: Quarter Books, 1982), 218.
4 N. N. E. Bray, *A Paladin of Arabia: The Biography of Brevet Lieut.-Colonel G. E. Leachman* (London: Unicorn Press, 1936), 412–13.
5 The best analysis of this remains Satia, *Spies in Arabia*, 31, 113, 150, 157, 160, 252, 350.
6 Winstone, *Leachman,* vii.
7 Quoted in Winstone, *Leachman*, 222.
8 Quoted in Winstone, *Leachman*, 180–81. Italics added for emphasis.
9 Rory McCarthy, "Saddam Makes an Exhibition of Himself."
10 N. N. E. Bray, *A Paladin of Arabia.*
11 For a survey of OR history in particular, see P. M. S. Blackett, "Scientists at the Operational Level," (1941), reprinted in 1948 in "Operational Research," *Advancement of Science* 17 (1948), collected in *Studies of War: Nuclear and Conventional* (Edinburgh and London: Oliver & Boyd, 1962); O. M. Solandt, "Observation, Experiment, and Measurement in Operational Research," *Journal of the Operations Research Society of America* 3, no. 1 (February 1955); Terry Copp, ed., *Montgomery's Scientists: Operational Research in Northwest Europe* (Waterloo, ON: Laurier Centre for Military Strategic and Disarmament Studies, 2000); and Maurice Kirby, *Operational Research in War and Peace: The British Experience from the 1930s to 1970s* (London: Imperial War College, 2003). On the rise of scientists in warfare, see Gregg Herken, *Cardinal Choices: Presidential Science Advisors from the Atomic Bomb to SDI* (Stanford, CA: Stanford University Press, 2000). For a representation of this body of work for Britain, see Ronald Clark, "Science and Technology, 1919–1945," in *A Guide to the Sources of British Military History*, ed. Robert Higham (Berkeley and Los Angeles: University of California Press, 1971), 542–65; for the United States, see Alex Roland, "Technology and War: The Historiographical Revolution of the 1980s," *Technology and Culture* 34, no. 1 (1993): 117–34. See also Jason S. Ridler, *Maestro of Science: Omond M. Solandt and Government Science in War and Hostile Peace, 1939–1956* (Toronto: University of Toronto Press, 2015).
12 In this way it paralleled the growth of OR as well, with men like P. M. S. Blackett rising to the position of influencing strategic debates on the use of Armadas in the Battle of the Atlantic. See note 11.
13 Isabell Hull, *Absolute Destruction: Military Culture and the Practices of War in Imperial German* (Ithaca, NY: Cornell University Press, 2005).

14 Notable exclusion to this rule is the sublime and short work by Barry N. Katz, *Foreign Intelligence: Research and Analysis in the Office of Strategic Services, 1942–1945* (Cambridge, MA: Harvard University Press, 1989), which covers a small cadre of expatriate experts from Europe.
15 An introduction to these organizations must include Bruce Westrate, *The Arab Bureau: British Police in the Middle East, 1916–1920* (University Park, PA: Penn State Press, 1992); William Mackenzie, *The Secret History of SOE* (New York: Little, Brown Books, 2002); M. R. D. Foot, *An Outline History of the Special Operations Executive* (London: Mandarin, 1990); A. R. B. Linderman, *Rediscovering Irregular Warfare: Colin Gubbins and the Origins of Britain's Special Operation Executive* (Norman: University of Oklahoma Press, 2016); Richard Harris Smith, *OSS: The Secret History if America's First Central Intelligence Agency* (New York: Rowman & Littlefield, 2005; originally published 1972); Douglas Waller, *Wild Bill Donovan: The Spymaster Who Created the OSS and Modern American Espionage* (New York: Free Press, 2011); Douglas Waller, *Disciples: The World War II Missions of the CIA Directors Who Fought for Wild Bill Donovan* (New York: Simon & Schuster, 2015); Ralph H. Smuckler, *A University Turns to the World: A Personal History of the Michigan State University International Story* (East Lansing: Michigan State University Press, 2003); and Robert Scigliano and Guy H. Fox, *Technical Assistance in Vietnam: The Michigan State University Experience* (New York: Praeger, 1965). A series of MSUG reports are available at United States Assistance and International Development website, https://www.usaid.gov/who-we-are; Christopher Lamb, James Douglas Orton, Michael C. Davies, and Theodore T. Pikulsky, *Human Terrain Teams: An Organization for Sociocultural Knowledge in Irregular Warfare* (Washington, DC: The Institute of World Politics Press, 2013); and Montgomery McFate and Janice H. Laurence, eds., *Social Science Goes to War: The Human Terrain System in Iraq and Afghanistan* (Oxford and New York: Oxford University Press, 2015).

Part I: Mavericks of the Great War

1 Michael Howard, "Men against Fire," in *Makers of Modern Strategy: From Machiavelli to the Nuclear Age*, ed. Peter Paret and Michael Howard (Princeton, NJ: Princeton University Press, 1986), 510–26.
2 Siegfried Sassoon, *Memoirs of an Infantry Officer* (London: Faber & Faber, 1930), 217.
3 See Paul Fussell, *The Great War and Modern Memory* (London: Oxford University Press, 1975).
4 Jonathan Vance, *Death So Noble: Memory, Meaning and the First World War* (Vancouver: University of British Columbia Press, 2001).
5 Quoted in D. C. Watt, *Too Serious a Business: European Armed Forces and the Approach to the Second World War*, preface to the introduction.

Chapter 1: "Those Who Dream in Daylight": T. E. Lawrence and the Impact of a Maverick of War

1 T. E. Lawrence, *Seven Pillars of Wisdom* (London: Penguin Books, 2000; originally printed in 1926), 23.

2 Quoted in Harold Orlans, *T. E. Lawrence: Biography of a Broken Hero* (Jefferson, NC: McFarland, 2002), 29.

3 Orlans, *T. E. Lawrence*. See Xenaphon, *Anabasis*, trans. H. G. Dkyns, (Project Gutenberg, 2013), http://www.gutenberg.org/files/1170/1170-h/1170-h.htm.

4 Scott Anderson, *Lawrence in Arabia: War, Deceit, Imperial Folly and the Making of the Modern Middle East* (New York: Double Day, 2013), 261.

5 Quoted in Basil Liddell Hart, *Lawrence of Arabia* (Cambridge, MA: Da Capo, 2009; 1935), 137.

6 James Schneider, *Guerrilla Leader: T. E. Lawrence and the Arab Revolt* (New York: Bantam, 2011), 80–107.

7 Quoted in Schneider, *Guerrilla Leader*, 124.

8 Lawrence, *Seven Pillars of Wisdom*, 317.

9 Lawrence, *Seven Pillars of Wisdom*, 317.

10 Orlans, *T. E. Lawrence*, 32–35.

11 Jeremy Wilson, *Lawrence of Arabia: The Authorized Biography* (London: Heinemann, 1988), 483.

12 Bruce Westrate, *The Arab Bureau: British Police in the Middle East, 1916–1920* (University Park, PA: Penn State Press, 1992), 104; and Malcolm Brown, ed., *T. E. Lawrence in War and Peace: An Anthology of the Military Writings of Lawrence of Arabia* (London: Greenhill Books, 2005), 142.

13 Azar Gat, *A History of Military Thought: From the Enlightenment to the Cold War* (Oxford: Oxford University Press, 2001), 672–75.

14 Williamson Murray, *Military Adaptation in War with Fear of Change*, (Cambridge: Cambridge University Press, 2011), 59.

15 John E. Mack, *A Prince of Our Disorder: The Life of T. E. Lawrence* (Cambridge, MA: Harvard University Press, 1998), 3–36.

16 Wilson, 33.

17 Wilson, 25.

18 After suffering a broken leg, he studied voraciously reading on archeology, including Austen Henry Layard's excavations on Nineveh in Mesopotamia. Wilson, 28. These were likely Austen Henry Layard, *Nineveh and Its Remains: With an Account of a Visit to the Chaldaean Christians of Kurdistan, and the Yezidis, or Devil-Worshippers; and an Enquiry into the Manners and Arts of the Ancient Assyrians*, vol. I and II (London: John Murray, 1849 and 1850).

19 Wilson, 25–26; Hart, *Lawrence of Arabia*, 6.

20 Wilson, 25–26; Hart, *Lawrence of Arabia*, 6.

21 He passed his Oxford entrance exams but failed to get a St. John's College scholarship. He did win the Meyricke Exhibition due to his Welsh birth. But his grades were not high enough to be exempt from responsions (exams taken before entering university), and he was forced to write on the historical work of Xenophon, Caesar's military campaigns, and algebra. Wilson, 41–42.

22 Wilson, 42, 43.

23 https://answers.yahoo.com/question/index?qid=20150219115836AAhhLb1Wilson 45.

24 Wilson, 52.

25 Wilson, 55.
26 Wilson, 53.
27 Quoted in Wilson, 53.
28 Wilson, 57.
29 Wilson, 63
30 Hart, *Lawrence of Arabia*, 9.
31 Wilson, 62.
32 Wilson, 59–60.
33 Wilson, 61.
34 Wilson, 62.
35 Wilson, 64.
36 Wilson, 69.
37 Hart, *Lawrence of Arabia*, 9.
38 Wilson, 74.
39 Wilson, 104.
40 Wilson, 115–18.
41 Wilson, 87.
42 Wilson, 92–97.
43 Wilson, 99.
44 Wilson, 100.
45 Wilson, 111.
46 Wilson, 112–13.
47 Wilson, 115.
48 Wilson, 118–19.
49 Wilson 100.
50 Quoted in Wilson, 134.
51 Wilson, 137.
52 Wilson, 141.
53 Wilson, 146.
54 Wilson, 143.
55 Quoted in Orlans, *T. E. Lawrence*, 20.
56 Orlans, *T. E. Lawrence*, 19.
57 "However, Clausewitz was intellectually so much the master of them, and his book so logical and fascinating, that unconsciously I accepted his finality until a comparison of Kuhne and Foch disgusted me with soldiers, wearied me of the officious glory, making me critical of all their light." But that would come later, when the horror of the Western Front also killed two of his brothers. At the time, his interest had been "abstract, concerned with theory and philosophy of warfare especially from the metaphysical side." Lawrence, *Seven Pillars of Wisdom*, 193.
58 Hart, *Lawrence of Arabia*, 128.
59 Wilson, 189.
60 Quoted in Wilson, 174–75.
61 Wilson, 189.
62 Wilson, 251.
63 Wilson, 251.

64 Quoted in Orlans, *T. E. Lawrence*, 27–28.
65 Quoted in Orlans, *T. E. Lawrence*, 29.
66 "Syria: The Raw Material," reprinted in *T. E. Lawrence in War and Peace: An Anthology of the Military Writings of Lawrence of* Arabia, ed. Malcolm Brown (London: Greenhill Books, 2005), 105.
67 Wilson, 323–24.
68 Wilson, 326.
69 Lawrence, *Seven Pillars of Wisdom*, 4.
70 Hart, *Lawrence of Arabia*, 107.
71 Hart, *Lawrence of Arabia*, 106.
72 Quoted in Asprey, 179.
73 Quoted in Orlans, *T. E. Lawrence,* 29.
74 Edmund V. D'Auvergne, *The Prodigious Marshal: Being the Life and Extraordinary Adventures of Maurice de Saxe, Marshal of France, Son of the King of Poland, Conqueror of the English, Pretender to the Dukedom of Kurland, and Universal Lover* (New York: Dodd, 1931), 43.
75 Gat, *History of Military Thought*, 32.
76 Gat, *History of Military Thought*, 32.
77 See David Bell, *The First Total War: Napoleon's Europe and the Birth of Warfare as We Know It* (New York: Mariner Books, 2008), 21–51.
78 Quoted in John Manchip White, *Marshal of France: The Life and Times of Maurice, Comte de Saxe [1696–1750]* (London: Hamish Hamilton, 1962), 263.
79 Maurice de Saxe, *Reveries on the Art of War* (1756), translation unknown, accessed April 2, 2015, www.bellum.nu, http://web.archive.org/web/20080205095610/ http://www.bellum.nu/literature/desaxe001.html.
80 Richard Preston and S. F. Wise, *Men in Arms: A History of Warfare and Its Interrelationships with Society*, 4th edition (New York: Holt, 1979), 144–45.
81 Quoted in David Bell, *The First Total War: Napoleon's Europe and the Birth of Warfare as We Know It* (Kindle Edition), 40.
82 Quoted in John Manchip White, *Marshal of France: The Life and Times of Maurice, Comte de Saxe [1696–1750]* (London: Hamish Hamilton, 1962), 72.
83 Lawrence, *Seven Pillars of Wisdom*, 195–96.
84 Quoted in Gat, *History of Military Thought*, 679.
85 Lawrence, *Seven Pillars of Wisdom*, 201.
86 Wilson, 395.
87 Scott Anderson, *Lawrence in Arabia: War, Deceit, Imperial Folly and the Making of the Modern Middle East* (New York: Double Day, 2013), 321.
88 See Wilson; Lawrence, *Seven Pillars of Wisdom.*
89 In Malcolm Brown, ed., *Lawrence of Arabia: The Selected Letters* (New York: W. W. Norton, 1980), 377–78.
90 Alex Danchev, *Alchemist of War: The Life of Basil Liddell Hart* (London: Weidenfeld Military, 1998), 45.
91 Michael Reynolds, *Hemingway: The 1930s* (New York: W. H. Norton, 1998), 75.
92 Reynolds, *Hemingway*, 279, 300.
93 See Andrew Birtle, *A History of Counterinsurgency and Contingency Operations in the US Army*, vol. 2, (Washington, DC: US Government Printing, 1997); and Crispin

Burke, "T. E. Lawrence: A Leadership Vignette for the Successful Counterinsurgent," *Small Wars Journal* (February 19, 2009), http://smallwarsjournal.com/jrnl/art/a-leadership-vignette-for-the-successful-counter-insurgent.

94 Cecil B. Currey, *Victory at Any Cost: The Genius of Vietnam's Gen. Vo Nguyen Giap* (Lincoln, NE: Potomac Books, 2005), 154.

95 Quoted in Schneider, *Guerrilla Leader*, 4.

96 See Gat, *A History of Military Thought*, 679.

97 A good summation of these attacks and challenges can be found in Karl E. Meyer and Shareen Blair Brysac, *Kingmakers: The Invention of the Modern Middle East* (New York: W. W. Norton, 2008), 196–98.

98 Richard J. Evans, *Telling Lies about Hitler: The Holocaust, History and the David Irving Trial* (London: Verso Books, 2002), 25.

99 The roots of Wilson's efforts began in 1971, and the result is a consummation of twenty years of study and reflection. Despite being out of print, it remains the best scholarly and readable account of Lawrence's life and times. Jeremy Wilson, *Lawrence of Arabia: The Authorized Biography of T. E. Lawrence* (New York: Atheneum, 1990).

100 US Army, *FM 3-24 and Counterinsurgency* (United States Government, 2006), 1–28.

Chapter 2: "The Lone and Hopeless Struggle": Wilhelm Wassmuss and the German Experiment in Islamic Insurgencies, 1914–1918

1 Percy Z. Cox. "The Death of Herr Wassmuss," *Journal of the Royal Central Asian Society* 19, no. 1 (1932): 151–55.

2 Christopher Sykes, *Wassmuss, "The German Lawrence": His Adventures in Persia during and after the War* (Leipzig: Bernard Tauchnitz, 1937), 182.

3 Jules Stewart, *The Kaiser's Mission to Kabul: A Secret Expedition to Afghanistan in World War I* (New York: I.B. Tauris, 2014), 133.

4 Sykes, *Wassmuss, "The German Lawrence"*, 55.

5 Peter Hopkirk, *On Secret Service East of Constantinople: The Plot to Bring down the British Empire* (New York: John Murray, 2004), 99.

6 Stewart, *The Kaiser's Mission to Kabul,* 138–37.

7 Stewart, *The Kaiser's Mission to Kabul*, 148.

8 Quoted in Stewart, *The Kaiser's Mission to Kabul*, 148.

9 Stewart, *The Kaiser's Mission to Kabul*, 150.

10 M. L. Hauner "Werner Otto von Hentig, 1886–1984," *Central Asian Survey* 3, no. 2 (January 1984): 139.

11 Hopkirk, *On Secret Service East of Constantinople*, 99.

12 Sykes, *Wassmuss, "The German Lawrence"*, 48.

13 Stewart, *The Kaiser's Mission to Kabul*, 126.

14 Marina Tolmacheva, C. H. Stigand, and Dagmar Weiler, *The Pate Chronicle: Edited and Translated from MSS 177,321,344, and 358 of the library of the University of Dar es Salaam* (Detroit: Michigan State University Press, 2010), 15–16.

15 Sykes, *Wassmuss, "The German Lawrence"*, 45.

16 Sykes, *Wassmuss, "The German Lawrence"*, 50.

17 Sykes, *Wassmuss, "The German Lawrence"*, 48.

18 Cox, "The Death of Herr Wassmuss," 151–55.
19 Kristian Coates Ulrichsen, *The First World War in the Middle East* (New York: Hurst, 2014), 24.
20 Cox, "The Death of Herr Wassmuss," 151–55.
21 Sykes, *Wassmuss, "The German Lawrence"*, 5, 53.
22 The most compelling case for the emergence of this strategic outlook remains Fritz Fischer's controversial work on Germany's war aims. As soon as German armies marched on France, "the German government, in collaboration with the general staff, was working out a far-reaching programme of revolution which was directed equally against the British Empire and Imperial Russia. These activities began immediately after the outbreak of war. The promotion of revolution as a means of warfare was an aspect of the war aim of breaking up the British and Russian Empires." It served immediate military and long-term political goals. Fritz Fischer, *Germany's Aims in the First World War* (New York: W. W. Norton, 1967), 120. As Jennifer Jenkins has noted, however, the role of revolution in Fischer's thesis was relatively quickly ignored in favor of contesting his arguments about the dominant fronts and dismissing the rebellions out of turn. But Fischer did not see them as ad hoc but as part of "all encompassing strategy of warfare and were a primary means for the achievement of German war aims" mostly focused on the east: Russia, Caucuses, and the Near East. It demonstrates a complex view of power and control, not limited to territory or conquest but indirect rule, economic dominance, as well as unique versions of controlling territory. Economic spheres would dominate the areas of Rumania, Turkey, Caucuses, and Germany. Feelers were sent to Persia and India. Destabilizing Russian and British empires would achieve these aims. So, instead of being isolated, it was actually a primary strategy of war. The first revolution that was part of war aims was *jihad* in the Islamic world. Fischer saw them as "pieces of a unified strategy." Jennifer Jenkins, "Fritz Fischer's 'Programme for Revolution': Implications for a Global History of Germany in the First World War," *Journal of Contemporary History* 48, no. 2 (2013): 403.
23 Anthony Sattin, *The Young T. E. Lawrence* (New York: Norton, 2015), 161–62.
24 Herman von Wissmann, *Afrika: Schilderungen und Rathschläge zur Vorbereitung für den Aufenthalt und Dienst in den Deutsche Schützgebieten* [Africa: Descriptions and Recommendations for Service in the German Protectorate], 1903.
25 Cultural historian Johannes Fabian noted this distinction, based on Wissmann's own writings. On the one hand, he could view the African peoples as quaint. "At Mirambo's I had a most friendly reception (with two bottles of champagne and a slaughtered ox). This, the most important negro I met in Africa, is thoroughly misjudged [verkannt, literally, 'misrecognized'] in Europe; I spent three extremely interesting days with this bellicose prince, who must inspire respect even in a European." And yet Fabian also notes what he describes as rare "flashes of humanity" in Wissmann's attitudes as revealed by his writing. Wissmann encountered a local woman. "[She had something] that made us forget that we had before us just a half-clothed negro woman from the savage interior, something that unconsciously made us behave toward her as to an elderly lady from our home country. The feeling of contempt, which the European often has when he first deals with savages, soon disappears; one no longer notices the people's nudity, and one also learns to distinguish faces, something that is very difficult in the beginning." Quoted in Johannes Fabian, "Remembering the Other: Knowledge and

Recognition in the Exploration of Central Africa," *Critical Inquiry* 26, no. 1 (Autumn 1999): 54–56. See Isabell Hull, *Absolute Destruction*.

26 It is understood that the campaigns of Paul von Lettow-Vorbeck were a mix of both conventional and guerrilla operations against British Imperial forces in Africa. But recent scholarship has demonstrated that it owed more to the conventional savvy of their commanding officer and the dominant German culture of the "offensive" than first appeared. Erick J. Mann, "The Schutztruppe and the Nature of Colonial Warfare during the Conquest of Tanganyika, 1889–1900," doctoral thesis, University of Madison-Wisconsin, May 1998.

27 D. Gaunt, *Massacres, Resistance, Protectors: Muslim–Christian Relations in Eastern Anatolia during World War I* (Piscataway, NJ: Gorgias Press, 2006), 62.

28 Lionel Gossman, *The Passion of Max von Oppenheim: Archeology and Intrigue in the Middle East from Wilhelm II to Hitler* (Cambridge: Open Book, 2013), xxiv.

29 Germany was too young to be anything but a minor player in the Great Game before the war. Her imperial warfare experience was primarily in Africa, and whatever innovative ideas emerged during the initial development of German East and South West Africa in 1889–1900, they were largely subsumed in the "German Way of Warfare" by 1914. There was no school of unconventional, unorthodox, or insurgent warfare. In fact, these were considered abhorrent and to be brutalized out of existence as Germany had done with the *franctieruers* in France and various tribal revolts in Africa since 1871. Yet, members of both the German and Turkish government, military, and diplomatic offices saw the strategy as worthy of trying. But it would be on the cheap. Here, the African experience is also intriguing. The German protection forces were led by Germans and filled by Africans because German blood would not be spilled in colonial territories, and African soldiers were cheaper. Propaganda, promises, and money would arrive instead of German soldiers and munitions.

30 Quoted in Fischer, *Germany's Aims in the First World War*, 121.

31 Thomas L. Hughes, "German Mission to Afghanistan, 1915–1916," *German Studies Review* 25, no. 3 (October 2002): 455.

32 Peter Paret, "Review of *Berlin, Kabul, Moskau: Oskar Ritter von Niedermayer und Deutschlands Geopolitik* by Hans-Ulrich Seidt," *Central European History* 37, no. 2 (2004): 304.

33 Hans-Ulrich Seidt, "From Palestine to the Caucasus-Oskar Niedermayer and Germany's Middle Eastern Strategy in 1918," *German Studies Review* 24, no. 1 (February 2001): 5.

34 Oskar von Niedermayer, *Under the Scorching Sun: Iran War Experiences of the German Expedition to Persia and Afghanistan*, trans. unknown (Dachau: Einhornverlag, 1925), 6.

35 Niedermayer, *Under the Scorching Sun*, 6.

36 Niedermayer, *Under the Scorching Sun,* 4–5.

37 Gossman, *The Passion of Max von Oppenheim*, 91–92. Sean McMeekin, *The Berlin-Baghdad Express: The Ottoman Empire and Germany's Bid for World Power, 1898–1918* (Cambridge, MA: Belknap Press of Harvard University Press, 2010), 215.

38 Walter Griesinger, *German Intrigues in Persia: The Diary of a German Agent: The Niedermayer Expedition through Persia to Afghanistan and India* (London: Hodder and Stoughton, 1918), 6.

39 McMeekin, *The Berlin-Baghdad Express*, 217.
40 McMeekin, *The Berlin-Baghdad Express*, 218.
41 Quoted from Zugmayer's captured diary in F. J. Mobley, *The History of the Great War, Based on Collected Documents, The Campaigns in Mesopotamia, Volume I: Outbreak of Hostilities, Campaign in Lower Mesopotamia*, (London: His Majesty's Stationery, 1923), 344.
42 Sykes, *Wassmuss, "The German Lawrence"*, 67, 70; Hopkirk, *On Secret Service East of Constantinople*, 87–89.
43 Quoted in Mobley, *The History of the Great War*, 344.
44 Quoted in Mobley, *The History of the Great War*, 344.
45 Niedermayer, *Under the Scorching Sun*, 17.
46 Antony Wynn, *Persia in the Great Game: Sir Percy Sykes, Explorer, Consul, Soldier, Spy* (London: John Murray, 2004), 248–72.
47 Wynn, *Persia in the Great Game*, 257; and Hopkirk, *On Secret Service East of Constantinople*, 107.
48 Hopkirk, *On Secret Service East of Constantinople*, 108; and Barbara Tuchman, *The Zimmerman Telegram*, 18.
49 Hopkirk, *On Secret Service East of Constantinople*, 105–09.
50 McMeekin, *The Berlin-Baghdad Express*, 221n*.
51 The full details of this group are unclear. Last names are used in most of the sources. There was a Dr. Max Otto Schoenemann in Kermanshah and a Chilean named Pugin and Fritz Seiler in Isfahan; explorer and zoologist Erich Zugmayer and Walter Griesinger were in Kerman. Sykes, *Wassmuss, "The German Lawrence"*, 71; and Wynn, *Persia in the Great Game,* 256.
52 Sykes, *Wassmuss, "The German Lawrence"*, 79.
53 Sykes, *Wassmuss, "The German Lawrence"*, 89–101.
54 F. J. Mobley, in Mobley, *The History of the Great War*, 179.
55 Sykes, *Wassmuss, "The German Lawrence"*, 93.
56 Sykes, *Wassmuss, "The German Lawrence"*, 95.
57 Sykes, *Wassmuss, "The German Lawrence"*, 74.
58 Gene R. Garthwaite, "The Bakhtiyari Khans, the Government of Iran, and the British, 1846–1915," *International Journal of Middle East Studies* 3, no 1 (January 1972): 40–41; and Hamadan Kirmanshah et al., "South Persian and the Great War," *Geographical Journal* 58, no. 2 (August 1921), 103.
59 Taline Ter Minassian and Tom Rees, trans., *Most Secret Agent of Empire: Reginald Teague-Jones, Master Spy of the Great Game* (Oxford: Oxford University Press, 2015), 54.
60 Oskar Ritter von Niedermayer, *Under the Burning Sun of Iran*, unattributed translation of Unter der Gut Sonnes Irans (Dachau: Einhornverlag, 1925), 13.
61 Mobley, *The History of the Great War*, 273.
62 Mobley, *The History of the Great War*, 274.
63 Sykes, *Wassmuss, "The German Lawrence"*, 98.
64 Sykes, *Wassmuss, "The German Lawrence"*, 102.
65 The British pushed for a pact and a signed agreement on December 13, 1915, of the new Ilkhan Gholam Hosain Khan with the title of Sardar Mohtesham, the Ilbeg, and some of the junior Khans. On February 15, 1916, more were signed by senior Khans in Tehran and the British minister. Payment of 1,500 and 1,000 to the top and

bottom. Garthwaite, "The Bakhtiyari Khans, the Government of Iran, and the British, 1846–1915," 41.

66 Sykes, *Wassmuss, "The German Lawrence"*, 104.

67 Willem Floor, "Borāzjān, a Rural Market Town in Bushire's Hinterland," *Iran* 42 (2004): 179.

68 Sykes, *Wassmuss, "The German Lawrence"*, 107.

69 Sykes, *Wassmuss, "The German Lawrence"*, 109.

70 Hopkirk, *On Secret Service East of Constantinople*, 148.

71 Hopkirk, *On Secret Service East of Constantinople*, 148.

72 V. Minorsky, review, "Wassmuss, 'The German Lawrence' by Christopher Sykes," *Bulletin of the School of Oriental Studies, University of London* 9, no. 1 (1937): 244–45.

73 Sykes, *Wassmuss, "The German Lawrence"*, 122.

74 Garthwaite, "The Bakhtiyari Khans, the Government of Iran, and the British, 1846–1915," 41.

75 Richard Popplewell, "British Intelligence in Mesopotamia, 1914–1916," *Intelligence and National Security* 5, no. 3 (April 1990): 163.

76 Sykes, *Wassmuss, "The German Lawrence"*, 139.

77 Percy Sykes, *A History of Persia, Volume II* (London: MacMillan, 1915), 450.

78 Percy Sykes, *A History of Persia, Volume II*, 444–45.

79 McMeekin, *The Berlin-Baghdad Express*, 275.

80 Sykes, *A History of Persia, Volume II*, 135.

81 Sykes, *A History of Persia, Volume II*, 450.

82 Hopkirk, *On Secret Service East of Constantinople*, 153.

83 It would reach, at peak, 8,000.

84 Percy Sykes, "South Persia and the Great War," *Geographical Journal* 58, no. 2 (August, 1921): 101–16; and Wynn, *Persia in the Great Game*.

85 Thomas L. Hughes, "German Mission to Afghanistan, 1915–1916," *German Studies Review* 25, no. 3 (October 2002): 468.

86 Hopkirk, *On Secret Service East of Constantinople*, 216–18.

87 Hopkirk, *On Secret Service East of Constantinople*, 216–18.

88 Rodney Carlisle, *Encyclopedia of Intelligence and Counterintelligence* (London: Taylor & Francis, 2004), 699.

89 Sykes, *Wassmuss, "The German Lawrence,"* 181–91.

90 Sykes, *Wassmuss, "The German Lawrence,"* 181–91.

91 The participants of both missions were painted as brave but foolish, their efforts the work of amateurs, incompetents, and their goals so grandiose as to be ridiculous, even foolish. Veteran British diplomat and political officer in the Middle East Sir Ronald Storrs also dismissed Oppenheim's efforts as no real threat. Historian Hans-Ulrich Seidt discussed this as the work of amateurs in his book *Berlin, Kabul, Moskau*. He said there were three main problems: insufficient preparations, inadequate resources, and poor organizations. "Anyone looking through the series of documents entitled 'Measures and incident against our enemies' in the archives of the *Aswärtiges Amt* and expecting to find a cool, calculated meticulously planned 'Grab for World Power' will be disappointed. There is no doubt that Max von Oppenheim was thinking boldly in terms of Germany's bid for world power and that he conceived and proposed to the Imperial government a comprehensive and complete plan for the Orient, based on the inciting of revolution. But this plan lacked both careful preparation and sound material groundwork. The personnel and material needed for its realization were not there. It was inevitable that Max von Oppenheim's dream of a 'Holy War' would be followed by a painful awakening." Quoted in Grossman, *The Passion of Max von Oppenheim*, Kindle edition, location 2512–23. Donald M. McKale, "'The Kaiser's Spy': Max von Oppenheim and the Anglo-German Rivalry before and during the First World War," *European History Quarterly* 27, no. 2 (April 1997): 199–219. Historian Milan Hauner argued German concepts of *jihad* were motivated by "wishful strategic considerations" more than anything else. Instead, Hauner argues that the mission's greatest impact was, in fact, after the war, with German intrigues throughout the interwar and Second World War seeded with the mission to Afghanistan, 1914–1915. Milan Hauner, "The Soviet Threat to Afghanistan and India 1938–1940," *Modern Asian Studies* 15, no. 3 (1981): 287.

92 The term used was *ein Schlag in Wasser*. Quoted in Tilman Lüdke, *Jihad Made in Germany: Ottoman and German Propaganda and Intelligence Operations in the First World War* (Munster: Lit Verlag, 2005), 186.

93 John H. Maurer, *Outbreak of the First World War: Strategic Planning, Crisis Decision Making, & Deterrence Failure* (Westport, CT: Greenwood Press, 1995), 1–128.

94 McMeekin, *The Berlin-Baghdad Express*, 278–79.

95 Grossman, *The Passion of Max von Oppenheim*, Kindle edition, location 2374.

96 Jeffrey Record, *Beating Goliath: Why Insurgencies Win* (Lincoln, NE: Potomac Books, 2009), introduction. A. R. B. Linderman is less convinced but admits it's possible. See A. R. B. Linderman, *Rediscovering Irregular Warfare: Colin Gubbins and the Origins of Britain's Special Operations Executive* (Norman: University of Oklahoma Press, 2015), 197n55.

97 H. A. R. Gibb, "*T. E. Lawrence* by Charles Edmonds; *Lawrence of Arabia* by R. H. Kiernan; *A Paladin of Arabia* by N. N. E. Bray; *Wassmuss: The German Lawrence* by Christopher Sykes, Review," *International Affairs* (Royal Institute of International Affairs 1931–1939) 15, no. 4 (July–August, 1936): 628.

Part II: Global War on Ignorance and the Axis: The Special Operations Executive and the Office of Strategic Services

1 See Andrew Birtle, *A History of Counterinsurgency and Contingency Operations in the US Army*, Vol. 2 (US Government Printing, 1997); and A. R. B. Linderman, *Rediscovering Irregular Warfare: Colin Gubbins and the Origins of Britain's Special Operation Executive* (Norman: University of Oklahoma Press, 2016).

2 Giles Milton, *Churchill's Ministry of Ungentlemanly Warfare: The Mavericks Who Plotted Hitler's Defeat* (New York: Picador, 2017), 87.

3 Olga Khazan, "Gentleman Reading Each Other's Mail: A Brief History of Diplomatic Spying," *The Atlantic*, June 17, 2013, https://www.theatlantic.com/international/archive/2013/06/gentlemen-reading-each-others-mail-a-brief-history-of-diplomatic-spying/276940/.

4 William Stevenson, *A Man Called Intrepid: The Incredible True Story of the Master Spy Who Helped Win World War II* (New York: Skyhorse, 2013), 172.

5 The National Archives in College Park, Maryland, has many of the OSS files available. See Office of Strategic Services Personnel Files from World War II, https://www.archives.gov/research/military/ww2/oss/personnel-files.html.
6 Richard Harris Smith, *OSS: The Secret History if America's First Central Intelligence Agency* (New York: Rowman & Littlefield, 2005; originally published 1972); and Fernaudo M. Lujan, "Wanted: PhDs Who Can Win a Bar Fight," *Foreign Policy*, March 2013, http://foreignpolicy.com/2013/03/08/wanted-ph-d-s-who-can-win-a-bar-fight/.

Chapter 3: "Dishonest Adventurers": Monty Woodhouse and the SOE in Greece during the Second World War

1 C. M. Woodhouse, *Something Ventured: An Autobiography* (New York: Harper Collins, 240), 18.
2 Luther Craig, "German Defensive Policy in the Balkans, a Case Study: The Build Up in Greece, 1943," *Balkan Studies* 23, no. 2 (1982): 403–19.
3 Mark Mazower, *Inside Hitler's Greece: The Experience of Occupation, 1941–1944* (New Haven, CT, and London: Yale University Press, 1993), 144–45.
4 On August 9, they, as well as republicans and others, left. They were flown from Greece. There were three communists: Tzimas, Despotopoulos, and Petros Roussos. Tsrimokos from EAM, Komninos Pyromaglou, and George Kartalis were three noncommunist guerillas. Siantos arrived to represent another influence of ELAS. Also included were British officers, including David Wallace, a friend of Anthony Eden's who'd been in Greece during the outbreak of war. Edward Myers, Bottom Sapper (self-published, 1984), 1–45.
5 Woodhouse, *Something Ventured*, 68.
6 Woodhouse, *Something Ventured*, 1.
7 Woodhouse, *Something Ventured*, 1.
8 "Monty Woodhouse: Obituary," *The Guardian*, February 19, 2001, accessed January 1, 2016, http://www.theguardian.com/news/2001/feb/20/guardianobituaries2.
9 Woodhouse, *Something Ventured*, 10.
10 Imperial War Museum Archive (hereafter IWM), "Woodhouse Interview on SOE Greece", Oral History 31579, Reel 1.
11 Woodhouse, *Something Ventured*, 7.
12 Artemis Cooper, *Patrick Leigh Fermor: An Adventure* (London: John Murray, 2012), 125.
13 Cooper, *Patrick Leigh Fermor*, 126.
14 IWM, Woodhouse Interview, Reel 1.
15 C. M. Woodhouse, *The Struggle for Greece, 1941–1949* (Chicago, IL: Ivan R. Dee, 1976; 2002), 11, 21.
16 Woodhouse, *The Struggle for Greece*, 22.
17 Ritchie Ovendale, "Orme Garton Sargent," in *Oxford Dictionary of National Biography* (Oxford, NY: Oxford University Press, 2004), 979.
18 Woodhouse, *Something Ventured*, 15–17.
19 Cooper, *Patrick Light Fermor*, 144.

20 Woodhouse, *Something Ventured*, 18.
21 Woodhouse, *Something Ventured*, 19.
22 Woodhouse, *Something Ventured*, 22.
23 Myers, *Bottom Sapper*, 1–31.
24 Woodhouse, *Something Ventured*, 23.
25 Woodhouse, *Something Ventured*, 24.
26 Woodhouse, *Something Ventured*, 24.
27 Woodhouse, *Something Ventured*, 29.
28 NAUK RG HS5/353, File Number SOE Greece No. 103, from October 1942 to April 1943, Sir Orme Sargent, deputy undersecretary of the Foreign Office, to unknown query on Greece, March 16, 1943.
29 NAUK HS5-307, Greece & the Aegean, Sep 42–Aug 43, AD3 to COS 11.9.42.
30 Woodhouse, *Something Ventured*, 31.
31 Woodhouse, *Something Ventured*, 32.
32 Woodhouse, *Something Ventured*, 35.
33 Woodhouse, *Something Ventured*, 36.
34 Woodhouse, *Something Ventured*, 36.
35 Woodhouse, *Something Ventured*, 40.
36 Woodhouse, *Something Ventured*, 41.
37 Woodhouse, *Something Ventured*, 41
38 Woodhouse, *The Struggle for Greece*, 6.
39 Woodhouse, *Something Ventured*, 44.
40 NAUK HS5-346 Greece CD & SO Files, File Number SOE Greece No. 98, narrative summary by Col. Myers from Harling War Diary, covering period September 30 to December 10.
41 Woodhouse, *Something Ventured*, 48.
42 Woodhouse, *Something Ventured*, 47.
43 Woodhouse, *Something Ventured*, 48.
44 NAUK HS5-346 Greece CD & SO Files, File Number SOE Greece No. 98, narrative summary by Col. Myers from Harling War Diary, covering period September 30 to December 10.
45 NAUK RG HS5/353, File Number SOE Greece No. 103, from October 1942 to April 1943, letter to E. Tsouderos regarding Gorgopotamos, Asopos, and Papadia, December 2, 1942.
46 Woodhouse, *Something Ventured*, 53.
47 Quoted in A. R. B. Linderman, *Rediscovering Irregular Warfare: Colin Gubbins and the Origins of Britain's Special Operation Executive* (Norman: University of Oklahoma Press, 2016), 159.
48 Woodhouse, *Something Ventured*, 54.
49 Woodhouse, *Something Ventured*, 57.
50 Woodhouse, *Something Ventured*, 57.
51 Woodhouse, *Something Ventured*, 58.
52 Woodhouse, *Something Ventured*, 58.
53 Woodhouse, *Something Ventured*, 60.
54 Woodhouse, *Something Ventured*, 61.

55 "If, however, we are to have our military operations completely subordinated in the manner suggested by the Foreign Secretary it should be clearly understood that SOE will be able to play no part whatsoever in cutting communications, 5th Column, rebellion or collection of intelligence: all of which are at present highly organized, coordinated, and controlled by British SOE officers in Greece. Furthermore, as and when the AXIS weaken or withdraw there will be Civil War for power instead of a controlled and coordinated anti-Axis action which only the presence of our British officers can ensure." HS5-307, Greece & the Aegean, Sep 42–Aug 43, Keble to J.O.S. March 15, 1943.
56 Woodhouse, *Something Ventured*, 62.
57 Sir Orme Sargent, deputy undersecretary of the Foreign Office, to unknown query on Greece, March 16, 1943; NAUK RG HS5/353, File Number SOE Greece No. 103, from October 1942 to April 1943.
58 NAUK RG HS5/353, File Number SOE Greece No. 103, from October 1942 to April 1943; Sir Orme Sargent, deputy undersecretary of the Foreign Office, to unknown query on Greece, March 16, 1943.
59 NAUK HS5-346 Greece CD & SO Files, File Number SOE Greece No. 98, Leeper to Sir Orme Sargent, "Greek Policy in the Coming Months" May 24, 1943.
60 See David Kilcullen, *The Accidental Guerrilla: Fighting Small Wars in the Midst of Big Ones* (Oxford: Oxford University Press, 2011), 25–54.
61 NAUK HS5-346 Greece CD & SO Files, File Number SOE Greece No. 98; Further Political Aspects of the Greek Resistance Movements, April 30, 1943.
62 NAUK HS5-346 Greece CD & SO Files, File Number SOE Greece No. 98, Orme Sargent to Leeper May 1943, letter.
63 NAUK HS5-346 Greece CD & SO Files, File Number SOE Greece No. 98, CD to D/HV Regarding Telegram No. 487/9 from Cairo May 20, 1943.
64 C. M. Woodhouse, *Apple of Discord: A Survey of Recent Greek Politics in Their International Setting* (London: Hutchinson, 1948), 135.
65 Woodhouse, *Something Ventured*, 66; and Woodhouse, *The Struggle for Greece*, 39.
66 Woodhouse, *Something Ventured*, 66.
67 Myers, *Bottom Sapper*, 40.
68 David Brewer, *Greece, the Decade of War: Occupation, Resistance, and Civil War* (New York: I. B. Tauris, 2016).
69 Lidia Santarelli, "Muted Violence: Italian War Crimes in Occupied Greece," *Journal of Modern Italian Studies* 9, no. 3 (2004), 294; and James Bugwyn, *Mussolini Warlord: Failed Dreams of Empire* (New York: Enigma Books, 2012).
70 Woodhouse, *Something Ventured*, 67.
71 NAUK HS5-268, Greece Anglo-Italian Relations in the Balkans, Lemon to Cairo 22/9. Italics added.
72 Woodhouse, *Something Ventured*, 68.
73 Kyriakos Nalmpantis, "Time on the Mountain: The Office of Strategic Services in Axis-Occupied Greece, 1943–1944," doctoral thesis, Kent State University, 2010, 26.
74 Woodhouse, *Something Ventured*, 70.
75 Nalmpantis, "Time on the Mountain," 116.
76 Woodhouse, *Something Ventured*, 70–72.

77 D. M. Condit, *Case Study in Guerrilla War: Greece during World War II* (Washington, DC: Department of the Army and Special Operations Research Office, 1961), 20.
78 NAUK HS5-281, Greece Conferences 1944, Mobility No. 140 of Feb 17.
79 NAUK HS5-281, Greece Conferences 1944, Mobility No. 140 of Feb 17, Renovation No. 147 of Feb 17.
80 NAUK HS5-281, Greece Conferences 1944, Mobility No. 151 Feb 18.
81 NAUK HS5-281, Discuss No. 96 of Feb 18.
82 NAUK HS5-281, Discuss No. 96 of Feb 18. Italics added.
83 NAUK HS5-281, Greece Conferences 1944, to Mobility from Cairo No. 194 of Feb 19.
84 NAUK HS5-281, Greece Conferences 1944, to Mobility from Cairo No. 194 of Feb 19.
85 NAUK HS5-281, Greece Conferences 1944, to Mobility from Cairo No. 221 of Feb 26.
86 NAUK HS5-281 Greece Conferences 1944, Mobility No. 178 of Feb 27.
87 NAUK HS5-281 Greece Conferences 1944, announcement on February 29, 1944.
88 Woodhouse, *Something Ventured*, 76.
89 NAUK HS5-281 Greece Conferences 1944, announcement on February 29, 1944.
90 Woodhouse, *Apple of Discord*, 188.
91 HS5-280 Greece Koutsaina Conference, Minutes of First Meeting, Mobility No. 326 of April 29, 1944.
92 HS5-280 Greece Koutsaina Conference, Mobility No. 329 of April 30, 1944.
93 He suggested the following: NORTHERN BOUNDARIES. Calamas River from its mouth to Soulopoulp. Thence along the main road to the North West corner of the Yannina Lake. Thence along the main road to the confluence of the Cours and Metzovitiko Rivers. EASTERN BOUNDARIES. Going upstream the course of the river Gouras to its source. Thence following the heights of the Peristeri up to the Calamas sources. Thence following the course of the river Kalarritikos to its confluence with the Arachthos river. Thence following the course of the Arachthos river to the suburbs of Arta, thence along the Arta Amphilochia main road to Menidi and thence to the sea opposite Menidi. SOUTHERN BOUNDARIES: Amvrakikos Bay. WESTERN BOUNDARIES. Ionian Sea. (HS5-280 Greece Koutsaina Conference, Mobility No. 329 of April 30, 1944).
94 NAUK HS5-281 Greece Conferences 1944, Woodhouse, and Wines "Notification," May 6, 1944; Nalmpantis "Time on the Mountain," 83.
95 HS-339 Greece Assessment of Situation in Greece Feb 1942, June 1944 SOE Greece No. 82, "C. M. Woodhouse, Situation in Greece Jan to May 1944 received 26 May 1944."
96 1010686 Greece: Successful Operations April, May, June 1944.
97 Woodhouse, *Something Ventured*, 80.
98 Woodhouse, *Something Ventured*, 81.
99 Woodhouse, *Something Ventured*, 81.
100 Woodhouse, *Something Ventured*, 85.
101 Woodhouse, *Something Ventured*, 85.

102 Woodhouse, *Something Ventured*, 85.
103 Woodhouse, *Something Ventured*, 87.
104 Woodhouse, *Something Ventured*, 91.
105 HS5-337 Greece Political Intelligence Reports Particularly Greek Islands, December 1942 to November 1944, Report on Political Situation Oct 3–10, 1944.
106 Woodhouse, *Something Ventured*, 94.
107 Woodhouse, *Something Ventured*, 94.
108 Woodhouse, *Something Ventured*, 95.
109 Woodhouse, *Something Ventured*, 96.
110 Woodhouse, *Something Ventured*, 103.
111 Stephen Kinzer, *All the Shah's Men: An American Coup and the Roots of Middle East Terror* (New York: John Wiley & Sons, 2008).
112 Quoted in Robert Asprey, *War in the Shadows: The Guerrilla in History*, Vol. II (Bloomington, IN: iUniverse, 2002), 190–91.
113 C. M. Woodhouse, *Something Ventured* (London: Granada, 1982), 1.
114 Woodhouse, *The Struggle for Greece*, xxii.
115 Woodhouse, *The Struggle for Greece*, xix.
116 Woodhouse, *The Struggle for Greece*, xx.
117 Woodhouse, *The Struggle for Greece*, xviii.

Chapter 4: "Despite the Handicap of Her Sex": Cora Du Bois, OSS Research and Analysis Chief in Southeast Asia, 1943–1945

1 Quoted in Susan Seymour, *Cora Du Bois: Anthropologist, Diplomat, Agent* (Lincoln and London: University of Nebraska Press, 2015), 168.
2 NARA RG 226 Entry NM-54 1 Research and Analysis Branch, Office of the Chief, General Correspondences, 1942–1946 Box 22, File 101 Burma. Cora Dubois, Kandy HQ, to Director, Office of Strategic Services, Washington, Attention: All Staff members of the Far East Division/R&A/Washington, Re: R&A/SEAC Outpost Letter #44.
3 Hilary Lapsley quoted in Seymour, *Cora Du Bois*, 42.
4 Seymour, *Cora Du Bois*, 51.
5 Seymour, *Cora Du Bois*, 51.
6 Seymour, *Cora Du Bois*, 80.
7 Seymour, *Cora Du Bois*, 98.
8 Quoted in Seymour, *Cora Du Bois*, 95.
9 Seymour, *Cora Du Bois*, 98.
10 Quoted in Seymour, *Cora Du Bois*, 132.
11 Seymour, *Cora Du Bois*, 138.
12 Seymour, *Cora Du Bois*, 142.
13 *OSS Exhibition Catalog* (Washington, DC: Center for the Study of Intelligence, n.d.), 32.
14 See Robin W. Winks, *Cloak and Gown: Scholars in the Secret War, 1939–1961* (New Haven, CT: Yale University press, 1996; second edition), 90–91, 123–24, 467–78;

and Barry N. Katz, *Foreign Intelligence: Research and Analysis in the Office of Strategic Services, 1942–1945* (Cambridge, MA: Harvard University Press, 1989), 1–57.
15 On the creation and arms of the OSS, see Richard Harris Smith, *OSS: The Secret History if America's First Central Intelligence Agency* (New York: Rowman & Littlefield, 2005; originally published 1972).
16 NARA RG 226 E177 Washington Research and Analysis and State OIR Records Box 4, File: War Report, Office of Strategic Services, War Report, Office of Strategic Services (OSS) Volume 1, Prepared by the History Project, Strategic Service Unit, Office of the Assistant Secretary of War, War Department, Washington, DC.
17 Quoted in Seymour, *Cora Du Bois*, 171.
18 Seymour, *Cora Du Bois*, 171.
19 Quoted Seymour, *Cora Du Bois*, 174.
20 Seymour, *Cora Du Bois*, 174.
21 Seymour, *Cora Du Bois*, 176.
22 Eric Bergerud, *Touched with Fire: The Land War in the South Pacific* (London and New York: Penguin, 1996), 55–104.
23 Quoted in Seymour, *Cora Du Bois*, 176.
24 Quoted in Seymour, *Cora Du Bois*, 178.
25 NARA RG 2 OSS Personnel Files, Julia McWilliams, https://nara-media-001.s3.amazonaws.com/arcmedia/oss/McWilliams_Child_Julia.pdf; Seymour, *Cora Du Bois*, 179.
26 NARA RG 2 OSS Personnel Files, Julia McWilliams. The single best work on the OSS in this region remains Maochun Yu, *OSS in China: Prelude to Cold War* (Annapolis, MD: Naval Institute Press, 2013).
27 Seymour, *Cora Du Bois*, 181.
28 NARA RG 226 Entry NM-54 1 Research and Analysis Branch, Office of the Chief, General Correspondences, 1942–1946 Box 24, Folder 1, First Progress Report, R&A/OSS, CBI/SEAC, March 1, 1944.
29 NARA RG 226 Entry NM-54 1 Research and Analysis Branch, Office of the Chief, General Correspondences, 1942–1946 Box 24, Folder 1, Capt. Spencer to Dr William Langer, RE: Future of CBI R&A, 6 May 1944. Capt. Spencer to Dr William Langer, RE: Future of CBI R&A, May 6, 1944.
30 NARA RG 226 Entry NM-54 1 Research and Analysis Branch, Office of the Chief, General Correspondences, 1942–1946 Box 24, Folder 1, John Coughlin, U.S. Army Experimental Station, Nazira, Assam, to Doctor Langer, May 9, 1944.
31 Representative of that can be seen in, NARA RG 226 Entry NM-54 1 Research and Analysis Branch, Office of the Chief, General Correspondences, 1942–1946 Box 24, Folder 1, Joseph Spencer to William L. Langer, Oct 25, 1944, and NARA RG 226 Entry NM-54 1 Research and Analysis Branch, Office of the Chief, General Correspondences, 1942–1946 Box 24, Folder 1, Joseph Spencer to William F. Langer, 7/11/44.
32 NARA RG 226 Entry NM-54 1 Research and Analysis Branch, Office of the Chief, General Correspondences, 1942–1946 Box 24, Folder 1, Joseph Spencer to William L. Langer, 6/11/44/.

33 NARA RG 226 Entry NM-54 1 Research and Analysis Branch, Office of the Chief, General Correspondences, 1942–1946, Box 24, Folder 1, Joseph Spencer to William L. Langer, June 11, 1944.
34 NARA RG 226 Entry NM-54 1 Research and Analysis Branch, Office of the Chief, General Correspondences, 1942–1946 Box 24, Folder 1, Lt. Cmdr. Turner H McBain, USNR to Brig. Gen. W. J. Donovan, Report on Trip to OSS Activities in CBI and SEAC, August 3, 1944.
35 NARA RG 226 Entry NM-54 1 Research and Analysis Branch, Office of the Chief, General Correspondences, 1942–1946 Box 24, Folder 1, Burton Fahs to William Langer, n.d., "Received Nov 16/44."
36 As one OSS official noted, "Women to China has been one of the hottest issues in the theater for two years and many of the ambitious have acquired badly burned fingers. Both General Stilwell and Ambassador Gauss bitterly oppose it. It is not a profitable issue to stick your neck out on." Yu, *OSS in China*, 553n104.
37 NARA RG 226 Entry NM-54 1 Research and Analysis Branch, Office of the Chief, General Correspondences, 1942–1946 Box 24, Folder 1, Burton Fahs to William Langer, n.d., "Received Nov 16/44."
38 NARA RG 226 Entry NM-54 1 Research and Analysis Branch, Office of the Chief, General Correspondences, 1942–1946 Box 22, File Outpost General I, 1944. W. L. Langer to General Donovan, Re: Problems of R & A Outposts, December 25, 1944.
39 NARA RG 226 Entry NM-54 1 Research and Analysis Branch, Office of the Chief, General Correspondences, 1942–1946 Box 23, File: China Theater, Charles B. Fahs to William L. Langer, Jan 16, 1945.
40 NARA RG 226 Entry NM-54 1 Research and Analysis Branch, Office of the Chief, General Correspondences, 1942–1946 Box 25, File: India Burma, William Langer to Col. John G. Coughlin, IBT, May 24, 1945.
41 NARA RG 226 Entry NM-54 1 Research and Analysis Branch, Office of the Chief, General Correspondences, 1942–1946 Box 21, File: Monthly Reports to Outposts, Cora Dubois, Monthly Report R&A/SEAC, May 31, 1945.
42 NARA RG 226 Entry NM-54 1 Research and Analysis Branch, Office of the Chief, General Correspondences, 1942–1946 Box 21, File: Monthly Reports to Outposts, Research and Analysis Branch Monthly Report to the Outposts For the Period May 1–May 31, 1945, June 5, 1945.
43 NARA RG 226 Entry NM-54 1 Research and Analysis Branch, Office of the Chief, General Correspondences, 1942–1946 Box 22, File Outpost General I, 1944, George C. Demas, Far East Theater Office, to SO, MO, OG, DDIS, R&A, SI, X-2, CD, MU, Schools and Training, Services, Security, R&D, Field Photographic, medical Services, Transportation, Communications, April 27, 1944.
44 NARA RG 226 Entry NM-54 1 Research and Analysis Branch, Office of the Chief, General Correspondences, 1942–1946 Box 23, File: Chungking, Lt. Col. R. B. Hall to Dr. William L. Langer, January 18, 1944.
45 Troy James Sacquety, "The Organizational Evolution of OSS Detachment 101 in Burma, 1942–1945," doctoral thesis, Texas A&M University, May 2008, 267.

46 NARA RG 226 Entry NM-54 1 Research and Analysis Branch, Office of the Chief, General Correspondences, 1942–1946 Box 23, File: China Theater. Charles B. Fahs to William L. Langer, January 16, 1945.
47 NARA RG 226 Entry NM-54 1 Research and Analysis Branch, Office of the Chief, General Correspondences, 1942–1946 Box 22, File Outpost General I, 1944. O. C. Doering (unnamed, but mentioned in cover sheet), Functions and Proposed Personnel of R&A Outposts in SEAC and CBI, n.d., but no later than March 27, 1944.
48 The poaching included the following people: John T., Stark, Roy Jones, Gordon Heid, John M. Corbett, and Robert Jones: Jones was the only one with research background. Heid "knows your own pet area, Cora, and should be very useful to you. He spent seven years as a field geologist for the Standard Oil Company of New Jersey in Sumatra, Java, Madera, Borneo, and New Guinea. He speaks Malay. His departure is a blow for we could have used him to advantage in a series of forthcoming JANIS studies that are demanded of us." NARA RG 226 E54 53 Correspondences with Outposts Box 2, File: Outgoing. John Appleman to CDB and Joseph Spencer February 23, 1945, SEAC assignment.
49 NARA RG 226 Entry NM-54 1 Research and Analysis Branch, Office of the Chief, General Correspondences, 1942–1946 Box 25, File: India Burma, John Coughlin to William L. Langer, May 8, 1945.
50 NARA RG 226 Entry NM-54 1 Research and Analysis Branch, Office of the Chief, General Correspondences, 1942–1946 Box 25, File: India Burma. William Langer to Col. John G. Coughlin, IBT, May 24, 1945.
51 NARA RG 226 E54 53 Correspondences with Outposts Box 1942–1946 2 (part II) File: Incoming, CDB to Dr. Langer, May 2, 1945.
52 NARA RG 226 E54 53 Correspondences with Outposts Box 1942–1946 2 (part II) File: Incoming, CDB to Dr. Langer, May 2, 1945.
53 NARA RG 226 Entry NM-54 1 Research and Analysis Branch, Office of the Chief, General Correspondences, 1942–1946 Box 25, File: India Burma. William Langer to Col. John G. Coughlin, IBT, May 24, 1945.
54 NARA RG 226 Entry NM-54 1 Research and Analysis Branch, Office of the Chief, General Correspondences, 1942–1946 Box 25, File: India Burma, Cora Du Bois to Dr. Burton Fahs, Re: Lubrications from IBT/R&A, May 22, 1945.
55 This report reads in part: "OSS specialists have been assigned to the Fourteenth Air Force and the Twentieth Bomber Command were they have been made available to A-2 OSS intelligence collected in other theaters as well as in Washington, and where they have collaborated in producing target analyses for air operations against Japan and Japanese controlled areas." Analysis of Incendiary Experience: "OSS fire damage experts have analyzed the success of various incendiary weapons especially in the European theater are expected to provide the basis for work in the Far East Theater, where these experts have been invited by the 20th and 21st Air Force Commands. Numbers Racket" on keeping tabs on production and stock of enemy's weapons. Food and Agro Work. "On the Spot" Intelligence and Studies. Early phases had agents in Europe to provide intelligence, Nothing on Japan. Photographic Intelligence Documentation. Services to OSS: R&A service to other branches. "These services have consisted of briefing and providing special reports, maps, and guides for OSS operatives in Europe and the Far

East." Map intelligence services and Field Memoranda, NARA RG 226 Entry NM-54 1 Research and Analysis Branch, Office of the Chief, General Correspondences, 1942–1946 Box 18, File 8: Achievements of R&A, Memorandum from Alvah V. Sulloway to William L. Langer, April 20, 1945.

56 Also, "Services similar to those performed for OSS operations have also been rendered to Theater Commanders in China, SEAC, and Burma—particularly through the program of Detachment 101 and Arakan Field Unit." NARA RG 226 Entry NM-54 1 Research and Analysis Branch, Office of the Chief, General Correspondences, 1942–1946 Box 18, File 8: Achievements of R&A, R&A/Far East Division in SEAC/IB and the China Theater [believed to be April 1945].

57 NARA RG 226 Entry NM-54 1 Research and Analysis Branch, Office of the Chief, General Correspondences, 1942–1946 Box 18, File 8: Achievements of R&A, R&A/Far East Division in SEAC/IB and the China Theater [believed to be April 1945].

58 Bob Bergin, "War of a Different Kind: OSS and Free Thai Operations in World War II," *Studies in Intelligence* 55, no. 4 (December 2011), 11–22, accessed at *CIA Library of Intelligence*, May 11, 2017, https://www.cia.gov/library/center-for-the-study-of-intelligence/csi-publications/csi-studies/studies/vol.-55-no.-4/pdfs-vol.-55-no.-4/Bergin-OSS%20and%20Free%20Thai-13Jan.pdf.

59 NARA RG 226 Entry NM-54 1 Research and Analysis Branch, Office of the Chief, General Correspondences, 1942–1946 Box 25, File: India Burma. Cora Du Bois to Dr. Burton Fahs, Re: Lubrications from IBT/R&A, May 22, 1945.

60 NARA RG 226 Entry NM-54 1 Research and Analysis Branch, Office of the Chief, General Correspondences, 1942–1946 Box 25, File: India Burma. Cora Du Bois to Dr. Burton Fahs, Re: Lubrications from IBT/R&A, May 22, 1945.

61 NARA RG 226 Entry NM-54 1 Research and Analysis Branch, Office of the Chief, General Correspondences, 1942–1946 Box 21, File: Monthly Reports to Outposts, Cora Dubois, Monthly Report R&A/SEAC, May 31, 1945.

62 NARA RG 226 Entry NM-54 1 Research and Analysis Branch, Office of the Chief, General Correspondences, 1942–1946 Box 21, File: Monthly Reports to Outposts, Research and Analysis Branch Monthly Report to the Outposts For the Period May 1–May 31, 1945, June 5, 1945.

63 NARA RG 226 Entry NM-54 1 Research and Analysis Branch, Office of the Chief, General Correspondences, 1942–1946 Box 25, File: India Burma. Cora Dubois, Progress Report, Research and Analysis Branch, May 1945, June 6, 1945.

64 NARA RG 226 Entry NM-54 1 Research and Analysis Branch, Office of the Chief, General Correspondences, 1942–1946 Box 25, File: India Burma, Cora Dubois, Progress Report, Research and Analysis Branch, May 1945, June 6, 1945.

65 Stelle joined in March of 1944, while Spencer was head of R&A in SEAC. NARA RG 226 Entry NM-54 1 Research and Analysis Branch, Office of the Chief, General Correspondences, 1942–1946 Box 24, Folder 1, First Progress Report, R&A/OSS, CBI/SEAC, March 1, 1944.

66 NARA RG 226 Entry NM-54 1 Research and Analysis Branch, Office of the Chief, General Correspondences, 1942–1946 Box 25, File: India Burma, Cora Du Bois to Dr. Burton Fahs, Re: Lubrications from IBT/R&A, May 22, 1945.

67 NARA RG 226 E54 53 Correspondences with Outposts Box 1942–1946 2 (part II) File: Incoming, Cora Dubois to Dr. Langer and Dr. Fahs, RE: Rangoon City Team, June 7, 1945.
68 The researchers were organized into an operational part of the offensive with intelligence capabilities, originally tried in Europe, to target areas of keen research value.
69 NARA RG 226 E54 53 Correspondences with Outposts Box 1942–1946 2 (part II) File: Incoming, Intelligence Officer to Strategic Service Officer, Re: Comments on R&A Theater Report for May, June 7, 1945.
70 NARA RG 226 E54 53 Correspondences with Outposts Box 1942–1946 2 (part II) File: Incoming, Cora Dubois to Burton Fahs, RE: Instructions for Microfiling, June 29, 1945.
71 Seymour, *Cora Du Bois*, 201.
72 Quoted in Seymour, *Cora Du Bois*, 236.
73 Seymour, *Cora Du Bois*, 201–37.
74 Quoted in Seymour, *Cora Du Bois*, 242.

Part III: Mavericks of Vietnam

1 Robert McNamara, *In Retrospect: The Tragedy and Lessons of Vietnam* (New York: Vintage Books, 1996), 32–33.

Chapter 5: Expert in Exile: Bernard Fall and Speaking Truth to Power in Vietnam

1 Dorothy Fall, *Bernard Fall: Memories of a Soldier Scholar* (Lincoln, NE: Potomac Books, 2006), 64–65.
2 Fall, *Bernard Fall*, 10.
3 Fall calls attention to this after the war, when he proposes changes to be made in German Youth Groups whose populace was made of 95 percent Hitler Youth. See Bernard Fall, "Possible Improvements of the GYA Program," July 28, 1947, File: Correspondences and Evidence Pertaining to the War Crimes Trial, esp. Krupp Trial May to August 1948. John F. Kennedy Library, hereafter JFK Library, Bernard Fall Papers, Box W-1 Series 2.3 WWII Nuremberg Trials.
4 Bernard Fall, *Last Reflections on a War* (Kindle edition), location 152 of 243; and Fall, *Bernard Fall*, 12.
5 This was not the case in other parts of Europe, especially Greece. See Gerhard Weinberg, "Some Myths about World War II," *Journal of Military History* 75 (July 2011): 706–7, 709, accessed October 21, 2015, http://h-diplo.org/essays/PDF/JMH-Weinberg-SomeMythsOfWWII.pdf.
6 Nicholas Atkin, *The French at War 1934–1944* (London: Longman, 2001), 52.
7 Atkin, *The French at War 1934–1944*, 52.
8 Stephen Cullen, "Legion of the Damned: the Milice Francaise, 1943–1945," *Military Illustrated: Past and Present* (March 2008), 1–3.
9 Fall, *Bernard Fall*, 16–17.
10 In H. R. Kedward, *In Search of the Maquis: Rural Resistance in Southern France, 1942–1944* (Oxford: Clarendon Press, 1993), 246.

11 Fall, *Bernard Fall*, 80. The groups he joined put Fall among dedicated middle-class fighters with the *Mouvement del Jeunesse Sionist* (MJS) or Zionist Youth Movement, the Éclaireurs Israélites de France (EIF), a prewar "scouting group," and the Armée Juive (AJ, Jewish Army).
12 Gordon Wright, "Reflections on the French Resistance (1940–1944)," *Political Science Quarterly* 77, no. 3 (September 1962): 339.
13 Susan Zuccotti, *The Holocaust, The French, and the Jews* (New York: Basic Books, 1993), 183, 243.
14 Fall, *Bernard Fall*.
15 Fall, *Bernard Fall*, 21–22.
16 The EIF and AJ both had connection with the maquis. Susan Zuccotti, *The Holocaust, The French, and the Jews* (New York: Basic Books, 1993), 275.
17 Fall, *Last Reflections on a War*, location 208 of 3352.
18 See Will Irwin, *The Jedburghs: The Secret History of the Allied Special Forces, France, 1944* (New York: Public Affairs, 2006); and Colin Beavan, *Operation Jedburgh: D-Day and America's First Shadow War* (London: Penguin, 2006).
19 Robert Aspry, *War in the Shadows, The Guerrilla in History, Volume I* (Bloomington, IN: iUniverse, 2002), 317.
20 Fall, *Bernard Fall*, 28.
21 Fall, *Bernard Fall*, 29.
22 Fall, *Bernard Fall*, 30–36.
23 Fall, *Bernard Fall*, 36.
24 William Manchester, *The Arms of Krupp: The Rise and Fall of the Industrial Dynasty that Armed Germany at War* (New York: Little, Brown, 2003), 631–32.
25 Office of the Chief of Counsel for War Crimes, Staff Evidence Analysis by Bernard Fall, September 16, 1947, Affidavit by Alfried Krupp, August 14, 1947, File: Correspondences and Evidence Pertaining to the War Crimes Trial, esp. Krupp Trial May to August 1948. JFK Library, Bernard Fall Papers, Box W-1 Series 2.3 WWII Nuremberg Trials.
26 Office of the Chief of Counsel for War Crimes, Staff Evidence Analysis by Bernard Fall, September 16, 1947, Affidavit by Alfried Krupp, August 14, 1947, File: Correspondences and Evidence Pertaining to the War Crimes Trial, esp. Krupp Trial May to August 1948. JFK Library, Bernard Fall Papers, Box W-1 Series 2.3 WWII Nuremberg Trials.
27 The IMT's final verdict referred to the Krupp firm as "This huge octopus with its body at Essen," quoted in Manchester, *The Arms of Krupp*, 657.
28 Fall and Joseph C. Pallenberg to Thayer, June 24, 1947, Memo Regarding Transportation, File March-June 1948, Correspondence and Evidence Pertaining to War Crimes Trial, esp. Krupp, JFK Library, Bernard Fall Papers, Box W-1 Series 2.3 WWII Nuremberg Trials. Starvation, TB, beatings, rape, and murder abounded within the festering population of slave labor that numbered 15,000 foreign workers (and grew to 35,000) and thousands more prisoners of war (POWs) and Jewish inmates. Desires for efficiency created minor respites and horror shows. Doctors and staff debated how illness and starvation effected production. Pregnancy spawned from rape of foreign women warranted the creation of abortion clinics on site. And the greatest targets for

violence were Russians and Jews. Russians were fed less and worked harder, including graveyard shifts between handful of hours of sleep and fed water posing as soup. They were also segregated from each for fear of subversion and sabotage. Jewish inmates with skilled labor were marched past the barbed wire of their concentration camps to factories. Worse, Krupp had established workshops using the labor of the death camps, particularly at Auschwitz, including the so-called Berthawerks, a howitzer plant named after Alfried Krupp's mother in Silesia, a factory built and worked by Jews. See Office of the Chief of Counsel for War Crimes, Staff Evidence Analysis by Bernard Fall April 6, 1947, Strength and Armament of the Work Police, from the Document Center at Herford, HQ Int. Div. File: January–March 47, Correspondence and Evidence of Pertaining to War Crimes Trials, Especially Krupp Trials. Office of the Chief of Counsel for War Crimes, Staff Evidence Analysis by Bernard Fall, April 11, 1947, Draft of a Request to be addressed by Kupke to the Reichsministry for Food, May 15, 1944, File: March–June 1948, Correspondence and Evidence Pertaining to War Crimes Trial, esp. Krupp, JFK Library, Bernard Fall Papers, Box W-1 Series 2.3 WWII Nuremberg Trials. See also Ulrich Herbert, *Hitler's Foreign Workers: Enforced Labor in Germany during the Third Reich* (Cambridge: Cambridge University Press, 1997), 214. Manchester, *The Arms of Krupp*, 450–52, 492, 520–22, 524.

29 Manchester, *The Arms of Krupp*, 450. At Essen, Krupp employed 600 members of the Gestapo and Work Police (Krupp's own security force), armed with machine guns, submachine guns, and small arms that made them the equivalent of a light battalion.

30 JFK Library, Bernard Fall Papers, Box W-1 Series 2.3 WWII Nuremberg Trials, Fall to Mr. Marcu [*sic*], Special Consultant, July 8, 1947, Memo Re: Trip to Northern Germany, File: Correspondences and Evidence Pertaining to the War Crimes Trial, esp. Krupp Trial May to August 1948.

31 JFK Library, Bernard Fall Papers.

32 In two years, Fall got a first-class experience in research and analysis in the most important trial of the century. It introduced him to methods, procedures, and analytical modes of thinking about war, economics, and ideology. Fall noted that this kind of work required "an excellent knowledge of the German language, of the German economic problems, of the Nazi organization and the technical, political, economic, military, and legal terminology and abbreviations, which could otherwise be the source of mistakes liable to change the sense of the documents concerned." JFK Library, Bernard Fall Papers, Box W-1 Series 2.3 WWII Nuremberg Trials, Document on Duties of Research Analyst, Trial Team III, File: Correspondences and Evidence Pertaining to the War Crimes Trial, esp. Krupp Trial May to August 1948.

33 JFK Library, Bernard Fall Papers, Box W-1 Series 2.3 WWII Nuremberg Trials. Letter Carbon of Child Services Officer, unknown recipient, no date, JFK Library, Bernard Fall Papers, Box W-1 Series 2.3 WWII Nuremberg Trials, File: "Correspondence."

34 Manchester, *The Arms of Krupp*, 650–55.

35 Quoted in Manchester, *The Arms of Krupp*, 657.

36 Quoted in Fall, *Bernard Fall*, 40.

37 Krupp was a proud member of the SS, and his papers revealed close to 70,000 foreign workers, 23,000 POWs, and nearly 5,000 concentration camp prisoners (almost exclusively Jews) for a slave labor force of est. 98,000 people. Manchester, *The Arms of Krupp*, 5, 11, 649–51.

38 Manchester, *The Arms of Krupp*, 5, 11, 649–51.

39 Bernard Fall, "The Case against Alfred Krupp," *Prevent World War III* (Summer 1951): 39.

40 Fall, "The Case against Alfred Krupp," 40.

41 At trial's end Fall focused on the future and studied for a year at the Sorbonne (1948–1949) before finding work as a Child Search Office for the International Refugee Organization in Munich (1949–1950), hoping to reunite children orphaned from the war with their parents, an orphan helping orphans, and did a stint as the manager of U.S. Army newspaper *Stars and Stripes* (1950–1951). Fall, *Bernard Fall*, 43.

42 Fall, *Bernard Fall*, 43–44.

43 He explored the depth of the German Army's unique role in German culture and politics, use of insurgencies during the Ruhr rebellion, key politicians, and more. Robert M. Kempner, former deputy chief of consul for war crimes, and other contacts in the Office, Chief of Counsel for War Crime (OCC), assisted in getting documents. These included Trial of Major War Criminals, Volume XXXV Document D-854. Bernard Fall, "Illegal Rearmament under the Weimar Republic," master's thesis, Political Science Syracuse University (June 1952), 137n156.

44 Fall included entire sections of the thesis to the "Steel Barons," notably Krupp. See Fall, "Illegal Rearmament under the Weimar Republic," 209–11.

45 Fall, "Illegal Rearmament under the Weimar Republic," 121.

46 Fall, "Illegal Rearmament under the Weimar Republic," ii.

47 Fall, "Illegal Rearmament under the Weimar Republic," 190.

48 Fall, "Illegal Rearmament under the Weimar Republic," 253.

49 During the First World War, Vandenbosch was General Pershing's translator. He later served with the OSS in Asian during the war, was a scholar of Southeast Asia and of the Dutch experience of colonialism in Indonesia, and part of the U.S. delegation to San Francisco who drafted the charter of the United Nations. Vandenbosch had just published a primer on the UN's structure and goals, and was beginning his research on what would become *South East Asia among the World Powers* when Fall became his student. Profile of Amry Vandenbosch at the Patterson School of Diplomacy and Commerce, University of Kentucky Website, accessed September 2, 2016, http://www.ukalumni.net/s/1052/index-no-right.aspx?sid=1052&gid=1&pgid=1109.

50 Fall, *Bernard Fall*, 56.

51 Fredrik Logevall, *Embers of War: The Fall of an Empire and the Making of America's of Vietnam* (New York: Random House, 2013), xx.

52 Logevall, *Embers of War*, 362.

53 Fall, *Bernard Fall*, 66–67.

54 Bernard Fall, *Street without Joy* (Harrisburg, PA: Stackpole Books, 1994; 1961), 256.

55 Fall, *Bernard Fall*, 67.

56 Fall, *Bernard Fall*, 68.

57 Fall, *Bernard Fall*, 69.

58 Fall, *Bernard Fall*, 70–72.

59 Fall, *Street without Joy*, 144; and "Chronology, 23 July 1953–5 August 1953," *Chronology of Intentional Events and Documents* 9, no. 15 (July 23–August 5, 1953): 472.
60 Fall, "Chronology, 23 July 1953–5 August 1953," 472.
61 Fall, "Chronology, 23 July 1953–5 August 1953," 472.
62 Fall, *Street without Joy*, 147.
63 Fall, *Street without Joy*, 151.
64 Fall, *Street without Joy*, 162.
65 Fall, *Street without Joy*, 165.
66 Fall, *Street without Joy*, 165.
67 Fall, *Street without Joy*, 168.
68 Fall, *Street without Joy*, 169–71.
69 Fall, *Bernard Fall*, 79–83.
70 Fall, *Street without Joy*, 271.
71 Fall, *Street without Joy*, 371.
72 Fall, *Bernard Fall*, 83.
73 Bernard Fall, "Indochina: The Seven Year Dilemma," *Military Review* XXXIII, no. 7 (October 1953): 30.
74 Bernard B. Fall, "Political Development of Viet-Nam, VJ-Day to the Geneva Cease-Fire," Doctoral Thesis, Syracuse University, 1955, iv.
75 Quoted in Fall, *Bernard Fall*, 92.
76 Fall, *Bernard Fall*, 92.
77 Fall, "Political Development of Viet-Nam, VJ-Day to the Geneva Cease-Fire," 60–229.
78 Fall, "Political Development of Viet-Nam, VJ-Day to the Geneva Cease-Fire," 237.
79 Quoted in Fall, "Political Development of Viet-Nam, VJ-Day to the Geneva Cease-Fire," 237–38.
80 Fall, "Political Development of Viet-Nam, VJ-Day to the Geneva Cease-Fire," 493.
81 Fall, "Political Development of Viet-Nam, VJ-Day to the Geneva Cease-Fire," 485.
82 Fall, "Political Development of Viet-Nam, VJ-Day to the Geneva Cease-Fire," 870.
83 Fall, "Political Development of Viet-Nam, VJ-Day to the Geneva Cease-Fire," 1001.
84 Quoted in Fall, *Bernard Fall*, 114.
85 Fall, *Bernard Fall*, 115.
86 Fall, *Bernard Fall*, 115.
87 Fall, *Bernard Fall*, 117.
88 Fall, *Bernard Fall*, 117.
89 Fall, *Bernard Fall*, 118.
90 Fall, *Bernard Fall*, 118.
91 Fall, *Bernard Fall*, 121.
92 Fall, *Bernard Fall*, 121.
93 Obituaries kept reporting village chiefs were dying, killed by "bandits" almost once a day. Then he found evidence in one year of 452 dead village officials. He made a map of the deaths, and another of reported guerrilla activity of communist cells in South Vietnam. They were the same areas. All of this happening from "criminal" element, because, of course, Diem had things locked. It was anything but the enemy communists. Fall, *Bernard Fall*.

94 Quoted in Fall, *Bernard Fall*, 123–24.
95 Fall, *Bernard Fall*, 123. JFK Library, Bernard Fall Papers, Box P-1 Papers and Reports by Fall, Bernard Fall, *The International Position of South Viet-Nam*, Part I: Thirteenth Conference of the Institute of Pacific Relations, Lahore, Pakistan, February 1958 (New York: Institute of Pacific Relations, 1958).
96 Fall, *The International Position of South Viet-Nam*, Part I.
97 Fall, *The International Position of South Viet-Nam*, Part I, 4.
98 Fall, *The International Position of South Viet-Nam*, Part I, 5.
99 Fall, *The International Position of South Viet-Nam*, Part III, 8.
100 "MAAG has five divisions: Joint Service Support; Comptroller; Combat Arms and Training and Organized Advisory Teams does the actual spade work of shaping the South Vietnamese Army in its American mold. There are American advisors attached to most South Vietnamese filed units and headquarters. They advise the Vietnamese unit commanders, most of whom have risen in at field and generals' ranks in less than five years, in tactics as well as supply, training, and maintenance. This writer has seen American advisory staffs attached to larger units, but single advisors are rotated to battalion or company headquarters as well."TERM was to survey equipment needs after French withdrawal, mostly covering U.S. equipment that had gone to the French. Other U.S. aid programs support the SV from Korea, the Philippines, and Taiwan. About 250 mill. discusses use of damaged and worn goods, too. NV complains about TERM saying it is cover for illegal smuggling of U.S. personnel. TERM is also a "whiphand" over military aid to SV. It's a leaver to break deadlocks with SV: not doing what the U.S. wants, TERM will take back gear. Fall, *The International Position of South Viet-Nam*, Part 3, 11–13.
101 Fall, *The International Position of South Viet-Nam*, Part III, 18.
102 Lansdale's success in the Philippines and knowledge of communist strategy made him an ideal advisor to Diem during the conflicts with the sects in 1954–1955 (Bohannan, as usual, was not mentioned). Fall, *The International Position of South Viet-Nam*, Part III, 18.
103 Fall, *The International Position of South Viet-Nam*, Part III, 22.
104 Fall, *The International Position of South Viet-Nam*, Part III, 23–24.
105 Fall, *The International Position of South Viet-Nam*, Part III, 23–24.
106 Fall, *The International Position of South Viet-Nam*, Part III, 25–26. Note: the work he's critiquing is MAAG HQ, Vietnam *Vietnamese History, People and Customs*, Saigon, March 1957. Fall, *The International Position of South Viet-Nam*, Part 3, 32n66.
107 Fall, *The International Position of South Viet-Nam*, Part IV, 1, 10.
108 Robert Fahs, "Back to a Forgotten Street: Bernard Fall and the Limits of Armed Intervention," *Prologue* 43, no. 1 (Spring 2011), accessed on May 7, 2015, http://www.archives.gov/publications/prologue/2011/spring/bernard-fall.html.
109 Quoted from reproduced document in Fahs, "Back to a Forgotten Street," accessed on May 13, 2013.
110 Fahs, "Back to a Forgotten Street."
111 Quoted in Fall, *Bernard Fall*, 190.
112 Quoted from FBI surveillance report, dated March 1, 1964, reprinted in Fall, *Bernard Fall*, 196.

113 Fall, *Bernard Fall*, 130.
114 Quoted in Fall, *Bernard Fall*, 134.
115 Quoted in Fall, *Bernard Fall*, 135.
116 Fall, *Bernard Fall*, 138.
117 Fall, *Bernard Fall*, 146–47.
118 Galula was invited to participate in the famous 1962 RAND symposium on counterinsurgency, attended by notable British practitioners from the Malaysian "Emergency" and hosted by Lansdale, Bohannan, Valeriano, and others who had served against the Huk. A. A. Cohen's biography of Galula remains the best monograph on the subject, establishing the professional friendship and shared ideas of the two, but little more. A. A. Cohen, *Galula: The Life and Writings of the French Officer Who Defined the Art of Counterinsurgency* (New York: Praeger, 2012).
119 Fall, *Bernard Fall*, 176.
120 Fall, *Bernard Fall*, 189–204.
121 When Maj. Gen. William P. Yarborough was informed, he contacted the FBI's assistant director to find out why Fall, who had an active lecture circuit including on U.S. military institutions, was now considered some kind of risk to the John F. Kennedy Center for Special Warfare. Hoover responded with a veiled threat to bring this up with the assistant chief of staff for intelligence, Department of the Army, instead of answering the question. When the Pentagon wrote back to Yarborough, they said he was an expert but critical of U.S. efforts and "that he has supported the French Government's position in Vietnam of negotiation between interested parties. He is in an excellent position to influence thinking on our efforts in Vietnam through his published writing and speaking appearances." Emphasis added, Fall, *Bernard Fall*, 200.
122 The general ignored the challenge of Fall's expertise, and Fall presented on July 29–30 in 1964. Yarborough told Fall's wife in the 1990s that "Bernard Fall was one of the acknowledged experts on Southeast Asia, Vietnam, Indochina. He was certainly one of those who had the necessary background, understanding, and expertise to help us and so, every early in the game, I contacted him along with other types that had been with the British in Malaya. Certainly, we wanted to know what had happened at Diem Bien Phu and placed like that and Bernard Fall had a grasp of the whole, only physical environment, but psychological and political environments. I had read *Street without Joy* and I felt that the lessons for the US Army in *Street without Joy* were many." Fall, *Bernard Fall*, 200.
123 He wrote from Cambodia on August 10, the Americans having been expelled by Prince Sihanouk. Attacks across the border of Vietnam grew. He even walked across the Vietnamese border himself, seeing just how poorly patrolled and open to insurgent movement the border had become. The Cambodians were terrified of the Viet Cong (VC). "Look at the VN army post there (a mile away)—they're so scared of the VCs they don't even come out and patrol the boundary. And look at the special housing for the 10 US advisors. They get brought in and out by helicopter. Nobody patrols." Fall, *Bernard Fall*, 207.
124 Neil Sheehan, *A Bright Shining Lie: John Paul Vann and America in Vietnam* (New York: Random House, 1988), 543.
125 Fall, *Bernard Fall*, 210.

126 Bernard B. Fall, "Vietnam Blitz: A Report on the Impersonal War," *New Republic* (October 9, 1965): 17–21.
127 Andrew Birtle, "PROVN, Westmoreland, and the Historians: A Reappraisal," *Journal of Military History* 72, no. 4 (October 2008): 1213.
128 Fall, *Bernard Fall*, 229.
129 Quoted in Fall, *Bernard Fall*, 229.
130 Quoted in Fall, *Bernard Fall*, 231–32.
131 Fall, *Bernard Fall*, 231–32. *Street without Joy* came out in a second edition and has never been out of print. Critics praised *Hell in a Very Small Place.* He edited and wrote an intro on a collection of Ho Chi Minh's writers, *Ho Chi Minh: On Revolution*. He wrote the entry on Vietnam for *Encyclopedia Britannica*, as Lawrence was asked to do so for guerrilla warfare. He published major pieces for *Horizon* magazine ("Two Thousand Years of War in Viet-Nam"), *Esquire* ("Seventeen Little Wars Nobody Talks About"), and *Foreign Affairs* ("Vietnam in the Balance").
132 Fall, quoted in Fall, *Bernard Fall*, 251–52.

Chapter 6: The Ad Man and the Wolf: The Victories and Defeats of Edward Lansdale and Charles Bohannan in Southeast Asia, 1945–1968

1 While Lansdale recalled that John Foster Dulles asked him to do this mission, it was actually Allen Dulles. See *Foreign Relations of the United States, 1952–1954*, Volume XIII, Part 1, Indochina (in two parts), 525. The Special Committee met in Mr. Kyes's office at 3:30 P.M. January 29, 1954, Office of the Historian of the State Department, accessed on January 2, 2016, https://history.state.gov/historicaldocuments/frus1952-54v13p1/d525.
2 *Foreign Relations of the United States, 1952–1954*, 525.
3 Quoted in Cecil B. Currey, *Edward Lansdale: The Unquiet American* (New York: Houghton Mifflin, 1988), 136.
4 Charles Ted Rutledge Bohannan (CTRB) Papers, hereafter, Box 1, File: Correspondence, Charles and Dorothy Bohannan, Edward Lansdale, "Dorothy: One Memory about Boh," November 18, 1982.
5 Edward G. Lansdale, *In the Midst of Wars: An American Mission in South East Asia* (Bronx, NY: Fordham University Press, 1972; 1991), 147.
6 Lansdale, *In the Midst of Wars*, 149.
7 CTRB Papers, "Dorothy: One Memory about Boh."
8 Currey, *Edward Lansdale*, 104; and Barbara Ehrenreich, *Bright-Sided: How the Relentless Promotion of Positive Thinking Has Undermined America* (New York: Henry Holt, 2009), 86–90, 133, 136, 140, 211, 228.
9 Forsyth Library Special Collections, Fort Hayes State University, Kansas, Cecil Currey Collection, hereafter CCC, Dorothy Bohannan interview by Cecil Currey, July 27, 1985.
10 Currey, *Edward Lansdale*, 9–12.
11 Claring Bohannan interview by Jason S. Ridler, May 10, 2011.

12 Clyde Kluckhon, *To the Foot of the Rainbow: A Tale of Twenty Five Hundred Miles of Wandering on Horseback through the Southwest Enchanted Land* (New York: The Century, 1927).

13 Alfred McCoy interviewed Bohannan for his book *Policing America's Empire*, where he described himself as an "expert" in Navajo folklore. Alfred McCoy, *Policing America's Empire: The United States, the Philippines, and the Rise of the Surveillance State* (Madison: University of Wisconsin Press, 2009), 377.

14 Jason Betzinez and Wilbur Sturtevant Nye, *I Fought with Geronimo* (Lincoln and London: University of Nebraska Press, 1959, 1987), 7.

15 Apache warriors made bows, spears, and arrows. According to James Parker, veteran of the Indian Wars and Medal of Honor winner, "[t]he lances were generally tipped with the blades of sabers taken from cavalry, while arrowheads were likewise filed from bits of steel and iron. In my time stone arrowheads had both been made for generations. Bows were fashioned from mulberry wood which was cut from second growth trees found along the base of the hills." James Parker, *The Old Army: Memories, 1872–1918* (Philadelphia, PA: Dorrance, 1929), 32.

16 Bob Utley and William Washburn, *Indian Wars* (New York: Mariner Books, 1977, 2002), 227.

17 In 1927, he was awarded the TH Huxley award for this groundbreaking work. He continued to build upon this research, established the *American Journal of Physical Anthropology*, and became the first curator of what would become the Smithsonian Institution National Museum of Natural History. Conducting research and expeditions across the world, from North America to Africa and Southeast Asia, Hrdlička's research between 1898 and 1903 focused on the remains of Asians and Native Americans and generated the first well-documented theory of the colonization of the American continent by the peoples of East Asia, across the Bering Strait, some 15,000 years ago. Donald J. Ortner, "Aleš Hrdlička and the Founding of the American Journal of Physical Anthropology: 1918," in *Histories of American Physical Anthropology in the Twentieth Century*, ed. Michael Little and Kenneth Kennedy (Lexington, MD: Lexington Books, 2010), 87–104.

18 Ortner, "Aleš Hrdlička and the Founding of the American Journal of Physical Anthropology." John L. Cotter and Anthony T. Boldurian, *Clovis Revisited: New Perspectives on Paleoindian Adaptation from Blackwater Draw, New Mexico* (Ephrata, PA: Science Press, 1999), 2.

19 Obituary, "Emerson Foote; Retired Ad Agency Executive," *Los Angeles Times*, July 9, 1992, accessed December 15, 2015, http://articles.latimes.com/1992-07-09/news/mn-2252_1_emerson-foote: Currey, *Edward Lansdale*, 15.

20 Jonathan Nashel, *Edward Lansdale's Cold War* (Amherst and Boston, MA: University of Massachusetts Press), 27–28.

21 Currey, *Edward Lansdale,* 16.

22 Personal History Memo from Edward G. Lansdale to Chief of SF Office, MIS, November 10, 1943. Much of his early military and OSS material was, it appears, legitimately lost in the wake of the ramping up of the U.S. war effort.

23 Currey, *Edward Lansdale*, 17–18.

24 Currey, *Edward Lansdale,* 17–18.

25 Currey, *Edward Lansdale,* 18–19.
26 From Lansdale's journal entry on November 10, 1946, quoted in Nashel, *Edward Lansdale's Cold War*, 115, 246n39.
27 Richard Harris Smith, *OSS: The Secret History of America's First Central Intelligence Agency*, 10, RG 226 Entry UD 92A COI/OSS Files, 1941–1946, Box 43, File 698, Memo Lansdale to Lt. Col. Carroll T. Harris, Subject: Available Agent, Now in Spain, December 29, 1942.
28 Robert Lapham and Bernard Norling, *Lapham's Raiders* (Lexington: University of Kentucky Press, 1996), 189.
29 John M. Carlisle, *Red Arrow Men: The 32nd Division on the Villa Verde Trail* (Detroit, MI: Arnold Powers, 1945), 152.
30 Ray C. Hunt and Bernard Norling, *Behind Japanese Lines: An American Guerrilla in the Philippines* (Lexington: University of Kentucky, 1993), 207.
31 "Cave Fighting on Luzon," *Intelligence Bulletin*, G-2, USAFPOA, no. 13 (April 6, 1945), http://cdm16040.contentdm.oclc.org/cdm/singleitem/collection/p4013coll8/id/2612/rec/107.
32 Carlisle, *Red Arrow Men*, 153.
33 Carlisle, *Red Arrow Men*, 153.
34 Carlisle, *Red Arrow Men,* 153.
35 Carlisle, *Red Arrow Men*, 151.
36 Bohannan, *I Am Ashamed: Confessions of a Citizen Soldier*, unpublished autobiography, Bohannan Private Papers, hereafter referred to as BPP.
37 Joseph Starr to Charles Bohannan, August 2, 1981, transcribed by Claring Bohannan.
38 Jason S. Ridler, "The Fertile Ground of Hell's Carnival: Charles T. R. Bohannan and the US Army's Counter Intelligence Corps' Investigations of War Criminals, Collaborators, and the Huk, in the Philippines 1945–1947," *Defense and Security Analysis* 33, no. 1 (2017): 15–29.
39 Currey, *Edward Lansdale*, 27–30.
40 Currey, *Edward Lansdale*, 27.
41 Recounted in Currey, *Edward Lansdale,* 32.
42 Theodore Friend, *Between Two Empires: The Ordeal of the Philippines, 1929–1946* (New Haven, CT: Yale University Press, 1965), 261–62.
43 Ridler, "The Fertile Ground of Hell's Carnival," 15–29; Currey, *Edward Lansdale,* 20–50.
44 Benedict J. Kerkvliet, *The Huk Rebellion: A Study of Peasant Revolt in the Philippines* (Lanham, MD: Rowman & Littlefield, 1977; reprinted 2002), 94.
45 Luis Taruc, *He Who Rides the Tiger: The Story of an Asian Guerrilla Leader* (New York: Praeger, 1967), 89.
46 Rufus Philips Papers, Charles Bohannan USAID Lecture, December 13, 1966, Session 3, Reel 2, 14.
47 William Pomeroy, *The Forest: A Personal Record of the Huk Guerrilla Struggle* (New York: International, 1963), 21.
48 Napoleon Valeriano, "Military Operations," *Counter Guerrilla Operations in Philippines Seminar at Fort Bragg* (June 15, 1961), 26, available at the Vietnam Center and

Archive Online, https://vva.vietnam.ttu.edu/repositories/2/digital_objects/398328; and Andrew J. Birtle, *US Army Counterinsurgency and Contingency Operations Doctrine, 1860–1941* (Washington, DC: Center for Military History, United States Army, 2003), 59.
49 Birtle, *US Army Counterinsurgency and Contingency Operations Doctrine*, 59.
50 Charles T. R. Bohannan and Napoleon D. Valeriano, *Counter Guerrilla Operations: The Philippine Experience* (New York: Praeger, 1962), 94.
51 Napoleon Valeriano, "Military Operations," *Counter Guerrilla Operations in Philippines Seminar at Fort Bragg* (June 15, 1961), 38.
52 For Lansdale's love of Paine, see Nashel, *Edward Lansdale's Cold War*, 107–08, 119.
53 HIA CTRB, Box 4, Folder: Bohannan's drafts.
54 Lansdale, *In the Midst of Wars*, 24–27.
55 Lansdale, *In the Midst of Wars*, 24–27.
56 Bohannan noted in a unpublished paper that "the truth of everything previously learned was confirmed. Every pertinent principle, and most of the techniques and tactics, could be derived from the experiences from 1899–1915. A few tactics were proven, such as the value of aerial re-supply, of light planes under the control[,] in fact virtually integral to command, of the local battalion commander; the value of and limitation of radio as contrast to other means of communications, etc. Among the more important re-affirmations were the success which counter-guerrilla forces could achieve against numerically superior guerrillas; the absolute importance of a cause, and of subordinating purely military considerations to winning the support of the people, etc." HIA CTRB Box 4, Folder: Bohannan's drafts.
57 Taruc disagreed, having become disillusioned with the hard-line communist attitudes, codified thinking, and rigid dogma disputed. But there was no arguing. Momentum and rhetoric ruled the day, called Huklandia. Taruc, *He Who Rides the Tiger*, 69–70.
58 Currey, *Edward Lansdale*, 56–134.
59 Charles Bohannan Collection, Box 4, Folder: Bohannan's drafts, Hoover Institution Archives, copyright Stanford University.
60 Bohannan and Valeriano, *Counter Guerrilla Operations,* 161.
61 Currey, *Edward Lansdale,* 97.
62 Birtle, *US Army Counterinsurgency and Contingency Operations Doctrine,* 63.
63 Birtle, *US Army Counterinsurgency and Contingency Operations Doctrine,* 63.
64 Bohannan and Valeriano, *Counter Guerrilla Operations*, 54.
65 This assessment is from intensive study on Bohannan's life. See, Jason S. Ridler. "Cowboy Academic: The Education of Charles T. R. Bohannan," unpublished paper 2015.
66 Birtle, *US Army Counterinsurgency and Contingency Operations Doctrine,* 160; and Charles Bohannan, "Anti-Guerrilla Operations," *The Annals of the American Academy of Political and Social Science* 341, no.1 (May 1962): 19-29.
67 Currey, *Edward Lansdale*, 126–29; and Nick Cullather, "America's Boy? Ramon Magsaysay and the Illusion of Influence," *Pacific Historical Review* 62, no. 3 (August 1993): 305–38.
68 Rufus Philips Papers, Bohannan Lecture FETA USAID, December 1966.
69 Currey, *Edward Lansdale,* 116–17.
70 HIA, Edward G. Lansdale Papers, hereafter referred to as EGL, Box 35, File: Bohannan.

71 Cecil Currey interview with John Dickson, January 1986, Forsyth Library Special Collections Fort Hayes State University, Kansas, Cecil Currey Collection.
72 Lansdale, *In the Midst of Wars*, 126–27.
73 Thomas Bass, *The Spy Who Loved Us: The Vietnam War and Pham Xuan An's Dangerous Game* (New York: Public Affairs, 2009), 78.
74 Ronald Spector, *Advice and Support: The Early Years, 1941–1960* (Washington, DC: Center for Military History, US Army, 1985), http://www.history.army.mil/html/books/091/91-1/CMH_Pub_91-1-B.pdf 241, 247. Lansdale, *In the Midst of Wars*, 264.
75 "United States–Vietnam Relations, 1945–1967," Final Report of the Secretary of Defense Vietnam Task Force, 1969, IV A.5 Tab 2, "Rebellion against My Diem," 5.
76 Bass, *The Spy Who Loved Us*, 89.
77 Spector, *Advice and Support*, 240. Lansdale also worked as part of TRIM, "but his activities were specialized." "United States–Vietnam Relations, 1945–1967," Final Report of the Secretary of Defense Vietnam Task Force, 1969, IV A.4, US Training of the Vietnamese National Army, 40, https://nara-media-001.s3.amazonaws.com/arcmedia/research/pentagon-papers/Pentagon-Papers-Part-IV-A-4.pdf.
78 Spector, *Advice and Support*, 240–41.
79 "United States–Vietnam Relations, 1945–1967," 42–43.
80 "United States–Vietnam Relations, 1945–1967," Final Report of the Secretary of Defense Vietnam Task Force, 1969, IV A.5 "Failure of the Geneva Settlement," 11.
81 "United States–Vietnam Relations, 1945–1967."
82 Bernard Fall, "Political Development of Viet-Nam, VJ-Day to the Geneva Cease-Fire," doctoral thesis, Syracuse University, 1955, 754–56.
83 Rufus Philips, *Why Vietnam Matters: An Eyewitness Account of Lessons Not Learned* (Lincoln, NE: Potomac Books, 2009), 91, 102–23.
84 Philips, *Why Vietnam Matters*, 27–28.
85 Philips, *Why Vietnam Matters*, 35.
86 EGL Papers, Box 35, File: OPERATION BROTHERHOOD.
87 Lansdale, *In the Midst of Wars*, 95.
88 Tim Weiner, "Lucien Conein, 79, Legendary Cold War Spy," *New York Times* (June 7, 1998), http://www.nytimes.com/1998/06/07/world/lucien-conein-79-legendary-cold-war-spy.html.
89 See Currey, *Edward Lansdale*, 156–85.
90 Spector, *Advice and Support*, 241.
91 Spector, *Advice and Support*, 241.
92 Quoted in Spector, *Advice and Support*, 243n52.
93 HIA CTRB, Box 4, Folder: Bohannan's drafts, Hoover Institution Archives, copyright Stanford University.
94 Spector, *Advice and Support*, 356.
95 Bernard B. Fall, *The International Position of South Viet-Nam*, Part 3 (New York: Institute of Pacific Relations, 1958), 18.
96 Philips, *Why Vietnam Matters*, 124–39.
97 Currey, *Edward Lansdale*, 1–3.
98 Philip E. Canton, *Diem's Final Failure: Prelude to America's War in Vietnam* (Lawrence: University Press of Kansas), 77.

99 Taylor in particular has been credited with interesting but unsuccessful innovative models of U.S. Army formations in the Cold War, including the Pentomic model built to be fought on an atomic battlefield but essentially refight the Second World War. Brian McAllister Linn, *The Echo of Battle: The Army's Way of War* (Cambridge, MA: Harvard University Press, 2007), 152–88.
100 "The Bay of Pigs Invasion and Its Aftermath, April 1961–October 1962," *US State Department, Office of the Historian*, https://history.state.gov/milestones/1961-1968/bay-of-pigs.
101 Currey, *Edward Lansdale*, 230.
102 CTRB Personal Papers, letter from Bohannan to Joseph Starr, August 13, 1981.
103 Lansdale to Bohannan, August 21, 1959. Cecil Currey collection at Fort Hayes State University Special Collections, from the Charles TR Bohannan Files. Bohannan pushed the need for legitimate political leadership, counterguerrilla training, civic action "attraction programs," psychological warfare units, and economic and domestic reform. In detail, this included the following:
1. Found a special counterguerrilla combat force from Lancero units within the Colombian Army; 2. Institute an effective military intelligence service and reorganize the civilian Servicio de Inteligencia Colombiana, (Colombian Intelligence Service [*sic*]); 3. Establish an effective government public information service with a covert psychological warfare capability; 4. Initiate a so-called "attraction" program, coordinated, through a Civil Affairs (G-5) section of the Armed Forces, in an effort to rehabilitate public opinion of Colombias, security forces; 5. Reorganize, train, equip, and deploy the National Police and rehabilitate their public image; 6. Emphasize national development and rehabilitation programs, particularly land settlement and government-community welfare ("self-help") projects.
Dennise Rempe, "The Past as Prologue? A History of US Counterinsurgency in Colombia, 1958–1966," Occasional Paper from the *Strategic Studies Institute* (March 2002), 5–6.
104 Birtle, *US Army Counterinsurgency and Contingency Operations Doctrine.*
105 "United States–Vietnam Relations, 1945–1967," Final Report of the Secretary of Defense Vietnam Task Force, 1969, IV A. 5, Evolution of the War, Origins of the Insurgency, "US Perceptions of the Insurgency, 1954–1960," 52–53.
106 "United States–Vietnam Relations, 1945–1967," 66–77.
107 Currey, *Edward Lansdale*, 227.
108 Amazingly, the Pentagon Papers, which Lansdale loathed and lamented, remain among the strongest caches of documents that serve as validators for his stance as a maverick who championed political and economic action rather than increased firepower. For the rivalries to his ideas, see "United States–Vietnam Relations, 1945–1967," Final Report of the Secretary of Defense Vietnam Task Force, 1969, IV B. 1, Evolution of the War, Origins of the Insurgency, "The Kennedy Commitments and Programs, 1961," i, iii, 13–14, 31, 35, 147.
109 Bohannan later said that Galula's work on Algeria, then classified, was "one of the most valuable books on counter-insurgency, based on personal experience, which I have seen yet. Galula managed to pacify the area, but didn't do one goddamn thing that was effective in terms of counter-insurgency. Immediately after he relinquished command of that company, the next two company commanders were knocked off within three

months. It is the clearest possible demonstration, to my way of thinking, that saturating an area with troops; doing nice things for the people in a sort of Lord of the Manor fashion, is not going to answer the problem when you have a well-developed insurgency; that only political means will do it." You had to know the aspirations of the people. You had to know what kind of country they wanted to live in and work toward it. If you don't, "you're not going to cut the mustard." RPP Bohannan Lecture, FETC/AID-UH December 13, 1966, FETC/AID-UH December 12, Session 1, Reel, 1, 26.
110 J. A. Koch, *The Chieu Hoi Program in South Vietnam, 1963–1971*, Report for the Advanced Research Project Agency (Santa Monica, CA: Rand, January 1973).
111 Philips, *Why Vietnam Matters*, 157–60.
112 Philips, *Why Vietnam Matters*, 157.
113 John Prados, "Kennedy and the Diem Assassination," *National Security Archive* (November 5, 2003), http://nsarchive.gwu.edu/NSAEBB/NSAEBB101/.
114 Currey, *Edward Lansdale*, 283–90.
115 Erik Bergerud, *The Dynamics of Defeat; The Vietnam War in Hau Nghia Province* (Boulder, CO: Westview Press, 1993), 11–45.
116 "United States–Vietnam Relations, 1945–1967," 16.
117 Quoted in Currey, *Edward Lansdale*, 297.
118 Quoted in Currey, *Edward Lansdale*, 294–96.
119 Quoted in Currey, *Edward Lansdale*, 294–96.
120 Currey, *Edward Lansdale*, 295.
121 Rufus Philips interview by Jason S. Ridler, February 13, 2012.
122 Hobart "Bo" Cleveland interview with Jason S. Ridler, June 15, 2012.
123 Currey, *Edward Lansdale*, 295.
124 Currey, *Edward Lansdale*, 297.
125 Currey, *Edward Lansdale*, 297.
126 Currey, *Edward Lansdale*, 304.
127 EGL Papers, Box 3, Lansdale to Ellsberg, September 15, 1975.
128 Bo to EGL, from San Juan, 13vi71, Forsyth Library Special Collections Fort Hayes State University, Kansas, Cecil Currey Collection.
129 Letter from Bohannan to Lansdale, July 29, 1982. HIAS Lansdale Papers, Box 2, File: Bohannan correspondences.
130 "Have you heard anything about the medal I was pushing through for you? Been blanked out on finding out myself, for some reason or other. Have you heard anything? If so, please let me know so I can take some further action, if necessary." Lansdale to Bohannan, January 23, 1957, Forsyth Library Special Collections Fort Hayes State University, Kansas, Cecil Currey Collection.
131 Dorothy Bohannan to Cecil Currey, Forsyth Library Special Collections Fort Hayes State University, Kansas, Cecil Currey Collection.
132 Forsyth Library Special Collections Fort Hayes State University, Kansas, Cecil Currey Collection. Interview with Dorothy Bohannan, July 27, 1985.

Part IV: Mavericks after Vietnam

1 As one historian noted, failure to understand the nature of the failure during Vietnam translated into limited interest from post-Vietnam soldiers and officials. "The failure of counterinsurgency in Vietnam meant that the Army of the 1970s would not seek to build on the innovations that had occurred but would rather turn away from them in an effort to rebuild and redefine an institution that had been shattered by the war in Vietnam." David Fitzgerald, *Learning to Forget: US Army Counterinurgency Doctrine and Practice from Vietnam to Iraq* (Stanford, CA: Stanford University Press, 2013), 39–59.

2 The literature on the origins of the American post-Vietnam RMA dialogue is vast. What follows is some key and representative literature on the larger themes and dialogues created by the subject. John Summers, *On Strategy: A Critical Analysis of the Vietnam War* (Novato, CA: Presidio, 1982); Andrew Krepinevich, *The Army and Vietnam* (Baltimore, MD, and London: Johns Hopkins Press, 1986); Michael A. Hennessy, *Strategy in Vietnam: The Marine Corps and Revolutionary Warfare in I Corps, 1965–1972* (Westport, CT, and London: Praeger, 1997); John Lovell, "Vietnam and the US Army: Learning to Deal with Failure," in *Democracy, Strategy, and Vietnam: Implications for American Policymaking*, ed. George K. Osborne, Asa A. Clark IV, Daniel J. Kaufman, and Douglas E. Lute (Lexington, MA, and Toronto: D. C. Heath, 1985), 130, 131–33; James F. Dunnigan and Raymond M. Macedonia, *Getting It Right: American Military Reform after Vietnam to the Persian Gulf and Beyond* (New York: William Morrow, 1993), 47; James Kitfield, *Prodigal Soldiers: How the Generation of Officers Born of Vietnam Revolutionized the American Style of War* (New York: Simon & Schuster, 1995); Richard M Swain, "Filling the Void: The Operational Art and the US Army," in *The Operational Art: Developments in the Theories of War*, ed. B. J. C. McKercher and Michael Hennessy (Westport, CT, and London: Praeger, 1996), 156; and Donn Starry, "To Change an Army," *Military Review* 63 (March 1983): 23.

3 Powell's doctrine was rooted in former secretary of defense Caspar Weinberg's own doctrine during the Reagan administration. They included such points as follows: (a) Have nonviolent measures been exhausted? (b) Is there a realistic exit strategy to bring forces back and avoid endless churning of forces? and (c) Do we have public support? Frank Hoffman, "A Second Look at the Powell Doctrine," *War on the Rocks* (February 20, 2014), https://warontherocks.com/2014/02/a-second-look-at-the-powell-doctrine/.

4 Mark Bowden, *Black Hawk Down: A Tale of Modern War* (New York: Signet, 1999).

5 Romeo Daillaire, *Shake Hands with the Devil: The Failure of Humanity in Rwanda* (New York: De Capo Press, 2003).

6 See Linda Polman, *We Did Nothing: Why the Truth Doesn't Always Come out When the UN Goes in* (London: Penguin, 1997).

Chapter 7: Prelude: Gertrude Bell and War in a "Devil's Cauldron"

1 David G. Hogarth, "Gertrude Lowthian Bell," *Geographical Journal* 68, no. 4 (October 26, 1926): 363–68.

2 Georgina Howell, ed. *Gertrude Bell, A Woman in Arabia: The Writings of the Queen of the Desert* (London: Penguin Books, 2015), xiii.

3 Bell's biographical material is vast, including collections of her own writing, much of which is available at Project Gutenberg and the Internet Archive, including her work in archaeology and poetry. The most successful of recent biographers remains Georgina Howell's *Gertrude Bell: Queen of the Desert, Shaper of Nations* (New York: Farrar, Straus, and Giroux, 2006). See also Hogarth, "Gertrude Lowthian Bell," 363–68.

4 Howell, *Gertrude Bell, A Woman in Arabia*, ix.

5 Howell, *Gertrude Bell, A Woman in Arabia*, 23.

6 Howell, *Gertrude Bell, A Woman in Arabia*, 138.

7 Gertrude Bell, *The Letters of Gertrude Bell*, vol. 1 (1927), available on Project Guttenberg, http://gutenberg.net.au/ebooks04/0400341h.html.

8 Howell, *Gertrude Bell, A Woman in Arabia*, 152–53.

9 Howell, *Gertrude Bell, A Woman in Arabia*, 152–53.

10 Quoted in Bruce Westrate, *The Arab Bureau: British Policy in the Middle East, 1916–1920* (University Park, PA: Penn State Press, 1992), 25.

11 Howell, *Gertrude Bell*, 241.

12 Howell, *Gertrude Bell*, 241.

13 Westrate, *The Arab Bureau*, 87–86.

14 Quoted in Priya Satia, *Spies in Arabia: The Great War and the Cultural Foundations of Britain's Covert Empire in the Middle East* (Oxford: Oxford University Press, 2009), 50–51.

15 Satia, *Spies in Arabia*, 100.

16 Satia, *Spies in Arabia*, 124.

17 Howell, *Gertrude Bell*, 179.

18 Satia, *Spies in Arabia*, 237.

19 Patrick Miller, "Building a Better Legacy: Contrasting the British and American Experience in Iraq," MA thesis, Naval Postgraduate School (December 2008), 34.

20 Howell, *Gertrude Bell*, 191.

21 Quoted in Ian Rutledge, *Enemy on the Euphrates: The Battle for Iraq* (London: Saqi Books, 2014), 221.

22 A good survey of this period is provided by Reeva Spector Simon and Eleanor H. Tejirian, eds., *The Creation of Iraq, 1914–1921* (New York: Columbia University Press, 2004).

23 Simon and Tejirian, *The Creation of Iraq, 1914–1921*.

24 Howell, *Gertrude Bell, A Woman in Arabia*, 166–75.

25 Gertrude Bell, *Review of the Civil Administration of Mesopotamia* (London: His Majesty's Stationery, 1920).

26 Howell, *Gertrude Bell, A Woman in Arabia*, 197.

27 Satia, *Spies in Arabia*, 209.

28 Amal Vinogradov, "The 1920 Revolt in Iraq Reconsidered: The Role of Tribes in National Politics," *International Journal of the Middle East* 3, no. 2 (April 1972): 134.

29 Howell, *Gertrude Bell, A Woman in Arabia*, 197–208.

30 Satia, *Spies in Arabia*, 239–62.

31 Satia, *Spies in Arabia*, 251.

32 Howell, *Gertrude Bell, A Woman in Arabia*, 208.

33 Howell, *Gertrude Bell, A Woman in Arabia*, 208.

34 Howell, *Gertrude Bell, A Woman in Arabia*, xiv.

35 Howell, *Gertrude Bell, A Woman in Arabia*, 255.

Chapter 8: Warlords, Commanders, and the Truth: Sarah Chayes in Afghanistan, 2002–2010

1 Sarah Chayes, *The Punishment of Virtue: Inside Afghanistan after the Taliban* (New York: Penguin Books, 2006), 300–15.
2 Chayes, *The Punishment of Virtue*, 300–15.
3 Tim Lewis, "Sarah Chayes: On Living in Afghanistan and Sleeping with a Kalashnikov," *The Guardian*, March 15, 2015, accessed May 31, 2017, https://www.theguardian.com/books/2015/mar/15/sarah-chayes-thieves-of-state-interview.
4 Lewis, "Sarah Chayes."
5 Sarah Chayes interview by Jason S. Ridler, January 23, 2013.
6 Declan Walsh, "American Activist Finds Her Calling in Afghan Hot Spot," *Globe Correspondent*, May 9, 2006, http://www.boston.com/news/world/asia/articles/2006/05/09/american_activist_finds_her_calling_in_afghan_hot_spot/.
7 Kari Neumeyer, "Chayes on Life in the Trenches," from "Removed" article at Medill News Site, March 27, 2001, recovered via PeaceCorps website, listed as October 14, 2002, http://peacecorpsonline.org/messages/messages/2629/1009535.html.
8 Quoted in Neumeyer, "Chayes on Life in the Trenches."
9 Richard Read, "Year after War Began, Afghans Still Suffering," *Oregon Live*, October 7, 2002, recovered by the PeaceCorps website, October 14, 2002, http://peacecorpsonline.org/messages/messages/2629/1009507.html.
10 Read, "Year after War Began, Afghans Still Suffering."
11 See Sean Maloney, *Enduring the Freedom* (Lincoln, NE: Potomac Books, 2006), 1–68; Lester Grau and Dodge Billingsley, *Operation Anaconda: America's First Major Battle in Afghanistan* (Lawrence: University Press of Kansas, 2011); and Aaron B. O'Connell, ed., *Our Latest Longest War: Losing Hearts and Minds* (Chicago, IL: University of Chicago Press, 2017).
12 Chayes, *The Punishment of Virtue*, 12.
13 Chayes, *The Punishment of Virtue*, 36.
14 Chayes, *The Punishment of Virtue*, 38.
15 Chayes, *The Punishment of Virtue*, 19.
16 Chayes, *The Punishment of Virtue*, 19.
17 Deena Hurwitz, Margaret Satterthwaite, and Douglas Ford, *Human Rights Advocacy Stories* (St. Paul, MN: Foundation Press, 2008), 518.
18 Akrem told Chayes later that there were about 600 rifles from the Pakistanis, plus sixty to a hundred rocket launchers. U.S. Army and CIA special forces, with communication gear mounted on Afghan trucks like "daddy long legs," helped organize the rabble of Shirzai's men for an assault on Kandahar. According to Akrem, who was with Shirzai at the airport, Shirzai's task was to secure the airport as Karzai headed for Kabul. Mullah Naqib, who had fought the Soviets and who decided not to contest the Taliban initially, would run Kandahar. According to Naqib, the BBC even announced it. But Shirzai had other plans. With the Taliban and most of al Qaeda gone, he attacked the city and gained control himself. Shirazi's men abandoned the airport for the city and moved fast and quick. Shirzai returned as fast as possible to secure his position in the city before Karzai was in Kabul. Taliban resistance was broken with air power. Linda Robinson, *One Hundred*

Victories: Special Ops and the Future of American Warfare (New York: Public Affairs, 2013), 10–11, 234; Robert L. Grenier, *88 Days to Kandahar: A CIA Diary* (New York: Simon & Schuster, 2016), 163–64, 189, 275; Walter L. Perry and David Kassing, *Toppling the Taliban: Air-Ground Operations in Afghanistan, October 2001 to June 2002* (Santa Monica, CA: RAND, 2016), 1–60; and Grau and Billingsley, *Operation Anaconda*, 70.

19 Chayes, *The Punishment of Virtue*, 25.

20 Chayes, *The Punishment of Virtue*, 54–570.

21 Sarah Chayes, "Breaking Ranks in Afghanistan," *Columbia Journalism Review*, December 11, 2003, http://www.alternet.org/story/17372/breaking_ranks_in_afghanistan.

22 Chayes, "Breaking Ranks in Afghanistan."

23 Chayes, *The Punishment of Virtue*, 60–61.

24 Chayes, *The Punishment of Virtue*, 72–73.

25 Chayes, *The Punishment of Virtue*, 73.

26 "Everyone stands up, and you shake hands all around, greeting each person in turn. If you know someone well, there is a kind of dance step you do: left hand to your friend's right shoulder, right hand to his waist. Then you take a half step back and let your right-hand slide across it and clasp it." Chayes, *The Punishment of Virtue*, 107–111.

27 Read, "Year after War Began, Afghans Still Suffering."

28 Sarah Chayes, "Letters from Kandahar," *Harvard Review* 23 (Fall 2002): 23.

29 Read, "Year after War Began, Afghans Still Suffering."

30 Read, "Year after War Began, Afghans Still Suffering."

31 Read, "Year after War Began, Afghans Still Suffering."

32 Sarah Chayes, "Rebuilding Akokolacha: Why America Must Get More Involved Not Less in Afghanistan," *Christian Science Monitor*, December 10, 2002, http://www.csmonitor.com/2002/1210/p12s01-coop.html.

33 Chayes, "Rebuilding Akokolacha."

34 Chayes, "Rebuilding Akokolacha."

35 Chayes, "Rebuilding Akokolacha."

36 "Interview with Sarah Chayes: Danger, Determination, and Destiny," *Frontline*, October 1, 2003. http://www.pbs.org/frontlineworld/stories/afghanistan/chayes.html.

37 Maloney, *Enduring the Freedom*, 99–114, 304.

38 Read, "Year after War Began, Afghans Still Suffering."

39 PRT efforts are detailed in Sean Maloney, *Fighting for Afghanistan: A Rogue Historian at War* (Annapolis, MD: US Naval Institute Press, 2011).

40 Maloney, *Fighting for Afghanistan*, 3–4.

41 "Interview with Sarah Chayes."

42 "Interview with Sarah Chayes."

43 "Interview with Sarah Chayes."

44 Chayes, *The Punishment of Virtue*, 25.

45 Chayes, *The Punishment of Virtue*, 26.

46 Chayes, *The Punishment of Virtue*, 27.

47 "Interview with Sarah Chayes."

48 Carter Malkasian, *War Comes to Garmser: Thirty-Years of Conflict on the Afghan Border* (Oxford: Oxford University Press, 2013, 2016), 78.

49 "Interview with Sarah Chayes."
50 See David Charters, Lee Windsor, and Brent Wilson, *Kandahar Tour: The Turning Point in Canada's Afghan Mission* (Toronto, ON: Wiley, 2010).
51 Geneva Collins, "Without a Parachute Ex-Reporter Finds Rewards in Relief Work," *Current*, September 20, 2004, recovered at http://peacecorpsonline.org/messages/messages/467/2023756.html.
52 Jerome Starkey and King Sengupta, "President Obama Ready to Cut Karzai Adrift," *The Independent*, January 23, 2009, http://www.independent.co.uk/news/world/politics/obama-ready-to-cut-karzai-adrift-1513407.html.
53 Chayes, *The Punishment of Virtue*, 317.
54 Quoted in "Uncertainty over Exit Date for Canadian Troops in Afghanistan," *Macleans*, November 2007, recovered at http://www.thecanadianencyclopedia.ca/en/article/uncertainty-over-exit-date-for-canadian-troops-in-afghanistan/.
55 Melanie Keveles, *Scrappy Startups: How 15 Ordinary Women Turned Their Unique Ideas into Profitable Businesses* (Santa Barbara, CA: Praeger, 2010), 129–43.
56 Sarah Chayes, *Thieves of State: Why Corruption Threatens Global Security* (New York: W. W. Norton, 2016), 35.
57 Lois L. Ross, *Canadian Development Report 2008: Fragile State or Failing Development* (Ottawa: North South Institute, 2007), 45n37.
58 Sarah Chayes, "The Perils of Delivering Aid in Afghanistan," *Globe and Mail*, August 15, 2008, https://www.theglobeandmail.com/opinion/the-perils-of-delivering-aid-in-afghanistan/article1059465/?page=all.
59 Chayes, *Thieves of State*, 37.
60 Bob Woodward, *Obama's Wars* (New York: Simon & Schuster, 2010), 70; and Chayes interview by Ridler.
61 *Bill Moyer Journal*, February 22, 2008, http://www.pbs.org/moyers/journal/02222008/watch2.html.
62 Chayes, *Thieves of State*, 37–39.
63 Sean Maloney, *War in Afghanistan: Eight Battles in the South* (Kingston: Canadian Defence Academy, 2012), 312–33.
64 Chayes, *Thieves of State*, 27.
65 Chayes interview by Ridler.
66 Chayes, *Thieves of State*, 38.
67 Rajiv Chandrasekaran, *Little America: The War within the War for Afghanistan* (New York: Vintage, 2012), 61.
68 Chayes, *Thieves of State*, 39.
69 Chayes, *Thieves of State*, 29.
70 David Kilculen, *The Accidental Guerrilla: Fighting Small War in the Midst of Big One* (Oxford: Oxford University Press, 2010).
71 Chayes, *Thieves of State*, 31.
72 Chayes, *Thieves of State*, 33.
73 Chayes, *Thieves of State*, 33.
74 Chayes, italics added, 41.
75 Maloney, *War in Afghanistan*, 333; and Christopher Lamb et al., *Human Terrain Teams: An Organization for Sociocultural Knowledge in Irregular Warfare* (Washington, DC: The Institute of World Politics Press, 2013), 19, 56, 64, 84, 124, 179, 186, 242, 333.

76 Chayes, *Thieves of State*, 42.
77 Chandrasekaran, *Little America*, 162.
78 Chayes, *Thieves of State*, 43.
79 Chayes, *Thieves of State*, 44.
80 Chayes, *Thieves of State*, 44.
81 Chayes, *Thieves of State*, 42.
82 "But where were the network diagrams for the district governors or the provincial police chief? What tribe was he? Who were his associates? Who did he pay kickbacks to? Which construction companies belonged to his family members? How was he facilitating the traffic of chromite or timber or opium? Did he have Karzai on speed dial who had he fought with during the last war? No one knew." Chayes, *Thieves of State*, 45.
83 These included recommending that soldiers ask about governance as part of their work in the field and funneling local intelligence about Afghan officials and government to ISAF and anonymous hotlines. They listed actions for deterring corruption for officers: don't directly contribute, don't meet with corrupt officials in ways that raise status (like at their homes, where they are hosts and are buying prestige). Don't renew contracts. Chayes, *Thieves of State*, 47.
84 High-echelon cases should be referred to the High Office of Oversight, for "prosecution by the Anti-Corruption Unit" in the attorney general's office, or the minister of the interior.
85 "Rigorous pursuit of an anticorruption approach would expose these conflicting agendas. Savage internal battles might result, or public embarrassment or nonparticipation or even obstruction by some NATO organizations. And Afghan frustration would only rise." Chayes, *Thieves of State*, 48.
86 Chayes, *Thieves of State*, 49.
87 Chayes, *Thieves of State*, 51.
88 Chayes, *Thieves of State*, 53.
89 Chayes, *Thieves of State*, 54.
90 Christopher D. Kolenda, *The Counterinsurgency Challenge: A Parable of Decision Making in Modern Conflict* (Mechanicsburg, PA: Stackpole Books, 2012); and Jack Tapper, *The Outpost: An Untold Story of American Valor* (New York: Little, Brown, 2012), 245–300.
91 Chayes, *Thieves of State*, 59.
92 Chayes, *Thieves of State*, 60.
93 Chayes, *Thieves of State*, 63.
94 Lewis, "Sarah Chayes."
95 Michael Hastings, "The Runaway General: The Profile That Brought Down McChrystal," *Rolling Stone*, June 22, 2010, http://www.rollingstone.com/politics/news/the-runaway-general-20100622.
96 Chayes interview by Ridler.
97 Paula Broadwell, *All In: The Education of General David Petraeus* (New York: Penguin Books, 2012).
98 Catherine Dale, who had been advisor to McChrystal's operational commander. Lesser time put in by Brooking's Institute's Steve Biddle and Max Boot of the Council of Foreign Relations. Chayes, *Thieves of State*, 136–37.
99 Others remained indifferent or challenging, including Special Representative for Afghanistan and Pakistan (SRAP) Richard Holbrooke. The stigma of Vietnam was

still rife for Holbrook, who saw interfering with government affairs carrying with it the ghost of Diem, assassinations, Project Phoenix, and worse. Vietnam obscured the lens of these officials, Chayes believed. Any effort to change government was stained with being compared to the failures or abuses on this front in Vietnam. Chayes interview by Ridler.
100 Joshua Partlow, *A Kingdom of Their Own: The Family Karzai and the Afghan Disaster* (New York: Random House, 2016).
101 Partlow, *A Kingdom of Their Own*.
102 The evidence, from wire taps of payoffs, financial records, and more, was solid. "Meyer told me Spranta (the National Security Advisor whose wire was taped with approval of the government) began to cry [upon hearing Salahi's bribe talk], exclaiming he would tell Karzai that not only should Salehi be dismissed, he should be arrested and prosecuted. With Karzai's approval, the attorney general signed out an arrest warrant, and Atmar's successor as interior minister, directed the MCTRF to carry out the arrest." Chayes, *Thieves of State*, 142.
103 Chayes, *Thieves of State*, 142.
104 See Partlow, *A Kingdom of Their Own*.
105 Chayes, *Thieves of State*, 144.

Chapter 9: British Pacifist versus American Pride: Emma Sky in Iraq, 2003–2010

1 Emma Sky, *The Unraveling: High Hopes and Missed Opportunities in Iraq* (New York: Public Affairs, 2015), 316.
2 Sky, *The Unraveling*, 320.
3 Sky, *The Unraveling*, 322–23.
4 Sky, *The Unraveling*, 335.
5 Sky, *The Unraveling*, 341.
6 Thomas Ricks, *Fiasco: The American Military Adventure in Iraq* (London: Penguin, 2006), 143–44, 170–71, 232–34, 279–90.
7 Sky, *The Unraveling*, 17.
8 Sky, *The Unraveling*, 17–18.
9 Richard Morris, *Cheshire: The Biography of Leonard Cheshire, VC, OM* (London: Viking Press, 2000).
10 Sky, *The Unraveling*, 20.
11 Sky, *The Unraveling*, 20.
12 Sky, *The Unraveling*, 20.
13 Sky, *The Unraveling*, 20.
14 Rajiv Chandrasekaran, *Imperial Life in the Emerald City: Inside Iraq's Green Zone* (New York: Vintage, 2006), 12–20.
15 Sky, *The Unraveling*, 3.
16 "Interview with Colonel William Mayville," *Frontline*, December 1, 2003, http://www.pbs.org/wgbh/pages/frontline/shows/beyond/interviews/mayville.html.
17 Her place was defended by Gurkhas with a private security company. She watched the Gurkhas argue with their Australian boss, who didn't want to give them more ammunition and wouldn't stay with them. They threw their weapons in a pile, and the

Aussie grabbed them and dumped them in his car. Sky gathered them to thank them for saving her life. She asked them to stay, said she'll get reinforcements from Baghdad, and warned they might not get better work. They agreed. The Aussie undid the good work and they all quit. Sky convinced most of them to stay. But the team leader left. Sky contacted British ambassador John Sawers, Bremer's deputy, and asked for support that had worked with the Gurkhas. British diplomat John Sawers visited the next day, took her with him on tour of Kurdistan, and met Meghan O'Sullivan, top member of Bremer's team and future figure in the creation of the surge. Sky, *The Unraveling*, 20–23.

18 Sky, *The Unraveling*, 26.

19 Fred Kaplan, *The Insurgents: David Petraeus and the Plot to Change the American Way of War* (New York: Simon & Schuster, 2013), 251–52.

20 Human Rights Watch, "Reversing Arabization of Kirkuk" in *Claims in Conflict: Reversing Ethnic Cleansing in Northern Iraq*, https://www.hrw.org/reports/2004/iraq0804/7=.htm.

21 Sky, *The Unraveling*, 28.

22 Sky, *The Unraveling*, 29.

23 Sky, *The Unraveling*, 29.

24 Sky, *The Unraveling*, 31.

25 Sky, *The Unraveling*, 32.

26 Sky, *The Unraveling*, 33.

27 Sky, *The Unraveling*, 36.

28 Sky, *The Unraveling*, 35–42.

29 The Bush administration arrived with promises to keep the military out of the nation-building they'd seen as a series of expensive entanglements during the 1990s in the Balkans and Africa. See Woodward's three-volume examination of the Bush administration at war, *Bush at War*, *Plan of Attack*, and *State of Denial*.

30 See Ricks, *Fiasco*, for a detailed account of the lack of strategic planning in place, approved of by the Bush administration.

31 Sky, *The Unraveling*, 42.

32 Sky, *The Unraveling*, 42.

33 Ricks, *Fiasco*, 143–44.

34 Kaplan, *The Insurgents,* 251–52.

35 Sky, *The Unraveling*, 48.

36 Sky, *The Unraveling*, 54–55.

37 James A. Baker III and Lee H. Hamilton, *The Iraq Study Group Report* (New York: Vintage Books, 2006), 18, 65.

38 Bob Woodward, *State of Denial* (New York: Simon & Schuster), 291.

39 In a strange inversion, the issue of what to do with returning soldiers is reminiscent of the failure of the Allied Controls Commission in Germany, which Fall wrote about. Failure to accommodate or engage the millions of returning soldiers in meaningful work fed the FreeCorps movement in 1920s Germany, where wartime soldiers returned to form private militias as independent powers on the street. Many flocked to Hitler's banner. Robert G. L. Waite, *The Vanguard of Nazism: The Free Corps Movement in Post War Germany, 1918–1923* (New York: W. W. Norton, 1953).

40 Sky, *The Unraveling*, 58.

41 "I wanted to describe how political disputes led to violence. But all General Sanchez wanted to hear about was projects and money spent. He spoke to us of the challenges in different parts of Iraq and the conditions necessary for the withdrawal of US forces. We were left slightly perplexed by his visit." Sky, *The Unraveling*, 59.
42 Sky, *The Unraveling*, 60–64.
43 Sky, *The Unraveling*, 67.
44 Sky, *The Unraveling*, 73.
45 Sky, *The Unraveling*, 73–80.
46 Sky, *The Unraveling*, 80–82.
47 Sky, *The Unraveling*, 82.
48 Sky, *The Unraveling*, 87.
49 These included Sir Jeremy Greenstock, Bremer's British equivalent for the British CPA members and his utter opposite. Bremer's relentless optimism was matched by Greenstock's cynical pragmatism on the rising tide of violence. Robert Blackwill, long-time friend of Bremer, sharp intellect, and National Security Advisor Condoleezza Rice's deputy, was a brilliant but strange man. He interrogated Sky on her knowledge of Iraqis and if she could ID the ethnicity of naked Iraqi men. But he was also among the earliest proponents of the need for more ground troops as violence escalated in September 2004. Woodward, *State of Denial*, 255; and Sky, *The Unraveling*, 92.
50 James Dobbins et al., *Occupying Iraq: A History of the Coalition Provisional Authority* (Santa Monica, CA: RAND National Security Research Division, 2009), 284.
51 Sky, *The Unraveling*, 93.
52 Sky, *The Unraveling*, 95.
53 Bing West, *No True Glory: A Frontline Account of the Battle for Fallujah*, (New York: Bantam, 2005; reprint 2011), 1–100.
54 Sky, *The Unraveling*, 97.
55 Yet, to most experts, it was now clear that America had no postwar plan for Iraq and had ignored all advice and evidence that their invasion would be met with resistance. Critiques of the war grew with the rising tide of violence. A petition from British officials and former diplomats to the British government (April 29, 2004) noted that "the conduct of the war made it clear there was no plan for the post-Saddam era. They noted that every Middle East expert had predicted that the occupation of Iraq by Coalition forces would be met with resistance [as did Dick Cheney during the First Gulf War]. Policy needed to take into account the nature and history of Iraq The military action of the Coalition should be guided by political objectives. They concluded saying there was no case for supporting policies which were doomed to fail." Sky, *The Unraveling*, 98, 101; and Ricks, *Fiasco*, 7–150.
56 Sky, *The Unraveling*, 101.
57 Sky, *The Unraveling*, 104.
58 She and Schilcher pushed the creation of a Kirkuk foundation with a special envoy to keep these fractions from deepening. Bremer backed the plan and it was even supported in theory by Sheikh Ghazi al-Yawar, the first president of Iraq, though funding difficulties killed the idea before it could be born. Sky, *The Unraveling*, 126.
59 Sky, *The Unraveling*, 126.
60 Sky, *The Unraveling*, 135.

61 Sky, *The Unraveling*, 136.
62 Among the most important works on the development of the surge, see Thomas E. Ricks, *The Gamble: General Petraeus and the American Military Adventure in Iraq* (New York: Penguin, 2010); Gentile, *Wrong Turn: America's Deadly Embrace of Counter-Insugency* (NewYork: The New Press, 2013); Kaplan, *The Insurgents*; and Peter R. Mansoor, *The Surge: My Journey with General David Petraeus and the Remaking of Iraq War* (New Haven, CT: Yale University Press, 2013).
63 Sky, *The Unraveling*, 139. Critique of Odierno's capacity for thinking outside of conventional warfare was most clearly made in Ricks, The Gamble.
64 Sky, *The Unraveling*, 148.
65 Sky, *The Unraveling*, 148.
66 Sky, *The Unraveling*, 151.
67 Sky, *The Unraveling*, 153.
68 Sky, *The Unraveling*, 153.
69 Sky, *The Unraveling*, 153.
70 Sky, *The Unraveling*, 159–60.
71 Sky, *The Unraveling*, 160.
72 Sky, *The Unraveling*, 160.
73 Sky, *The Unraveling*, 16.
74 Kaplan, *The Insurgents*, 254.
75 Kaplan, *The Insurgents*, 254.
76 Sky, *The Unraveling*, 173.
77 Sky, *The Unraveling*, 173.
78 Sky, *The Unraveling*, 183; and Niel Smith and Sean MacFarland, "Anbar Awakens: The Tipping Point," *Military Review* (March–April 2008): 41–52.
79 Sky, *The Unraveling*, 184.
80 Margaret Warner, "Emma Sky's Remarkable Rise in Iraq in a Virtually All-Male Sea of Military Men," *PBS News Hour*, 2015, http://www.pbs.org/newshour/updates/emma-sky-operating-virtually-male-sea-military-men/.
81 Sky, *The Unraveling*, 191.
82 Sky, *The Unraveling*, 193.
83 Sky, *The Unraveling*, 195.
84 "The work that Lambo had begun now became institutionalized within the Force Strategic Engagement Cell, which was headed up by Major General Paul newton and State Department foreign service officer Don Blome. Maliki agreed to establish a counterpart committee with Basim and Abu Mohamad as the key staff. They were given responsibility for vetting all the volunteers who wished to join the Iraqi security forces." See Sky, *The Unraveling*, 195–205.
85 Sky, *The Unraveling*, 199–201.
86 "General Falah described in graphic detail how he had survived an assassination in which Hazem al-Araji (the brother of a member of parliament) and an Iraqi battalion commander were clearly complicit. General Falah painted a picture of gangster-land around the Kadhimiya shrine. The director of the Dadrist office claimed he personally had phoned Condoleezza Rice to get the US troops withdrawn from the areas, and Jaysh al-Mahdi were bragging that they were stronger than the Iraqi security forces." Sky, *The Unraveling*, 213.

87 Sky, *The Unraveling*, 214.
88 Carter Malkasian, *Illusions of Victory: The Anbar Awakening and the Rise of the Islamic State* (London: Oxford University Press, 2017), 75.
89 Mansoor, *The Surge*, 296.
90 Sky, *The Unraveling*, 218.
91 Mansoor, *The Surge*, 137.
92 "He threatened not to sign the strategic partnership declaration with the US nor support the renewal of the UN Security Council resolution that provided the legal basis for Coalition forces." Sky, *The Unraveling*, 221.
93 Ned Parker, "US & Mahdi Army: Another Marriage of Convenience in Iraq," *The Seattle Times*, September 2007, http://old.seattletimes.com/html/iraq/2003882138_sadr13.html; and "Lt. Col. Patrick Frank Quote," *US Army*, https://www.army.mil/article/7019/Lt__Col__Patrick_Frank_quote.
94 Sky, *The Unraveling*, 228.
95 Sky, *The Unraveling*, 225.
96 Sky, *The Unraveling*, 227.
97 Sky, *The Unraveling*, 229.
98 Sky, *The Unraveling*, 229.
99 Mansoor, *The Surge*, 137.
100 Mansoor, *The Surge*, 137.
101 Sky, *The Unraveling*, 237.
102 Sky, *The Unraveling*, 237–41.
103 Sky, *The Unraveling*, 254.
104 Sky, *The Unraveling*, 256.
105 Ricks, *The Gamble*, 153–65.
106 Sky, *The Unraveling*, 257.
107 Sky, *The Unraveling*, 263.
108 Sky, *The Unraveling*, 65.
109 Mansoor, *The Surge*, 257.
110 Sky, *The Unraveling*, 296.
111 This included Minister of Defense Abdul Qadir al Obiedi, Minister of Interior Jawad Boulani, Chief of Staff of Army Babaker Zebari (Kurd), KRG Minister of Interior Karim Sanjari, and Minister of Peshmerga Sheikh Jafar.
112 Sky, *The Unraveling*, 296.
113 Sky, *The Unraveling*, 298.
114 Sky, *The Unraveling*, 302.
115 Sky, *The Unraveling*, 306–08.
116 Sky, *The Unraveling*, 306–08.
117 Sky, *The Unraveling*, 311.
118 Sky, *The Unraveling*, 313.
119 Amrita Madhukalya, "The Iraq War Ended the Idea of Pax Americana: Emma Sky," *Daily News and Analysis*, January 30, 2017, http://www.dnaindia.com/india/interview-the-iraq-war-ended-the-idea-of-pax-americana-emma-sky-2299607.

120 Carter Malkasian's recent monograph speaks to the limited return of the surge and how this incomplete victory contributed to the creation of ISIS and continued regional conflict. Malkasian, *Illusions of Victory*.

Conclusion

1 These would jump to £30,000 for individual support. Conversely, the bribe for the relief of Kut had an upper limit of £1,000,000. Wilson, *Lawrence of Arabia: The Authorized Biography* (London: William Heniman, 1989), 262, 478.
2 Priya Satia, *Spies in Arabia: The Great War and the Cultural Foundations of Britain's Covert Empire in the Middle East* (Oxford: Oxford University Press, 2008), 258, 302.
3 Edward Said, *Orientalism* (New York: Vintage, 2014; 1978), 255.
4 This emerged in discussions with British COIN experts during the 1962 RAND conference on counterinsurgency. *Counterinsurgency: A Symposium* April 16–20, 1962 (Santa Barbara, CA: Rand Corporation, 1963), https://www.rand.org/content/dam/rand/pubs/reports/2006/R412-1.pdf.
5 See Andrew Birtle, *US Army Counterinsurgency and Contingency Operations Doctrine, 1860–1941* (Washington, DC: Center for Military History, United States Army, 2003), both volumes.
6 An example of the lessons-learned approach can be seen in the recommended reading list of Bohannan's work on the Huk campaign. See Bohannan and Valeriano, *Counter-Guerrilla Warfare: The Philippines Experience* (Santa Barbara, CA: Praeger, 2007), 214–18.
7 Quoted in Robert Asprey, *War in the Shadows: The Guerrilla in History. Vol. II.* (Bloomington, IN: iUniverse, 2002), 190–91.
8 Jonathan Nashel, *Edward Lansdale's Cold War* (Amherst and Boston: University of Massachusetts Press, 2005).
9 Peter Hopkirk, *On Secret Service East of Constantinople: The Plot to Bring Down the British Empire* (New York: John Murray, 2004), 64.
10 See Robert Kromer, *The Bureaucracy Does Its Thing: Institutional Constraints on US-GVN Performance in Vietnam* (Santa Barbara, CA: RAND Corporation, August 1972); and Andrew Krepinevich, *The Army and Vietnam* (Baltimore, MD: Johns Hopkins University Press, 1988).
11 See David Grossman, *On Killing: The Psychological Cost of Learning to Kill in War and Society* (New York: Little, Brown, 1995).
12 See Aaron B. O'Connell, ed., *Our Latest Longest War: Losing Hearts and Minds in Afghanistan* (Chicago, IL: University of Chicago Press, 2017). Chayes and Sky make these claims in their own work.
13 Quoted in Asprey, *War in the Shadows*, 190–91.

Bibliography

Primary Sources

United Kingdom

Imperial War Museum

"C. M. Woodhouse interview on SOE Greece," Oral History 31579 Reel 1.

National Archives of the United Kingdom (Nauk), Kew

NAUK 1010686 Greece: Successful Operations April, May, June 1944

NAUK HS5-268 Greece Anglo-Italian Relations in the Balkans

NAUK HS5-280 Greece-Koutsaina

NAUK HS5-281 Greece Conferences 1944, Mobility No. 140 of Feb. 17

NAUK HS5-307 Greece Greece & The Aegean

NAUK HSS-339 Greece: Assessment of Situation in Greece Feb 1942 June 1944 SOE Greece No. 82

NAUK HS5-337 Greece Political Intelligence Reports Particularly Greek Islands

NAUK HS5-353 File Number SOE Greece

NAUK HS5-346 Greece-CD & SO Files

NAUK HS5-353 File Number SOE Greece No. 103

United States

National archives, College Park, Maryland

NARA RG 226 Entry NM-54 1 Research and Analysis Branch, Office off the Chief, General Correspondences, 1942–1946

NARA RG 226 E177 Washington Research and Analysis and State OIR Records

NARA RG 2 OSS Personnel Files, Julia McWilliams, available online at https://nara-media-001.s3.amazonaws.com/arcmedia/oss/McWilliams_Child_Julia.pdf, Seymour, 179

NARA RG 226 Entry UD 92A COI/OSS Files, 1941–1946

Office of Strategic Services Personnel Files from World War II, https://www.archives.gov/research/military/ww2/oss/personnel-files.html

University and Library Archives

Hoover Institute Archive, Stanford University, Stanford

Charles Ted Rutledge Bohannan Papers

Edward G. Lansdale Papers

John F. Kennedy Library Archive and Museum, Boston

Bernard Fall Papers

Forsyth Library Special Collections, Fort Hayes State University, Hayes
Cecil Currey Collection

Texas Tech University
Vietnam Center and Archive Online, https://vva.vietnam.ttu.edu/repositories/2/digital_objects/398328

Personal Papers
Charles T. R. Bohannan Papers
Rufus Philips Papers

Interviews
Claring Bohannan interview by Jason S. Ridler, May 10, 2011.
Rufus Philips interview by Jason S. Ridler February 13, 2012.
Hobart "Bo" Cleveland interview with the author, June 15, 2012.
Sarah Chayes Interview by Jason S. Ridler, January 23, 2013.

Secondary Sources
Doctoral and Masters Theses
Fall, Bernard. "Illegal Rearmament under the Weimar Republic." Master's thesis, Political Science Syracuse University, June 1952.

———. "Political Development of Viet-Nam, VJ-Day to the Geneva Cease-Fire." Doctoral thesis, Syracuse University, 1955.

Mann, Erick J. "The Schutztruppe and the Nature of Colonial Warfare during the Conquest of Tanganyika, 1889–1900." Doctoral thesis, University of Madison-Wisconsin, May 1998.

Miller, Patrick. "Building a Better Legacy: Contrasting the British and American Experience in Iraq." MA thesis, Naval Postgraduate School, December 2008.

Nalmpantis, Kyriakos. "Time on the Mountain: The Office of Strategic Services in Axis-Occupied Greece, 1943–1944." Doctoral thesis, Kent State University, May 2010.

Nesselhuf , F. Jon. "General Paul von Lettow-Vorbeck's East Africa Campaign: Maneuver Warfare on the Serengeti." Master of Arts (History), University of North Texas, May 2012.

Sacquety, Troy James. "The Organizational Evolution of OSS Detachment 101 in Burma, 1942–1945." Doctoral thesis, Texas A&M, May 2008.

Government Publications
United Kingdom

Bell, Gertrude. *Review of the Civil Administration of Mesopotamia.* London: His Majesty's Stationary, 1920.

Mobley, F. J. *The History of the Great War, Based on Collected Documents, The Campaigns in Mesopotamia, Volume I: Outbreak of Hostilities, Campaign in Lower Mesopotamia.* London: His Majesty's Stationery, 1923.

United States

Birtle, Andrew. *A History of Counterinsurgency and Contingency Operations in the US Army.* Vol. 2. US Government Printing, 1997.

Condit, D. M. *Case Study in Guerrilla War: Greece during World War II.* Washington, DC: Department of the Army and Special Operations Research Office, 1961.

Foreign Relations of the United States, 1952–1954. Vol. XIII, Part 1, Indochina in Two Parts, *Office of the Historian of the State Department.* Accessed on January 2, 2016, https://history.state.gov/historicaldocuments/frus1952-54v13p1/d525.

Office of Strategic Services Personnel Files from World War II, https://www.archives.gov/research/military/ww2/oss/personnel-files.html.

Spector, Robert. *Advice and Support: The Early Years, 1941–1960.* Lawrence: US Army Centre for Military History, 1985.

The Iraq Study Group Report. New York: Vintage Books, 2006.

"United States Vietnam Relations, 1945–1967." *Final Report of the Secretary of Defense Vietnam Task Force*, 1969.

US Army FM3-24 *Counterinsurgency* 2006.

Monographs and Articles

Anderson, Scott. *Lawrence in Arabia: War, Deceit, Imperial Folly and the Making of the Modern Middle East.* New York: Double Day, 2013.

Asprey, Robert. *War in the Shadows: The Guerrilla in History.* Vol. II. Bloomington, IN: iUniverse, 2002.

Atkin, Nicholas. *The French at War 1934–1944.* London: Longman, 2001.

Bell, David. *The First Total War: Napoleon's Europe and the Birth of Warfare as We Know It.* New York: Mariner Books, 2008.

Bergerud, Eric. *The Dynamics of Defeat: The Vietnam War in Hau Nghia Province.* Boulder, CO: Westview Press, 1993.

———. *Touched by Fire: The Land War in the South Pacific.* London and New York: Penguin, 1996.

Betzinez, Jason, and Wilbur Sturtevant Nye. *I Fought with Geronimo.* Lincoln and London: University of Nebraska Press, 1959, 1987.

Birtle, Andrew. "PROVN, Westmoreland, and the Historians: A Reappraisal." *Journal of Military History* 72 (October 4, 2008): 1213.

Blackett, P. M. S. "Scientists at the Operational Level." 1941. Reprinted in 1948 in "Operational Research." *Advancement of Science.* Vol. 17 1948, collected in *Studies of War: Nuclear and Conventional.* Edinburgh & London: Oliver & Boyd, 1962.

Bohannan, Charles T. R., and Napoleon Valeriano. *Counter Guerrilla Operations: The Philippine Experience.* New York: Praeger, 1962, 2006.

Bowden, Mark. *Black Hawk Down: A Tale of Modern War.* New York: Signet, 1999.

Bray, N. N. E. *A Paladin of Arabia: The Biography of Brevet Lieut.-Colonel G. E. Leachman.* London: Unicorn Press, 1936.

Brewer, David. *Greece, the Decade of War: Occupation, Resistance, and Civil War.* New York: I. B. Tauris, 2016.

Broadwell, Paula. *All In: The Education of General David Petraeus.* New York: Penguin Books, 2012.

Brown, Malcolm, ed. *T. E. Lawrence in War and Peace: An Anthology of the Military Writings of Lawrence of Arabia.* London: Greenhill Books, 2005.

Bugwyn, James. *Mussolini Warlord: Failed Dreams of Empire.* Enigma Books, 2012.

Burke, Crispin. "T. E. Lawrence: A Leadership Vignette for the Successful Counterinsurgent." *Small Wars Journal.* February 19, 2009. http://smallwarsjournal.com/jrnl/art/a-leadership-vignette-for-the-successful-counter-insurgent.

Canton, Philip E. *Diem's Final Failure: Prelude to America's War in Vietnam.* Lawrence: University Press of Kansas, 2003.

Carlisle, John M. *Red Arrow Men: The 32nd Division on the Villa Verde Trail.* Detroit, MI: Arnold Powers, 1945.

Chandrasekaran, Rajiv. *Imperial Life in the Emerald City: Inside Iraq's Green Zone.* New York: Vintage, 2006.

———. *Little America: The War within the War for Afghanistan.* New York: Vintage, 2012.

Charters, David, Lee Windsor, and Brent Wilson. *Kandahar Tour: The Turning Point in Canada's Afghan Mission.* Toronto: Wiley, 2010.

Chayes, Sarah. "Rebuilding Akokolacha: Why America Must Get More Involved—Not Less—in Afghanistan." *Christian Science Monitor*, December 10, 2002.

———. "Breaking Ranks in Afghanistan." *Columbia Journalism Review*, December 11, 2003, http://www.alternet.org/story/17372/breaking_ranks_in_afghanistan.

———. "Interview with Sarah Chayes: Danger, Determination, and Destiny." *Frontline*, October 1, 2003. http://www.pbs.org/frontlineworld/stories/afghanistan/chayes.html.

———. *The Punishment of Virtue: Inside Afghanistan after the Taliban.* New York: Penguin Books, 2006.

———. "The Perils of Delivering Aid in Afghanistan." *Globe and Mail*, August 15, 2008.

———. *Thieves of State: Why Corruption Threatens Global Security.* New York: W. W. Norton, 2016.

Cohen, A. A. *Galula: The Life and Writings of the French Officer Who Defined the Art of Counterinsurgency.* New York: Praeger, 2012.

Collins, Geneva. "Without a Parachute Ex-Reporter Finds Rewards in Relief Work." *Current*, September 20, 2004, http://peacecorpsonline.org/messages/messages/467/2023756.html.

Cooper, Artemis. *Patrick Leigh Fermor: An Adventure* London: John Murray, 2012.

Copp, Terry, ed. *Montgomery's Scientists: Operational Research in Northwest Europe.* Waterloo, ON: Laurier Centre for Military Strategic and Disarmament Studies, 2000.

Counterinsurgency: A Symposium. April 16–20, 1962. Santa Barbara, CA: Rand Corporation, https://www.rand.org/content/dam/rand/pubs/reports/2006/R412-1.pdf.

Cox. Percy Z. "The Death of Herr Wassmuss." *Journal of the Royal Central Asian Society* 19, no. 1 (1932): 151–55.

Craig, Luther. "German Defensive Policy in the Balkans. A Case Study: The Build Up in Greece, 1943." *Balkan Studies* 23, no. 2 (1982): 403–19.

Cullen, Stephen. "Legion of the Damned: The Milice Francaise, 1943–1945." *Military Illustrated: Past and Present* (March 2008).

Currey , Cecil B. *Victory at Any Cost: The Genius of Vietnam's Gen. Vo Nguyen Giap*. Lincoln, NE: Potomac Books, 2005.

Danchev, Alex. *Alchemist of War: The Life of Basil Liddell Hart*. London: Weidenfeld Military, 1998.

D'Auvergne, Edmund V. *The Prodigious Marshal: Being the Life and Extraordinary Adventures of Maurice de Saxe, Marshal of France, Son of the King of Poland, Conqueror of the English, Pretender to the Dukedom of Kurland, and Universal Lover*. New York: Dodd, 1931.

Dobbins, James, Seth G. Jones, Benjamin Runkle, and Siddarth Mohandas. *Occupying Iraq: A History of the Coalition Provisional Authority*. Santa Monica, CA: RAND National Security Research Division, 2009.

E. G. R. "Obituary: Hermann von Wissmann." *Geographical Journal* 26, no. 2 (August, 1905): 227–330.

Ehrenreich, Barbara. *Brightisded: How the Relentless Promotion of Positive Thinking Has Undermined America*. New York: Henry Holt, 2009.

Evans, Richard J. *Telling Lies about Hitler: The Holocaust, History and the David Irving Trial*. London: Verso Books, 2002.

Fabian, Johannes. "Remembering the Other: Knowledge and Recognition in the Exploration of Central Africa." *Critical Inquiry* 26, no. 1 (Autumn 1999): 49–69.

Fahs, Robert. "Back to a Forgotten Street: Bernard Fall and the Limits of Armed Intervention." *Prologue* 43, no. 1 (Spring 2011). Accessed on May 7, 2015, http://www.archives.gov/publications/prologue/2011/spring/bernard-fall.html.

Fall, Bernard. "The Case against Alfred Krupp." *Prevent World War III* (Summer 1951).

———. "Indochina: The Seven Year Dilemma." *Military Review* XXXIII, no. 7 (October 1953).

———. *The International Position of South Viet-Nam*, Parts 1–3. New York: Institute of Pacific Relations, 1958.

———. "Vietnam Blitz: An Impersonal War." *New Republic*, October 9, 1965, 17–21.

———. *Street without Joy*. Mechanicsburg, PA: Stackpole Books, 1994; 1961.

———. *Last Reflections on a War*. Mechanicsburg, PA: Stackpole, 2000; Kindle edition.

Fall, Dorothy. *Bernard Fall: Memoir of a Soldier Scholar*. Lincoln, NE: Potomac Books, 2006.

Fischer, Fritz. *Germany's Aims in the First World War*. New York: Norton, 1967.

Floor, Willem. "Borāzjān, a Rural Market Town in Bushire's Hinterland." *Iran* 42 (2004): 179–200.

Frank, Patrick. "Lt. Col. Patrick Frank Quote." *US Army,* https://www.army.mil/article/7019/Lt__Col__Patrick_Frank_quote.

Friend, Theodore. *Between Two Empires: The Ordeal of the Philippines, 1929–1946*. New Haven, CT: Yale University Press, 1965.

Fussell, Paul. *The Great War and Modern Memory*. London: Oxford University Press, 2000; 1975.

Garthwaite, Gene R. "The Bakhtiyari Khans, the Government of Iran, and the British, 1846–1915." *International Journal of Middle East Studies* 3, no. 1 (January 1972): 24–44.
Gat, Azar. *A History of Military Thought.* Oxford: Oxford University Press, 2001.
Gaunt, D. *Massacres, Resistance, Protectors: Muslim–Christian Relations in Eastern Anatolia During World War I.* Piscataway, NJ: Gorgias Press, 2006.
Gibb , H. A. R. "*T. E. Lawrence* by Charles Edmonds; *Lawrence of Arabia* by R. H. Kiernan; *A Paladin of Arabia* by N. N. E. Bray; *Wassmuss: The German Lawrence* by Christopher Sykes, Review." *International Affairs (Royal Institute of International Affairs 1931–1939)* 15, no. 4 (July–August 1936): 628.
Gossman, Lionel. *The Passion of Max von Oppenheim: Archeology and Intrigue in the Middle East.* Cambridge: Open Book, 2013.
Griesinger, Walter. *German Intrigues in Persia: The Diary of a German Agent: The Niedermayer Expedition through Persia to Afghanistan and India.* London: Hodder and Stoughton, 1918.
Grau, Lester, and Dodge Billingsley. *Operation Anaconda: America's First Major Battle in Afghanistan.* Lawrence: University Press of Kansas, 2011.
Grenier, Robert L. *88 Days to Kandahar: A CIA Diary.* New York: Simon & Schuster, 2016.
Grossman, David. *On Killing: The Psychological Cost of Learning to Kill in War and Society.* New York: Little, Brown, 1995.
Harris Smith, Richard. *OSS: The Secret History if America's First Central Intelligence Agency.* New York: Rowman & Littlefield, 2005; originally published 1972.
Hart, Basil Liddell. *Lawrence of Arabia.* Boston, MA: Da Capo, 2009; 1935.
Hauner, M. L. "Werner Otto von Hentig, 1886–1984." *Central Asian Survey* 3, no. 2 (January 1984): 287–309.
Hauner, Milan. "The Soviet Threat to Afghanistan and India 1938–1940." *Modern Asian Studies* 15, no. 3 (1981): 287.
Hennessy, Michael A. *Strategy in Vietnam: The Marine Corps and Revolutionary Warfare in I Corps, 1965–1972.* Wesport and London: Praeger, 1997.
Herbert, Ulrich. *Hitler's Foreign Workers: Enforced Labor in Germany during the Third Reich.* Cambridge: Cambridge University Press, 1997.
Herken, Gregg. *Cardinal Choices: Presidential Science Advisors from the Atomic Bomb to SDI.* Stanford, CA: Stanford University Press, 2000.
Hogarth, David G. "Gertrude Lowthian Bell." *Geographical Journal* 68, no. 4 (October 26, 1926): 363–68.
Hopkirk, Peter. *On Secret Service East of Constantinople: The Plot to Bring Down the British Empire.* New York: John Murray, 2004.
Howell, Georgina. *Gertrude Bell: Queen of the Desert, Shaper of Nations.* New York: Farrar, Straus, and Giroux, 2006.
Hughes, Thomas L. "German Mission to Afghanistan, 1915–1916." *German Studies Review* 25, no. 3 (October 2002): 447–76.
Hull, Isabell. *Absolute Destruction: Military Culture and the Practices of War in Imperial German.* Ithaca, NY: Cornell University Press, 2005.

Human Rights Watch. "Reversing Arabization of Kirkuk." In *Claims in Conflict: Reversing Ethnic Cleansing in Northern Iraq*. https://www.hrw.org/reports/2004/iraq0804/7.htm.

Hunt, Ray C., and Bernard Norling. *Behind Japanese Lines: An American Guerrilla in the Philippines.* Lexington: University of Kentucky, 1993.

Hurwitz, Deena, Margaret Satterthwaite, and Douglas Ford. *Human Rights Advocacy Stories.* St. Paul, MN: Foundation Press, 2008.

"Interview with Colonel William Mayville." *Frontline.* December 1, 2003. http://www.pbs.org/wgbh/pages/frontline/shows/beyond/interviews/mayville.html.

Jenkins, Jennifer. "Fritz Fischer's 'Programme for Revolution': Implications for a Global History of Germany in the First World War." *Journal of Contemporary History* 48, no. 2 (2013): 397–497.

Kaplan, Robert. *The Insurgents: David Petraeus and the Plot to Change the American Way of War*. New York: Simon & Schuster, 2013.

Katz, Barry N. *Foreign Intelligence: Research and Analysis in the Office of Strategic Services, 1942–1945*. Cambridge, MA: Harvard University Press, 1989.

Kerkvliet, Benedict J. *The Huk Rebellion: A Study of Peasant Revolt in the Philippines* Lanham, MD: Rowman & Littlefield, 1977; reprinted 2002.

Keveles, Melanie. *Scrappy Startups: How 15 Ordinary Women Turned Their Unique Ideas into Profitable Businesses*. Santa Barbara, CA: Praeger, 2010.

Kilcullen, David. *The Accidental Guerrilla: Fighting Small Wars in the Midst of Big Ones*. London, Oxford: Oxford University Press, 2011.

Kirby, Maurice. *Operational Research in War and Peace: The British Experience from the 1930s to 1970s*. London: Imperial War College, 2003.

Percy Sykes. "South Persia and the Great War." *Geographical Journal* 58, no. 2 (August 1921): 101–116.

Kitfield, James. *Prodigal Soldiers: How the Generation of Officers Born of Vietnam Revolutionized the American Style of War.* New York: Simon & Schuster, 1995.

Kedward , H. R. *In Search of the Maquis: Rural Resistance in Southern France, 1942–1944*. Oxford: Clarendon Press, 1993.

Kerkvliet, Benedict J. *The Huk Rebellion: A Study of Peasant Revolt in the Philippines*. Lanham, MD: Rowman & Littlefield, 1977; reprinted 2002.

Kluckhon, Clyde. *To the Foot of the Rainbow: A Tale of Twenty Five Hundred Miles of Wandering on Horseback through the Southwest Enchanted Land.* New York: Century, 1927.

Koch, J. A. *The Chieu Hoi Program in South Vietnam, 1963–1971*. Report for the Advanced Research Project Agency, Rand Publication. January 1973.

Kolenda, Christopher D. *The Counterinsurgency Challenge: A Parable of Decision Making in Modern Conflict*. Mechanicsburg, PA: Stackpole Books, 2012.

Krepinevich, Andrew. *The Army and Vietnam.* Baltimore, MD: Johns Hopkins University Press, 1988.

Kundras, Birthe. "From the Herero to the Holocaust? Some Remarks on the Current Debate." *Africa Spectrum* 40, no. 2 (2005): 299–308.

Lamb, Christopher, James Douglas Orton, Michael C. Davies, and Theodore T. Pikulsky. *Human Terrain Teams: An Organization for Sociocultural Knowledge in Irregular Warfare*. Washington, DC: Institute of World Politics Press, 2013.

Lansdale, Edward G. *In the Midst of Wars: An American Mission in South East Asia*. Bronx, NY: Fordham University Press, 1991; 1972.

Lapham Robert, and Bernard Norling. *Lapham's Raiders*. Lexington: University of Kentucky Press, 1996.

Lawrence, T. E. "Evolution of a Revolt." *Army Quarterly and Defence Journal* (October 1920), reprinted by the Combat Studies Institute. http://usacac.army.mil/cac2/cgsc/carl/download/csipubs/lawrence.pdf.

———. *Seven Pillars of Wisdom*. London: Penguin Books, 2000; originally printed in 1926.

Lewis, Tim. "Sarah Chayes: On Living in Afghanistan and Sleeping with a Kalashnikov." *The Guardian* (March 15, 2015). Accessed May 31, 2017. https://www.theguardian.com/books/2015/mar/15/sarah-chayes-thieves-of-state-interview.

Linderman, A. R. B. *Rediscovering Irregular Warfare: Colin Gubbins and the Origins of Britain's Special Operation Executive*. Norman: University of Oklahoma Press. 2016.

Logevall, Fredrik. *Embers of War: The Fall of an Empire and the Making of America's of Vietnam*. New York: Random House, 2013.

Lovell, John. "Vietnam and the US Army: Learning to Deal with Failure." In *Democracy, Strategy, and Vietnam: Implications for American Policymaking*, edited by George K. Osborne, Asa A. Clark IV, Daniel J. Kaufman, and Douglas E. Lute, 121–54. Lexington, MA, and Toronto, ON: D. C. Heath, 1985.

Lüdke, Tilman. *Jihad Made in Germany: Ottoman and German Propaganda and Intelligence Operations in the First World War*. Münster: Lit Verlag, 2005.

Lujan, Fernaudo M. "Wanted: PhDs Who Can Win a Bar Fight." *Foreign Policy* (March 2013). http://foreignpolicy.com/2013/03/08/wanted-ph-d-s-who-can-win-a-bar-fight/.

Mack, John E. *A Prince of Our Disorder: The Life of T. E. Lawrence*. Harvard, MA: Harvard University Press, 1998.

Madhukalya, Amarita. "The Iraq War Ended the Idea of Pax Americana: Emma Sky." *Daily News and Analysis*, January 30, 2017. http://www.dnaindia.com/india/interview-the-iraq-war-ended-the-idea-of-pax-americana-emma-sky-2299607.

Malkasian, Carter. *War Comes to Garmser: Thirty-Years of Conflict on the Afghan Border*. Oxford: Oxford University Press, 2016; 2013.

———. *Illusion of Victory: The Anbar Awakening and the Rise of the Islamic State*. London: Oxford University Press, 2017.

Maloney, Sean. *Enduring the Freedom: A Rogue Historian in Afghanistan*. Lincoln, NE: Potomac Books, 2006.

———. *Fighting for Afghanistan: A Rogue Historian at War*. Annapolis, MD: US Naval Institute Press, 2011.

———. *War in Afghanistan: Eight Battles in the South*. Kingston, ON: Canadian Defence Academy, 2012.

Manchester, William. *The Arms of Krupp: The Rise and Fall of the Industrial Dynasty That Armed Germany at War*. New York: Little, Brown, 2003.

Manchip White, John. *Marshal of France: The Life and Times of Maurice, Comte de Saxe [1696–1750]*. London: Hamish Hamilton, 1962.

Mansoor, Peter. *The Surge: My Journey with General David Petraeus and the Remaking of Iraq War*. New Haven, CT: Yale University Press, 2013.
Mazower, Mark. *Inside Hitler's Greece: The Experience of Occupation, 1941–1944*. New Haven, CT, and London: Yale University Press, 1993.
McCarthy, Rory. "Saddam Makes an Exhibition of Himself," *The Guardian*, January 10, 2003. https://www.theguardian.com/world/2003/jan/10/worlddispatch.iraq.
McCoy, Alfred. *Policing America's Empire: The United States, the Philippines, and the Rise of the Surveillance State*. Madison: University of Wisconsin Press, 2009.
McKale, Donald M. "'The Kaiser's Spy': Max von Oppenheim and the Anglo-German Rivalry before and during the First World War." *European History Quarterly* 27, no. 2 (April 1997): 199–219.
McMeekin, Sean. *The Berlin-Baghdad Express the Ottoman Empire and Germany's Bid for World Power, 1898–1918.* Cambridge, MA: The Belknap Press of Harvard University Press, 2010.
Meyer, Karl E., and Shareen Blair Brysac. *Kingmakers: The Invention of the Modern Middle East.* New York: W. W. Norton, 2008.
Milton, Giles. *Churchill's Ministry of Ungentlemanly Warfare: The Mavericks Who Plotted Hitler's Defeat*. New York: Picador, 2017.
Minorsky, V. Review, "Wassmuss, 'The German Lawrence' by Christopher Sykes." *Bulletin of the School of Oriental Studies, University of London* 9, no. 1 (1937): 244–45.
"Monty Woodhouse: Obituary." *The Guardian,* February 19, 2001. Accessed January 1, 2016. http://www.theguardian.com/news/2001/feb/20/guardianobituaries2.
Morris, Richard. *Cheshire: The Biography of Leonard Cheshire, VC, OM*. London: Viking Press, 2000.
Myers, Edward. *Bottom Sapper*. Self-published, 1984.
Nashel, Jonathan. *Edward Lansdale's Cold War*. Amherst and Boston, MA. University of Massachusetts Press, 2005.
Neumeyer, Kari. "Chayes on Life in the Trenches." from "removed" article at Medill News Site, March 27, 2001, Recovered via PeaceCorps website, listed as October 14, 2002.
Niedermayer, Oskar von. *Under the Scorching Sun: Iran War Experiences of the German Expedition to Persia and Afghanistan*. Dachau: Einhornverlag, 1925.
Nigmann, Ernst. *German Schutztruppe in East Africa: History of the Imperial Protectorate Force, 1889–1911.* Translated by Robert E. Dohrenwend. Nashville, TN: Battery Press, 2005; originally published by Ernst Siegfried Mittler and Sohn, 1911.
O'Connel, Aaron. *Our Latest Longest War: Losing Hearts and Minds in Afghanistan.* Edited by Aaron B. Chicago, IL: University of Chicago Press, 2017.
Orlans, Harold. *T. E. Lawrence: Biography of a Broken Hero*. Jefferson, NC: McFarland, 2002.
Ortner, Donald J. "Aleš Hrdlička and the Founding of the *American Journal of Physical Anthropology: 1918.*" In *Histories of American Physical Anthropology in the Twentieth Century*, edited by Michael Little and Kenneth Kennedy, 87–104. Lexington, KY: Lexington Books, 2010.
OSS Exhibition Catalog. Washington, DC: Center for the Study of Intelligence, n.d.

Ovendale, Ritchie. "Orme Garton Sargent." *Oxford Dictionary of National Biography*, Oxford, New York: Oxford University Press, 2004.

Paret, Peter. Review of *Berlin, Kabul, Moskau: Oskar Ritter von Niedermayer und Deutschlands Geopolitik* by Hans-Ulrich Seidt, in *Central European History*. Vol. 37, no. 2 (2004): 304.

Parker, James. *The Old Army: Memories, 1872–1918*. Philadelphia, PA: Dorrance, 1929.

Parker, Ned. "US & Mahdi Army: Another Marriage of Convenience in Iraq." *The Seattle Times*, September 2007. http://old.seattletimes.com/html/iraq/2003882138_sadr13.html.

Partlow, Joshua. *A Kingdom of Their Own: The Family Karzai and the Afghan Disaster.* New York: Random House, 2016.

Perry, Walter L., and David Kassing. *Toppling the Taliban: Air-Ground Operations in Afghanistan, October 2001 to June 2002*. Santa Monica, CA: RAND, 2016.

Philips, Rufus. *Why Vietnam Matters: An Eyewitness Account of Lessons Not Learned* Lincoln, NE: Potomac Books, 2009.

Pomeroy, William. *The Forest: A Personal Record of the Huk Guerrilla Struggle*. New York: International, 1963.

Popplewell, Richard. "British Intelligence in Mesopotamia, 1914–1916." *Intelligence and National Security* 5, no. 3 (April 1990), 139–72

Prados, John. "Kennedy and the Diem Assassination." *National Security Archive* 5 (November 2003). http://nsarchive.gwu.edu/NSAEBB/NSAEBB101/.

Preston, Richard, and S. F. Wise. *Men in Arms: A History of Warfare and Its Interrelationships with Society*, 4th ed. New York: Holt, 1979.

Read, Richard. "Year after War Began, Afghans Still Suffering." *Oregon Live*, October 7, 2002, recovered by the PeaceCorps website, October 14, 2002. http://peacecorpsonline.org/messages/messages/2629/1009507.html.

Record, Jeffrey. *Beating Goliath: Why Insurgencies Win.* Lincoln, NE: Potomac Books, 2009.

Rempe, Dennise. "The Past as Prologue? A History of US Counterinsurgency in Colombia, 1958–1966." Occasional Paper from the *Strategic Studies Institute*, March 2002, 5–6.

Reynolds, Michael. *Hemingway: The 1930s.* New York: W. W. Norton, 1998.

Ricks, Thomas. *Fiasco: The American Military Adventure in Iraq*. New York: Penguin, 2006.

———. *The Gamble: General Petraeus and the American Military Adventure in Iraq.* New York: Penguin, 2010.

Ridler, Jason S. *Maestro of Science: Omond M. Solandt and Government Science in War and Hostile Peace, 1939–1956.* Toronto, ON: University of Toronto Press, 2015.

———. "The Fertile Ground of Hell's Carnival: Charles T. R. Bohannan and the US Army's Counter Intelligence Corps' Investigations of War Criminals, Collaborators, and the Huk, in the Philippines 1945–1947." *Defense and Security Analysis* 33, no. 1 (2017): 15–29.

Ridler, Jason S., and Greg Liedtke. "Berlin's African Experiment: Hermann von Wissmann and Imperial Germany's Initial View of Colonial Warfare," unpublished paper.

Robinson, Linda. *One Hundred Victories: Special Ops and the Future of American Warfare.* New York: Public Affairs, 2013.

Roland, Alex. "Technology and War: The Historiographical Revolution of the 1980s." *Technology and Culture* 34, no. 1 (1993): 117–34.

Ross, Lois L. *Canadian Development Report 2008: Fragile State or Failing.* Ottawa: Development North South Institute, 2007.

Rutledge, Ian. *Enemy on the Euphrates: The Battle for Iraq.* London: Saqi Books, 2014.

Said, Edward. *Orientalism.* New York: Vintage, 2014; 1978.

Santarelli, Lidia. "Muted Violence: Italian War Crimes in Occupied Greece." *Journal of Modern Italian Studies* 9, no. 3 (2004): 280–99.

Satia, Priya. *Spies in Arabia: The Great War and the Cultural Foundations of Britain's Covert Empire in the Middle East* (Oxford: Oxford University Press, 2009).

Sattin, Anthony. *The Young T. E. Lawrence.* New York: W. W. Norton, 2015.

Sassoon, Siegfried. *Memoirs of an Infantry Officer.* London: Faber & Faber, 1930.

Saxe, Maurice de. *Mes rêveries,* (Amsterdam et a Leipzig: n.p.,1757), reproduced at the Internet Archive,https://archive.org/details/mesrveries01saxe.

Schneider, James. *Guerrilla Leader: T. E. Lawrence and the Arab Revolt.* New York: Bantam, 2011.

Seidt, Hans-Ulrich. "From Palestine to the Caucasus-Oskar Niedermayer and Germany's Middle Eastern Strategy in 1918." *German Studies Review* 24, no. 1 (February 2001): 1–18.

Seymour, Susan. *Cora Du Bois: Anthropologist, Diplomat, Agent.* Lincoln and London: University of Nebraska Press, 2015.

Sheehan, Neil. *A Bright Shining Lie: John Paul Vann and America in Vietnam.* New York: Random House, 1988.

Simon, Reeva Spector, and Eleanor H. Tejirian, eds. *The Creation of Iraq, 1914–1921.* New York: Columbia University Press, 2004.

Sky, Emma. *The Unraveling: High Hopes and Missed Opportunities in Iraq.* New York: Public Affairs, 2015.

Smith, Niel, and Sean MacFarland. "Anbar Awakens: The Tipping Point." *Military Review* (March–April 2008): 41–52.

Smith, Richard Harris. *OSS: The Secret History if America's First Central Intelligence Agency.* New York: Rowman & Littlefield, 2005; 1972.

Solandt, O. M. "Observation, Experiment, and Measurement in Operational Research." *JORS* 3, no. 1 (February 1955).

Starkey, Jerome, and Kim Sengupta. "President Obama Ready to Cut Karzai Adrift." *The Independent*, January 23, 2009. http://www.independent.co.uk/news/world/politics/obama-ready-to-cut-karzai-adrift-1513407.html.

Starry, Donn. "To Change an Army." *Military Review* 63 (March 1983): 23.

Stewart, Jules. *The Kaiser's Mission to Kabul: A Secret Expedition to Afghanistan in World War I.* New York: I. B. Tauris, 2014.

Sykes, Christopher. *Wassmuss: The German 'Lawrence': His Adventures in Persia during and after the War.* Leipzig: Bernhard Tauchnitz, 1937.

Sykes, Percy. *A History of Persia, Volume II.* London: MacMillan, 1915.

Tapper, Jake. *The Outpost: An Untold Story of American Valor*. New York: Little, Brown, 2012.

Taruc, Luis. *He Who Rides the Tiger: The Story of an Asian Guerrilla Leader*. New York: Praeger, 1967.

"The Bay of Pigs Invasion and Its Aftermath, April 1961–October 1962." *US State Department, Office of the Historian*. https://history.state.gov/milestones/1961-1968/bay-of-pigs.

Tuchman, Barbara. *The Zimmerman Telegram*. New York: Random House, 1995; 1958.

"Uncertainty over Exit Date for Canadian Troops in Afghanistan." *Macleans*. November 2007.

Utley, Bob, and William Washburn. *Indian Wars*. Mariner Books, 2002; 1977.

Vinogradov, Amal. "The 1920 Revolt in Iraq Reconsidered: The Role of Tribes in National Politics." *International Journal of the Middle East* 3, no. 2 (April 1972).

Waite, Robert G. L. *The Vanguard of Nazism: The Free Corps Movement in Post War Germany, 1918–1923*. New York: W. W. Norton, 1953.

Walsh, Declan. "American Activist Finds Her Calling in Afghan Hot Spot." *Globe Correspondent* (May 9, 2006). http://www.boston.com/news/world/asia/articles/2006/05/09/american_activist_finds_her_calling_in_afghan_hot_spot/.

Watt, D. C. *Too Serious a Business: European Armed Forces and the Approach to the Second World War*. Berkeley: University of California Press, 1935.

Weinberg, Gerhard L. "Some Myths about World War II." *Journal of Military History* 75 (July 2011): 706–707, 709. Accessed October 21, 2015. http://h-diplo.org/essays/PDF/JMH-Weinberg-SomeMythsOfWWII.pdf.

Weiner, Tim. "Lucien Conein, 79, Legendary Cold War Spy." *New York Times*, June 7, 1998. http://www.nytimes.com/1998/06/07/world/lucien-conein-79-legendary-cold-war-spy.html.

West, Bing. *No True Glory: A Frontline Account of the Battle for Fallujah*. New York: Bantam, 2005; reprint 2011.

Westrate, Bruce. *The Arab Bureau: British Police in the Middle East, 1916–1920*. University Park, PA: Penn State Press, 1992.

Wilson, Jeremy. *Lawrence of Arabia: The Authorized Biography of T. E. Lawrence*. London: Heinemann, 1988.

Winks, Robin W. *Cloak and Gown: Scholars in the Secret War, 1939–1961*. New Haven, CT: Yale University press, 1996.

Winstone, H. F. V. *Leachman: O. C. Desert*. London: Quarter Books, 1982.

Wissmann, Herman von. *Afrika: Schilderungen und Rathschläge zur Vorbereitung für den Aufenthalt und Dienst in den Deutsche Schützgebieten* [Africa: Descriptions and Recommendations for Service in the German Protectorate], 1903.

Woodhouse, C. M. *Apple of Discord: A Survey of Recent Greek Politics in Their International Setting*. London: Hutchinson, 1948.

———. *The Struggle for Greece, 1941–1949*. Chicago, IL: Ivan R. Dee, 1976; 2002.

———. *Something Ventured: An Autobiography*. New York: HarperCollins, 1982, 240.

———. *Obama's Wars*. New York: Simon & Schuster, 2010.

Woodward, Bob. *State of Denial*, New York: Simon & Schuster, 2006.

Wright, Gordon. "Reflections on the French Resistance 1940–1944." *Political Science Quarterly* 77, no. 3 (September 1962).

Wynn, Antony. *Persia in the Great Game: Sir Percy Sykes, Explorer, Consul, Soldier, Spy.* London: John Murray, 2004.

Xenaphon, *Anabasis.* Translated by H. G. Dkyns, 2013. Project Gutenberg. http://www.gutenberg.org/files/1170/1170-h/1170-h.htm.

Zuccotti, Susan. *The Holocaust, the French, and the Jews.* New York: Basic Books, 1993.

Index

J

K

About the Author

Jason S. Ridler is a historian, writer, and improv actor. He received his doctorate in war studies from the Royal Military College of Canada and is the author of *Maestro of Science*, the biography of early atomic warfare expert Dr. Omond M. Solandt (University of Toronto Press, 2015). He is a teaching fellow at Johns Hopkins University and a lecturer for Norwich University, where he teaches and designs classes on historical inquiry and change in military affairs. His historical and military works have appeared in *War on the Rocks*, *Small Wars and Insurgencies*, *Diplomacy and Statecraft*, and other fine journals. As a writer of fiction he has published over sixty short stories, and his crime series *The Brimstone Files* is available from Night Shade Press. He has performed and produced sketch comedy and improv shows for theaters around the Bay Area of San Francisco, including the Exit Theater, PianoFight, and Pan Theater, and often performs with local group SOMETHING. A former punk rock musician and cemetery groundskeeper, Dr. Ridler currently resides in Berkeley, California. Follow his efforts at *Soldiers & Scholars* on Facebook and Ridlerville at WordPress.